GRAMMAR AND BEYOND

Randi Reppen

with Deborah Gordon

1

CAMBRIDGE
UNIVERSITY PRESS

CAMBRIDGE
UNIVERSITY PRESS

University Printing House, Cambridge CB2 8BS, United Kingdom

One Liberty Plaza, 20th Floor, New York, NY 10006, USA

477 Williamstown Road, Port Melbourne, VIC 3207, Australia

314–321, 3rd Floor, Plot 3, Splendor Forum, Jasola District Centre, New Delhi – 110025, India

79 Anson Road, #06–04/06, Singapore 079906

Cambridge University Press is part of the University of Cambridge.

It furthers the University's mission by disseminating knowledge in the pursuit of education, learning and research at the highest international levels of excellence.

www.cambridge.org
Information on this title: www.cambridge.org/9780521142939

© Cambridge University Press 2012

First published 2012

20 19 18 17 16 15 14 13 12 11 10 9 8

Printed in Malaysia by Vivar Printing

A catalog record for this publication is available from the British Library

ISBN 978-0-521-14293-9 Student's Book 1
ISBN 978-0-521-14304-2 Student's Book 1A
ISBN 978-0-521-14307-3 Student's Book 1B
ISBN 978-0-521-27988-8 Workbook 1
ISBN 978-0-521-27989-5 Workbook 1A
ISBN 978-0-521-27990-1 Workbook 1B
ISBN 978-1-107-69431-6 Teacher Support Resource Book with CD-ROM 1
ISBN 978-0-521-14330-1 Class Audio CD 1
ISBN 978-1-139-06183-4 Writing Skills Interactive 1

Book design and layout services: TSI Graphics
Art direction: Adventure House, NYC
Audio production: John Marshall Media

Contents

Appendices

Introduction to *Grammar and Beyond*

Grammar and Beyond is a research-based and content-rich grammar series for beginning- to advanced-level students of North American English. The series focuses on the grammar structures most commonly used in North American English, with an emphasis on the application of these grammar structures to academic writing. The series practices all four skills in a variety of authentic and communicative contexts. It is designed for use both in the classroom and as a self-study learning tool.

Grammar and Beyond Is Research-Based

The grammar presented in this series is informed by years of research on the grammar of written and spoken North American English as it is used in college lectures, textbooks, academic essays, high school classrooms, and conversations between instructors and students. This research, and the analysis of over one billion words of authentic written and spoken language data known as the *Cambridge International Corpus*, has enabled the authors to:

- Present grammar rules that accurately represent how North American English is actually spoken and written

- Identify and teach differences between the grammar of written and spoken English

- Focus more attention on the structures that are commonly used, and less attention on those that are rarely used, in written and spoken North American English

- Help students avoid the most common mistakes that English language learners make

- Choose reading and writing topics that will naturally elicit examples of the target grammar structure

- Introduce important vocabulary from the Academic Word List

Grammar and Beyond Teaches Academic Writing Skills

Grammar and Beyond helps students make the transition from understanding grammar structures to applying them in their academic writing.

In the Student's Books

At Levels 1 through 3 of the series, every Student's Book unit ends with a section devoted to the hands-on application of grammar to writing. This section, called Grammar for Writing, explores how and where the target grammar structures function in writing and offers controlled practice, exposure to writing models, and a guided but open-ended writing task.

At Level 4, the most advanced level, the syllabus is organized around the academic essay types that college students write (e.g., persuasive, cause and effect) and is aimed at teaching students the grammar, vocabulary, and writing skills that they need in order to be successful at writing those kinds of essays.

Online

Grammar and Beyond also offers *Writing Skills Interactive*, an interactive online course in academic writing skills and vocabulary that correlates with the Student's Books. Each unit of the writing skills course focuses on a specific writing skill, such as avoiding sentence fragments or developing strong topic sentences.

Special Features of *Grammar and Beyond*

Realistic Grammar Presentations

Grammar is presented in clear and simple charts. The grammar points presented in these charts have been tested against real-world data from the *Cambridge International Corpus* to ensure that they are authentic representations of actual use of North American English.

Data from the Real World

Many of the grammar presentations and application sections in the Student's Book include a feature called Data from the Real World, in which concrete and useful points discovered through analysis of corpus data are presented. These points are practiced in the exercises that follow.

Avoid Common Mistakes

Each Student's Book unit features an Avoid Common Mistakes section that develops students' awareness of the most common mistakes made by English language learners and gives them an opportunity to practice detecting and correcting these errors in running text. This section helps students avoid these mistakes in their own work. The mistakes highlighted in this section are drawn from a body of authentic data on learner English known as the *Cambridge Learner Corpus*, a database of over 35 million words from student essays written by nonnative speakers of English and information from experienced classroom teachers.

Academic Vocabulary

Every unit in *Grammar and Beyond* includes words from the Academic Word List (AWL), a research-based list of words and word families that appear with high frequency in English-language academic texts. These words are introduced in the opening text of the unit, recycled in the charts and exercises, and used to support the theme throughout the unit. The same vocabulary items are reviewed and practiced in *Writing Skills Interactive*, the online writing skills course. By the time students finish each level, they will have been exposed several times to a carefully selected set of level-appropriate AWL words, as well as content words from a variety of academic disciplines.

Series Levels

The following table provides a general idea of the difficulty of the material at each level of *Grammar and Beyond*. These are not meant to be interpreted as precise correlations.

	Description	TOEFL IBT	CEFR Levels
Level 1	beginning	20 – 34	A1 – A2
Level 2	low intermediate to intermediate	35 – 54	A2 – B1
Level 3	high intermediate	55 – 74	B1 – B2
Level 4	advanced	75 – 95	B2 – C1

Components for Students

Student's Book

The Student's Books for Levels 1 through 3 teach all of the grammar points appropriate at each level in short, manageable cycles of presentation and practice organized around a high-interest unit theme. The Level 4 Student's Book focuses on the structure of the academic essay in addition to the grammar rules, conventions, and structures that students need to master in order to be successful college writers. Please see the Tour of a Unit on pages xvi–xix for a more detailed view of the contents and structure of the Student's Book units.

Workbook

The Workbook provides additional practice of the grammar presented in each unit of the Student's Book. The exercises offer both discrete and consolidated practice of grammar points and can be used for homework or in class. Each unit also offers practice correcting the errors highlighted in the Avoid Common Mistakes section in the Student's Book to help students master these troublesome errors. Self-Assessment sections at the end of each unit allow students to test their mastery of what they have learned.

Writing Skills Interactive

This online course provides graduated instruction and practice in writing skills, while reinforcing vocabulary presented in the Student's Books. Each unit includes a vocabulary review activity, followed by a short text that builds on the theme presented in the Student's Book and provides an additional context for the vocabulary. The text is followed by an animated interactive presentation of the target writing skill of the unit, after which students have the opportunity to practice the target skill in three different activities. Each unit closes with a quiz, which allows students to assess their progress.

Teacher Resources

Teacher Support Resource Book with CD-ROM

This comprehensive book provides a range of support materials for instructors, including:

- Suggestions for applying the target grammar to all four major skill areas, helping instructors facilitate dynamic and comprehensive grammar classes

- An answer key and audio script for the Student's Book

- A CD-ROM containing:

  - Ready-made, easily scored Unit Tests

  - PowerPoint presentations to streamline lesson preparation and encourage lively heads-up interaction

Class Audio CD

The class audio CD for each level provides the Student's Book listening material for in-class use.

Teacher Support Website

www.cambridge.org/grammarandbeyond

The website for *Grammar and Beyond* contains even more resources for instructors, including:

- Unit-by-unit teaching tips, helping instructors plan their lessons

- Downloadable communicative activities to add more in-class speaking practice

- A monthly newsletter on grammar teaching, providing ongoing professional development

We hope you enjoy using this series, and we welcome your feedback! Please send any comments to the authors and editorial staff at Cambridge University Press, at grammarandbeyond@cambridge.org.

About the Authors

Randi Reppen is Professor of Applied Linguistics and TESL at Northern Arizona University (NAU) in Flagstaff, Arizona. She has over 20 years experience teaching ESL students and training ESL teachers, including 11 years as the Director of NAU's Program in Intensive English. Randi's research interests focus on the use of corpora for language teaching and materials development. In addition to numerous academic articles and books, she is the author of *Using Corpora in the Language Classroom* and a co-author of *Basic Vocabulary in Use*, 2nd edition, both published by Cambridge University Press.

Deborah Gordon, creator of the Grammar for Writing sections, has more than 25 years' experience teaching ESL students and training ESL teachers in the United States and abroad. She is currently an ESL instructor at Santa Barbara City College and a TESOL Certificate instructor at the University of California, Santa Barbara Extension. Deborah is coauthor of *Writers at Work: From Sentence to Paragraph*, published by Cambridge University Press, among many other titles.

Corpus Consultants

Michael McCarthy is Emeritus Professor of Applied Linguistics at the University of Nottingham, UK, and Adjunct Professor of Applied Linguistics at the Pennsylvania State University. He is a co-author of the corpus-informed *Touchstone* series and the award-winning *Cambridge Grammar of English*, both published by Cambridge University Press, among many other titles, and is known throughout the world as an expert on grammar, vocabulary, and corpus linguistics.

Jeanne McCarten has over 30 years of experience in ELT/ESL as a teacher, publisher, and author. She has been closely involved in the development of the spoken English sections of the *Cambridge International Corpus*. Now a freelance writer, she is co-author of the corpus-informed *Touchstone* series and *Grammar for Business*, both published by Cambridge University Press.

Advisory Panel

The ESL advisory panel has helped to guide the development of this series and provided invaluable information about the needs of ESL students and teachers in high schools, colleges, universities, and private language schools throughout North America.

Neta Simpkins Cahill, Skagit Valley College, Mount Vernon, WA

Shelly Hedstrom, Palm Beach State College, Lake Worth, FL

Richard Morasci, Foothill College, Los Altos Hills, CA

Stacey Russo, East Hampton High School, East Hampton, NY

Alice Savage, North Harris College, Houston, TX

Acknowledgments

The publisher and authors would like to thank these reviewers and consultants for their insights and participation:

Marty Attiyeh, The College of DuPage, Glen Ellyn, IL

Shannon Bailey, Austin Community College, Austin, TX

Jamila Barton, North Seattle Community College, Seattle, WA

Kim Bayer, Hunter College IELI, New York, NY

Linda Berendsen, Oakton Community College, Skokie, IL

Anita Biber, Tarrant County College Northwest, Fort Worth, TX

Jane Breaux, Community College of Aurora, Aurora, CO

Anna Budzinski, San Antonio College, San Antonio, TX

Britta Burton, Mission College, Santa Clara, CA

Jean Carroll, Fresno City College, Fresno, CA

Chris Cashman, Oak Park High School and Elmwood Park High School, Chicago, IL

Annette M. Charron, Bakersfield College, Bakersfield, CA

Patrick Colabucci, ALI at San Diego State University, San Diego, CA

Lin Cui, Harper College, Palatine, IL

Jennifer Duclos, Boston University CELOP, Boston, MA

Joy Durighello, San Francisco City College, San Francisco, CA

Kathleen Flynn, Glendale Community College, Glendale, CA

Raquel Fundora, Miami Dade College, Miami, FL

Patricia Gillie, New Trier Township High School District, Winnetka, IL

Laurie Gluck, LaGuardia Community College, Long Island City, NY

Kathleen Golata, Galileo Academy of Science & Technology, San Francisco, CA

Ellen Goldman, Mission College, Santa Clara, CA

Ekaterina Goussakova, Seminole Community College, Sanford, FL

Marianne Grayston, Prince George's Community College, Largo, MD

Mary Greiss Shipley, Georgia Gwinnett College, Lawrenceville, GA

Sudeepa Gulati, Long Beach City College, Long Beach, CA

Nicole Hammond Carrasquel, University of Central Florida, Orlando, FL

Vicki Hendricks, Broward College, Fort Lauderdale, FL

Kelly Hernandez, Miami Dade College, Miami, FL

Ann Johnston, Tidewater Community College, Virginia Beach, VA

Julia Karet, Chaffey College, Claremont, CA

Jeanne Lachowski, English Language Institute, University of Utah, Salt Lake City, UT

Noga Laor, Rennert, New York, NY

Min Lu, Central Florida Community College, Ocala, FL

Michael Luchuk, Kaplan International Centers, New York, NY

Craig Machado, Norwalk Community College, Norwalk, CT

Denise Maduli-Williams, City College of San Francisco, San Francisco, CA

Diane Mahin, University of Miami, Coral Gables, FL

Melanie Majeski, Naugatuck Valley Community College, Waterbury, CT

Jeanne Malcolm, University of North Carolina at Charlotte, Charlotte, NC

Lourdes Marx, Palm Beach State College, Boca Raton, FL

Susan G. McFalls, Maryville College, Maryville, TN

Nancy McKay, Cuyahoga Community College, Cleveland, OH

Dominika McPartland, Long Island Business Institute, Flushing, NY

Amy Metcalf, UNR/Intensive English Language Center, University of Nevada, Reno, NV

Robert Miller, EF International Language School San Francisco – Mills, San Francisco, CA

Marcie Pachino, Jordan High School, Durham, NC

Myshie Pagel, El Paso Community College, El Paso, TX

Bernadette Pedagno, University of San Francisco, San Francisco, CA

Tam Q Pham, Dallas Theological Seminary, Fort Smith, AR

Mary Beth Pickett, Global-LT, Rochester, MI

Maria Reamore, Baltimore City Public Schools, Baltimore, MD

Alison M. Rice, Hunter College IELI, New York, NY

Sydney Rice, Imperial Valley College, Imperial, CA

Kathleen Romstedt, Ohio State University, Columbus, OH

Alexandra Rowe, University of South Carolina, Columbia, SC

Irma Sanders, Baldwin Park Adult and Community Education, Baldwin Park, CA

Caren Shoup, Lone Star College – CyFair, Cypress, TX

Karen Sid, Mission College, Foothill College, De Anza College, Santa Clara, CA

Michelle Thomas, Miami Dade College, Miami, FL

Sharon Van Houte, Lorain County Community College, Elyria, OH

Margi Wald, UC Berkeley, Berkeley, CA

Walli Weitz, Riverside County Office of Ed., Indio, CA

Bart Weyand, University of Southern Maine, Portland, ME

Donna Weyrich, Columbus State Community College, Columbus, OH

Marilyn Whitehorse, Santa Barbara City College, Ojai, CA

Jessica Wilson, Rutgers University – Newark, Newark, NJ

Sue Wilson, San Jose City College, San Jose, CA

Margaret Wilster, Mid-Florida Tech, Orlando, FL

Anne York-Herjeczki, Santa Monica College, Santa Monica, CA

Hoda Zaki, Camden County College, Camden, NJ

We would also like to thank these teachers and programs for allowing us to visit:

Richard Appelbaum, Broward College, Fort Lauderdale, FL

Carmela Arnoldt, Glendale Community College, Glendale, AZ

JaNae Barrow, Desert Vista High School, Phoenix, AZ

Ted Christensen, Mesa Community College, Mesa, AZ

Richard Ciriello, Lower East Side Preparatory High School, New York, NY

Virginia Edwards, Chandler-Gilbert Community College, Chandler, AZ

Nusia Frankel, Miami Dade College, Miami, FL

Raquel Fundora, Miami Dade College, Miami, FL

Vicki Hendricks, Broward College, Fort Lauderdale, FL

Kelly Hernandez, Miami Dade College, Miami, FL

Stephen Johnson, Miami Dade College, Miami, FL

Barbara Jordan, Mesa Community College, Mesa, AZ

Nancy Kersten, GateWay Community College, Phoenix, AZ

Lewis Levine, Hostos Community College, Bronx, NY

John Liffiton, Scottsdale Community College, Scottsdale, AZ

Cheryl Lira-Layne, Gilbert Public School District, Gilbert, AZ

Mary Livingston, Arizona State University, Tempe, AZ

Elizabeth Macdonald, Thunderbird School of Global Management, Glendale, AZ

Terri Martinez, Mesa Community College, Mesa, AZ

Lourdes Marx, Palm Beach State College, Boca Raton, FL

Paul Kei Matsuda, Arizona State University, Tempe, AZ

David Miller, Glendale Community College, Glendale, AZ

Martha Polin, Lower East Side Preparatory High School, New York, NY

Patricia Pullenza, Mesa Community College, Mesa, AZ

Victoria Rasinskaya, Lower East Side Preparatory High School, New York, NY

Vanda Salls, Tempe Union High School District, Tempe, AZ

Kim Sanabria, Hostos Community College, Bronx, NY

Cynthia Schuemann, Miami Dade College, Miami, FL

Michelle Thomas, Miami Dade College, Miami, FL

Dongmei Zeng, Borough of Manhattan Community College, New York, NY

Tour of a Unit

Grammar in the Real World presents the unit's grammar in a **realistic** context using **contemporary** texts.

Notice activities draw students' attention to the **structure**, guiding their own **analysis** of form, meaning, and use.

UNIT 11

Conjunctions: *And, But, Or*; *Because*

Time Management

1 Grammar in the Real World

A Do you have enough time for school, work, and family? Read the article below. What is one way to manage your time well?

Time for Everything

Many adults say they want more time. They are busy with work, family, **and** school, **and** they often don't get everything done. People feel stressed **because** there is not enough time to do it all. However, there are some simple ways to manage your time well **and** avoid stress.

One way is to identify the important **or** necessary tasks for that day. Then create a schedule **or** a "to do" list.[1] When you finish your important tasks, you can move on to the next, less important ones. Soon your tasks are done, **and** there is hopefully some extra time for fun activities.

Another way is to do important tasks on the same days every week. For example, you can do your laundry every Monday, **and** go to the gym on Tuesday and Thursday mornings before work or school. Always do the tasks on the same days. That way, you can plan around these important tasks **and** have time for other things. Some people don't like schedules, lists, or weekly plans. Instead, they use the notes or calendar features on their cell phones. Put a reminder[2] for the task on your phone, **but** don't forget to do it!

These ideas can help you improve your time management.[3] When you make plans and complete them, you feel good **and** can do more.

To Do:
grocery shopping
laundry
walk the dog

Monday	Tuesday
7:00 laundry	8:00 gym
9:00 work	10:00 class

[1]**"to do" list:** a list of things you need to do | [2]**reminder:** something that helps someone remember, like an alarm on a phone | [3]**time management:** being in control of your time; planning and using your time well

122

Conjunctions: *And, But, Or*; *Because*

B **Comprehension Check** Answer the questions. Use the article to help you.

1. What do most adults not have enough of?
2. What are two ways to manage your time?
3. What happens when people make plans and complete them?

C *Notice* Find the words *and, but, or,* and *because* in the article. Then complete the sentences.

1. They are busy with work, family, _____ school.
2. People feel stressed _____ there is not enough time to do it all.
3. Some people don't like schedules, lists, _____ weekly plans.
4. Put a reminder for the task on your phone, _____ don't forget to do it!

2 And, But, Or

▶ **Grammar Presentation**

And, but, and *or* are coordinating conjunctions. They connect words, phrases, and clauses.	People are busy with family **and** work. I like to exercise, **but** I don't have time for it every day. She studies in the morning **or** after work.

2.1 *And, But, Or* for Connecting Words and Phrases

Connecting Words	**Time and money** are valuable. She sleeps only **five or six** hours a night.
Connecting Phrases	I always **make a schedule and look at it often.** I have "to do" lists **on my computer but not on my phone.** Do you work **during the day or at night**?

2.2 *And, But, Or* for Connecting Clauses

First Clause		Second Clause
You have more time in your day,	and	you feel less stressed.
Some people use their time well,	but	other people do not.
You can make a list,	or	you can schedule tasks on the same days.

Time Management 123

The *Grammar Presentation* begins with an **overview** that describes the grammar in an **easy-to-understand** summary.

xvi

2.3 Using *And, But, Or*

a. Use *and*, *but*, and *or* to connect words, phrases, and clauses.	Time **and** money are valuable. He has time **but** not money. Do you use schedules, **or** do you make "to do" lists?
b. Use *and* to join two or more ideas.	Maria makes time for school, family, **and** work. I study **and** work every day. I make a "to do" list, **and** I check the list often during the day.
c. Use *but* to show contrast or surprising information.	José works hard, **but** he also has fun. He always makes a schedule, **but** he rarely follows it.
d. Use *or* to show a choice of two alternatives.	You can make lists **or** schedules. I exercise **or** do laundry after I study. Is he at school **or** at work?
e. Use a comma when *and*, *but*, and *or* connect two clauses.	My family gets together at night, **and** we talk about our day. Sonya wakes up early, **but** she is always late for work.

▶ **Grammar Application**

Exercise 2.1 Choosing *And, But, Or*

A Read the sentences about two types of people. Complete the sentences with *and*, *but*, or *or*. Add commas where necessary.

The Organized Person

1. Every day I wake up *and* I make a long "to do" list.
2. I usually use the "notes" feature on my phone for important tasks _____ I always do them.
3. I don't like to forget appointments _____ be late.
4. I like to be busy _____ I feel good when I get things done.

The Disorganized Person

5. Sometimes I make lists _____ I usually lose them.
6. I have a lot of appointments _____ a lot of things to do every day.
7. I try to be on time _____ I am often late for appointments.
8. I am always busy _____ I don't get things done.

B *Over to You* Read the sentences in A with a partner. Which statements are true for you? Tell your partner.

Exercise 2.4 Vocabulary Focus: Expressions with *And* and *Or*

Data from the Real World

English has many expressions using *and* and *or*. The nouns usually occur in the order they appear below.	Do you like peanut butter and jelly? NOT ~~Do you like jelly and peanut butter?~~	
Common "noun *and* noun" expressions for food	cream **and** sugar salt **and** pepper bread **and** butter	peanut butter **and** jelly fish **and** chips
Common "noun *and* noun" expressions for relationships	mom **and** dad brother **and** sister husband **and** wife	Mr. **and** Mrs. father **and** son mother **and** daughter
Other common "noun *and* noun" expressions	night **and** day men **and** women name **and** address	ladies **and** gentlemen boys **and** girls
Common expressions with *or*	cash **or** credit	coffee **or** tea
Common "adjective *and* adjective" expressions	black **and** white old **and** new	nice **and** warm

A Complete the questions.

1. Do you like _cream_ and sugar with your coffee?
2. Do your _____ and dad live in the United States?
3. Do you have brothers and _____ ?
4. Do you work _____ and day?
5. Do you like black and _____ movies?
6. Do you think _____ and women have really different interests?
7. Do you put salt and _____ on your food?
8. Do you usually pay with _____ or credit?
9. Do you ever eat peanut butter and _____ sandwiches?
10. Do you prefer _____ or tea?

A **wide variety** of exercises introduce new and stimulating content to keep students engaged with the material.

Students learn to *Avoid Common Mistakes* based on research in student writing.

▶ **Grammar Application**

Exercise 3.1 Cause-and-Effect Relationships with *Because*

Match the effect on the left with the cause on the right.

1. John is tired ___c___
2. Tanya is usually late _____
3. Dan is often hungry _____
4. Eric walks slowly _____
5. Sue takes her brother to school _____
6. Maya and Sara sleep late _____
7. Jack takes classes at night _____

a. because his foot hurts.
b. because he never eats breakfast.
c̶. because he doesn't sleep enough.
d. because he works during the day.
e. because she doesn't put reminders on her phone.
f. because their mother doesn't have time.
g. because their alarm clocks don't work.

Exercise 3.2 ◄)) The Position of *Because*

Put *because* in the correct place in each sentence. Add commas where necessary. Then listen and compare your answers.

Bob, Jamal, Tony, and Leo are roommates. They study at the local community college. Each roommate has a problem with time.

           because
1. Leo works at night ʌ he goes to school during the day.
2. Tony can only study in the mornings he thinks more clearly then.
3. Bob's alarm clock doesn't work he is always late.
4. Jamal can't study at home his roommates are too noisy.
5. Leo forgets to write his assignments down he often misses them.
6. Tony and Jamal sometimes miss class they play basketball instead.

4 | Avoid Common Mistakes ⚠

1. Do not use a comma when you join two words or two phrases.
Lisa creates a schedule ̷ and a list every day.

2. Use a comma when you join two clauses with *and*, *but*, and *or*.
I need to study for the test and then I have to work!
         ^

3. Use *and to* add information. Use *but to* show a contrast. Use *or* to show a choice.
      but
Sam is always late, and he gets his work done.

4. Do not use a comma if *because* is in the second part of the sentence.
Jake is always on time ̷ because he takes the 8:00 bus to school every day.
But do use a comma if *because* is in the first part of the sentence.
Because Lily makes a daily schedule ̖ she never forgets to do her tasks.

5. Use *because* to state the reason (cause) for something. The other part of the sentence states the result (effect).
  Because Kylie writes her assignments on her calendar,
Kylie writes her assignments on her calendar ~~because she doesn't forget them.~~
  Kylie doesn't forget her assignments because
Because Kylie doesn't forget her assignments; she writes them on her calendar.

Editing Task

Read the story about Professor Kwan's class on time management. Find and correct 9 more mistakes.

A Useful Class

    Every year, Professor Kwan teaches a class on time management. Many students like to take her class. Sometimes the class fills up quickly/because it is so popular. Students know that they need to register early – in person and online. This is the first lesson of the time-management class.

5   In this class, Professor Kwan talks about different ways for students to organize their time. Her students often complain about the stress they have but how little

After studying what **common mistakes** to avoid, students apply the information in **editing tasks**.

> *Grammar for Writing* connects the unit's grammar to specific **applications** in writing.

> The final writing exercise **brings everything together** as students apply their knowledge of the unit's grammar in a level-appropriate **writing task.**

5 Grammar for Writing

Describing the Way You Do Something

Writers use *and, but, or,* and *because* to combine ideas and to show relationships between ideas. They can use these conjunctions to write about something they do regularly.

Remember:

- **Use *and, but,* or *or* to combine words, phrases, or clauses.**
  I usually do my homework on the bus <u>and</u> on my lunch break.
  She does her homework at night, <u>but</u> sometimes she falls asleep.
  His homework is never late <u>or</u> incomplete.

- **Use *because* to show a cause-and-effect relationship between two sentences.**
  She has very little time <u>because</u> she has two jobs.

Pre-writing Task

1 Read the paragraph below. When and where does the writer do her homework? Why?

Doing My Homework

I'm always busy(because)I work and I take classes.
I don't have a lot of time for homework because of this.
Because my homework is important, I do it in the library
before or after my class. The library opens at 7:00 a.m.,
5 and my class starts at 8:00 a.m. The library is quiet at
7:00 a.m. because it is often empty then. Sometimes I ask
the librarians for help. They are usually very nice and
helpful, but sometimes they are busy with their work.
After class, the library is full, but it is still a good place
10 to study.

2 Read the paragraph again. Circle the conjunctions *and, but, or,* and *because.* Which conjunctions connect words? Which connect phrases? Which connect clauses?

Writing Task

1 *Write* Use the paragraph in the Pre-writing Task to help you write about something you need to do regularly. Do you schedule time for this activity? When and where do you do this activity? Explain why. Write about how you:

- clean house
- do dishes
- do homework
- do laundry
- exercise

- go food shopping
- make meals
- pay bills
- take care of children

Use *and, but, or,* and *because* to combine ideas and show relationships between ideas.

2 *Self-Edit* Use the editing tips below to improve your sentences. Make any necessary changes.

1. Did you use conjunctions to write about something you do regularly?
2. Did you use *and, but,* and *or* to connect words, phrases, or clauses?
3. Did you use *because* to show cause-and-effect relationships?
4. Did you avoid the mistakes in the Avoid Common Mistakes chart on page 130?

> A **Pre-writing Task** uses a model to guide students' **analysis** of grammar in **writing.**

Statements with Present of *Be*

Tell Me About Yourself

1 Grammar in the Real World

A How do you introduce yourself to your instructors? What information do you give?
Read the conversation between an adviser and a student. What are two interesting facts
about Jun-Ho?

First Meeting with an Adviser

Jun-Ho	Hello, Mr. Garcia. I**'m** Jun-Ho. Sorry I**'m** late for our meeting.
Mr. Garcia	That**'s** OK. Nice to meet you, Jun-Ho. Please have a seat.
5 Jun-Ho	Thanks.
Mr. Garcia	First, I**'m** glad that you**'re** here. As your adviser, I**'m** here to help you. I can help you choose your classes, and I can help you with any problems.
10 Jun-Ho	Thanks, I need your help. I have lots of questions about courses, instructors, and my program.
Mr. Garcia	Good! But first I'd like to know more about you. Tell me about yourself.
Jun-Ho	Sure. I**'m** 19, and I**'m** a graduate of Central High School. I**'m** from South Korea originally.
15	
Mr. Garcia	I see. What **are** some of your interests?
Jun-Ho	Well, I**'m** interested in cars and music. And I really like computers. My major **is** computer science.
Mr. Garcia	Great. You know, the college has lots of clubs. It**'s** a good way to meet people and practice English.
20	
Jun-Ho	Well, I**'m** pretty busy most of the time. My brother and I **are** salesclerks in my uncle's store. We**'re** really interested in his business. I don't have much free time.
Mr. Garcia	OK. I understand. Now, let's talk about your academic plans . . .

B *Comprehension Check* Circle the correct words.

1. Mr. Garcia is **a student / an adviser**.

2. Jun-Ho is from **South Korea / the United States**.

3. Jun-Ho is a salesclerk in his uncle's **store / restaurant**.

C *Notice* Complete the sentences. Use the conversation to help you.

1. I _____ Jun-Ho. Sorry I _____ late.

2. My major _____ computer science.

3. My brother and I _____ salesclerks. We _____ really interested in his business.

2 | Present of *Be*: Affirmative Statements

▶ Grammar Presentation

Be links ideas.	I 'm a student .

2.1 Full Forms (with Subject Pronouns)

SINGULAR			PLURAL		
Subject	*Be*		**Subject**	*Be*	
I	**am**		We		
You	**are**	late.	You	**are**	from Seoul.
He She It	**is**		They		
		difficult.			

▶▶ Capitalization and Punctuation Rules: See page A1.

2.2 Contractions (with Nouns and Subject Pronouns)

SINGULAR		
I am	→	I'**m**
You are	→	You'**re**
He is	→	He'**s**
Jun-Ho is	→	Jun-Ho'**s**
She is	→	She'**s**
His mother is	→	His mother'**s**
It is	→	It'**s**
My name is	→	My name'**s**

PLURAL		
We are	→	We'**re**
You are	→	You'**re**
They are	→	They'**re**

2.3 Using Present of *Be*

a. The verb *be* "links" ideas. You can use *be* to link nouns or pronouns with words that give information about them.	Jun-Ho is a student. They are from California.
b. Use the full forms of *be* in academic writing.	I **am** a computer science major. I **am** in your grammar class.
c. Use contractions of *be* in conversation and informal writing.	**I'm** Mr. Garcia. **They're** sick today.
d. You can use *be* + noun • to talk about occupations.	He's **a teacher**. They're **students**.
• to identify things.	It's an **English class**. My hobbies are **baseball and music**. My major is **math**.
e. You can use *be* + number to talk about ages.	My sister is **18**. His parents are **49** years old.
f. You can use *be* + adjective • to talk about nationalities.	I'm **Canadian**. His parents are **South Korean**.
• to describe people and things.	Jun-Ho is **tall**. My sister is **sick**. Our reading class is **interesting**.

2.3 Using Present of *Be* *(continued)*

g. You can use *be* + preposition

• to talk about hometowns and places.	*My parents are **from Seoul**.* *I'm **from California**.*
• to talk about where people and things are.	*She is **at home**.* *We are **in Los Angeles**.*
• to talk about the groups, such as teams or clubs, that people are in.	*My friends and I are **in a band**.* *He is **on the basketball team**.*

▶ # Grammar Application

Exercise 2.1 Present of *Be*: Full Forms

A Complete the sentences about a student, using *am*, *is*, and *are*.

1. My name is Ling. I _am_ a student at the University of Florida.
2. My friend Ana and I _____ in Science 101.
3. Mr. Johnson _____ a good instructor.
4. The class _____ interesting.
5. My classmates _____ crazy about science.
6. Ana _____ smart.
7. Ana and I _____ seniors this year.

B Look at the underlined word(s). Circle the subject pronoun that replaces the underlined words.

1. My college is in Detroit, Michigan. **It / She** is a good school.
2. Jorge and Lisa are in Grammar 110. **They / We** are in a fun class.
3. Mrs. Chapple is a great teacher. **It / She** is also very nice.
4. Marcos is crazy about grammar. **He / They** is never late for class.
5. My brother is smart. **He / It** is an excellent student.
6. My mother is a nurse. **She / It** is always very busy.
7. My sister and I are sick. **She / We** are at home today.

C Complete the student's online profile. Use the full forms of *be* (*am*, *is*, *are*).

My name __*is*__ Cindy Wang. I _____ from
    (1)   (2)
Jackson, Illinois. My parents _____ from China
                                    (3)
originally. I _____ 20 years old. I _____ now
            (4)   (5)
a student at the University of Texas. My major _____
                                                  (6)
public health. My favorite subjects _____ math and
                                        (7)
biology. I _____ interested in sports and drawing.
          (8)
My friend Bev and I _____ servers in a restaurant on
                        (9)
weekends. My sister _____ still a high school student in Illinois.
                        (10)

D *Over to You* Complete the sentences with the correct full form of *be* and the information about you. Then read your sentences to your partner. How many of your sentences are the same?

1. My name _____ _____ .
                (be)   (name)
2. I _____ from _____ .
      (be)   (country)
3. I _____ _____ .
      (be)   (age)
4. My major _____ _____ .
                (be)   (subject)
5. My favorite class _____ _____ .
                        (be)   (name of class)
6. I _____ interested in _____ .
      (be)   (name of things)
7. I _____ .
    (Tell one more thing about yourself. Remember to use *be*.)

Exercise 2.2 Present of *Be*: Contractions

A Complete the sentences with *'m*, *'s*, or *'re*.

1. *Ana* Hi, I _'m_ Ana.
                (1)

   Ron Hi, Ana. My name_____ Ron. Nice to meet you.
                            (2)

   Ana It_____ nice to meet you, too.
              (3)

   Ron I_____ in Ms. Cook's class.
            (4)

   Ana She_____ my teacher, too. You_____ in
              (5)   (6)
   my class.

   Ron Great. I think we_____ in Room 9.
                            (7)

2. *Sara* Excuse me. I'm lost. My teacher_____ Mr. Martinez.
             ₍₈₎

   Ron Mr. Martinez? He_____ in Room 10.
          ₍₉₎

   Ana Room 10_____ over there. On the right.
          ₍₁₀₎

   Sara Oh, thanks.

   Ana You_____ welcome.
          ₍₁₁₎

3. *Ana* Ron, this is my friend Cathy. We_____ friends from
          ₍₁₂₎
          high school.

   Ron Hi, Cathy.

   Cathy Hi, Ron!

   Ana Cathy_____ on the basketball team. She_____ a
          ₍₁₃₎   ₍₁₄₎
          great player.

   Ron Really? I_____ a big basketball fan.
          ₍₁₅₎

   Ana Well, come to our next game. It_____ on Friday.
          ₍₁₆₎

B ***Pair Work*** Introduce yourself to your partner. Use contractions. Then introduce your
partner to a classmate.

Hi, I'm Alex. This is Hong-yin. He's from Texas. He's on the soccer team.

3 | Present of *Be*: Negative Statements

▶ Grammar Presentation

3.1 Full Forms

SINGULAR		
Subject	***Be + Not***	
I	**am not**	
You	**are not**	in class.
He She It	**is not**	

PLURAL		
Subject	***Be + Not***	
We You They	**are not**	students.

3.2 Negative Contractions

SINGULAR		PLURAL	
I am not →	I**'m not**	We are not →	We**'re not** / We **aren't**
You are not →	You**'re not** / You **aren't**	You are not →	You**'re not** / You **aren't**
He is not →	He**'s not** / He **isn't**	They are not →	They**'re not** / They **aren't**
She is not →	She**'s not** / She **isn't**		
It is not →	It**'s not** / It **isn't**		

Data from the Real World

In conversation, people usually use **'s not** and **'re not** after pronouns.	He**'s not** 21. She**'s not** in class. They**'re not** here.	
They usually use **isn't** and **aren't** after names and nouns.	Carlos **isn't** 21. Louise **isn't** in class. The boys **aren't** here.	

He/She isn't/   He's/She's not/
They aren't   They're not

▶ Grammar Application

Exercise 3.1 Present of *Be:* Negative Statements with Full Forms

A Complete the sentences. Use *am not, is not,* or *are not.*

1. My roommate and I _are not_ math majors.

2. My friends _____ in my business class.

3. My cousin _____ married.

4. You _____ late.

5. My friend _____ in the library.

6. I _____ interested in chemistry.

7. Our instructor _____ from the United States.

8. The students _____ interested in history.

B *Over to You* Write six negative sentences about yourself. Use the full form of *be*.

1. I _am not_ a teacher.

2. I _____ from _____ .

3. I _____ interested in _____ .

4. I _____ a/an _____ major.

5. I _____ a/an _____ .

6. I _____ in _____ .

C *Pair Work* Read your sentences to a partner. Are any of your sentences the same?

Exercise 3.2 Affirmative or Negative?

A Read the online profiles. Complete the sentences with the correct affirmative or negative form of *be*. Use contractions when possible.

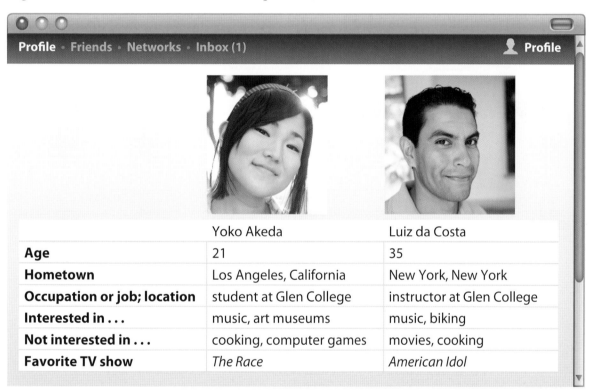

○ ○ ○		
Profile · **Friends** · **Networks** · **Inbox (1)**		👤 **Profile**

	Yoko Akeda	Luiz da Costa
Age	21	35
Hometown	Los Angeles, California	New York, New York
Occupation or job; location	student at Glen College	instructor at Glen College
Interested in . . .	music, art museums	music, biking
Not interested in . . .	cooking, computer games	movies, cooking
Favorite TV show	*The Race*	*American Idol*

1. Yoko _is_ 21. She _'s not_ 35.

2. Yoko and Luiz _____ the same age.

3. Luiz _____ an instructor. He _____ a student.

4. Yoko _____ from New York. She _____ from Los Angeles.

5. Luiz _____ from New York. He _____ from Los Angeles.

6. They _____ from Chicago.

7. They _____ interested in music.

   They _____ interested in cooking.

8. Luiz _____ interested in movies.

9. *American Idol* _____ Yoko's favorite TV show.

10. *The Race* _____ Yoko's favorite TV show. It _____ Luiz's favorite show.

B 🔊 Listen. Where are these people? Complete the sentences with the correct pronouns and forms of *be*. Use contractions when possible.

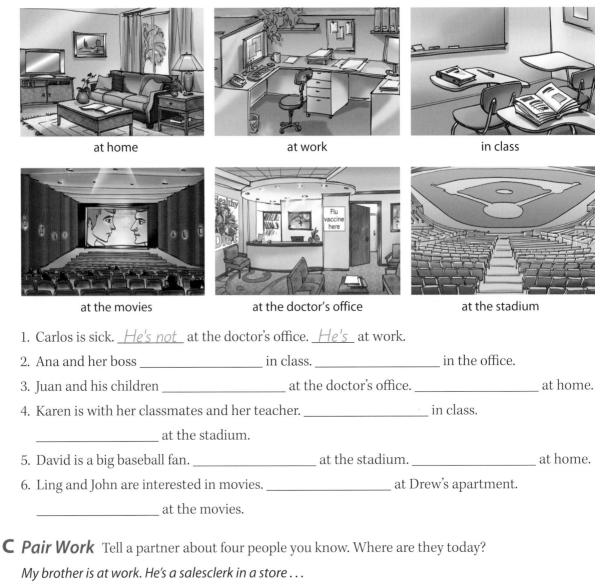

at home   at work   in class

at the movies   at the doctor's office   at the stadium

1. Carlos is sick. *He's not* at the doctor's office. *He's* at work.

2. Ana and her boss _____ in class. _____ in the office.

3. Juan and his children _____ at the doctor's office. _____ at home.

4. Karen is with her classmates and her teacher. _____ in class.

   _____ at the stadium.

5. David is a big baseball fan. _____ at the stadium. _____ at home.

6. Ling and John are interested in movies. _____ at Drew's apartment.

   _____ at the movies.

C *Pair Work* Tell a partner about four people you know. Where are they today?

My brother is at work. He's a salesclerk in a store . . .

Exercise 3.3 Negative of *Be*

Complete the conversations. Use *'s not* and *'re not* after pronouns and *isn't* and *aren't* after names and nouns.

1. *Sara*   Hello. Accounting Department.

   Ben   Louise?

   Sara   No, it's Sara. Louise *isn't* here.
   (1)

   She _____ at work today.
   (2)

2. *Sam*   Oh, no! My wallet _____ in my bag!
            (3)
            It's on the bus!

   Man   No, it _____ on the bus.
            (4)
            Look, here it is.

3. *Lara*   Where are your brothers? The game's on TV,

             and they _____ here.
                        (5)
   Joe   They _____ interested in baseball.
                   (6)
            They _____ interested in sports.
                   (7)

4 | Avoid Common Mistakes ⚠

1. Use *be* to link ideas.

   is
He an engineering student.
  ^

2. Use *be* + *not* to form negative statements with *be*. Do not use *be* + *no*.

    not
Ana is ~~no~~ a science teacher.

3. A statement has a subject. Do not begin a statement with *be*.

She is
~~Is~~ my sister's best friend.

Editing Task

Correct nine more mistakes about Amy. Rewrite the sentences.

1. This my friend. *This is my friend.* _____

2. Her name Amy. _____

3. Amy and I roommates. _____

4. She 27. _____

5. She is no a student. _____

6. Is a science teacher. _____

7. Is very nice and very smart. _____

8. Amy is no in school today. _____

9. She sick. _____

10. Is at home. _____

5 | Grammar for Writing ✏

Writing About a Person

Writers often use the verb *be* when they describe people.
Remember:

- **Be + noun can tell an occupation or identify people.**
  Marisol is my friend. She is a graduate student.

- **Be + number can tell a person's age.**
  Marisol is not old. She is only 28 years old.

- **Be + adjective tells a person's nationality or describes a person.**
  Marisol is Peruvian. She is very friendly.

- **Be + preposition can give a location or tell a group that a person belongs to.**
  Marisol is from California. She is in Paris right now. She is on a soccer team.

Pre-writing Task

1 Read the paragraph below. Who is the important person?

An Important Person in My Life

My sister (is) an important person in my life. Her name is Lila. She is 23 years old. She is a nurse at Cottage Hospital. Her interests are dancing and music. She is not interested in sports. She is tall. Her hair is long, and she is very beautiful. She is also very funny. She is still single. She and I are good friends. We are together often.

2 Read the paragraph again. Circle every form of the verb *be*. How many times does the verb *be* appear in the paragraph?

Writing Task

1 *Write* Use the paragraph in the Pre-writing Task to help you write about an important person in your life. Write at least four things about this person. For example, tell about the person's age, occupation, nationality, appearance, personality, or interests.

2 *Self-Edit* Use the editing tips below to improve your sentences. Make any necessary changes.

1. Did you use the verb *be* to tell many things about the important person in your life?
2. Did you use the correct form of *be* in your sentences?
3. Did your sentences all have a subject?
4. Did you avoid the mistakes in the Avoid Common Mistakes chart on page 11?

UNIT 2

Yes/No Questions and Information Questions with *Be*

Schedules and School

1 Grammar in the Real World

A What is your class schedule? Read and listen to the conversations below. Are Yuko's and Juan's classes the same?

Conversation A (Monday)

Yuko So, **is your next class writing?**

Juan No, it's reading.

Yuko Really? My next class is reading, too. **Are you in my class?** It's at 1:30.

Juan Maybe. **Is your class in Building H?**

Yuko Yes, it's in Building H, Room 308.

Juan Then I'm in your class, too!

Yuko Hmm. **Where's Building H?**

Juan It's on the hill, over there.

Yuko Oh, OK. **What time is it?**

Juan It's 1:20. Uh-oh. We're late!

Yuko No, we aren't.

Juan **Are you sure?**

Yuko Yes. Class is at 1:30.

Juan Oh, you're right. That's good. Let's go.

Conversation B (Thursday)

Yuko Hey, Juan. **How are you?**

Juan I'm OK. **How are you?**

Yuko I'm fine, thanks.

Juan **How are your classes?**

Yuko They're fine, but they're all really big.

Juan Really? **How many students are in your classes?**

Yuko About 25 to 30. **Is that unusual?**

Juan No, it isn't. **Who's your grammar teacher?**

Yuko Mr. Walters. He's funny, but his class is difficult.

Juan So, **when's your next class?**

Yuko Let me see. Today's Thursday. Computer lab is at 3:00.

Juan **When is it over?**

Yuko At 4:15. Let's meet after that.

B Comprehension Check Read the sentences. Circle *True* or *False*.

Conversation A

1. Yuko and Juan are in Building H now.   True   False

2. They are late for class.   True   False

Conversation B

3. Mr. Walters is Yuko's grammar teacher.   True   False

4. Computer lab is over at 4:15.   True   False

C Notice Find the questions in the conversations. Complete the questions.

1. _____ you in my class?

2. _____ your class in Building H?

3. _____ that unusual?

4. _____ you sure?

Which words are at the beginning of the questions?

2 | Yes / No Questions and Short Answers with *Be*

▶ Grammar Presentation

A *Yes / No* question is a question you can answer with *Yes* or *No*.	"Is Yuko's class in Building H?" "Yes, it is." / "No, it isn't."

2.1 Singular *Yes / No* Questions

Be	Subject	
Am	I	
Are	you	in class?
Is	he / she / it	

2.2 Singular Short Answers

AFFIRMATIVE				NEGATIVE		
	Subject	**Be**			**Subject**	**Be + Not**
	I	**am**.			I	**am not**.
Yes,	you	**are**.		No,	you	**are not**.
	he / she / it	**is**.			he / she / it	**is not**.

2.3 Plural *Yes* / *No* Questions

Be	Subject	
Are	we you they	late?

2.4 Plural Short Answers

AFFIRMATIVE				NEGATIVE		
	Subject	*Be*			Subject	*Be + Not*
Yes,	we you they	**are**.		No,	we you they	**are not**.

2.5 Negative Short Answers: Contractions

SINGULAR			PLURAL		
No, I am not.	→	No, I**'m not**.	No, we are not.	→	No, we**'re not**. No, we **aren't**.
No, you are not.	→	No, you**'re not**. No, you **aren't**.	No, you are not.	→	No, you**'re not**. No, you **aren't**.
No, he is not.	→	No, he**'s not**. No, he **isn't**.	No, they are not.	→	No, they**'re not**. No, they **aren't**.
No, she is not.	→	No, she**'s not**. No, she **isn't**.			
No, it is not.	→	No, it**'s not**. No, it **isn't**.			

2.6 Using *Yes / No* Questions and Short Answers with *Be*

a. Use a question mark at the end of questions.	*Is reading class hard?*
b. Put the verb *be* before the subject in *Yes / No* questions.	STATEMENT SUBJECT VERB *Reading class is at 1:30.* YES / NO QUESTION *Is reading class at 1:30?*
c. Use pronouns in short answers.	*"Is reading class hard?"* *"Yes, it is."*
d. Do not use contractions in short answers with *yes*.	*"Is class at 1:30?"* *"Yes, it is."* NOT *"Yes, it's."*
e. Use contractions in short answers with *no*.	*"Is Yuko late?"* *"No, she's not."* OR *"No, she isn't."*
f. Say *I don't know, I think so,* or *I don't think so* when you don't know or are not sure of the answer. Say *I don't know* when you don't know the answer. *I think so* means "maybe yes." *I don't think so* means "maybe no."	*"Is the library closed?"* *"I don't know."* OR *"I think so."* OR *"I don't think so."*

▶ # Grammar Application

Exercise 2.1 Singular *Yes / No* Questions and Answers

A Circle the correct verbs to make questions. Then complete the answers with the correct pronoun and form of *be*. Use contractions when possible.

1. **(Is)/ Are** your writing class in the morning? Yes, _it is_ .
2. **Am / Are** you free on Fridays after lunch? No, _I'm not_ .
3. **Are / Is** you always on time? Yes, _I am_ .
4. **Is / Are** your teacher busy today? Yes, _he is_ .
5. **Is / Are** you interested in sports? No, _I'm not_ .
6. **Are / Is** your roommate in your class? No, _she isn't_ .
7. **Is / Am** this an English class? Yes, _it is_ .
8. **Is / Are** your next class in this building? No, _it's not_ .

B Write two questions and two answers about each picture. Use the words in parentheses.

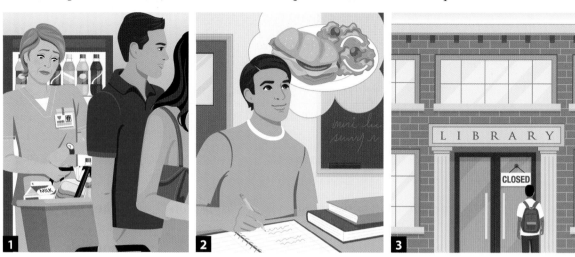

1. a. (late) _Is she late?_   _Yes, she is._
   b. (at home) _is the at home_ _____
2. a. (hungry) _i She hngre_ _____
   b. (at the store) _is he o the Store?_ _____
3. a. (open) _is the libory open?_ _____
   b. (a white building) _____ _____

Exercise 2.2 Plural Yes/No Questions and Answers

Complete the conversation between two students, John and Eric. Then practice their conversation with a partner.

John (your teachers / friendly) _Are your teachers friendly?_ _____

 Eric (yes) _Yes, they are._ _____

John (you and your classmates / happy) _____

 Eric (yes) _____

John (the homework assignments / easy) _____

 Eric (no) _____

John (your classmates / on time) _____

 Eric (no) _____

John (you and your friends / busy) _____

 Eric (yes) _____

John (the exams / difficult) _____

 Eric (yes) _____

Exercise 2.3 Singular and Plural *Yes / No* Questions and Answers

Read the paragraph from Julio's essay. Then write questions and answers about it. Use full forms of *be*.

Julio and Paulo

My roommate and I are in the English program at our college. Paulo is from Brazil, and I am from Venezuela. Paulo is a very good student, and he is very smart. I am a good student, but I am a little lazy. My classes are on Mondays, Wednesdays, and Fridays. Paulo's classes are every day from Monday to Friday. We are always busy, but on the weekend we relax.

1. Paulo and Julio / college students

   Are Paulo and Julio college students? Yes, they are.

2. they / from the same country

   _____

3. they / good students

   _____

4. Paulo / smart

   _____

5. Paulo / lazy

   _____

6. Julio's classes / every day from Monday to Friday

   _____

3 | Information Questions with *Be*

▶ Grammar Presentation

Use the question words *who, what, when, where,* and *how* to ask for information.	*What's your name?* *Who is the teacher?* *Where are the classrooms?*

3.1 Information Questions

SINGULAR SUBJECTS			PLURAL SUBJECTS		
Wh- Word	*Be*	Subject	*Wh-* Word	*Be*	Subject
Who		your teacher?	**Who**		your teachers?
What		your major?	**What**		your plans?
When	**is**	our exam?	**When**	**are**	your exams?
Where		the building?	**Where**		your books?
How		your class?	**How**		your classes?

3.2 Contractions with Singular Subjects

Who is	→	**Who's**
What is	→	**What's**
When is	→	**When's**
Where is	→	**Where's**
How is	→	**How's**

3.3 Using Information Questions with *Be*

a. Put a question mark (?) at the end of information questions.	*Who are those students?*
b. Put the question word first in an information question.	***What** is your name?*
c. Answer information questions with information. Don't answer with *Yes* or *No*.	*"When is grammar class?"* **"At 10:00."**
d. In conversations, most answers are not complete sentences. They are short answers.	*"Who's your teacher?"* **"Mr. Jones."**
e. Note that with singular subjects it is common to use the contracted form of *is* with the question word.	*What**'s** your name?* *Where**'s** your class?*

3.4 Using *Wh-* Words with *Be*

a. Use *who* to ask about people.	***Who's** our teacher?* ***Who** are your friends?*	*Ms. Williams.* *Marie and Elsa.*
b. Use *what* to ask about things.	***What** are your favorite classes?* ***What's** your phone number?*	*Grammar and writing.* *It's 368-555-9823.*
c. Use *where* to ask about places.	***Where's** your class?* ***Where** are you from?* ***Where** are your friends?*	*It's in Building H.* *Brazil.* *They're in the computer lab.*

3.4 Using *Wh-* Words with *Be* (continued)

d. Use *when* to ask about days or times.	**When's** your exam? **When** is lunch? **When** are our exams?	It's February 14. At noon. Next week.
e. Use *how* to ask about health or opinions.	**How's** your mother? **How's** school?	She's well. Great!
f. Use *how much* to ask about cost and amount. Use *how many* to ask about numbers. Use *how old* to ask about age.	**How much** is the movie? **How many** students are here? **How old** are your brothers?	Eight dollars. Twelve. They're 17 and 15.

▶ # Grammar Application

Exercise 3.1 Information Questions with *Be*

A Complete the conversation between Joe and his mother. Use the correct *Wh-* word. Use contractions of *be*.

Mother   <u>What's</u> your roommate's name?
(1)

Joe   Mike.

Mother   _____ he from?
(2)

Joe   Chicago.

Mother   _____ his major?
(3)

Joe   I don't know. Mom, my history class is in five minutes.

Mother   _____ your instructor?
(4)

Joe   I don't know his name. It's the first class.

Mother   _____ your class over?
(5)

Joe   At 4:30. Please don't call before that.

B Complete the questions with *How, How much, How many,* or *How old*. Use the correct form of *be*.

1. <u>How are</u> you?   I'm fine, thanks.
2. _____ you?   I'm 23.
3. _____ the textbook?   It's $26.
4. _____ students _____ in your English class?   Thirty.
5. _____ the sandwiches?   They're $5.75.

Exercise 3.2 Information Questions and Answers

Write questions about the tuition bill. Then write answers in complete sentences.

Plains Community College

Spring Semester   February 1–May 28
Name: Jason Armenio   **Student ID Number:** 452319
Major: History   **Total class credits:** 15

      Tuition: $ 600.00   ($40.00 per credit)
      Parking permit: $ 20.00
      Health Services Fee: $ 17.00
    Total: $ 637.00

IMPORTANT DATES
First day of classes: February 1 **Tuition payment due:** January 31
Spring Break: March 29–April 3   **Final Exams:** May 24–28

1. (What / the college's name) _What is the college's name? It's Plains Community College._

2. (What / the student's name) _____

3. (When / the spring semester) _____

4. (What / his major) _____

5. (How much / the tuition) _____

6. (How much / the parking permit) _____

7. (What / the total) _____

8. (When / final exams) _____

Exercise 3.3 More Information Questions and Answers

Pair Work With a partner, write five questions to ask your classmates. Ask questions about their classes, schedules, and school. Then interview your classmates. Write their answers in the chart.

Interview Questions	Your Classmates' Answers
1. *When are your classes?*	*My classes are on Monday and Wednesday.*
2. when is First day of classes?	My classes start February
3. where is spring Break	
4.	
5.	
6.	

4 Avoid Common Mistakes ⚠

1. **Begin a question with a capital letter. End with a question mark.**

   W   *?*
   ~~w~~here is Karla~~.~~

2. **Remember that a question has a subject and a verb.**

   is
   Where Room 203?

3. **Don't use contractions with short *Yes* answers to *Yes / No* questions.**

   I am
   "Are you tired?" "Yes, ~~I'm~~."

4. **Make sure the subject and verb agree.**

   Are
   ~~Is~~ John and Pedro here?

5. **Put the verb after the question word in information questions.**

   When is the writing class?
   ~~When the writing class is?~~

Editing Task

Find and correct the mistakes in these questions and answers about your school.

     W
1. ~~w~~here is your school?

2. What is the school's name.

3. How much the tuition is?

4. "your school expensive." "Yes, it's."

5. What your major?

6. Is you a good student?

7. When summer break is?

8. Is all your classes difficult?

5 | Grammar for Writing ✏

Using Questions to Get Information About a Topic

Writers use questions to get information about topics they want to write about. First, they think of the information that they want to know. Then they ask the questions that will give them that information.

Remember:

Question word order and statement word order are different.

	SUBJECT	VERB	
Statement	*Paulo*	*is*	*at the library.*

	VERB	SUBJECT	
Yes/No Question	*Is*	*Paulo*	*at the library?*

	WH- WORD	VERB	SUBJECT
Information Question	*Where*	*is*	*Paulo?*

Pre-writing Task

1 Read the paragraph below.

My Classmate Javier

Javier is a college student. His school is in Orlando, Florida. His major is business. His business classes are all interesting. His first language is Spanish. His birthday is on June 11. His interests are computers and soccer. He is married, and his wife's name is Violeta. She is not a student.

2 Write the questions the writer asked Javier to get information before writing the paragraph.

Writer's Questions	Javier's Answers
1. Are __you a student__ ?	Yes, I am.
2. Where _____ ?	It's in Orlando, Florida.
3. What _____ ?	It's business.
4. How _____ ?	They're all interesting.
5. What _____ ?	It's Spanish.
6. When _____ ?	It's on June 11.
7. What _____ ?	Computers and soccer.

8. _____ married?   Yes, I am.

9. What _____ ?   Violeta.

10. _____ a student?   No, she isn't.

Writing Task

1 *Write* Use the paragraph in the Pre-writing Task to help you write about a classmate or a friend. Decide on the information you want to know. Then write at least six questions to find out the answers. Interview the person, and then write your paragraph.

2 *Self-Edit* Use the editing tips below to improve your sentences. Make any necessary changes.

1. Did you use questions to find out information about your classmate?
2. Did you use the correct word order for *Yes / No* questions?
3. Did you use the correct word order for information questions?
4. Did you avoid the mistakes in the Avoid Common Mistakes chart on page 23?

UNIT 3

Count Nouns; *A/An*; *Have* and *Be*

Gadgets

1 Grammar in the Real World

A Do you have a cell phone? If so, is your cell phone like these phones? Read the web page. Which phone is best for you?

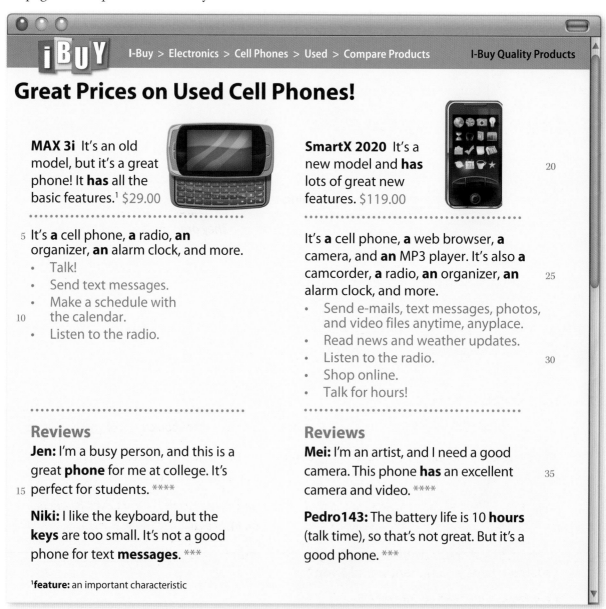

iBUY   I-Buy > Electronics > Cell Phones > Used > Compare Products   I-Buy Quality Products

Great Prices on Used Cell Phones!

MAX 3i It's an old model, but it's a great phone! It **has** all the basic features.[1] $29.00

5 It's **a** cell phone, **a** radio, **an** organizer, **an** alarm clock, and more.
- Talk!
- Send text messages.
- Make a schedule with
10 the calendar.
- Listen to the radio.

SmartX 2020 It's a new model and **has** lots of great new features. $119.00   20

It's **a** cell phone, **a** web browser, **a** camera, and **an** MP3 player. It's also **a** camcorder, **a** radio, **an** organizer, **an**   25 alarm clock, and more.
- Send e-mails, text messages, photos, and video files anytime, anyplace.
- Read news and weather updates.
- Listen to the radio.   30
- Shop online.
- Talk for hours!

Reviews

Jen: I'm a busy person, and this is a great **phone** for me at college. It's
15 perfect for students. ****

Niki: I like the keyboard, but the **keys** are too small. It's not a good phone for text **messages**. ***

Reviews

Mei: I'm an artist, and I need a good camera. This phone **has** an excellent   35 camera and video. ****

Pedro143: The battery life is 10 **hours** (talk time), so that's not great. But it's a good phone. ***

[1]**feature:** an important characteristic

26

B *Comprehension Check* Answer the questions. Circle *Yes* or *No*. Use the web page to help you.

1. Are the two phones new models?   Yes   No
2. Is the MAX 3i $29.00?   Yes   No
3. Is the SmartX 2020's camera good?   Yes   No

C *Notice* Circle the correct words. Use the web page to help you.

1. The MAX 3i is **a** / **an** old model.
2. Jen is **a** / **an** busy person.
3. The battery life is 10 **hour** / **hours**.
4. This is a great **phone** / **phones** for me.

2 | Nouns; *A/An*

▶ Grammar Presentation

Nouns are words for people, places, and things.	*I'm an* **artist**. *It's an electronics* **store**. *It is a great* **phone**. *They are great* **phones**.

2.1 Singular and Plural Nouns

Singular Nouns	Plural Nouns
It's a **camera**.	*They are* **cameras**.
It's a good **product**.	*They are good* **products**.

2.2 Singular Nouns

a. Count nouns have singular and plural forms.	*a book – three books* *one phone – two phones*
b. Use *a* before singular count nouns that begin with a consonant sound (*b, c, d, f, g,* etc.).	*a* **cell phone** *a* **web browser** *a* **screen** *a* **camera**
c. Use *an* before singular count nouns that begin with a vowel sound (*a, e, i, o, u*).	*an* **address book** *an* **advertisement** *an* **MP3** *player* *an* **update**
Note: Some nouns that begin with the letter *u* have a consonant sound ("you").	*a* unit *a* university

▶▶ Indefinite and Definite Articles: See page A19.

2.3 Plural Nouns

a. Add -*s* to most singular nouns to form plural nouns.	*a model – two models* *a camera – two cameras* *a key – keys* *a student – students*
b. Add -*es* to nouns that end in -*ch*, -*sh*, -*ss*, -*z*, and -*x*.	*watch – watches* *class – classes* *dish – dishes* *tax – taxes*
c. With nouns that end in consonant + *y*, change the *y* to *i* and add -*es*.	*battery – batteries* *accessory – accessories*
d. With nouns that end in -*ife*, change the ending to -*ives*.	*life – lives* *knife – knives*

2.4 Irregular Plural Nouns

a. Some plural nouns have irregular forms. ⬤ These are the most common irregular plural nouns in academic writing.	*man – men* *woman – women* *child – children* *person – people* *foot – feet* *tooth – teeth*
b. Some nouns have the same form for singular and plural.	*one fish – two fish* *one sheep – two sheep*
c. Some nouns are only plural. They do not have a singular form.	*clothes* *jeans* *scissors* *headphones* *pants* *sunglasses*

▶❙ Spelling Rules for Noun Plurals: See page A2.

2.5 Proper Nouns

Proper nouns are the names of specific people, places, and things. They begin with capital letters.	*Jenny* *Mr. Johns* *Ms. Thorson* *Canada* *Dallas* *Chester College* *San Francisco Herald*

▶❙ Capitalization and Punctuation Rules: See page A1.

▶ Grammar Application

Exercise 2.1 *A* or *An*

A Write *a* or *an* next to each noun.

1. _*a*_ pencil
2. _____ eraser
3. _____ camera
4. _____ grammar book
5. _____ laptop
6. _____ marker
7. _____ address book
8. _____ calculator
9. _____ wallet
10. _____ notebook

B *Over to You* Ask and answer questions about things in the classroom. Use *a* or *an*. Make a list of the new words you learn.

    A What's the word for this in English?

    B It's a desk. / I don't know. Let's ask the teacher.

Exercise 2.2 Plural Nouns

A Look at this store advertisement. Write the plural form of the nouns. For nouns that have only one form, leave the space blank.

Shop at The Mart

This week's sale prices

Electronics		School Supply*ies*		Clothes and Accessory____	
battery_____	$3–$5	dictionary_____	$5.95–$29.95	dress_____	$19–$89
calculator_____	$8–$75	scissors_____	$2.95–$10	belt_____	$13–$39
headphones_____	$5–$65	notebook_____	75¢–$3.50	sunglasses_____	$10–$20
cell phone_____	$60–$200			purse_____	$19–$129
computer_____	$300–$999			jeans_____	$29–$80
video camera_____	$400–$1,000				

B *Pair Work* Practice asking and answering questions about the items in A with a partner.

    A How much are the belts?

    B They're $13 to $39.

Exercise 2.3 ◄)) Pronunciation Focus: Plural Nouns

For nouns that end in the sounds /s/, /ʃ/, /tʃ/, /dʒ/, /ks/, and /z/, say /əz/ in the plural. These nouns have an extra syllable in the plural form.		**/əz/**
	/s/	cla**ss** – classes
	/ʃ/	di**sh** – dishes
	/tʃ/	wat**ch** – watches
	/dʒ/	messa**ge** – messages
	/ks/	bo**x** – boxes
	/z/	qui**z** – quizzes
For most other nouns, say /s/ or /z/ in the plural.		**/s/ or /z/** book – books pho**ne** – phones accessor**y** – accessories

A 🔊 Listen. Check (✓) the nouns with an extra syllable in the plural form.

✓ 1. purse – purses   ☐ 4. door – doors   ☐ 7. page – pages

☐ 2. bag – bags   ☐ 5. size – sizes   ☐ 8. closet – closets

☐ 3. map – maps   ☐ 6. computer – computers   ☐ 9. phone – phones

B Write the plural form of these nouns. Do they have an extra syllable? Check (✓) *Yes* or *No*.

	Extra Syllable?				Extra Syllable?	
	Yes	No			Yes	No
1. desk __desks__	☐	✓	8. brush _____		☐	☐
2. tax _____	☐	☐	9. dictionary _____		☐	☐
3. CD player _____	☐	☐	10. match _____		☐	☐
4. case _____	☐	☐	11. chair _____		☐	☐
5. orange _____	☐	☐	12. quiz _____		☐	☐
6. penny _____	☐	☐	13. pen _____		☐	☐
7. student _____	☐	☐	14. garage _____		☐	☐

Exercise 2.4 Proper Nouns

Write answers to the questions. Use proper nouns.

1. What's the capital of the United States? _It's Washington, D.C._ _____

2. What's your last name? _____

3. What's the name of the street where you live? _____

4. What's the name of your hometown? _____

5. What's the name of your favorite movie? _____

6. What's your favorite store? _____

7. What's the name of your school or college? _____

8. What's your teacher's name? _____

3 | *Be* with *A / An* + Noun

▶ Grammar Presentation

3.1 Using *Be* with *A / An* + Noun

a. You can use *be* with *a / an* + noun to tell:

- what something is.
- what something is like.
- who someone is.
- what someone is like.

*It's **a** cell phone. It's **an** MP3 player, too.*
*It's **a** great phone.*
*Jon is **a** friend from college.*
*He's **a** nice guy.*

b. You can use *be* + *a / an* + noun to say a person's occupation.

*Jenny is **a** businesswoman.*
*Pedro is **an** architect.*

c. Don't use *a / an* with plural nouns.

*They're cell phone**s**.*
NOT ~~They are a cell phones.~~

Pronunciation note: *A* and *an* are not usually stressed. *a* = /ə/ and *an* = /ən/
/ə/ CELL phone   /ən/ ARchitect

▶ Grammar Application

Exercise 3.1 *A / An* + Noun

Complete the conversation with *a* or *an*.

A Is that <u>*a*</u> new cell phone? Is it <u>*an*</u> MP3 player, too?
(1)   (2)

B Yes. It's my new toy. It's <u>*a*</u> smart phone.
(3)

A Cool. Oh, look! Is that <u>*an*</u> e-mail?
(4)

B No, it's <u>*a*</u> text message from Jeff.
(5)

A Jeff? Is he <u>*a*</u> friend?
(6)

B Yes, from high school. He's now <u>*an*</u> engineering
(7)

student at <u>*a*</u> university in Florida. He's in town
(8)

with his brother, Dan. Dan's <u>*an*</u> artist.
(9)

A Wow. So, where are they?

B They're at <u>*a*</u> coffee shop near here. Let's go see them.
(10)

A That sounds like fun. Let's get <u>*a*</u> taxi.
(11)

Exercise 3.2 A / An + Noun: Occupations

A Match the occupations and the pictures. Write the correct letter next to the names. Then complete the sentences below. Make some occupations plural.

| a. chef | b. electrician | c. engineer | d. mechanic | e. pharmacist | f. receptionist |

1. Mike __c__

2. Carl __a__

3. Julia __b__

4. Jody and Bryan __d__

5. Sarah __e__

6. Ana and Peter __f__

1. Mike _is an engineer._
2. Carl _is an chef_
3. Julia _is an electrition_
4. Jody and Bryan _one an mechanic_
5. Sarah _is a pharmacist_
6. Ana and Peter _are an receptionist_

B *Over to You* Write sentences about people you know.

1. I am _a student. I'm also a part-time salesclerk._
2. My friend is ___a student___
3. My neighbor is ___doctor___
4. My friends are ___mona___ and ___Vi___ . They ___are classmates___
5. My classmate's name is ___mona___ . He / She ___She is from Sout Arabie___
6. My ___Brother___ is ___a student in TXT___
   (family member)

4 | *Have*

▶ Grammar Presentation

<table>
<tr><td>*Have* can show possession. It can also mean "to experience."</td><td>He **has** a nice apartment. (possession)
My friends and I **have** a good time together. (experience)</td></tr>
</table>

4.1 *Have*

Subject	*Have*	
I We You They	**have**	a camera.
He She It	**has**	

4.2 Using *Have*

a. Use *have* + noun to show: • possession or ownership. • relationships. • parts of a whole.	I **have** a car. She **has** a friend from Chile. The website **has** helpful links.
b. It can also mean "to experience" or "to take part in an activity."	We **have** fun in class. They **have** lunch at 12:30.

▶ Grammar Application

Exercise 4.1 *Have*

Complete the sentences. Use *have* or *has*.

1. Big Electric is an electronics store. It usually __has__ good prices.

2. The store is very large. It __has__ four floors.

3. The first floor __have__ computers and phones.

4. The second floor __have__ video game consoles and video games.

5. The third and fourth floors __have__ TVs, sound systems, and entertainment systems.

6. Big Electric also __has__ a website.

7. The website sometimes __has__ special sale prices.

8. Customers __have__ a lot of fun shopping here.

Exercise 4.2 *Have* and *Be*

Complete the sentences from a student essay. Use *have, has, am, is,* or *are*.

My Favorite Gadget

Let me tell you about my laptop. It __is__ an old laptop, but it __has__ a good
(1)   (2)

computer. It only weighs four pounds, so it __is__ not very heavy. It __is__
(3)   (4)

great speakers, and it also __has__ a bright, colorful screen. So it __is__ great for
(5)   (6)

movies and for music. It __is__ also good for e-mail. I __am__ a student, so my
(7)   (8)

laptop __is__ very important for me. I use it to do almost all my homework. This
(9)

laptop also __has__ a webcam. I use it to talk to my friends in Mexico. I __have__ a lot
(10)   (11)

of friends there, and we __are__ very happy to see each other and talk over
(12)

the Internet. Sometimes I __have__ problems with my computer. For example, the
(13)

battery __is__ not very strong. Also, the computer __is__ slow. I want a new
(14)   (15)

one, but good laptops __are__ very expensive.
(16)

5 | Avoid Common Mistakes ⚠

1. Use *a* or *an* to say a person's job.

        an
    Jody is ^ artist.

2. Use *a* or *an* to say what kind of a person someone is.

        a
    She's ^ nice person.

3. Use *are* after plural nouns. Remember: *people*, *men*, *women*, and *children* are plural.

               are
    The people in my class ~~is~~ nice.

          are
    His children ~~is~~ smart.

4. Use *are* with two nouns joined with *and*.

            are
    My clock and my radio ~~is~~ on my desk.

5. Use *has* with a singular subject.

      has
    Tom ~~have~~ a great laptop.

Editing Task

Find and correct nine more mistakes about the Lim family.

                         are
1. The people in my neighborhood ~~is~~ nice.

          are
2. My neighbors ~~is~~ very friendly.

          are
3. Tom and Nancy Lim ~~is~~ my neighbors.

      is a
4. Nancy ~~is~~ computer programmer.

      is a
5. Tom ~~is~~ cell phone designer.

         are
6. Their children ~~is~~ Joe and Cathy.

          are
7. Joe and Cathy ~~is~~ students at Hatfield College.

      an
8. Joe is ^ student in the computer department.

      has
9. He ~~have~~ a lot of classes this year.

      is a
10. Cathy ~~is~~ busy architecture student.

6 | Grammar for Writing

Writing About a Favorite Place

Writers often use *be* and *have* to give information about people, places, and things. These verbs can help you clearly explain your ideas.

Remember:

- ***Be*** + noun and ***have*** + noun give different information.

- ***Be*** + noun can identify and describe people and things.

    He *is* my brother.   Oaxaca *is* a city.

- ***Have*** + noun can show:

    possession or relationship

    I *have* a cat.   I *have* a cousin.

    experience

    My friend and I *have* a good time together.

    parts of a whole

    That website *has* many interesting links.

Pre-writing Task

1 Read the paragraph below. What places can you visit in this city?

My Favorite City

I <u>have</u> a favorite <u>city</u>. The city (is Giza,) Egypt.

It <u>has</u> a lot of beautiful monuments. It also <u>has</u>

a lot of <u>museums</u> and beautiful <u>parks</u>. My favorite

park (is Orman Park.) Giza <u>has</u> a fast and <u>clean</u>

subway system.

2 Read the paragraph again. Circle *be* + noun. Underline *have* + noun.

I have a favorite city. The city is Rio, Brasil.
It has a lot of beoutiful landscapes. It also has
a lot of Beaches. My favorite Beach is copacabana
Rio has all the beaches very clean.

Writing Task

1 *Write* Use the paragraph in the Pre-writing Task to help you write about a favorite city or place. Write about the places and things that make this place special.

2 *Self-Edit* Use the editing tips below to improve your sentences. Make any necessary changes.

1. Did you use sentences with *be* and *have* to tell about your favorite place?
2. Did you use *be* to describe people and things?
3. Did you use *have* to show possession and experience?
4. Did you avoid the mistakes in the Avoid Common Mistakes chart on page 35?

Demonstratives and Possessives

The Workplace

1 | Grammar in the Real World

A Can you name five things that you use in an office? Read the conversation. How many different office things do the speakers mention in the conversation?

First Day at the Office

Robert Hello, Claudia. I'm Robert. Welcome to **our** company!

Claudia Hello, Robert. It's nice to meet you.

Robert **This** is **your** desk. **That**'s the closet for **your** coat. Let me show you around.

5 *Claudia* Thanks.

Robert Office supplies, like paper, folders, and CDs, are in **those** cabinets over there. The printers are here, and **this** is the only copy machine. The paper is in **these** drawers below the printers.

Claudia   Thanks. **That**'s good to know.

10   Robert   Now, let me introduce you to Keung. He's on **your** team. Keung, **this** is Claudia. She's **our** new sales manager.

Keung   Nice to meet you, Claudia.

Claudia   Nice to meet you, Keung. **Those** photographs are beautiful. Are you a photographer?

15   Keung   Well, photography is **my** hobby. **Those** pictures are from **my** trip to Thailand.

Claudia   **That** photograph on the left is great. What is it?

Keung   It's the Royal Palace in Bangkok, **my** favorite place.

Claudia   **That**'s a great picture, too.

20   Keung   **Those** little girls are **my sister's** children. She lives in Bangkok.

Robert   Sorry to interrupt, but we have a management meeting in 10 minutes. It's in the conference room. It's **this** way, down the hall. Let's get some coffee before the meeting.

Claudia   OK. See you later, Keung.

25   Keung   Wait. Robert, are **these your** reports?

Robert   Yes, they are. Thanks. I need them for the meeting.

B *Comprehension Check*   Match the two parts of the sentences about the conversation.

1. Claudia _C_   a. are in the cabinets.

2. Keung _e_   b. are his sister's children.

3. The little girls in the photograph _b_   c. is a new employee.

4. Office supplies _a_   d. is in the conference room.

5. The meeting _d_   e. is on her team.

C *Notice*   Find the sentences in the conversation and circle the correct words.

1. The paper is in **these** / **this** *drawers* below the printers.

2. **Those** / **That** *photograph* on the left is great.

3. **That** / **Those** little *girls* are my sister's children.

4. It's **this** / **these** *way*, down the hall.

Now look at the nouns in *italics*. What words come before the singular nouns? What words come before the plural nouns?

2 Demonstratives (*This, That, These, Those*)

▶ Grammar Presentation

> The demonstratives are *this*, *that*, *these*, and *those*. We use demonstratives to "point to" things and people.
>
> **This** is my desk.
> **Those** desks are for new employees.

2.1 Demonstratives with Singular and Plural Nouns

SINGULAR				PLURAL			
This / That	Noun	Verb		*These / Those*	Noun	Verb	
This	drawer	is	empty.	**These**	cabinets	are	for supplies.
That			for paper.	**Those**			locked.

2.2 Demonstratives Used Without Nouns

SINGULAR			PLURAL		
This / That	Verb		*These / Those*	Verb	
This	is	for you.	**These**	are	from your co-workers.
That		my desk.	**Those**		for us.

2.3 Using Demonstratives with Singular and Plural Nouns

a. Use *this* for a person or thing <u>near</u> you (a person or thing that is <u>here</u>).

This desk is Amanda's.
This paper is for the printer.

b. Use *that* for a person or thing <u>not near</u> you (a person or thing that is <u>there</u>).

That desk is Janet's.
That printer is a color printer.

c. Use *these* for people or things <u>near</u> you (people or things that are <u>here</u>).

These reports are for the meeting.
These students are in your English class.

d. Use *those* for people or things <u>not near</u> you (people or things that are <u>there</u>).

Those folders are the sales reports.
Those soccer players are great.

e. Use *this*, *that*, *these*, and *those* before nouns to identify and describe people and things.

This photo is my favorite.
That little girl in the photo is my sister's daughter.
These charts are helpful.
Those papers are important.

2.4 Using Demonstratives with *Be*

a. You can use *this*, *that*, *these*, and *those* as pronouns to identify things.

This is the only copy machine.
= *This copy machine is the only copy machine.*

That is the color printer.
= *That printer is the color printer.*

These are the reports for the meeting.
= *These reports are the reports for the meeting.*

Those are my keys.
= *Those keys are my keys.*

b. You can only use *this* and *these* as pronouns to introduce people.

A This is Claudia.
B Hi, Claudia! Nice to meet you.

A These are my co-workers, Mena and Liz.
B Hello. Nice to meet you.

c. In informal speaking, use the contraction *that's* instead of *that is*.

That's a nice picture.

2.5 Questions with Demonstratives

a. To identify people, ask questions with *Who is . . . ?* If it's clear who you are talking about, you can omit the noun.

Who is that new teacher?
Who is that?

b. To identify things, ask questions with *What is . . . ?* If it's clear what you are talking about, you can omit the noun.

What is that noise?
What is that?

c. To ask about a price, use *How much is / are . . . ?* If it's clear what you are talking about, you can omit the noun.

How much is this printer?
How much is this?
How much are these printers?
How much are these?

d. After questions with *this* and *that*, answer with *it* for things and *he* or *she* for people.

"How much is **this** copier?" "**It's** $100."

"Who is **that** lady?" " **She**'s my boss."

e. After questions with *these* and *those*, answer with *they*.

"Are **these** your reports?" "Yes, **they** are."

"Who are **those** people?" "**They**'re my co-workers."

▶ Grammar Application

Exercise 2.1 Demonstratives with Singular and Plural Nouns

Help Margo describe her office. Write *this* or *these* for things that are near her, and *that* or *those* for things that are <u>not</u> near her.

1. ___This___ phone is new.
2. ___That___ closet is for her coat.
3. ___These___ books are about business.
4. ___This___ computer is old.
5. ___These___ pens are very good.
6. ___That___ window is open.
7. ___These___ papers are for the meeting.
8. ___That___ cabinet is for paper clips, folders, and general office things.
9. ___That___ picture is a photograph of her family.
10. ___These___ folders are for the sales reports.

Exercise 2.2 More Demonstratives with Singular and Plural Nouns

Pair Work What's in your pocket? What's in your bag? Tell your partner using *this* and *these*. Then your partner repeats everything using *that* and *those*.

A *This is a cell phone. These are keys. This is a pen. These are pencils. This is a paper clip.*

B *OK. That's a cell phone. Those are keys. That's a pen. Those are pencils. That's a paper clip.*

Exercise 2.3 Demonstratives Without Nouns

A Which noun isn't necessary? Cross out the noun. Check (✓) the sentences where you cannot cross out the noun.

Jane	How much are these (1) ~~memory sticks~~?
Salesclerk	$30.
Jane	Thank you. That's a nice (2) *computer.* ✓
Lisa	Yes, it has a big screen. What's that (3) *thing* on the front?
Salesclerk	It's the webcam. And here's the headphone jack.
Jane	Yeah. Is this (4) ~~model~~ a new model?
Salesclerk	No. This (5) ~~model~~ is an old model. That's why it's on sale. That's (6) *the new model* over there.
Jane	Oh, I see. Hey, these (7) ~~headphones~~ are great headphones.
Lisa	Yeah? Buy them!
Jane	Hmm . . . They're $250. No, thank you!

B 🔊 Listen to the conversation and check your answers.

Exercise 2.4 Questions and Answers with Demonstratives

Circle the correct words.

1. *A* How much is **these /(that)** printer, please?   *B* **(It's)/ They're** $220.
2. *A* Excuse me, how much are **(these)/ this** scanners?   *B* **It's /(They're)** $150.
3. *A* How much is **those /(this)** electronic dictionary?   *B* **It's / They're** $100.
4. *A* Excuse me, how much are **that /(those)** pens?   *B* **It's / They're** $4.
5. *A* How much are **these / that** laptops?   *B* **It's / They're** on sale. **It's / They're** $300.
6. *A* How much is **those / that** digital photo frame?   *B* **It's / They're** $60.

Exercise 2.5 More Questions and Answers with Demonstratives

Pair Work Look around your classroom. In each box, write the names of three more things you see.

	Near Me	Not Near Me
Singular	*a desk, . . .*	*a map, . . .*
Plural	*books, . . .*	*windows, . . .*

Ask your partner *Yes/No* questions about the things above. Answer with *it* (singular) or *they* (plural).

A Is **that** a map of Iowa?
B No, **it**'s not. **It**'s a map of Illinois.

A Are **these** books new?
B Yes, **they** are.

Exercise 2.6 Vocabulary Focus: Responses with *That's*

You can use short responses with *That's* + adjective in conversations.	A I have a new job. B *That's* great! / *That's* good!	A My printer is broken. B *That's* too bad.
Here are common adjectives to use with *that's*.	excellent good great OK terrible too bad	interesting nice wonderful

Write a response with *That's* + adjective. Use the adjectives above.

1. It's a holiday tomorrow. _That's nice._

2. We're on the same team! _____

3. Business isn't very good this year. _____

4. Patricia's not here today. She's sick. _____

5. I have a new laptop! _____

6. This cell phone has a dictionary. _____

3 Possessives and *Whose*

▶ Grammar Presentation

Possessives show that someone possesses (owns or has) something.	A *Is this **Diane's** desk?* B *No, it's **my** desk. **Her** desk is in the other office. **Her boss's** desk is in that office, too.*

3.1 *My, Your, His, Her, Its, Our, Their*

Subject	Possessive	
I	my	I'm not ready for class. **My** desk is very messy.
you	your	You are very organized. **Your** desk is so neat.
he	his	He is a new employee. **His** old job was in Hong Kong.
she	her	She isn't in the office now. **Her** computer is off.
it	its	It is a new company. **Its** president is Mr. Janesh.
we	our	We have the reports. **Our** boss wants to read them now.
you	your	You are co-workers. **Your** office is on the second floor.
they	their	They are at the office. **Their** boss is on vacation.

▶◀ Subject and Object Pronouns: See page A18.

3.2 Possessive Nouns

a. Add 's to singular nouns to show possession.	The **manager's** name (one manager) The **boss's** ideas (one boss)
b. Add an apostrophe (') to plural nouns ending in -s to show possession.	The **managers'** names (more than one manager) The **bosses'** ideas (more than one boss)
c. For irregular plural nouns, add 's to show possession.	The **men's** books (more than one man) The **children's** room (more than one child)
d. *My, your, his, her, our,* and *their* can come before a possessive noun.	**my friend's** job **our parents'** names

▶◀ Capitalization and Punctuation Rules: See page A1.

3.3 *Whose?*

a. We can use *whose* to ask who owns something. We can use it with singular and plural nouns.	***Whose*** *jacket is this?* *I think that's* **Kana's** *jacket.*
b. We often use *whose* with *this, that, these,* and *those*.	***Whose*** *papers are* ***those****?* *Oh! They're* **my** *papers. Thank you.*

3.4 Using Possessives

a. Use the same possessive form before a singular noun or a plural noun.	**SINGULAR** **PLURAL** **my** friend **my** friends **her** report **her** reports the **boss's** report the **boss's** reports
b. Use a possessive to show that someone owns something.	**her** pen **their** folders **Rachel's** car
c. Use a possessive to show that someone has something.	**your** name **my** birthday **Jared's** job
d. Use a possessive to show relationships between people.	**my** sister **his** boss **Claudia's** co-worker
e. Use a possessive noun to talk about places and countries.	The **city's** population **Japan's** prime minister

Grammar Application

Exercise 3.1 Possessives

Ben sends an e-mail to Dora and attaches some pictures. He describes them. Complete the e-mail. Use the possessive form of the pronoun in parentheses – *my, his, her, its, our, their* – or *'s*.

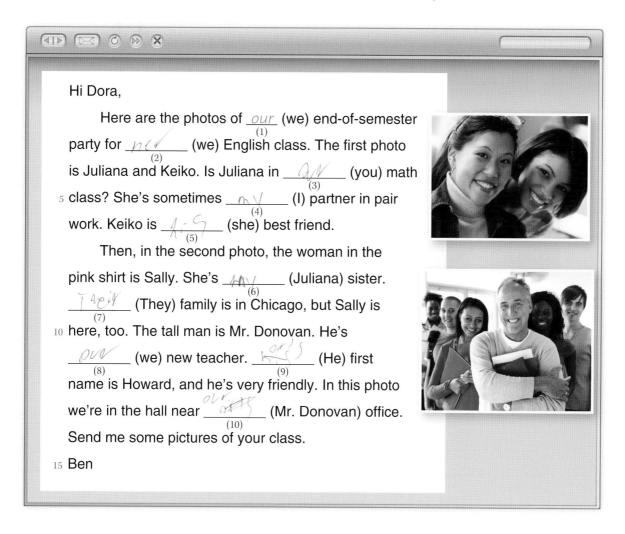

Hi Dora,

Here are the photos of __our__ (we) end-of-semester
party for __our__ (we) English class. The first photo
(2)
is Juliana and Keiko. Is Juliana in __our__ (you) math
(3)
5 class? She's sometimes __my__ (I) partner in pair
(4)
work. Keiko is __her__ (she) best friend.
(5)
Then, in the second photo, the woman in the
pink shirt is Sally. She's __Juliana's__ (Juliana) sister.
(6)
__Their__ (They) family is in Chicago, but Sally is
(7)
10 here, too. The tall man is Mr. Donovan. He's
__our__ (we) new teacher. __His__ (He) first
(8)   (9)
name is Howard, and he's very friendly. In this photo
we're in the hall near __Mr. Donovan's__ (Mr. Donovan) office.
(10)
Send me some pictures of your class.

15 Ben

Exercise 3.2 Possessive 's or s'?

A Circle the correct form of the possessive (*'s* or *s'*) in the sentences.

1. My **co-worker's** / **co-workers'** name is Krista.
2. **Krista's** / **Kristas'** last name is Logan.
3. She has two managers. Her **manager's** / **managers'** names are Tom and Sara.
4. **Sara's** / **Saras'** family is from Colombia.
5. She has two brothers. Her **brother's** / **brothers'** names are José and Carlos.

6. **Tom's / Toms'** wife is from New Jersey. Her name is Jessica.

7. Jessica and Tom have a daughter. Their **daughter's / daughters'** name is Danielle.

8. They have two cats. The **cat's / cats'** names are Sam and Max.

B *Pair Work* Tell a partner about someone you know at work or about a friend at school. Use the sentences in A as a model.

Exercise 3.3 Questions with *Whose* and *Who's*

A Complete the questions about the people in the photos with *Whose* and *Who's*. Then answer the questions.

Name: Ling Yang
Nationality: Chinese
Birthday: October 2
Best friend: Leila
Major: Nursing
Interests: yoga, art

Name: Ki-woon Do
Nationality: South Korean
Birthday: June 5
Best friend: Nora
Major: Business
Interests: soccer, movies

Name: Missolle Beauge
Nationality: Haitian
Birthday: April 7
Best friend: Lona
Major: Computers and Technology
Interests: music, cooking

1. ___Whose___ best friend is Leila? ___Leila is Ling's best friend.___
2. ___whose___ birthday is in June? ___Ki-woon birthday is in June___
3. ___who's___ Chinese? ___Ling is from Chinese___
4. ___whose___ major is Business? ___Ki-woon. missolle is Haitia___
5. ___who's___ Haitian? _____
6. ___who's___ from South Korea? ___Ki-woon is from South Korea___
7. ___whose___ major is Nursing? ___Ling Yong major is Nursing___
8. ___whose___ birthday is in October? ___Ling Yon's birthday is in oct___
9. ___who's___ interested in soccer? ___Ki-woon is interested in soccer___
10. ___whose___ interests are music and cooking? ___Missolle interests are music or cook___

B *Pair Work* Ask and answer other questions about the people in A.

A *Whose best friend is Nora?*
B *Nora is Ki-woon's best friend.*

4 | Avoid Common Mistakes ⚠️

1. Use *this* and *that* for singular things and people.

This
~~These~~ printer is $79.

That
~~Those~~ man is my manager.

2. Use *these* and *those* for plural things and people.

These
~~This~~ folders are for the meeting.

Those
~~That~~ women are on my team.

3. *Its* is possessive. *It's* is a contraction for *it is*.

Its   *It's*
He works for a small company. ~~It's~~ name is Z-Tech. ~~Its~~ on Main Street.

4. Use *'s* (singular) or *s'* (plural) with possessive nouns.

mother's   *co-workers'*
Tomorrow is her ~~mother~~ birthday.   I don't know my ~~co-workers~~ birthdays.

5. Use the same possessive form before a singular noun or a plural noun.

her
Justine enjoys spending time with ~~hers~~ co-workers.

Editing Task

Find and correct eight more mistakes in this conversation.

A Hi. I'm sorry to interrupt you, but where's the manager's office?

B It's next to Claudia's office.

A Where is that? I don't know Claudia.

B Oh, it's down this hallway right here. Turn left after you pass those two elevators.

A Oh, OK. You mean it's near the two assistants' offices?

B That's right. Do you know them?

A Yes, I do.

B Then please give them a message. Their folders are on my desk.

5 | Grammar for Writing

Writing About Things and People's Possessions

Writers use demonstratives and possessives to explain who people are and what they own. They also use them to describe the location of people and things in a place.

Writers often use demonstratives and possessives to describe people and things in pictures. Remember:

- **Use *this* and *these* for things and people <u>near</u> you.**

  This is my boss, Serena.   *These are my co-workers, Jon and Marquesa.*

- **Use *that* and *those* for things and people <u>not near</u> you.**

  That office over there is Jon's office.   *Those offices over there are empty.*

- **Use possessives before a noun or nouns to show the relationships between people and things.**

  Serena's boss is there.   *Her name is Maxie.*   *Our office is here.*

Pre-writing Task

1 Read the e-mail below. What does the writer describe?

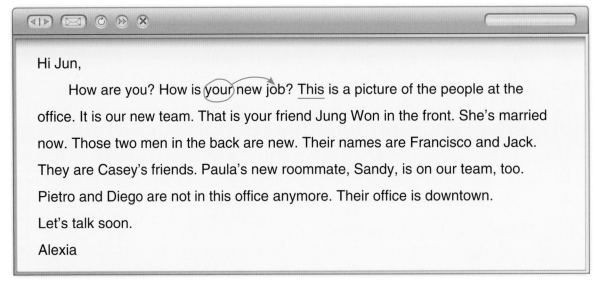

Hi Jun,

How are you? How is your new job? This is a picture of the people at the office. It is our new team. That is your friend Jung Won in the front. She's married now. Those two men in the back are new. Their names are Francisco and Jack. They are Casey's friends. Paula's new roommate, Sandy, is on our team, too. Pietro and Diego are not in this office anymore. Their office is downtown.

Let's talk soon.

Alexia

2 Read the e-mail again. Circle the possessives and draw an arrow to the things or people the possessives go with. Then underline the demonstratives. Notice the writer's use of *our*. Who does the writer mean by *our*?

Writing Task

1 *Write*   Find a picture of people in your life. Write an e-mail about them. Use the e-mail in the Pre-writing Task to help you.

Use sentences with demonstratives and possessives. Use sentences such as:

- This is a picture of _____ .
- This / That is _____ .
- These / Those (people, things) are _____ .
- This / That (person, thing) is _____ .

2 *Self-Edit*   Use the editing tips below to improve your sentences. Make any necessary changes.

1. Did you use demonstratives and possessives to write about people and their relationships in your pictures?
2. Did you use *this* and *these* for things and people near you?
3. Did you use *that* and *those* for things and people <u>not</u> near you?
4. Did you use possessives before a noun or nouns to show the relationships between people and things?
5. Did you avoid the mistakes in the Avoid Common Mistakes chart on page 49?

1 Grammar in the Real World

A Do you use a social networking website? Which one? Read the web article about a social networking site for jobs. Are these websites useful for employers?

NEWS

SEARCH

Social Networking for Jobs

Sometimes, social networking[1] websites are for sending news, messages, and photos to friends. They're like **big** bulletin boards on the Internet. Now social networking websites are for work, too. **Unemployed**[2] people can find jobs there, and companies can find **new** workers. Some sites also have a lot of
5 very **useful** information about jobs and careers.

Here is the story of two people who use JobsLink, a social networking website.

Julia is a **hardworking** student at a **large** community college. She's very **busy** with her courses, but she is also **ambitious**.[3] Her career goal is to be an
10 accountant. She has a profile on a social networking website for business professionals. Her profile has a link[4] to her résumé.

Ricardo is an employer. He has a **small** business. His accounting office needs a **new** accountant. He's interested in Julia's profile on JobsLink. She's **young**, but she's an **excellent** student. Ricardo contacts Julia by e-mail. She has an
15 interview with Ricardo. He thinks that Julia is **friendly** and **smart**. Soon, Julia has a **new** job. Julia and Ricardo are **happy** with the social networking website.

[1]**social networking:** meeting and talking to people on the Internet | [2]**unemployed:** not having a job that earns money | [3]**ambitious:** wanting success | [4]**link:** a word or image on a website that can take you to another document or website

B *Comprehension Check* Answer the questions. Use the article to help you.

1. What is JobsLink?
2. Is Julia a student or an instructor?
3. Is Ricardo an employee or an employer?
4. Who has an interview with Ricardo?

C *Notice* The nouns in each sentence are underlined. Circle the word that describes each noun. These words are adjectives.

1. It's like a big <u>bulletin board</u>.
2. He has a small <u>business</u>.
3. Julia is a hardworking <u>student</u> at a large <u>community college</u>.
4. Julia has a new <u>job</u>.

Do the adjectives come before or after the nouns?

2 | Adjectives

▶ Grammar Presentation

Adjectives describe or give information about nouns – people, places, things, and ideas.	*I found a **good** job.* (*Good* describes *job*.) *This website is **helpful**.* (*Helpful* describes *this website*.)

2.1 Adjectives

a. Adjectives can come before nouns.

	ADJECTIVE	NOUN
He owns a	**small**	**business**.
She has a	**new**	**job**.

b. Adjectives can come after the verb *be*. They describe the subject.

SUBJECT	BE	ADJECTIVE
Julia	**is**	**smart**.
They	**are**	**young**.

c. Adjectives have the same form when they describe singular or plural nouns.

	ADJECTIVE	NOUN (SINGULAR)
He needs a	**good**	**accountant**.

	ADJECTIVE	NOUN (PLURAL)
He needs two	**good**	**accountants**.

2.2 Using Adjectives

a. When using an adjective before a singular noun:

• use *a* before adjectives that begin with a consonant[1] sound.	*They work for **a big** company.* *She has **a long** résumé.* ***A new** student is in my class.*
• use *an* before adjectives that begin with a vowel[2] sound.	*He has **an interesting** blog.* *She's **an ambitious** businessperson.* *That's **an excellent** idea!*

b. You can use adjectives to describe:

• color	*a **blue** suit*	*an **orange** skirt*
• age	*a **new** website*	*an **old** résumé*
• size	*a **tall** building*	*a **small** phone*
• shape	*a **wide** street*	*a **round** window*
• opinions	*a **great** job*	*an **excellent** student*
• length of time	*a **short** meeting*	*a **long** vacation*

c. You can use *very* to make the adjective stronger. *The meeting was **very long**.*

Reminder:
[1]Consonants: the letters *b, c, d, f, g, h, j, k, l, m, n, p, q, r, s, t, v, w, x, y, z*
[2]Vowels: the letters *a, e, i, o, u*

Data from the Real World

These adjectives are used after the verb *be*.	*afraid, alone, asleep, awake*
Do *not* use them before a noun.	*Ahmed is asleep.* NOT *Ahmed is ~~the asleep man~~.*

▶ Grammar Application

Exercise 2.1 Adjective + Noun

A Rewrite the sentences with the adjectives in parentheses.

1. James is an engineer. (unemployed) _James is an unemployed engineer._

2. James is a person. (hardworking) _____

3. This is a website. (useful) _____

4. It has jobs. (interesting) _____

5. This is a company. (large) _____

6. James can send his résumé. (new) _____

B Write sentences about the people and things in parentheses. Use your own ideas and some of the adjectives from the box. Remember to put the adjectives before the nouns.

ambitious	busy	friendly	interesting	popular	unusual
big	difficult	good	kind	smart	useful

1. (company) _Microsoft is a big company._____

2. (person) _____

3. (website) _____

4. (job) _____

5. (employer) _____

6. (student) _____

Exercise 2.2 Vocabulary Focus: Opposites with Adjective + Noun and *Be* + Adjective

asleep / awake	good / bad	old / new (things)	*My office isn't **loud**. It's **quiet**.*
big / little	happy / sad	old / young (people or animals)	*Please be **early**. Don't be **late**.*
big / small	hot / cold	short / long	*This résumé is **old**, but that one*
early / late	loud / quiet	short / tall	*is **new**.*

Note: *Big* has two opposites, *little* and *small*. *Short* has two opposites, *tall* and *long*. *Tall* is for height. *Long* is for length, distance, or time.

Old has two opposites, *new* and *young*. *New* is for things, and *young* is for people or animals.

A Complete the sentences with their opposites. Use adjectives from the Vocabulary Focus box.

1. I'm not asleep right now. I'm _awake_ .

2. This is a _____ phone message. It's not old.

3. The office is very _____ . There are only two people here. It isn't big.

4. The office building is _____ . It isn't short. It has 50 floors.

5. Today isn't bad. This is a _____ day! I have a new job!

6. Do you have a _____ ruler? This one is short.

B *Pair Work* Work with a partner. Make sentences with adjectives from the Vocabulary Focus box. Your partner makes sentences with the opposite adjectives. Take turns.

A *This isn't a little book.*
B *It's a big book.*

A *I'm tall.*
B *Maria is short.*

C Complete the e-mail. Use the adjectives from the box.

~~excited~~	happy	interesting	long	young
friendly	helpful	late	old	

Hi Ramon,

How are you? I'm very __excited__ about my new job. My work hours are
(1)
_____ . For example, I usually work from 8:00 a.m. until 6:00 p.m.
(2)
But I'm _____ because it's an _____ job. I am a research
(3)   (4)
assistant in a hospital. My office is on the tenth floor. It's an _____ building.
(5)
It's 60 years old. My boss is _____ — he's only 30. He's _____
(6)   (7)
and _____ when I have questions.
(8)
That's all for now. It's _____ at night and I'm tired. Please write soon.
(9)

Take care,
Jack

Exercise 2.3 Vocabulary Focus: Nationality Adjectives

Ending in -*an* or -*ian*		Ending in -*ish*	Ending in -*ese*	Ending in -*i*
African	Indian	British	Chinese	Iraqi
American	Indonesian	Danish	Japanese	Israeli
Australian	Italian	English	Lebanese	Kuwaiti
Austrian	Korean	Irish	Portuguese	Omani
Brazilian	Mexican	Polish	Sudanese	Pakistani
Canadian	Nigerian	Scottish	Vietnamese	Qatari
Chilean	Peruvian	Spanish		Saudi
Egyptian	Russian	Swedish		Yemeni
Ethiopian	Syrian	Turkish		
German	Venezuelan			

Exceptions: Dutch (from the Netherlands), Filipino (from the Philippines), French (from France), Greek (from Greece), Swiss (from Switzerland), Thai (from Thailand)

A Complete the sentences. Use nationality adjectives.

1. Paula is from Brazil. She's _Brazilian_ .
2. My co-workers are from Chile. They're _____ .
3. Hakim is from Kuwait. He's _____ .
4. Alex is from Germany. He's _____ .
5. Vinh is from Vietnam. He's _____ .
6. Sarah is from England. She's _____ .

B *Over to You* Write three sentences about yourself. Then write sentences about three people from other countries. Remember to capitalize the names of countries and languages.

My name is Claudia. I'm from Mexico. I'm Mexican.

3 Questions with *What . . . like?* and *How* + Adjective

▶ Grammar Presentation

Questions with *What . . . like?* and *How* + adjective ask for a description. They are usually answered with an adjective.	A "What is Arizona like?" B "It's beautiful." A "How deep is the Grand Canyon?" B "It's very deep."

3.1 Questions with *What . . . like?*

What + Be	Subject	Like	Answers with Adjectives
What is **What's**	New York	**like?**	It's **big**.
What are	the restaurants		They're **expensive**.

3.2 Questions with *How* + Adjective

How	Adjective	Be	Subject	Answers with Adjectives
How	**old**	is	the company?	It's 40 years **old**.
	tall	is	Jack?	He's 6 feet (1.80 meters) **tall**.
	long	are	the lines?	They're not **long**. They're very **short**.
	cold	is	the water?	It's not very **cold**. It's **warm**.

▶ Grammar Application

Exercise 3.1 Questions with *What . . . like?*

A Complete the conversation about the city of St. Louis. Use *What . . . like* in the questions. Then choose an answer from the box.

It's very cold, and it's snowy.	They're good and not too expensive.
It's an old Midwestern city in Missouri.	They're very friendly.

John I have exciting news! I have a new job!

Erica That's great!

John Well, the bad news is this: It's in St. Louis. It's not here in Chicago.

Erica Wow! <u>What's</u> St. Louis <u>like</u> ?

(1)   (1)

John _____

(2)

Erica _____ the weather _____

(3)   (3)

in the winter?

John _____

(4)

Erica _____ the people _____?

(5)   (5)

John _____

(6)

Erica _____ the restaurants _____?

(7)   (7)

John _____

(8)

B ◀)) Listen to the conversation and check your answers.

C *Over to You* Write questions with *What . . . like in your city?* Then answer the questions with *It's* or *They're*.

1. (the weather) _*What's the weather like in your city? It's very hot in the summer.*_

2. (traffic) _____

3. (the people) _____

4. (the parks) _____

5. (the restaurants) _____

6. (the shopping) _____

Exercise 3.2 Questions with *How* + Adjective

A Complete these questions with *How* and an adjective from the box. Then ask and answer the questions with a partner.

    A How old is your city?   *B It's really old. It's about 200 years old.*

bad	cold	crowded	expensive	hot	~~old~~

1. _____*How old*_____ is your city?
2. _____ is it in the summer?
3. _____ is it in the winter?
4. _____ is the downtown area with people?
5. _____ are the apartments?
6. _____ is the traffic?

B *Pair Work* Write six questions about a city to ask your partner. Write two with *What . . . like?* and three with *How* + adjective. Your partner chooses a city. Then you ask the questions and guess the city.

1. What *are winters like in this city?*_____
2. What _____
3. What _____
4. How _____
5. How _____
6. How _____
7. Let me guess. Is this city _____

4 Avoid Common Mistakes ⚠️

1. An adjective can come before the noun it describes or after the verb *be*.

    long meeting   *is*

I have a ~~meeting long~~ every Wednesday. This meeting important.

2. Adjectives do not have plural forms.

    wonderful

I have three ~~wonderfuls~~ employees.

3. Use *an* before adjectives that begin with a vowel sound. Use *a* before adjectives that begin with a consonant sound.

    an   *a*

My sister is ~~a~~ ambitious person. She's ~~an~~ hardworking employee.

4. Nationality adjectives begin with a capital letter.

    Danish

Sven is from Denmark. He's ~~danish~~.

Editing Task

Find and correct nine more mistakes in these profiles from a social networking website.

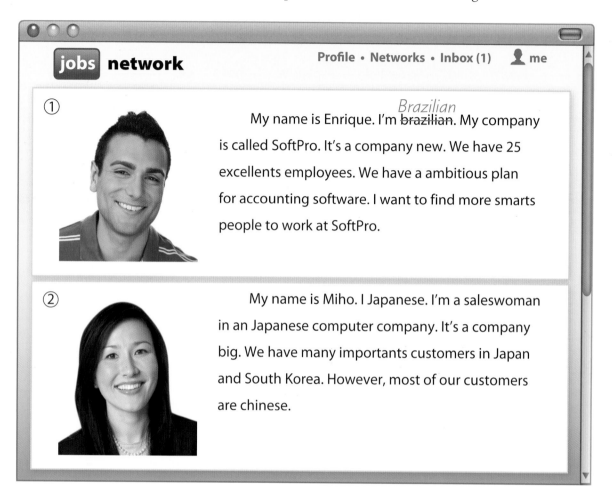

① My name is Enrique. I'm ~~brazilian~~ *Brazilian*. My company is called SoftPro. It's a company new. We have 25 excellents employees. We have a ambitious plan for accounting software. I want to find more smarts people to work at SoftPro.

② My name is Miho. I Japanese. I'm a saleswoman in an Japanese computer company. It's a company big. We have many importants customers in Japan and South Korea. However, most of our customers are chinese.

5 | Grammar for Writing

Writing About Skills and Qualities

Writers use adjectives to describe their professional skills and their personal qualities. Remember:

- **Use adjectives before nouns and after *be* to describe the nouns.**
  Your boss is a <u>busy</u> person.   *Everyone in my office is <u>friendly</u>.*

- **Use *very* to make your statement stronger. But be careful not to use it too much, or the statements all become weaker.**
  My communication skills are <u>very</u> good.

Pre-writing Task

1 Read the paragraph below. How many qualities does the writer describe?

My Nursing Goal

My goal is to be a nurse for (young) children. I have a lot of useful qualities for nursing. I am a very friendly person. I love people, and I am very good with young children and small babies. I am also patient. I am a very hardworking person, and I am strong. My communication skills are good. I am smart. My science class grades are high. These qualities are very important for successful nurses.

2 Read the paragraph again. Circle the adjectives. Then draw an arrow from the adjectives to the nouns they describe. With which adjectives does the writer use *very*? Why?

Writing Task

1 *Write* Write about your ideal job. What are your professional skills and personal qualities? What makes you special for that job? Use the paragraph in the Pre-writing Task and the sentences below to help you write about your goal.

Use sentences such as:
- My goal is to be _____ (occupation).
- I have a lot of useful qualities for _____ (career).
- I am _____ (qualities).
- I am also a/an _____ person.

2 *Self-Edit* Use the editing tips below to improve your sentences. Make any necessary changes.

1. Did you use adjectives to write about your professional and personal skills and qualities?
2. Did you use both adjective + noun and *be* + adjective combinations?
3. Did you use *very* to make some of your statements stronger?
4. Did you avoid the mistakes in the Avoid Common Mistakes chart on page 59?

Prepositions

Around the House

1 Grammar in the Real World

A What's it like to have a houseguest? Maya is away, but her friend Cathy is her houseguest for the weekend. Read Maya's note to Cathy. Do you think Cathy is happy right now?

Hi Cathy,

    I'm happy you're **in** the apartment this weekend. My cat Fluffy is glad you're here, too. Please use my bedroom. Clean towels and sheets are **in** the closet. There's an extra blanket **in** the drawer **under** the bed.

5   I'm sorry the refrigerator's empty, but the supermarket's **across** the street. The car keys are **on top of** the refrigerator. The car's out of gas,[1] but the gas station's close, just two blocks away **on** Main Street.

    The TV's **in** the cabinet **near** the window. The remote control's **on** the counter **next**
10 **to** the coffee maker. (I think the batteries are dead. ☹)

    I'm sorry about the cat food **on** the floor. Fluffy's very messy. ☺ The vacuum cleaner's **in** the closet. It's old but it works.
15 The cleaning supplies are **behind** the plant. The garbage cans are **outside** the front door, **in front of** the garage.

    See you **on** Sunday evening. My bus arrives **at** 5:30 p.m. So expect me **between**
20 6:00 and 7:00.

Love,
Maya

P.S. I'm **at** my sister's house.
Her phone number is (212) 555-8749.

[1]**out of gas:** without gas

B *Comprehension Check* Match the two parts of the sentences about the note.

1. Maya is   a. on the floor.
2. The car is   b. at her sister's house.
3. The cat food is   c. in the closet.
4. Clean towels are   d. out of gas.
5. Cathy is   e. in the apartment.

C *Notice* Complete the sentences. Use the note to help you.

1. Clean towels and sheets are _____ the closet.
2. The car keys are _____ the refrigerator.
3. The remote control is _____ the counter _____ the coffee maker.
4. See you _____ Sunday evening.
5. My bus arrives _____ 5:30 p.m.

Which sentences tell you when something happens? Which sentences tell you where something is?

2 | Prepositions of Place: Things at Home and in the Neighborhood

▶ Grammar Presentation

| Prepositions can show place. They can tell you where someone or something is. | *The remote control is **next to** the coffee maker.*
*My home is **near** the train station.* |

2.1 Things at Home

in

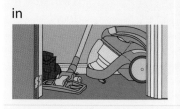

The vacuum cleaner is **in** the closet.

on / on top of

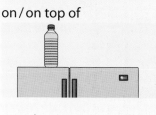

The bottle is **on** the refrigerator.

The bottle is **on top of** the refrigerator.

under

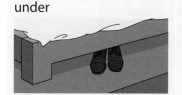

The shoes are **under** the bed.

behind

The cleaning supplies are **behind** the plant.

2.1 Things at Home *(continued)*

above

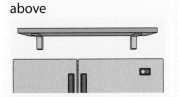

The shelf is **above** the refrigerator.

next to / near

The book is **next to** the lamp.

The lamp is **near** the window.

in front of

The garbage can is **in front of** the garage.

between

The car keys are **between** the watch and the wallet.

2.2 Things in the Neighborhood

in front of

The man is **in front of** the bakery.

between

The bank is **between** the restaurant and the delicatessen.

behind

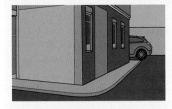

The car is **behind** the building.

across from

The woman is **across from** the bank.

next to / near

The coffee shop is **next to** the post office.

The coffee shop is **near** the bakery.

outside

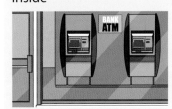

The garbage can is **outside** the door.

at

The children are **at** the zoo.

inside

The ATMs are **inside** the bank.

▶ Grammar Application

Exercise 2.1 Prepositions of Place: Things at Home

A Complete the sentences with prepositions of place and the words in the box. Use the picture to help you. Sometimes more than one answer is possible.

coffee maker	counter	door	floor	gym bag	refrigerator	table

Sean I need my cell phone. Where is it?

Jon It's _on the table_ .
        (1)

Sean Thanks. Now, where's my gym bag?

Jon It's _____ .
        (2)

Sean OK. Oh, and I need my wallet. Where's that?

Jon It's _____ .
        (3)

Sean And my keys. Where are my keys?

Jon They're _____ .
        (4)

Sean Now, where's my laptop? I need my laptop.

Jon It's _____ .
        (5)

Sean Is the newspaper outside the front door?

Jon No, it's _____ .
        (6)

Sean And where are my books for school?

Jon They're _____ .
        (7)

Sean Hey. How about a cup of coffee?

Jon Sure. Where's the coffee?

Sean It's _____ .
        (8)

B Write questions with *Where* and answers. Use the picture in A to answer the questions.

1. (radio) _Where's his radio? It's on/on top of the refrigerator._

2. (watch) _____

3. (glasses) _____

4. (headphones) _____

5. (notebook) _____

C *Pair Work* Ask your partner about where things are in his or her home. Write six
questions. Then answer your partner's questions. Use the words from the box.

bed	coffee maker	desk	remote control	sofa
clothes	computer	refrigerator	rug	

A Where's your TV?
B It's in the living room. It's next to the bookshelf.

Exercise 2.2 Prepositions of Place: Things in the Neighborhood

A Write sentences about the places in this neighborhood. Use four more of the
prepositions from the box.

above	at	between	next to
across from	~~behind~~	in front of	outside

1. the gas station / the supermarket *The gas station is behind the supermarket.*

2. the camera store / the shoe store and the coffee shop _____

3. the red car / the gas station _____

4. the shopping carts / the supermarket _____

5. the bookstore / the bank _____

B 🔊 Listen. Where are these places? Write sentences. Use and reuse the prepositions from the box in A.

1. The parking lot is *in front of the supermarket.*
2. The hair salon is _____
3. The movie theater is _____
4. The park is _____
5. The post office is _____

C *Pair Work* Ask and answer questions about your school and the area around the school.

A *Where's the post office?*   *A* *Is the school across from the bank?*
B *It's across from the school.*   *B* *No, it's next to the library.*

3 | Prepositions of Place: Locations and Other Uses

▶ Grammar Presentation

Certain prepositions commonly appear with some locations.	Maya's sister lives **in San Diego**. She lives **on Market Street**. Her home is **at 606 Market Street**.

3.1 *In, On,* and *At* with Locations

in + neighborhood ... + city / town ... + state ... + country	I live **in Midtown**. I live **in Miami**. My hometown is **in Ohio**. Montreal is **in Canada**. **What state** is Seattle **in?**
on + street	I live **on Main Street**. The restaurant is **on Grand Avenue**. **What street** is the movie theater **on?**
at + address	I live **at 1298 Seventh Avenue**. We met **at 405 Broadway**.

3.2 Ordinal Numbers with Streets and Floors

1 first	7 seventh	13 thirteenth	19 nineteenth
2 second	8 eighth	14 fourteenth	20 twentieth
3 third	9 ninth	15 fifteenth	21 twenty-first
4 fourth	10 tenth	16 sixteenth	30 thirtieth
5 fifth	11 eleventh	17 seventeenth	31 thirty-first
6 sixth	12 twelfth	18 eighteenth	32 thirty-second

Use ordinal numbers with some streets.	I live on **Third Avenue**. My apartment is on **Ninth Street**.
Use *on* + *the* + ordinal number + *floor*.	The doctor's office is **on the second floor**. I live **on the fifteenth floor**.

3.3 Common Expressions with Prepositions

at home (*or* home)	Maya is not **at home** this weekend. NOT Maya is not ~~at the home~~ this weekend.
at work	She is not **at work** today. NOT Maya is not ~~at the work~~ today.
at school / college in school / college	It's 10:30. Cathy's **at school** right now. (= in the building) I'm a student. I'm still **in school**. (= still a student)
in class / in a meeting	Tom is **in class**. (= in the classroom)
on campus	The bookstore is **on campus**.
across the street	The student center is **across the street**.

▶ # Grammar Application

Exercise 3.1 *In, On,* and *At* with Locations

A *Pair Work* Complete the questions with the correct prepositions. Then write the full answers to the questions. Use your own ideas. Check your answers with a partner.

1. Are we _in_ Canada right now? _____

2. What town or city are we _____ ? _____

3. Are we still _____ Broad Street? _____

4. Are you _____ 25 Madison Avenue? _____

5. Are the restrooms _____ the first floor? _____

6. What street is this school _____ ? _____

B Complete the paragraphs about a student. Use *in*, *on*, or *at*.

My name is Blanca González, and I am from Mexico. My hometown is __*in*__ Mexico. Now I live _____ the United
(1)   (2)
States. I live _____ Waltham, Massachusetts. It's near
(3)
Boston. My apartment is _____ 399 Moody Street. My
(4)
parents also live in Waltham, _____ 147 Hope Avenue.
(5)
They are only two minutes away from my apartment.

I have three roommates. Our apartment is _____ the third floor. There is a
(6)
large supermarket _____ my street. There are also several gas stations _____ my
(7)   (8)
neighborhood. It's noisy _____ the street, but it's OK _____ our apartment. During
(9)   (10)
the day I study accounting. In the evenings I work at a restaurant _____ Watertown.
(11)
That's a town next to Waltham.

Exercise 3.2 *In, On,* and *At* with Locations and Ordinal Numbers

A *Over to You* Complete the information about your home and school. Use the information in parentheses.

1. My hometown is _____*in*_____ ____*Illinois*____ .
(preposition)   (state or country)

2. My hometown is between _____ and _____ .
(one city/town)   (another city/town)

3. Now I live _____ _____ .
(preposition)   (neighborhood)

4. My home is _____ _____ .
(preposition)   (street name)

5. I live _____ _____ .
(preposition)   (address – You can give an imaginary address.)

6. My home is near _____ .
(a place or building)

7. My classroom is _____ _____ _____ floor.
(preposition)   (+ *the*)   (ordinal number)

8. My school is across the street from _____ .
(a place)

B *Pair Work* Share your information with a partner.

Exercise 3.3 Expressions with *In, On,* and *At*

Complete the cell phone conversations. Use *in, on,* or *at*. Sometimes more than one answer is possible.

1. *Ashley* Hi, this is Ashley.

    Sarah Hi. This is Sarah. Where are you?

    Ashley I'm __at__ work. How about you? Are

    you _____ home?

    Sarah No, I'm _____ the movie

    theater _____ Fourth Street, and

    I'm cold.

    Ashley Oh, sorry. I'm late. I'm on my way.

2. *Rodrigo* Hi, it's me.

    Bob Hi. Where are you? Are you _____

    class?

    Rodrigo No. Class starts in two minutes.

    I'm _____ campus, but I think my

    backpack's _____ my closet.

    Can you bring it?

    Bob Sure. No problem. I'm still _____ the

    apartment.

3. *Alan* Hey. Where are you? Are you _____ class?

    Inga No. I'm _____ campus. Class starts in

    five minutes.

    Alan OK. I'm _____ home, but I'll be _____ work tonight.

    Inga OK, thanks for the reminder. I won't wait for you for dinner.

4. *Joseph* Mike? It's Joseph. Are you _____ school today?

    Mike Hi, Joseph. Yes. I'm _____ the library.

    Joseph Well, I'm _____ the coffee shop _____ Sullivan Street.

    Are you free?

    Mike Sure. See you in five minutes.

4 | Prepositions of Time

▶ Grammar Presentation

Prepositions can tell you about when something happens.	Maya returns **on** Sunday. Her bus arrives **at** 5:30 p.m. Cathy expects her **between** 6:00 and 7:00.

4.1 *In, On, At*

Use *in* + parts of the day	Cathy always goes for a walk **in the afternoon**. On Mondays, I work **in the morning**.
Use *in* + month	My birthday is **in December**. Vietnam is beautiful **in April**.
Use *in* + season	Waltham is very cold **in the winter**. Please visit me **in the spring**.

 People also say, for example, "in winter" and "in spring," but "in the winter" and "in the spring" are more common.

Use *on* + date In dates, write the number, but say the ordinal number.	I'll see you **on July 1**. My class ends **on May 20**.	(on July first) (on May twentieth)

 People also say, for example, "the twentieth of May," but "May twentieth" is more frequent.

Use *on* + day	See you **on Monday**. Our class begins **on Friday**.	
Use *at* + specific time	The bank opens **at 7:00**. I usually wake up **at 5:30**.	(at seven / at seven o'clock) (at five-thirty / at half past five)

4.2 Questions with Days, Dates, and Times

You can ask questions about days, dates, or times with: *When is / are . . .* *What day is . . .* *What time is . . .* You can give shorter or longer answers to questions about days, dates, and times.	"**When is** Independence Day?" "It's on July 4. / On July 4. / July 4." "**What time is** your class?" "It's at 8:00. / At 8:00. / 8:00."

▶ Grammar Application

Exercise 4.1 *In, On, At* with Time

A Circle the correct preposition.

1. In my state, it's very cold **at** / **in** the winter and very hot **at** / **in** the summer.

2. The warm weather usually starts **on** / **in** April.

3. Unfortunately, it rains a lot **in** / **on** the spring.

4. The first day of summer is **in** / **on** June.

5. In the summer, the sun goes down late **at** / **in** the evening.

6. It's still sunny when I finish my class **on** / **at** 7:00.

7. I usually stay up late **on** / **in** Fridays and look at the stars.

8. I like to wake up **on** / **at** 6:30 on Saturdays because the weather is still cool **in** / **at** the morning.

Data from the Real World

People often give approximate times with *around* or *about*.	*See you around 6:30.* (= 6:20–6:40) *Call me about 6:15.* (= 6:10–6:20)
You can use *between* + two times.	*I'll see you between 6:00 and 7:00.*

B Complete the conversation. Use *in, on, at, around,* or *between*. Sometimes more than one answer is possible.

Alex Let's get together next week. Let's have lunch __*on*__ Monday.
(1)

I'm free _____ 12:30 and 2:30.
(2)

Sam Monday? That's my brother's birthday. We always have lunch

together _____ my brother's birthday.
(3)

Alex How about _____ Tuesday?
(4)

Sam Well, I have class _____ the afternoon on Tuesday.
(5)

It's _____ 1:00. It usually finishes _____ 2:15.
(6)   (7)

Let's meet _____ Wednesday.
(8)

Alex Great. Let's meet _____ Wednesday then,
(9)

_____ 1:00.
(10)

C *Over to You* Write six sentences about dates that are special for you. Then share your sentences with a partner.

My mother's birthday is on July 16. My favorite holiday is Independence Day. It's on July 4.

Exercise 4.2 Questions with Days, Dates, and Times

A Unscramble the words to make questions about the Expo.

1. the / Expo / is / When

   When is the Expo?

2. day / What / is / the concert

   _____

3. the students / do / a break / When / have

   _____

4. the Career Fair / What / is / day

   _____

5. is / lunch / When

   _____

6. the welcome / is / time / What

   _____

VALE COMMUNITY COLLEGE

Music Industry Expo
Thursday, April 22, 7 p.m.–10 p.m.

Concert
Friday, April 23, 9 a.m.–5 p.m.

──────── Friday ────────

9:00 Welcome
9:30 "The Business of Music"
10:30 "Becoming a Songwriter"
11:15–11:30 Break
11:30 Talk by Sound Engineer
12:30–1:30 Lunch
1:30 "Writing Music for the Movies"
2:30–4:30 Career Fair
4:30 New Music Software

B *Pair Work* Ask and answer the questions in A with a partner.

A When is the Expo?
B It's on Thursday, April 22.

5 | Avoid Common Mistakes ⚠

1. Use *in* + month, but use *on* + date or day.

   My birthday is ~~in~~ *on* May 10. My sister's birthday is ~~on~~ *in* May, too, but it's not ~~in~~ *on* the same day.

2. Use *at* + time.

   My bus arrives *at* 9:00.

3. Use *on* + street name. Use *at* + address.

   My house is ~~in~~ *on* Gorge Avenue. It's ~~on~~ *at* 1276 Gorge Avenue.

4. Use *on* + *the* + ordinal number + *floor*.

   My office is ~~in~~ *on the* third floor.

Editing Task

Find and correct nine more mistakes in this e-mail about a birthday celebration.

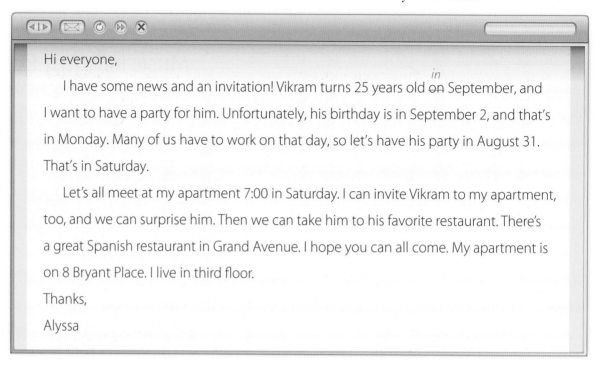

Hi everyone,

    I have some news and an invitation! Vikram turns 25 years old ~~on~~ *in* September, and I want to have a party for him. Unfortunately, his birthday is in September 2, and that's in Monday. Many of us have to work on that day, so let's have his party in August 31. That's in Saturday.

    Let's all meet at my apartment 7:00 in Saturday. I can invite Vikram to my apartment, too, and we can surprise him. Then we can take him to his favorite restaurant. There's a great Spanish restaurant in Grand Avenue. I hope you can all come. My apartment is on 8 Bryant Place. I live in third floor.

Thanks,

Alyssa

6 | Grammar for Writing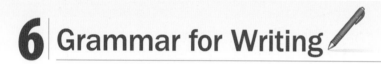

Using Prepositions

Writers use prepositions of place and time when they write invitations. Remember:

- **The prepositions *in*, *on*, and *at* have many different meanings.**

  The party is <u>on</u> the ninth.   *My house is <u>on</u> Kellogg Street.*   *The invitation is <u>on</u> the kitchen counter.*

- **A lot of prepositions are two or more words.**

  I live <u>next to</u> Surma.   *The bus stop is <u>in front of</u> the bank.*

Pre-writing Task

1 Read the e-mail invitation. What is it an invitation for? When is the party? Where is the party?

> Hi Raul,
>
> You're invited (to) a graduation party for Claudia at my house on Saturday, the ninth. The party is at 6:00 p.m. I have a new apartment. It's at 616 Campana Way. My apartment is on the third floor. My building doesn't have a parking lot. You can park in the parking lot behind the bank. The bank is across from the gas station on Kellogg Street.
>
> See you soon!
> Daniel

2 Read the e-mail invitation again. Circle all the prepositions. Then complete the top of the invitation.

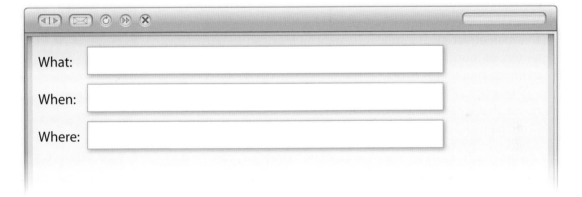

What: _____

When: _____

Where: _____

Writing Task

1 *Write* Write an e-mail invitation to a special party. What is the reason for the party? Where is the party? When is the party? Where is parking, or where is a bus stop near the party? Use the e-mail in the Pre-writing Task to help you. Use prepositions of place and time from the unit.

2 *Self-Edit* Use the editing tips below to improve your sentences. Make any necessary changes.

1. Did you use time and location prepositions in your e-mail invitation?
2. Did you use *in*, *on*, and *at* correctly?
3. Did you use any prepositions that are two or three words?
4. Did you avoid the mistakes in the Avoid Common Mistakes chart on page 73?

There Is and There Are

Local Attractions

1 Grammar in the Real World

A Do you know a lot about the old areas of your town? Read the blog about a historic street in Los Angeles. What are some fun things to do there?

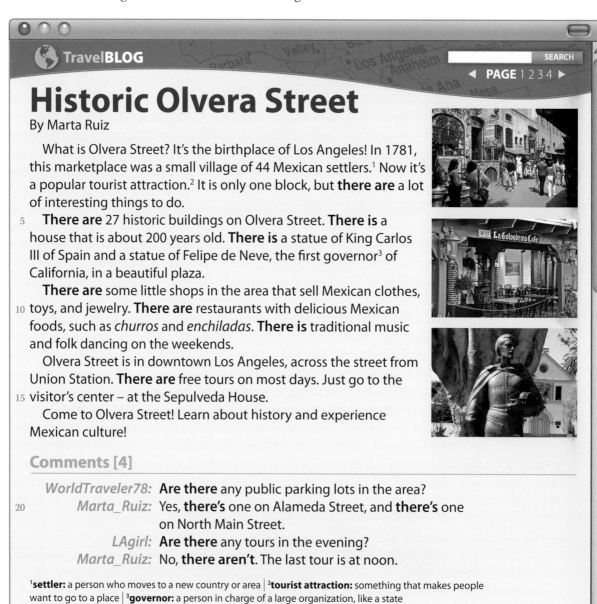

TravelBLOG   SEARCH

◄ PAGE 1 2 3 4 ►

Historic Olvera Street

By Marta Ruiz

What is Olvera Street? It's the birthplace of Los Angeles! In 1781, this marketplace was a small village of 44 Mexican settlers.[1] Now it's a popular tourist attraction.[2] It is only one block, but **there are** a lot of interesting things to do.

5   **There are** 27 historic buildings on Olvera Street. **There is** a house that is about 200 years old. **There is** a statue of King Carlos III of Spain and a statue of Felipe de Neve, the first governor[3] of California, in a beautiful plaza.

There are some little shops in the area that sell Mexican clothes, 10 toys, and jewelry. **There are** restaurants with delicious Mexican foods, such as *churros* and *enchiladas*. **There is** traditional music and folk dancing on the weekends.

Olvera Street is in downtown Los Angeles, across the street from Union Station. **There are** free tours on most days. Just go to the 15 visitor's center – at the Sepulveda House.

Come to Olvera Street! Learn about history and experience Mexican culture!

Comments [4]

WorldTraveler78:	**Are there** any public parking lots in the area?
20 *Marta_Ruiz:*	Yes, **there's** one on Alameda Street, and **there's** one on North Main Street.
LAgirl:	**Are there** any tours in the evening?
Marta_Ruiz:	No, **there aren't**. The last tour is at noon.

[1]**settler:** a person who moves to a new country or area │ [2]**tourist attraction:** something that makes people want to go to a place │ [3]**governor:** a person in charge of a large organization, like a state

B *Comprehension Check* Match the two parts of the sentences about Olvera Street.

1. Olvera Street was
2. It's a tourist attraction
3. There are a lot of
4. There are some
5. The last tour is

a. little shops in the area.
b. interesting things to do.
c. at noon.
d. in downtown Los Angeles.
e. a small village in 1781.

C *Notice* Find these words in the text. Do they come after *there is* or *there are*? Write the words in the correct columns.

a lot of interesting things to do traditional music	27 historic buildings restaurants	a statue of King Carlos III

There is . . .	There are . . .

Now circle the correct words in these two sentences about *there is* and *there are*.

The writer uses **_There is_ / _There are_** with singular nouns. She uses **_There is_ / _There are_** with plural nouns.

2 | There Is / There Are

▶ Grammar Presentation

There is and *There are* tell you that something or someone exists or that something is a fact.	**There's** *a statue of King Carlos III in this plaza.* **There are** *free tours on most days.*

2.1 Affirmative Statements

There	Be	Subject	Place/Time		Contraction
There	**is**	a parking lot a free tour	on Alameda Street. at 10:00.		There is → There's
	are	some little shops free tours	in the area. on most days.		

2.2 Negative Statements

There	Be + Not/No	Subject	Place/Time
There	**isn't**	a bank	in Union Station.
	is no	bank	
	isn't	a show	at 8:00.
	is no	show	
	's no	bank	in Union Station.
		show	at 8:00.
	aren't	any cars	on Olvera Street.
	are no	cars	
	aren't	any tours	in the evening.
	are no	tours	

para worlo holove "actividoes"

2.3 Using *There Is / There Are*

a. Use *There is / There are* to say that something or someone exists or to introduce a fact or a situation.

> **There are** a lot of interesting things to do in this area.
> **There's** an article by Marta Ruiz on this website.
> **There are** two questions from readers.

b. Use *There is / There are* to tell the location of something or someone.

> **There's** a parking lot on the corner.
> **There are** some Mexican restaurants on the next block.
> **There's a** tour guide at the door.

c. Use *There is / There are* to tell when an event happens.

> **There's** an art show at 8:00.
> **There are** concerts on the weekend.

d. Use the full forms in academic writing, but in speaking, use contractions.

> **There's** music in the plaza.
> **There's** no free parking on this street.

In informal speech, people often say *There're* instead of *There are*, but don't write it.

> **There are** a lot of museums in Los Angeles.
> NOT ~~**There're**~~ a lot of museums in Los Angeles.

e. Use *There is* when there are two or more nouns and the first noun is singular.

> SINGULAR NOUN   PLURAL NOUN
> **There's** a <u>jewelry store</u> and two <u>restaurants</u> on this street.

Use *There are* when there are two or more nouns and the first noun is plural.

> PLURAL NOUN   SINGULAR NOUN
> **There are** two <u>restaurants</u> and a <u>jewelry store</u> on this street.

f. You can use *some* with a plural noun after *There are*.

> **There are some** shops around the corner.

2.3 Using *There Is / There Are* (continued)

g. For negative statements, you can use *There isn't* and *There aren't*. The full forms *is not* and *are not* are not often used.	***There isn't*** *a bad restaurant on this street.* ***There aren't*** *any parking spaces here.*
OR You can use *There is / There are* + *no*.	***There's no*** *fee at this parking lot.* ***There are no*** *hotels around here.*
You can use *any* in negative statements with *There aren't*.	***There aren't any*** *traffic lights on Olvera Street.*
h. You can use *There is* and *There are* to introduce new people, places, and things.	INTRODUCTION MORE INFORMATION ***There is*** *an old house on the street.* ***It's*** *now a museum.*
You can use *It is / It's* and *They are / They're* to give more information.	***There are*** *a lot of shops on Olvera.* ***They are*** *all very nice.*

▶ Grammar Application

Exercise 2.1 Affirmative Statements

A Complete the sentences from an e-mail. Use *There's* or *There are*.

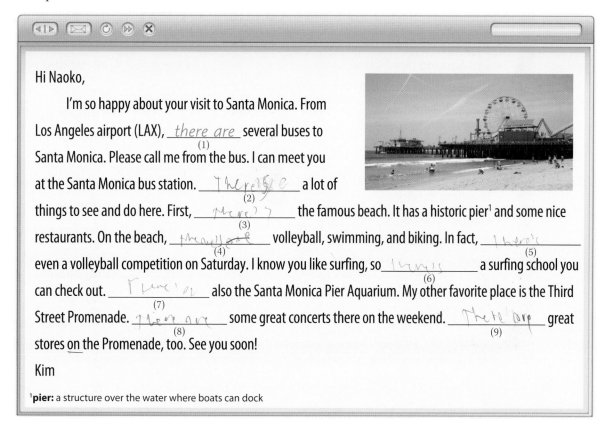

Hi Naoko,

I'm so happy about your visit to Santa Monica. From Los Angeles airport (LAX), *there are* several buses to
(1)
Santa Monica. Please call me from the bus. I can meet you at the Santa Monica bus station. ___There are___ a lot of
(2)
things to see and do here. First, ___There's___ the famous beach. It has a historic pier[1] and some nice
(3)
restaurants. On the beach, ___there are___ volleyball, swimming, and biking. In fact, ___There's___
(4)   (5)
even a volleyball competition on Saturday. I know you like surfing, so___There's___ a surfing school you
(6)
can check out. ___There's___ also the Santa Monica Pier Aquarium. My other favorite place is the Third
(7)
Street Promenade. ___There are___ some great concerts there on the weekend. ___There are___ great
(8)   (9)
stores on the Promenade, too. See you soon!

Kim

[1]**pier:** a structure over the water where boats can dock

B *Over to You* What is your favorite city? Fill in the chart with some of the interesting places in your favorite city.

There is . . .	There are . . .
There is o beotiful country	*There are Privleges becouse no army*

C *Pair Work* Tell your partner what is in your favorite city. Use your information from B. Take turns.

    A *There's an art museum.*

    B *There are several big parks.*

Exercise 2.2 Affirmative and Negative Statements

A Look at the hotel information. Complete the sentences. Use *There is / are* and *There isn't / aren't*.

Comfort Hotel

- $10 parking (for 24 hours)
- $7.95 wireless Internet service (per day)
- Free breakfast
- Free coffee in the lobby
- Outdoor pool
- Fitness room
- Business services
- Conference center
- Meeting rooms (4)
- Ice machines in the hallways
- Park views
- Restaurant

1. ___*There isn't*___ free parking.
2. ___*There are*___ business services.
3. _____ an indoor pool.
4. _____ six meeting rooms.
5. _____ any free wireless Internet service.
6. _____ any ocean views.
7. _____ a fitness room.
8. _____ any refrigerators in the rooms.
9. _____ a restaurant.
10. _____ a conference center.

B *Over to You* What doesn't exist in your town or city? Look at the places in the box. Add your own ideas. Write six sentences about your town or city. Use *There is no* and *There aren't any*.

aquarium	cheap restaurants	historic houses	park	statues
beach	free parking	library	public pool	tourist attractions
bus station	~~gas stations~~	museums	river	train station

1. *There aren't any gas stations.* _____
2. _____
3. _____
4. _____
5. _____
6. _____
7. _____

Exercise 2.3 *There Is / There Are* or *It Is / They Are*

A Read Mi-Sun's description of her town on her blog. Complete the sentences. Use *There's*, *There are*, *It's*, or *They're*.

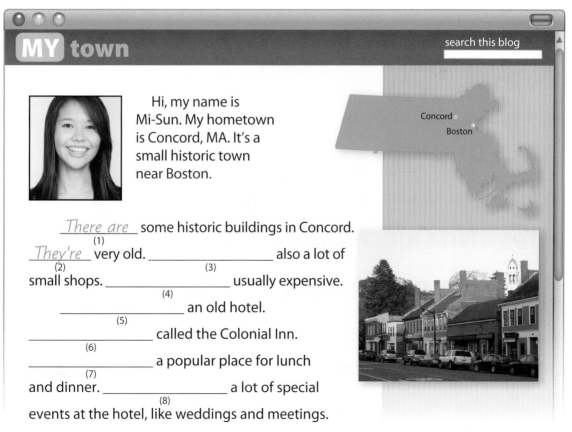

search this blog

MY town

Hi, my name is Mi-Sun. My hometown is Concord, MA. It's a small historic town near Boston.

Concord
Boston

There are some historic buildings in Concord.
(1)
They're very old. _____ also a lot of
(2)   (3)
small shops. _____ usually expensive.
(4)
_____ an old hotel.
(5)
_____ called the Colonial Inn.
(6)
_____ a popular place for lunch
(7)
and dinner. _____ a lot of special
(8)
events at the hotel, like weddings and meetings.

_____ often live music at night. I like
(9)
to go and listen to jazz.

_____ a national park by the
(10)
Concord River. _____ beautiful
(11)
and peaceful. _____ always lots of
(12)
tourists at the park. It has a famous bridge – Old
North Bridge. Also, _____ a very
(13)
famous statue of a minuteman next to the bridge.
The soldier was called a "minuteman" because
he could get ready in a minute. A historic battle
happened there in 1775. I often walk there
with friends.

B ◀)) Listen to Mi-Sun and check your answers.

C *Over to You* Write four pairs of sentences about your town or city. Use *There's / There are* in the first sentence. Use *It's* or *They are* in the second sentence to add more information.

> *There's a big park in my city. It's on State Street.*

1. _____
2. _____
3. _____
4. _____

3 | Yes / No Questions with *There Is / There Are*

▶ Grammar Presentation

Yes / No Questions with *There is / There are* can ask about people, things, and events.	**Is there** *a tour guide in this museum?* **Are there** *any concerts on Friday?*

3.1 *Yes/No* Questions and Short Answers

Be	There	Subject	Place/Time	Short Answers
Is		a visitor's center	on Olvera Street?	Yes, **there is**.
	there	a performance	at 6:00?	No, **there isn't**.
Are		any parking lots	in the area?	Yes, **there are**.
		any tours	in the evening?	No, **there aren't**.

3.2 Using *Yes/No* Questions and Short Answers with *There Is / There Are*

a.	You can use *any* with a plural noun in *Yes/No* questions with *Are there*.	*"**Are there any** hotels on Alameda Street?"* *"**Are there any** concerts on weekdays?"*
b.	In affirmative short answers, don't use the contractions *there's* or *there're*.	*"Yes, **there is**."* NOT *"Yes, ~~there's~~."* *"Yes, **there are**."* NOT *"Yes, ~~there're~~."*
c.	You can use *It is / They are* to say more after a short answer.	*"Is there a visitor's center on Olvera Street?"* *"Yes, there is. **It is** at the Sepulveda House."* *"Are there any parking lots in the area?"* *"Yes, there are. **They are** on Alameda Street."*

3.3 Longer Answers with *There Is / There Are*

a.	In longer answers with *There is*, you can use *one* instead of repeating *a* + singular noun.	*Is there a visitor's center on Olvera Street?* *Yes, there's **one** in the Sepulveda House.* *No, there isn't **one** on Olvera Street.*
b.	In longer answers with *There are*, you can use *some/any* instead of repeating *some/any* + plural noun.	*Are there any public parking lots in the area?* *Yes, there are **some** on Alameda Street.* *No, there aren't **any** in the area.*

▶ Grammar Application

Exercise 3.1 Yes/No Questions and Answers

A Read the TV schedule and complete the questions and answers. Use *Are there any* and *Is there a* for the questions. Then write short answers.

T.V. tonight			Page 5
6:30 p.m.	News: *Weather report*	11:15 p.m.	Movie: *Where Is Jimmy Jones?*
7:00 p.m.	Talk show: *The Guy Norris Show*	1:00 a.m.	Music: *The Dixonville Festival*
8:00 p.m.	Documentary: *Antarctica*	2:00 a.m.	Music: *Jazz with Kenny Delmot*
9:00 p.m.	Movie: *The Long Road*	3:00 a.m.	Comedy: *The Watson Family*

1. __*Are there any*__ movies on TV tonight?   Yes, there _____ two movies. There's one at 9:00 and one at 11:15.

2. __*Is there a*__ talk show?   Yes, _____ one at 7:00.

3. _____ music shows?   Yes, there _____ . There's one at _____ and one at _____ .

4. _____ sports shows?   _____ .

5. _____ documentary?   _____ one at 8:00.

6. _____ kids' show?   _____ .

7. _____ comedy show?   _____ .

8. _____ news program?   _____ .

B *Pair Work* Write questions about events in your city or town. Use *Is there a/an* and *Are there any*. Then ask and answer the questions with a partner. Write the answers to the questions with your partner.

A Are there any good movies this weekend?

B Yes, there are two good movies.

1. (art festival) _____

2. (jazz concerts) _____

3. (baseball game) _____

4. (dance performance) _____

5. (new paintings at the museum) _____

6. (good movies) _____

C Answer each question with *yes* in three different ways. Give information about your own area, if possible.

1. Is there a mall in this town?

   Yes, there's one on Westwood Avenue. Yes, there's a mall on Westwood Avenue.
   Yes, it's on Westwood Avenue.

2. Is there a good coffee shop nearby?

   _____

3. Is there an art museum?

   _____

4. Is there a nice park?

   _____

5. Is there a sports stadium?

   _____

6. Is there a big movie theater?

   _____

4 Avoid Common Mistakes ⚠

1. Use *There is* with singular nouns. Use *There are* with plural nouns.

There ~~are~~ *is* a music festival this week.   There ~~is~~ *are* musicians from different countries at the festival.

2. *There is* and *There are* introduce <u>new</u> people, places, and things. *It is* and *They are* give more information.

There is a small building on Thomas Street. ~~There~~ *It* is the town museum.

~~They~~ *There* are three large cities in Texas. They are Houston, San Antonio, and Dallas.

3. Use the full forms in academic writing. Do not use the contractions.

~~There's~~ *There is* a wonderful museum in downtown Philadelphia.

~~There's~~ *There is* no bank in the train station.

4. In informal speaking, people often say *There are* very quickly, so it sounds like *They're*. Don't confuse them in writing.

~~They're~~ *There are* some great shows this weekend.

Editing Task

Find and correct seven more mistakes in this article about New York City's famous park.

New York City's Central Park

New York City is an expensive place to visit, but there ~~are~~ *is* one place that is always free: Central Park. There is a very big park. In fact, it is about 2.5 miles (4 km) long and 0.5 miles (0.8 km) wide. There is over 843 acres[1] in the park. There is fields, ponds, and lakes. Visitors enjoy different kinds of sports and events here. There are walkers,

5 joggers, skaters, bicyclists, and bird-watchers. There are a zoo and two ice-skating rinks. There's also an outdoor theater. The theater has "Shakespeare in the Park" summer festivals. There is a swimming pool in the summer, too. Throughout the year,

10 they're horse-and-carriage rides. Every year, there is over 25 million visitors. They are happy to visit a fun and free New York City tourist attraction.

[1] **843 acres:** 1.32 square miles or 3.41 square kilometers

5 | Grammar for Writing

Writing About Places

Writers use *There is* and *There are* when they describe places. Remember:

- **You can follow *There is* / *There are* sentences with *It is* / *They are* sentences. These sentences give more information.**
  There are some mountains near my town. They are very tall.

- **Use *some* in affirmative statements and *any* or *no* in negative statements.**
  There are some big trees near my house.   *There are not any buses on my street. There are no traffic lights.*

Pre-writing Task

1 Read the paragraph below. What kind of place does the writer describe? What is in the place?

Elwood Park

There is a big park near my apartment. It is very beautiful. There is a playground in the park. It always has a lot of children. There are also some small lakes. One lake is for swimming. It has a little beach. The other lakes do not have any beaches. They are for fishing. There are some small boats to rent. There is a fountain in the center of the park. It is a very cool place to be in the summer. There are not any food stands, but there are a lot of picnic tables.

2 Read the paragraph again. Underline *There* and circle the pronouns *It* and *They*. Draw an arrow from the *It* and *They* pronouns to the nouns that they refer to.

Writing Task

1 *Write* Use the paragraph in the Pre-writing Task to help you write about a place that you like. Where is this place? What is in it? What is missing? What is special about the place? You can write about:

- a park
- a neighborhood in your town or city
- a street in your town or city
- the downtown or city center

- a museum
- a special building
- a beach or hill near your home
- your school or place of work

Use sentences such as:

- There are _____ . They are _____ .
- There is _____ . It is _____ .
- There is / are not any _____ .
- There are some _____ .

2 *Self-Edit* Use the editing tips below to improve your sentences. Make any necessary changes.

1. Did you use *There is / There are* sentences to describe a place?
2. Did you use *It is / They are* sentences to give more information?
3. Did you use *some* with affirmative statements and *any* or *no* with negative statements?
4. Did you avoid the mistakes in the Avoid Common Mistakes chart on page 85?

1 | Grammar in the Real World

A Is there someone very old in your family? Read the magazine article about places where people live a long time. Why do some people have a long life?

A Long, Healthy Life

On the Japanese island of Okinawa, many people **live** to be over 100 years old. Researchers[1] **find** this in several places around the world, including Sardinia, Italy; Icaria, Greece; the Nicoya Peninsula of Costa Rica; and Loma Linda, California. Why do people in these areas **live** so long? The answer **is** lifestyle.[2] This list **shows** six lifestyle habits[3] that **are** common in these places.

1. People in these areas **move** around a lot. They **don't exercise** in a gym, but they **walk** a lot during the day. They **use** their bodies and **live** actively.
2. They **have** a purpose in their lives. Some **spend** time with grandchildren. Others **do** gardening or volunteer work.[4]
3. They **relax**. **Every day**, they **take** time to rest and relax. They **rarely feel** stressed.[5]
4. They **eat** lots of vegetables, and they **usually don't eat** meat.
5. They **have** many friends. They **are** part of an active social group.
6. They **feel** close to their families.

[1]**researcher:** a person who studies something to learn detailed information about it | [2]**lifestyle:** the way people live; how people eat, sleep, work, exercise | [3]**habit:** something you do or the way you act regularly | [4]**volunteer work:** work without pay, usually to help other people or an organization | [5]**stressed:** very nervous or worried

B *Comprehension Check* Answer the questions.

1. Why do people in some areas live so long? *habits*
2. Do these people feel stressed? *They rarely feel stressed*
3. Do they eat much meat?
   They usually don't eat meat

C *Notice* Find the sentences in the article. Complete the sentences with the correct words.

1. People in these areas _____ ~~don't~~ *help* around a lot.
2. They _____ *don't* _____ exercise in a gym.
3. They _____ *walk* _____ a lot during the day.
4. _____ , they _____ time to rest and relax.

Find the places you use *don't*. What words show time?

2 | Simple Present: Affirmative and Negative Statements

▶ Grammar Presentation

The simple present describes habits, routines, and facts.	*In some cultures, people **live** to be 100 years old. These people **exercise** and **eat** very well.*

2.1 Affirmative Statements

SINGULAR			PLURAL		
Subject	**Verb**		**Subject**	**Verb**	
I You	eat	vegetables every day.	We You They	eat	vegetables every day.
He She It	eats				

2.2 Negative Statements

SINGULAR					PLURAL			
Subject	*Do / Does* + *Not*	Base Form of Verb			Subject	*Do + Not*	Base Form of Verb	
I You	**do not** **don't**	**eat**	a lot of meat.		We You They	**do not** **don't**	**exercise**	in the morning.
He She It	**does not** **doesn't**							

2.3 Using Simple Present and Time Expressions

a.	Use simple present to talk about things that regularly happen, such as habits and routines.	*Okinawans usually **eat** fruits and vegetables.* *We **don't eat** meat.* *He **doesn't drive** to work.*
b.	When you talk about things that regularly happen, use time expressions such as *every day*, *every* + day, *in the morning / afternoon / evening*, *at night*, and *at 6:30*.	*They take long walks **every day**.* *She takes long walks **every Saturday**.* *We take naps **in the afternoon**.* *I watch TV **at night**.* *Our family eats dinner **at 6:30**.*
	An -*s* after the day of the week / *morning* / *afternoon* / *evening* or *weekend* means the action or event always happens.	***On Saturdays**, I work in a restaurant.* *I take long walks **on weekends**.*
	Use *from ... to ...* to say how long something happens.	*I work **from** 8:00 **to** 5:00.*
c.	Time expressions usually come at the end of the sentence. If the time expression is at the beginning of the sentence, use a comma after it.	*I visit my grandparents **in the summer**.* ***In the summer**, I visit my grandparents.* ***In June**, I take a break from school.*
d.	You can also use the simple present to talk about facts.	*Okinawans **live** long lives.*

2.4 Spelling Rules for Adding *-s*, *-es*, and *-ies* to Verbs

a. Add *-s* to most verbs.
  Add *-s* to verbs ending in a vowel[1] + *-y*.

drinks, rides, runs, sees, sleeps
buys, pays, says

b. Add *-es* to verbs ending in *-ch, -sh, -ss, -x*.
  Add *-es* to verbs ending in a consonant[2] + *-o*.

teaches, pushes, misses, fixes
does, goes

c. For verbs that end in a consonant + *-y*, change the *y* to *i* and add *-es*.

cry → *cries*
study → *studies*

d. Some verbs are irregular.

be → *am / are / is*
have → *has*

Reminder:
[1]Vowels: the letters *a, e, i, o, u*
[2]Consonants: the letters *b, c, d, f, g, h, j, k, l, m, n, p, q, r, s, t, v, w, x, y, z*
▶▶ Spelling and Pronunciation Rules for Simple Present: See page A20.

Data from the Real World

Here are some of the most frequent simple present verbs:

be	do	get	know	see	come	want
have	say	go	think	make	take	give

▶ # Grammar Application

Exercise 2.1 Simple Present Statements

Complete the sentences with the correct form of the verbs in parentheses.

1. My grandparents _live_ (live) healthy lifestyles.

2. My grandfather _____ *goes* _____ (go) for a walk every morning.

3. In the afternoon, he ___ *Checks* ___ (check) his e-mail and ___ *walkeg* ___ (work) in his garden.

4. My grandmother _____ *is* _____ (be) also active.

5. She ___ *works* ___ (work) part-time in a hotel.

6. She ___ *does* ___ (do) volunteer work at a local school three days a week.

7. Before dinner, they ___ *relaxs* ___ (relax) in the living room.

8. They ___ *eat* ___ (eat) healthy food, and they ___ *don't smoke* ___ (not smoke).

Exercise 2.2 More Simple Present Statements

Complete the statements with the affirmative or negative form of the verbs in parentheses.

1. Tran and his roommate, Edgar, _have_ (have) a lot to do every week.

2. They often ___feel___ (feel) stressed during the week.

3. Tran ___works___ (work) long hours at a department store.

4. He ___can't see___ (not see) his family very much.

5. Tran and Edgar both ___takes___ (take) night classes at the community college.

6. They usually ___don't have___ (not have) time to cook dinner.

7. For dinner, they often ___eat___ (eat) fast food like hamburgers and French fries.

8. Edgar ___can't have___ (not have) a job.

9. Every morning, he ___goes___ (go) online to look at job listings.

10. Edgar usually ___run___ (run) in the afternoon.

11. On the weekends, Edgar and Tran ___relax___ (relax) with friends.

Exercise 2.3 More Simple Present Statements

A *Over to You* Complete the sentences about yourself. Use affirmative or negative forms of the verbs in the box.

do	eat	feel	live	sleep
drink	exercise	have	read	spend

1. I ___feel___ stressed during the week.

2. I ___have___ good friends in my town.

3. I ___live___ very actively.

4. I ___exercise___ in a gym.

5. I ___eat___ a lot of meat.

6. I ___do not sleep___ about eight hours every night.

7. I ___spend___ a lot of time online or on the computer.

8. I ___do___ volunteer work in my area.

9. I ___drink___ a lot of water every day.

10. I ___read___ the newspaper in the morning.

B *Pair Work* Share your sentences with a partner. Then change partners. Tell your new partner about your classmate.

   A *Ari feels stressed during the week.*

   B *Maria doesn't feel stressed during the week.*

Exercise 2.4 ◀)) Pronunciation Focus: -s and -es

Say /s/ after /f/, /k/, /p/, and /t/ sounds.	*laughs, drinks, walks, sleeps, writes, gets*
Say /z/ after /b/, /d/, /g/, /v/, /m/, /n/, /l/, and /r/ sounds and all vowel sounds.	*grabs, rides, hugs, lives, comes, runs, smiles, hears, sees, plays, buys, goes, studies*
Say /əz/ after /tʃ/, /ʃ/, /s/, /ks/, /z/, and /dʒ/ sounds.	*teaches, pushes, kisses, fixes, uses, changes*
Pronounce the vowel sound in *does* and *says* differently from *do* and *say*.	*do* /duː/ → *does* /dʌz/ *say* /seɪ/ → *says* /sez/

A ◀)) Listen and repeat the verbs in the chart above.

B Read about Staci's week. Underline the verbs that end in *-s* or *-es*.

     Staci <u>goes</u> to school from Monday to Friday from 7:30 a.m. to 11:30 a.m. Then she rushes to work. She works at a hospital until 8:00 p.m. In the evening, Staci <u>catches</u> a bus to go home. On her way home, she listens to music and relaxes. She <u>eats a q</u>uick dinner with her family. Then she reads to her children and checks their homework. If she isn't too tired, she finishes her own homework. Staci usually falls asleep by 10:00 p.m.

C 🔊 Listen to the information about Staci's week and check (✔) the sounds of the verbs in the boxes below. Then practice saying the verbs.

	/s/	/z/	/əz/
1. goes		✔	
2. rushes		✓	✓
3. works	✓	✓	
4. catches		✓	✓
5. listens		✓	✓
6. relaxes			✓
7. eats	✓		
8. reads		✓	
9. checks		✓	
10. finishes			✓
11. falls		✓	

D *Pair Work* Ask and answer the questions with a partner. Then tell the class about your partner.

1. What are two of your healthy habits?
2. What do you do to relax?

Paulo eats healthy food, and he doesn't smoke or drink. To relax, he listens to music.

Exercise 2.5 Using Time Expressions with Simple Present

	Sunday	Monday	Tuesday	Wednesday	Thursday	Friday	Saturday
Morning	Off	Get up 6:30 a.m. Work 7:30 a.m.–2:30 p.m.	Get up 6:30 a.m. Work 7:30 a.m.–2:30 p.m.	Get up 6:30 a.m. Work 7:30 a.m.–2:30 p.m.	Get up 6:30 a.m. Work 7:30 a.m.–2:30 p.m.	Get up 6:30 a.m. Work 7:30 a.m.–2:30 p.m.	Off
Afternoon	Visit parents	Yoga		Yoga			Do homework
Evening			Class 7:15–9:45 p.m.		Class 7:15–9:45 p.m.		
	Bed at 11:00 p.m.	Bed at 11:00 p.m.	Bed at 11:00 p.m.	Bed at 11:00 p.m.	Bed at 11:00 p.m.	Bed at 11:00 p.m.	

A Look at Allie's schedule on p. 94, and complete the sentences about it. Use the correct time expressions.

Time	Part of Day / Day of Week
at (time)	*in the* (morning / afternoon / evening)
from (time) *to* (time)	*on* (day of week)

Use *at* (time) and *from* (time / day) *to* (time / day) to indicate exact times and days.
Use *on* (day of week) or *in the* (morning / afternoon / evening) to indicate the day or part of day.

1. Allie goes to yoga _on Mondays and Wednesdays_ . (days)
2. She works _from Monday to Friday_ . (days)
3. She works _from 7:30 am to 2:30 pm_ . (times)
4. She has classes _on Thursday and Thursdays_ . (days)
5. Her classes are _from 7:45pm to 9:15pm_ . (times)
6. Her days off are _on Saturdays_ . (days)
7. She visits her parents _on Sunday_ . (day)
8. During the week, she usually goes to bed _at 11:00 pm_ and wakes up _at 6:30_ . (times)
9. She does her homework _on Saturdays_ . (day)

B *Over to You* Think about your schedule. Complete the sentences below. Make them true for you.

1. I take classes (days) _on Mondays, Tuesdays, Wednesdays, and Thursdays_ .
2. My classes are (time) _9:00 am o 3 pm_ .
3. I work (days) _all days_ .
4. I work (time) _unehopm_ .
5. During the week, I go to sleep (time) _11:30 pm_ .
6. On the weekends, I go to sleep (time) _2:00 am_ .
7. On Sundays, I get up (time) _10 am &pm_ .
8. I do my homework (time) _8 pm_ .

3 Statements with Adverbs of Frequency

▶ **Grammar Presentation**

Adverbs of frequency describe how often something happens.	*Our neighbors **never drive** to work.* *They **always ride** their bikes.*

3.1 Adverbs of Frequency

Negative					Positive
0%					100%
never	rarely	sometimes	often	usually	always

Rarely is not frequently used.

3.2 Adverbs of Frequency

Subject	Adverb of Frequency	Verb	
I You We They	always usually often sometimes rarely never	work	10 hours a day.
He She It		works	

Adverbs of Frequency with *Be*

Subject	*Be*	Adverb of Frequency	
I	am	always usually often sometimes rarely never	tired.
You We They	are		
He She It	is		

3.3 Using Adverbs of Frequency

a. Adverbs of frequency usually come after the verb *be*.	I *am often* busy in the afternoon. She *is usually* tired in the morning.
b. Adverbs of frequency usually come before other verbs.	My parents **rarely eat** meat. Cristina **often rides** her bike to work. He **doesn't usually watch** TV.
c. *Sometimes*, *usually*, and *often* can come before the verb OR at the beginning or end of a sentence.	We **sometimes cook** for our family. **Sometimes** we **cook** for our family. We **cook** for our family **sometimes**.
d. Do not begin or end sentences with *always* and *never*.	Your grandparents are **always** active. NOT **Always** your grandparents are active. NOT Your grandparents are active **never**.

▶ # Grammar Application

Exercise 3.1 Adverbs of Frequency with Simple Present

Unscramble the words to make sentences.

1. happy / My / always / is / brother / at work.
   My brother is always happy at work.

2. music. / He / listen to / does / not / often
   He does not after listen to music.

3. slows down. / never / He
   He never slows down

4. sometimes / He / seven / works / a week. / days
   He works sometimes works days a week.

5. takes / He / a day off. / rarely
   He takes rarely a day off

6. starts / in / work / He / at 3:00 / usually / the afternoon.
   He usually starts in work in at 3:00 the afternoon

7. until 1:00 a.m. / doesn't / He / usually / finish
   He doesn't usually finish until 1:00 a.m

8. is / tired. / rarely / My brother
   My brother is rarely tired.

Exercise 3.2 More Adverbs of Frequency with Simple Present

A *Over to You* Read the sentences and check (✔) the boxes. Make them true for you.

Talk About Your Lifestyle

	never	sometimes	often	usually	always
1. I get eight hours of sleep at night.					
2. I fall asleep easily.					
3. I wake up at night.					
4. I exercise three times a week.					
5. I have dinner with friends on the weekend.					
6. I watch TV at night.					
7. I go to the library one day a month.					
8. I go away for vacation.					

B *Pair Work* Take turns saying your sentences from A with a partner.

A I never get eight hours of sleep at night. How about you, Olga?
B I sometimes get eight hours of sleep at night.

4 | Avoid Common Mistakes ⚠️

1. For affirmative statements with *he/she/it*, use the base form of the verb + *-s* / *-es*.

relaxes
He ~~relax~~ after lunch.

2. For affirmative statements with *I/you/we/they* or a plural noun, use the base form of the verb.

go
My parents ~~goes~~ out to dinner every Friday night.

3. In negative statements, use *do not* / *don't* or *does not* / *doesn't* + the base form of the verb.

jog
Maria does not ~~jogs~~ after dark.

4. Do not use *do* or *does* in negative statements with *be*.

am not
I ~~don't be~~ in an active social group.

5. Do not use *be* with a simple present verb.

I ~~am~~ exercise on Tuesdays.

Editing Task Find and correct 10 more mistakes in the letter.

Dear Pedro,

How are you? I'm fine. I'm in Vermont with my aunt and uncle. They ~~lives~~ *live* on a farm. The lifestyle here is very different. They are dairy farmers, so they are work hard every day. They usually get up at 4:30 a.m. They go to the barn and milk the cows. Cows makes a lot of noise in the

5 morning, so they usually wakes me up. Of course, I do not gets up until about 7:00 a.m. At 9:00, my uncle cook a wonderful breakfast. We all eat together. After that, he and I goes to the barn and works there. My aunt usually stay in the house. In the afternoon, there is more work. At night, I am

10 really tired, so I always goes to bed at 8:30! Usually my aunt and uncle don't be tired. They usually go to bed late!

I hope your vacation is fun. See you soon!

Your friend,

15 Oscar

5 | Grammar for Writing ✏

Writing About Daily Life

Writers use the simple present with adverbs of frequency to write about routines and daily habits in people's lives.

Remember:

- **Use adverbs of frequency to show how often you do things.**

  I _usually_ exercise in the mornings.   _Sometimes_ he goes for a run before breakfast.

- **Use _never_ or the negative simple present to show things you don't do. Don't use _never_ and the negative simple present together.**

  They _never_ work on the weekends.   We _do not_ stay up late during the week.

Pre-writing Task

1 Read the paragraph below. When do the routines in the paragraph happen? How are the writer's routines and her husband's routines different?

Different Routines

My husband and I <u>have</u> very different routines. My husband (usually) goes to bed early. Sometimes he watches TV and then goes to bed around 9:00. I never go to bed early. I usually check my e-mail. I often surf the Internet. I never watch TV, but I sometimes read. Then, around midnight, I drink some warm milk and go to sleep. My husband always gets up early. He goes for a run, and then he makes coffee. When the coffee is ready, I get up.

2 Read the paragraph again. Underline the simple present verbs and circle the adverbs of frequency. Complete the chart.

The writer's routines	The writer's husband's routines
	goes to bed early

Writing Task

1 *Write* Use the paragraph in the Pre-writing Task to help you write about some of your routines, or compare your routines with the routines of another person. Think about your favorite time of day. What do you usually do or not do during this time? What does the other person usually do or not do?

Use sentences such as:

- I often _____ .
- She never _____ .
- We usually _____ .
- Sometimes I _____ .

2 *Self-Edit* Use the editing tips below to improve your sentences. Make any necessary changes.

1. Did you use the simple present and adverbs of frequency to write about daily life?
2. Did you use adverbs of frequency to show how often these daily routines happen?
3. Did you use *never* or *do not / does not* to show things that don't ever happen?
4. Did you avoid the mistakes in the Avoid Common Mistakes chart on page 99?

Simple Present Yes / No Questions and Short Answers

Daily Habits

1 Grammar in the Real World

A Do you get enough sleep? Do you have trouble sleeping? Read the news article below about sleeping habits. Answer the survey questions.

Do most people get enough sleep?

If you think "no," you are correct. The National Sleep Foundation's 2010 Sleep in America™ poll[1] shows that sleep is a problem for many people. About 75 percent agree that poor sleep can affect their work or family relationships. How are your sleep habits? To find out, answer the survey[2] questions below.

	Yes	No
1. **Do** you **fall asleep** in 30 minutes or less?	❑	❑
2. **Do** you **have** trouble falling asleep?	❑	❑
3. **Do** you **suffer** from insomnia?[3]	❑	❑
4. **Does** stress **keep** you awake?	❑	❑
5. **Do** you **take** any sleep medication?	❑	❑
6. **Do** you **wake up** during the night?	❑	❑
7. **Do** you **wake up** too early in the morning?	❑	❑
8. **Do** you **feel** very tired in the morning?	❑	❑
9. **Do** you **get** at least seven hours of sleep each night?	❑	❑
10. **Do** you **get** more sleep on the weekends?	❑	❑

[1]**poll:** a short questionnaire, usually one question | [2]**survey:** a set of questions to find out people's habits or beliefs about something | [3]**suffer from insomnia:** find it difficult to get to sleep or to sleep well

B *Comprehension Check* Circle the correct answer.

1. This article is about **health / sleep** habits.

2. Sleep is a **problem / hobby** for many people.

3. Many people believe poor sleep can affect their **work / friends**.

C *Notice* Find the questions in the news article, and choose the correct word to complete the questions. Then underline the subject of each sentence.

1. **Do / Does** most people get enough sleep?

2. **Do / Does** you suffer from insomnia?

3. **Do / Does** stress keep you awake?

Notice the use of *do* and *does*. Which word do you use for singular subjects? Which word do you use for plural subjects?

2 | Simple Present *Yes / No* Questions and Short Answers

▶ Grammar Presentation

You can use simple present questions to ask about habits, routines, and facts.	*Do* you **wake up** early? *Does* she **suffer** from insomnia?

2.1 *Yes / No* Questions

Do / Does	Subject	Base Form of Verb	
Do	I you we they	**fall asleep**	in 30 minutes?
Does	he she it		

2.2 Short Answers

AFFIRMATIVE				NEGATIVE			
Yes	Subject	*Do/Does*		*No*	Subject	*Do/Does + Not*	
Yes,	I you we they	**do.**		No,	I you we they	**do not.** **don't.**	
	he she it	**does.**			he she it	**does not.** **doesn't.**	

2.3 Using Simple Present *Yes/No* Questions and Answers

a. For simple present *Yes/No* questions, use *Do* or *Does* with the base form of the verb.	***Do*** you **feel** tired every morning? ***Does*** he **wake up** during the night?
b. People usually use contractions in negative short answers.	*"Do you watch TV all night?"* *"No, I **don't**."*
Be careful! Negative full forms are very strong. You can sound angry.	*"No, I **do not!**"* (This can sound angry.)
c. You can give longer answers to *Yes/No* questions. It's friendly to give more information.	*"Do you fall asleep easily?"* *"Yes, I usually fall asleep in about 15 minutes."* *"No, I often stay awake for an hour."*
You can also give a short answer and then give more information in a separate sentence.	*"Yes, I do. I usually fall asleep in about 15 minutes."* *"No, I don't. I often stay awake for an hour."*
d. Some questions do not have a simple *yes* or *no* answer. You can answer *Well, . . .* and give a longer answer in speaking.	*"Do you live with your family?"* *"**Well**, I live with my aunt and uncle."*
Do not use *Well, . . .* to answer questions in academic writing, for example in compositions or tests.	*"Does the average college student get a lot of sleep?"* *"The average student gets about six hours of sleep."* NOT *"Well, the average student gets about six hours of sleep."*

▶ Grammar Application

Exercise 2.1 Yes/No Questions and Short Answers

A Complete the questions with *Do* or *Does*. Then write short answers. Make them true for you.

1. __*Do*__ you get up early?   *Yes, I do./No, I don't.*

2. _____ the sun wake you up?   _____

3. _____ your alarm clock play music? _____

4. _____ you often go back to sleep?   _____

5. _____ you like mornings?   _____

6. _____ you sleep until noon on the weekends? _____

7. _____ you usually stay up past midnight?   _____

8. _____ you study late at night?   _____

B *Pair Work* Ask and answer the questions in A. Give short answers to your partner's questions.

A *Do you get up early?*

B *No, I don't.*

Exercise 2.2 More Yes / No Questions and Short Answers

A Complete the conversations about other habits. Write questions with the words in parentheses. Then complete the short answers.

Conversation 1

Lucy ___*Do you and your brother share*___ (you and your
          (1)
brother/share) the cooking?

Malia No, _____ . I'm always busy with school.
               (2)

Lucy So, _____ (your
                        (3)
brother/do) all the cooking?

Malia Yes, _____ . He's a great cook.
                (4)

Lucy _____ (he/work)
                    (5)
in a restaurant?

Malia No, _____ .
               (6)

Lucy Oh, _____ (he/go)
                       (7)
to cooking school?

Malia No, _____ . He just loves food.
               (8)

Conversation 2

Lucy _____ (your grandparents/live) nearby?
                  (1)

Malia Yes, _____ . They live next door.
                (2)

Lucy Nice. _____ (you and your family/see) them often?
                          (3)

Malia No, _____ . They're at the hospital a lot.
               (4)

Lucy Oh, I'm sorry. _____ (they/need) help?
                                (5)

Malia No, _____ . They're fine. They work there. They volunteer at the hospital.
               (6)

Lucy Oh? _____ (they/visit) patients and help the nurses?
                       (7)

Malia No, _____ . They both work in the hospital gift shop.
               (8)

B *Pair Work* Practice the conversations in A with a partner.

Exercise 2.3 🔊 Pronunciation Focus: *Do you . . . ?*

In speaking, people often say *Do you* very fast.
It can sound like one word ("D'you").
Always write *Do you* as two words, but say it fast so it sounds like one word ("D'you").

A 🔊 Listen to the questions about people's music habits. Repeat the questions. Say *Do you* fast, as one word.

Do you fall asleep with music on?

Do you like loud music?

Do you dance when you listen to music?

Do you listen to music all the time?

Do you study with music on?

Do you sing along to music?

Do you have an MP3 player?

B *Pair Work* Ask and answer the questions in A. Give a short answer first, and then give more information in a second sentence. Use *Well, . . .* for some answers.

A *Do you like loud music?*   A *Do you listen to music all the time?*
B *No, I don't. I prefer soft music.*   B *Well, I don't listen to music when I'm in class.*

Exercise 2.4 Yes / No Questions in a Survey

A *Over to You* Write questions for these habits. Then ask your classmates these questions. Write their names in the chart.

Who . . . ?		Name
falls asleep with the TV on	1. *Do you fall asleep with the TV on?*	_____
falls asleep to music	2. _____	_____
talks in his or her sleep	3. _____	_____
dreams a lot	4. _____	_____
remembers his or her dreams	5. _____	_____
walks in his or her sleep	6. _____	_____
hits the "snooze" button[1] 2 or 3 times	7. _____	_____
gets enough sleep	8. _____	_____

[1]**snooze button:** a button on an alarm clock that stops the alarm for a short time and makes the alarm ring again in a few minutes

B *Pair Work* Tell a partner about four classmates and their sleeping habits.

Delia talks in her sleep.

3 | Avoid Common Mistakes ⚠

1. Use *Do* with plural subjects and with *you*.

Do
~~Does~~ your roommates stay up late?

2. Use *Does* with singular subjects (except *you*).

Does
~~Do~~ this alarm clock work?

3. Use *Do* / *Does* in simple present questions with *have*.

Do you have
~~Have you~~ an MP3 player?

4. Do not use *Do* / *Does* in questions with *be*.

Is
~~Do~~ your cell phone new?

5. Do not use *Be* with other simple present verbs.

Do
~~Are~~ you agree?

Editing Task

Find and correct seven more mistakes in these questions about sleeping habits.

Do you have
1. ~~Have you~~ trouble falling asleep?

2. Are you sleep on your stomach, your back, or your side?

3. Have you a TV in your bedroom?

4. Does you dream in color or in black-and-white?

5. Do a dream ever scare you?

6. Does loud noises wake you up at night?

7. Do you a light sleeper or a deep sleeper?

8. Does you fall asleep quickly?

4 Grammar for Writing ✒

Writing Survey Questions About Habits and Routines

Writers use simple present *Yes/No* questions in surveys to find out about people's daily habits and routines.
Remember:

- **Start your questions with *Do* and *Does*.**
  <u>Do</u> you eat breakfast before work?   <u>Does</u> your workplace have coffee?

- **You can use *ever* or *usually* in your questions to find out how often things happen.**
  Do you <u>ever</u> work at night?   Does your homework <u>usually</u> take an hour or more?

Pre-writing Task

1 *Pair Work* Read the paragraphs below and the survey questions that a student wrote about living with others. Ask and answer the questions with a partner. Take turns.

Habits at Home

Most people do not live alone. They live with their parents, their families, or friends. There are many wonderful things about living with other people. For example, there is always somebody that you can talk to when you feel sad or angry. The house can be a comfortable place. However, sometimes there are problems when many people live
5 together. For example, people argue a lot, or the house is very noisy all the time. Good communication is important. Everyone can talk to each other and solve problems. Here are some questions about living situations. Please answer the questions. What is your living situation like? Is your living situation a good one?

    1. <u>Do</u> the <u>people</u> in your home help with the housework and chores?
10   2. Do the people in your home (usually) help each other when there are problems?
    3. Do you ever spend time together and talk about your lives?
    4. Do the people in your home usually enjoy each other's company?
    5. Does everyone eat meals together?
    6. Do you think that you have a good living situation?

15   The answers to these questions are important. I believe that people who answer *yes* to these questions have good living situations.

2 Read the paragraphs and the questions again. Underline the subject and *do* or *does* in the questions. Circle *ever* and *usually*.

Writing Task

1 *Write* Write a short paragraph and some survey questions about people's habits or things they do every day. Use the paragraphs and survey in the Pre-writing Task to help you. Choose one topic below:

- food-shopping routines
- homework or study habits
- morning or evening routines
- getting to work or school
- mealtime routines
- your own idea

Think about what you know about the topic and what you want to find out. At the end, give your survey to your classmates. Write about what you find out.

2 *Self-Edit* Use the editing tips below to improve your sentences. Make any necessary changes.

1. Did you use the simple present to talk about a topic and write survey questions about that topic?
2. Did you use *Do* and *Does* correctly?
3. Did you use *ever* or *usually* in some of your questions?
4. Did you avoid the mistakes in the Avoid Common Mistakes chart on page 107?

Simple Present Information Questions

Cultural Holidays

1 | Grammar in the Real World

A What is your favorite holiday or celebration? Read the interview about a Mexican holiday. What is the Day of the Dead?

Coffee ☕ Time | TODAY'S TOPIC Mexico's DAY OF THE DEAD

Michelle	Hello, everyone! This is *Coffee Time*. Our topic today is celebrations around the world. Today our guest is Elena Lopez, from a university in Mexico. She's here to tell us about the Day of the Dead. Welcome, Dr. Lopez!
Dr. Lopez	Thank you. It's nice to be here.
Michelle	First of all, **where do people celebrate the Day of the Dead?**
Dr. Lopez	They celebrate it in many parts of the world, such as in Mexico.
Michelle	**When do people celebrate it, and how do they celebrate it?**
Dr. Lopez	Well, the Day of the Dead takes place on two days: November 1 and 2. We remember our dead relatives – our ancestors[1] – and friends. People build little altars[2] in the home and in public schools. They also clean and decorate the graves.[3]
Michelle	**What do they put on these altars and graves?**
Dr. Lopez	They put candles, food, drinks, flowers, and pictures of the dead. There are sweets in the shape of skulls,[4] too. The traditions are a little different in every region of Mexico.
Michelle	What do the different things mean?
Dr. Lopez	Well, for example, the candles are a guide for our ancestors. They guide them home. There are bells, too. They call the dead.
Michelle	**What do the skulls symbolize?[5]** Do they symbolize death?
Dr. Lopez	Well, yes. But they also symbolize rebirth,[6] according to the first Day of the Dead thousands of years ago.

(line numbers: 5, 10, 15, 20, 25)

[1]**ancestor:** any member of your family from long ago | [2]**altar:** a type of table that people use in religious ceremonies | [3]**grave:** a place where you bury a dead person or people, usually under the ground | [4]**skull:** the bones of the head around the brain | [5]**symbolize:** use a sign or mark to represent something | [6]**rebirth:** a new period of growth of something

B *Comprehension Check* Choose the correct answers.

1. On the Day of the Dead, people remember _____.
   a. their parents   b. their dead relatives   c. their children

2. People put pictures of the dead _____.
   a. on altars   b. on sweets   c. on skulls

3. The Day of the Dead takes place _____.
   a. every month   b. one day a year   c. on November 1 and 2

4. People _____ their ancestors' graves.
   a. decorate   b. paint   c. celebrate

C *Notice* Answer the questions with the correct question word. Use the interview to help you.

1. Which word asks a question about **time**?   What   When   Where

2. Which word asks a question about **places**?   What   When   Where

3. Which word asks a question about **things**?   What   When   Where

What word comes after *when*, *where*, and *what*?

2 | Simple Present Information Questions

▶ Grammar Presentation

Information questions begin with a *Wh-* word (*Who*, *What*, *When*, *Where*, *Why*, or *How*). They ask for information and cannot be answered with a simple *yes* or *no*.	***Where*** *do people celebrate the Day of the Dead?* ***When*** *do Americans celebrate Independence Day?*

2.1 Information Questions

Wh- word	Do / Does	Subject	Base Form of Verb	
Who			**see**	at school?
What	**do**	I you we they	**eat**	at parties?
When			**celebrate**	that holiday?
What time			**begin**	the celebration?
Where		he she it	**study**	for school?
Why	**does**		**live**	at home?
How			**meet**	new people?

2.2 Using Simple Present Information Questions

a. Use a *Wh-* word with *do* before *I, you, we, they,* and plural nouns.	***When do*** *you celebrate the holiday?*
Use a *Wh-* word with *does* before *he, she, it,* and singular nouns.	***Why does*** *she study Spanish?*
b. Use simple present information questions to ask for specific information.	*"**Where** do you live?" "I live in Mexico City."* *"**What time** do you start work?" "8:30."*
c. Use simple present information questions to ask about habits, facts, traditions, and regular activities.	*"**When** do they celebrate the Day of the Dead?"* *"In November."* *"**Why** does she travel to Mexico every year?"* *"Because she has family there."*
d. You can answer information questions with a short or long answer.	*"**What** do you eat on Thanksgiving?"* Short answer: *"Turkey and pie."* Long answer: *"I eat turkey and pie."*

2.3 Using *Wh-* Words

a. Use *Who* to ask about people.	*"**Who** do you remember on the Day of the Dead?"* *"I remember my grandmother."*
b. Use *What* to ask about things.	*"**What** do you study?"* *"Spanish and history."*
c. Use *When* to ask about time (days, months, years, seasons, parts of the day).	*"**When** do you celebrate Chinese New Year?"* *"In January or February."*
d. Use *What time* to ask about clock time.	*"**What time** does your class finish?"* *"4:30. / Five o'clock."*
e. Use *Where* to ask about places.	*"**Where** does she work?"* *"At the University of Mexico."*
f. Use *Why* to ask about reasons.	*"**Why** do you like celebrations?"* *"Because they're always fun."*
g. Use *How* to ask about manner – the way people do something.	*"**How** do you celebrate your birthday?"* *"We eat at my favorite restaurant."*

▶ Grammar Application

Exercise 2.1 Questions with *Who, What, When, Where, How*

A Complete the questions with *Who*, *What*, *When*, *Where*, or *How* and *do* or *does*.

1. A *Where* *do* people celebrate the Day of the Dead?   B In Mexico.

2. A _____ _____ they celebrate the Day of the Dead?   B On November 1 and 2.

3. A _____ _____ they remember?   B Their dead relatives and friends.

4. A _____ _____ they decorate?   B Graves and altars.

5. A _____ _____ they put pictures of the dead?   B On altars.

6. A _____ _____ they decorate the graves?   B With flowers, candles, food, and drinks.

B *Over to You* Unscramble the words and add *do* or *does* to make questions. Then write answers that are true for you.

1. what celebration / you / like / the best / ?

   A *What celebration do you like the best?*

   B _____

2. when / you / celebrate / it / ?

   A _____

   B _____

3. who / you / celebrate / it / with / ?

   A _____

   B _____

4. what / you / usually / do / ?

   A _____

   B _____

5. where / you / celebrate / it / ?

A _____

B _____

6. what / you / usually / eat / ?

A _____

B _____

7. when / it / usually / end / ?

A _____

B _____

C *Pair Work* Ask and answer the questions in B with a partner.

Exercise 2.2 Questions with *When* and *What Time*

A Complete the questions with *When* or *What time* and *do* or *does*.

1. A __When__ __do__ you graduate?   B On June 15.
2. A _what time do_ you have the ceremony?   B At 3:30.
3. A _when does_ Sandi turn 21?   B Next Saturday.
4. A _what time_ her birthday party start?   B At 7:00.
5. A _when do_ you celebrate Thanksgiving in the   B At the end of November.
   United States?
6. A _when does_ your family usually have the meal?   B In the late afternoon.
7. A _what time do_ you usually start cooking on that day? B At about 8:00 a.m.

B *Pair Work* Ask and answer the questions in A with a partner.

Exercise 2.3 Asking Information Questions

A Read the paragraph about a holiday celebration in Massachusetts. Write information questions using the words in parentheses. Find the verbs in the paragraph, and use the information to write your questions. Remember to use *do* and *does* in your questions.

One of my favorite holidays is Patriots' Day in the Boston, Massachusetts, area. Every year, Boston residents celebrate Patriots' Day on the third Monday of April. On this day, people remember the beginning of the American Revolutionary War. Many towns have parades and speeches.[1] The second important event is the Boston Marathon.[2] The marathon happens every year on Patriots' Day. The race starts around 10:00 a.m. in Hopkinton and ends in Boston. Thousands of people watch runners from all over the world. The third event is the special Patriots' Day baseball game. The Boston Red Sox play a team from another town. The game starts around 11:00 a.m. in Boston.

[1]**speech:** a formal talk | [2]**marathon:** a race in which people run 26 miles and 385 yards (42.195 kilometers)

1. (what / people / celebrate) _What do people celebrate on the third Monday of April?_
2. (what / people / remember) _what do people remember beginning of the American revolution_
3. (what / towns / have) _what to towns have parades and speechs_
4. (when / marathon / happen) _when do marathon happen from all over the world_
5. (what time / marathon / start) _what time do marathon start 10m._
6. (where / marathon / start) _where did marathon Stor_
7. (who / people / watch) _who people watchy_

B *Pair Work* Ask and answer the questions in A with a partner.

A What do people celebrate on the third Monday of April?
B They celebrate Patriots' Day.

Exercise 2.4 🔊 Pronunciation Focus: Intonation in Questions

In information questions, our voice usually *goes down*. We call this falling intonation.	Where do you go on va**ca**tion?
	Why do you stay **home**?
	When do you see your **re**latives?
In *Yes / No* questions, our voice often *goes up*. We call this rising intonation.	Do you celebrate Me**mo**rial Day?
	Is that your favorite day of the **year**?
	Does she work at **night**?

A 🔊 Listen to the questions and answers. Mark the questions with ↗ for rising intonation and ↘ for falling intonation.

1. **A** Excuse me. Are you from Japan? ↗

   B Yes, I am. I'm from Tokyo.

2. **A** Can I ask you some questions? ↘

   B Sure!

3. **A** What's your favorite holiday in Japan? ↗

   B New Year's Day.

4. **A** Why is it your favorite? ↗

   B Because we have special food for the holiday, and we relax all day.

5. **A** Do you help your mother with the cooking? ↗

   B Yes, I do. We also see all our relatives on New Year's Day.

6. **A** Do you play any special games? ↗

   B No, not really. But we watch some special TV programs.

7. **A** What else do you do on New Year's Day? ↘

   B Well, we read all our holiday cards then.

8. **A** Do you really save all the cards to open on the same day? ↘

   B Yes, it's a special custom.

B 🔊 Listen and repeat the questions.

Exercise 2.5 Information Questions in Titles

Data from the Real World

We often use information questions in the titles of academic articles and books. The article or book answers the question.	*Why Do We Laugh?* *How Does a Computer Work?* *When Do People Watch TV?*
Titles with *How? What?* and *Why?* are very frequent.	How do/does? What do/does? Why do/does?

A Read the quotations from academic articles. Choose a title for each article from the box.

Why Do People Celebrate Holidays?	What Do Teens Search for on the Internet?
How Do People Make New Friends?	Why Does a Bird Learn to Sing?
When Does a Child Become an Adult?	~~What Do Children Like to Eat?~~
Why Do We Dream?	Why Do We Grow Old?

1. *What Do Children Like to Eat?*
"Children prefer food that is not very hot or very strong in flavor."

5. _____
"Most searches are about movie stars, singers, and sports personalities."

2. _____
"Birds need to communicate with other birds."

6. _____
"We make friends with people we have something in common with, often at work or school."

3. _____
"We need to bring people together to remember good and bad events in our cultures."

7. _____
"We dream because our minds need to rest."

4. _____
"Our body is a machine. It works hard every day, year after year."

8. _____
"Teenagers are young adults, and the years 16 to 18 are very important."

B *Over to You*   Do you know more about the topics in A? Tell a partner.

A lot of children don't like spicy food.

3 | Questions with *How Often*

▶ Grammar Presentation

Questions with *How often* ask about how many times something happens.	*How often does she travel to Mexico?* *How often do you see your family?*

3.1 Questions with *How Often*

How Often	Do/Does	Subject	Base Form of Verb	
How often	**do**	I/you/we/they	**take**	a vacation?
	does	he/she/it	**receive**	a gift?

3.2 Using Questions with *How Often*

a. Use questions with *How often* to ask how many times something happens.	***How often** do you run in a marathon?* ***How often** does your family eat together?*
b. The answers are often frequency expressions.	*All the time.* *Every day.* *Every weekend.* *Every other week.* *Once a week.* *Twice a month.* *Three times a month.* *Several times a year.* *A few times a year.* *Once in a while.* *Almost never.*

▶ Grammar Application

Exercise 3.1 Questions with *How Often*

A Use the words to write questions with *How often*. Then write short answers. Make them true for you.

1. you / drink coffee

   Question: _How often do you drink coffee?_

   Answer: _Every day._

2. you / drink soda

   Question: _How often do yo drink s_

   Answer: _____

3. you / eat breakfast alone

   Question: _How Answer eat breakfaa_

   Answer: _____

4. your family / go out to a nice restaurant

Question: _A͟y͟f͟ ͟y͟/͟n͟y͟o͟_

Answer: _____

5. your friends / eat at a fast-food restaurant

Question: _____

Answer: _____

6. your relatives / visit your home

Question: _____

Answer: _____

B *Pair Work* Ask and answer the questions in A with a partner.

C *Over to You* Use *How often* to write your own questions. Use words from the box and your own ideas. Then ask your partner the questions.

board game	hiking	movie	swimming	TV
gym	library	music concert	text message	

1. *How often do you watch TV past midnight?*

2. _____

3. _____

4. _____

5. _____

6. _____

4 | Avoid Common Mistakes ⚠

1. In simple present information questions, use *do* or *does* before the subject.

do
Where you work?

does
Why he drink so much coffee?

2. Use *do* or *does*, not *is* or *are*, with the verb.

does
What time ~~is~~ the concert begin?

3. Do not use *-s* on the verb with *he* / *she* / *it* or a singular noun.

go
Where does Tom ~~goes~~ to school?

Editing Task

Find and correct seven more mistakes in these questions about Thanksgiving traditions in the United States.

How Do You Celebrate Thanksgiving?

1. *do*
   How you celebrate Thanksgiving?

   Answer: We eat a very big meal: turkey, mashed potatoes, vegetables, and pies for dessert.

2. Where do you celebrates Thanksgiving?

   Answer: We usually go to my aunt and uncle's house.

3. What are you does during Thanksgiving Day?

   Answer: We usually go to a high school football game in the morning. Then we go to
   my aunt and uncle's house and watch TV.

4. What you watch on TV?

   Answer: Football, of course! It's a Thanksgiving tradition.

5. What time are you usually have your meal?

   Answer: We usually have our meal at about 6:00 p.m.

6. What you do on the Friday after Thanksgiving?

   Answer: I don't go shopping! I usually sleep late and then go to the gym.

7. Why people celebrate Thanksgiving?

   Answer: Because it's a special day to be together with our families. We also remember
   the first Thanksgiving with the Pilgrims[1] and the Native Americans.

[1]**Pilgrims:** the English people who sailed to America and began living in Massachusetts in 1620

5 | Grammar for Writing ✏

Using Questions to Write About Special Days

Writers use information questions in the simple present to help them think of ideas about a topic. They use the answers to help them write their paragraphs.

Remember:

- **Start your questions with *Who, What, When, Where, What time, Why,* or *How*.**

  What do you do on your birthday?   *When do you eat your Thanksgiving meal?*

- **Use *How often* to find out specific information about how frequently people do things.**

  How often does your daughter visit for Mother's Day?

Pre-writing Task

1 Read the student's paragraph below. Have you ever celebrated Mardi Gras?

Mardi Gras

what

Mardi Gras is a popular celebration. It takes place once a year for several days in February or March. Many people celebrate it around the world. The celebrations are all different. For example, in the United States, New Orleans is famous for its Mardi Gras celebrations. During Mardi Gras, people wear colorful costumes and march in parades. Some parades are at night. Marchers throw colorful necklaces to the people watching the parades. The beads are very popular. There is a lot of jazz music and dancing. People love Mardi Gras because it is a good time to relax and enjoy life.

2 Read the paragraph again. Notice how the sentences answer information questions about Mardi Gras. Find a sentence that gives an answer for each of these *wh-* words: *What, When, Who,* and *Why.* Write the correct *wh-* word above the sentences you find.

Writing Task

1 *Write* Use the paragraph in the Pre-writing Task to help you write about a special day in your life. Make a list of information questions about your special day. Use the answers as you write.

2 *Self-Edit* Use the editing tips below to improve your sentences. Make any necessary changes.

1. Did you use information questions about your special day to help you think of ideas?
2. Did you use the answers from the questions to help you write your paragraph?
3. Did you use *Wh-* words and *do / does* in your questions?
4. Did you avoid the mistakes in the Avoid Common Mistakes chart on page 120?

Conjunctions: *And, But, Or*; *Because*
Time Management

1 Grammar in the Real World

A Do you have enough time for school, work, and family? Read the article below. What is one way to manage your time well?

Time for Everything

Many adults say they want more time. They are busy with work, family, **and** school, **and** they often don't get everything 5 done. People feel stressed **because** there is not enough time to do it all. However, there are some simple ways to manage your time well **and** avoid stress.

One way is to identify the important **or** 10 necessary tasks for that day. Then create a schedule **or** a "to do" list.[1] When you finish your important tasks, you can move on to the next, less important ones. Soon your tasks are done, **and** there is hopefully some 15 extra time for fun activities.

Another way is to do important tasks on the same days every week. For example, you can do your laundry every Monday, **and** go to the gym on Tuesday and 20 Thursday mornings before work or school. Always do the tasks on the same days. That way, you can plan around these important tasks **and** have time for other things. Some people don't like schedules, lists, 25 or weekly plans. Instead, they use the notes or calendar features on their cell phones. Put a reminder[2] for the task on your phone, **but** don't forget to do it!

These ideas can help you improve your 30 time management.[3] When you make plans and complete them, you feel good **and** can do more.

To Do:

grocery shopping

laundry

walk the dog

Monday	Tuesday
7:00 laundry	8:00 gym
9:00 work	10:00 class

[1]**"to do" list:** a list of things you need to do | [2]**reminder:** something that helps someone remember, like an alarm on a phone | [3]**time management:** being in control of your time; planning and using your time well

B *Comprehension Check* Answer the questions. Use the article to help you.

1. What do most adults not have enough of?
2. What are two ways to manage your time?
3. What happens when people make plans and complete them?

C *Notice* Find the words *and*, *but*, *or*, and *because* in the article. Then complete the sentences.

1. They are busy with work, family, _____ school.

2. People feel stressed _____ there is not enough time to do it all.

3. Some people don't like schedules, lists, _____ weekly plans.

4. Put a reminder for the task on your phone, _____ don't forget to do it!

2 | *And, But, Or*

▶ Grammar Presentation

And, *but*, and *or* are coordinating conjunctions. They connect words, phrases, and clauses.	*People are busy with family **and** work.* *I like to exercise, **but** I don't have time for it every day.* *She studies in the morning **or** after work.*

2.1 *And, But, Or* for Connecting Words and Phrases

Connecting Words	***Time and money** are valuable.* *She sleeps only **five or six** hours a night.*
Connecting Phrases	*I always **make a schedule and look at it often**.* *I have "to do" lists **on my computer but not on my phone**.* *Do you work **during the day or at night**?*

2.2 *And, But, Or* for Connecting Clauses

First Clause		Second Clause
You have more time in your day,	**and**	you feel less stressed.
Some people use their time well,	**but**	other people do not.
You can make a list,	**or**	you can schedule tasks on the same days.

2.3 Using *And, But, Or*

a. Use *and*, *but*, and *or* to connect words, phrases, and clauses.	Time **and** money are valuable. He has time **but** not money. Do you use schedules, **or** do you make "to do" lists?
b. Use *and* to join two or more ideas.	Maria makes time for school, family, **and** work. I study **and** work every day. I make a "to do" list, **and** I check the list often during the day.
c. Use *but* to show contrast or surprising information.	José works hard, **but** he also has fun. He always makes a schedule, **but** he rarely follows it.
d. Use *or* to show a choice of two alternatives.	You can make lists **or** schedules. I exercise **or** do laundry after I study. Is he at school **or** at work?
e. Use a comma when *and*, *but*, and *or* connect two clauses.	My family gets together at night, **and** we talk about our day. Sonya wakes up early, **but** she is always late for work.

▶ # Grammar Application

Exercise 2.1 Choosing *And, But, Or*

A Read the sentences about two types of people. Complete the sentences with *and*, *but*, or *or*. Add commas where necessary.

The Organized Person

1. Every day I wake up*, and* I make a long "to do" list.

2. I usually use the "notes" feature on my phone for important tasks _____ I always do them.

3. I don't like to forget appointments _____ be late.

4. I like to be busy _____ I feel good when I get things done.

The Disorganized Person

5. Sometimes I make lists _____ I usually lose them.

6. I have a lot of appointments _____ a lot of things to do every day.

7. I try to be on time _____ I am often late for appointments.

8. I am always busy _____ I don't get things done.

B *Over to You* Read the sentences in A with a partner. Which statements are true for you? Tell your partner.

Exercise 2.2 Punctuating Sentences with *And, But, Or*

A Correct the sentences below about ways to add time to a busy day. Add capital letters, periods, and commas as necessary.

1. a. Jane wants to read more but she doesn't have the time

      Jane wants to read more, but she doesn't have the time.

   b. now she listens to audiobooks in the car and during her breaks at work

      _____

   c. she listens to a book or a podcast every day and feels good about herself

      _____

2. a. James is very busy and often doesn't do his homework or study

      _____

   b. he worries about his grades and gets very upset

      _____

   c. finally, he talks about his problem with a classmate and they decide to help each other

      _____

   d. he and his classmate now talk on the phone every day and work on their homework together

      _____

B *Group Work* Make a list of four study tips. Use *and*, *but*, and *or* in your sentences.

Exercise 2.3 More *And, But, Or*

Good time management includes time for fun activities. Complete the sentences with your ideas about things you do for fun. Use *and*, *but*, or *or*.

1. On the weekends, I *watch TV and garden* _____.

2. Once a day, I _____.

3. In the evenings, I _____.

4. Sometimes I _____.

Exercise 2.4 Vocabulary Focus: Expressions with *And* and *Or*

Data from the Real World

English has many expressions using *and* and *or*. The nouns usually occur in the order they appear below.	*Do you like peanut butter and jelly?* NOT *~~Do you like jelly and peanut butter?~~*	
Common "noun *and* noun" expressions for food	cream **and** sugar salt **and** pepper bread **and** butter	peanut butter **and** jelly fish **and** chips
Common "noun *and* noun" expressions for relationships	mom **and** dad brother **and** sister husband **and** wife	Mr. **and** Mrs. father **and** son mother **and** daughter
Other common "noun *and* noun" expressions	night **and** day men **and** women name **and** address	ladies **and** gentlemen boys **and** girls
Common expressions with *or*	cash **or** credit	coffee **or** tea
Common "adjective *and* adjective" expressions	black **and** white old **and** new	nice **and** warm

A Complete the questions.

1. Do you like _cream_ and sugar with your coffee?
2. Do your _____ and dad live in the United States?
3. Do you have brothers and _____ ?
4. Do you work _____ and day?
5. Do you like black and _____ movies?
6. Do you think _____ and women have really different interests?
7. Do you put salt and _____ on your food?
8. Do you usually pay with _____ or credit?
9. Do you ever eat peanut butter and _____ sandwiches?
10. Do you prefer _____ or tea?

B *Pair Work* Take turns asking and answering the questions in A with a partner. Use complete sentences in your answers.

> *A Do you like cream and sugar with your coffee?*
>
> *B I like sugar, but I don't like cream.*

3 | *Because*

▶ Grammar Presentation

Because introduces the reason for or cause of something.	EFFECT CAUSE *People feel stressed* **because** *there is not enough time.*	

3.1 *Because* for Connecting Clauses

a. *Because* shows a cause-and-effect relationship.	EFFECT CAUSE *I am always late* **because** *I don't like to get up early.*
Clauses with *because* must have a subject and a verb.	SUBJECT VERB *Some people send e-mail reminders* **because** **they** **want** *to remember their tasks.*
b. A clause with *because* is <u>not</u> a complete sentence. It needs the main clause to form a complete sentence.	MAIN CLAUSE *I am always late* **because** *I don't like to get up early.* NOT *I am always late.* **Because** ~~*I don't like to get up early*~~.
c. *Because* can come before or after the main clause. Use a comma when *because* comes first in a sentence.	MAIN CLAUSE **Because** *I don't like to get up early* **,** *I am always late.* MAIN CLAUSE *I am always late* **because** *I don't like to get up early.*
d. In speaking, you can answer a question starting with *because*. Do not do this in writing.	*Why are you at school?* Say: **Because** *I want to learn English.*

▶ Grammar Application

Exercise 3.1 Cause-and-Effect Relationships with *Because*

Match the effect on the left with the cause on the right.

1. John is tired __c__
2. Tanya is usually late _____
3. Dan is often hungry _____
4. Eric walks slowly _____
5. Sue takes her brother to school _____
6. Maya and Sara sleep late _____
7. Jack takes classes at night _____

a. because his foot hurts.
b. because he never eats breakfast.
c. because he doesn't sleep enough.
d. because he works during the day.
e. because she doesn't put reminders on her phone.
f. because their mother doesn't have time.
g. because their alarm clocks don't work.

Exercise 3.2 ◀)) The Position of *Because*

Put *because* in the correct place in each sentence. Add commas where necessary. Then listen and compare your answers.

Bob, Jamal, Tony, and Leo are roommates. They study at the local community college. Each roommate has a problem with time.

1. Leo works at night *because* he goes to school during the day.

2. Tony can only study in the mornings he thinks more clearly then.

3. Bob's alarm clock doesn't work he is always late.

4. Jamal can't study at home his roommates are too noisy.

5. Leo forgets to write his assignments down he often misses them.

6. Tony and Jamal sometimes miss class they play basketball instead.

Exercise 3.3 Combining Sentences with *Because*

Label each clause with *C* for "cause" and *E* for "effect." Then combine the sentences with *because*. Do not change the order of the clauses.

1. _*E*_ Brendon does well in class.   _*C*_ He studies every day.

    Brendon does well in class because he studies every day.

2. _*C*_ Tanya's alarm clock does not work.   _*E*_ She is often late for work.

    Because Tanya's alarm clock does not work, she is often late for work.

3. _____ Alan has three reminders about   _____ He doesn't want to forget about it.
              the meeting on his phone.

    _____

4. _____ Wanda is always hungry at work.   _____ She doesn't have time for lunch.

    _____

5. _____ Karin starts work very early.   _____ She drinks a lot of coffee.

    _____

6. _____ Blanca works during the day.   _____ She takes night classes.

    _____

7. _____ Jared keeps a "to do" list.   _____ He has a lot of work.

    _____

Exercise 3.4 Giving Reasons with *Because*

Complete the sentences. Make them true for you.

1. I take English classes because _____.

2. I wake up at _____ because _____.
                    (time)

3. I live in _____ because _____.
                (town/city)

4. I like _____ because _____.
             (class)

5. I go to bed at _____ because _____.
                      (time)

4 Avoid Common Mistakes ⚠️

1. **Do not use a comma when you join two words or two phrases.**

   Lisa creates a schedule ~~,~~ and a list every day.

2. **Use a comma when you join two clauses with *and*, *but*, and *or*.**

   I need to study for the test ⌃and then I have to work!

3. **Use *and to* add information. Use *but* to show a contrast. Use *or* to show a choice.**

   but

   Sam is always late, ~~and~~ he gets his work done.

4. **Do not use a comma if *because* is in the second part of the sentence.**

   Jake is always on time ~~,~~ because he takes the 8:00 bus to school every day.

   But do use a comma if *because* is in the first part of the sentence.

   Because Lily makes a daily schedule ⌃she never forgets to do her tasks.

5. **Use *because* to state the reason (cause) for something. The other part of the sentence states the result (effect).**

   Because Kylie writes her assignments on her calendar,

   ~~Kylie writes her assignments on her calendar because~~ she doesn't forget them.

   Kylie doesn't forget her assignments because

   ~~Because Kylie doesn't forget her assignments,~~ she writes them on her calendar.

Editing Task

Read the story about Professor Kwan's class on time management. Find and correct 9 more mistakes.

A Useful Class

Every year, Professor Kwan teaches a class on time management. Many students like to take her class. Sometimes the class fills up quickly ⌿because it is so popular. Students know that they need to register early – in person and online. This is the first lesson of the time-management class.

5   In this class, Professor Kwan talks about different ways for students to organize their time. Her students often complain about the stress they have but how little

time they have. Professor Kwan always tells her students to buy a calendar. She says students can use an electronic calendar but a paper calendar. Because her students get organized they use their calendar every day. She tells students to find time to study

10 at least once a day – either after school and at night. When students plan their time well, they feel in control and confident.

This is not the only thing that Professor Kwan teaches in the class. Students have a lot of stress because it is also important to find time to relax, and exercise. Professor Kwan's class is so popular, because all students need help with time management. At the

15 end of her class, students have less stress and they have great time-management skills!

5 | Grammar for Writing ✏️

Describing the Way You Do Something

Writers use *and*, *but*, *or*, and *because* to combine ideas and to show relationships between ideas. They can use these conjunctions to write about something they do regularly. Remember:

- **Use *and, but,* or *or* to combine words, phrases, or clauses.**
  I usually do my homework on the bus <u>and</u> on my lunch break.
  She does her homework at night, <u>but</u> sometimes she falls asleep.
  His homework is never late <u>or</u> incomplete.

- **Use *because* to show a cause-and-effect relationship between two sentences.**
  She has very little time <u>because</u> she has two jobs.

Pre-writing Task

1 Read the paragraph below. When and where does the writer do her homework? Why?

Doing My Homework

I'm always busy (because) I work and I take classes.

I don't have a lot of time for homework because of this.

Because my homework is important, I do it in the library

before or after my class. The library opens at 7:00 a.m.,

5 and my class starts at 8:00 a.m. The library is quiet at

7:00 a.m. because it is often empty then. Sometimes I ask

the librarians for help. They are usually very nice and

helpful, but sometimes they are busy with their work.

After class, the library is full, but it is still a good place

10 to study.

2 Read the paragraph again. Circle the conjunctions *and*, *but*, *or*, and *because*. Which conjunctions connect words? Which connect phrases? Which connect clauses?

Writing Task

1 *Write* Use the paragraph in the Pre-writing Task to help you write about something you need to do regularly. Do you schedule time for this activity? When and where do you do this activity? Explain why. Write about how you:

- clean house
- do dishes
- do homework
- do laundry
- exercise
- go food shopping
- make meals
- pay bills
- take care of children

Use *and*, *but*, *or*, and *because* to combine ideas and show relationships between ideas.

2 *Self-Edit* Use the editing tips below to improve your sentences. Make any necessary changes.

1. Did you use conjunctions to write about something you do regularly?
2. Did you use *and*, *but*, and *or* to connect words, phrases, or clauses?
3. Did you use *because* to show cause-and-effect relationships?
4. Did you avoid the mistakes in the Avoid Common Mistakes chart on page 130?

Simple Past Statements
Success Stories

1 | Grammar in the Real World

A Do you know people who don't give up easily? Read the article below. What do you learn about this band?

A Band That Didn't Give Up[1]

Writers, artists, singers, and inventors[2] often feel discouraged[3] when others tell them they are not good enough. Some people give up. Others, like a group of young musicians in the 1960s,
5 don't let it stop them.

In December 1961, a record company executive[4] **traveled** to Liverpool, England. He **went** to listen to a new rock 'n' roll band. The executive **thought** the band **had** talent and
10 **invited** them to an audition[5] in London. The group **went** to London and **played** on New Year's Day 1962. After the audition, they **went** home and **waited** for a phone call. They **didn't hear** any news for weeks.

15 Finally, the company executive **told** the band manager, "Guitar groups are on the way out,[6] Mr. Epstein." So the record company **didn't give** the band a contract.[7]

But the band **didn't give up**. In the end, they **signed** a contract with another company and **became** a very famous band: The Beatles.

[1]**give up:** stop trying | [2]**inventor:** someone who designs or create new things | [3]**discouraged:** not confident to try again | [4]**executive:** person in a high position in a company who manages and makes decisions | [5]**audition:** short performance given to show ability | [6]**out:** not fashionable; not popular | [7]**contract:** written legal agreement

B Comprehension Check Are these sentences true or false? Use the article to help you. Correct the false sentences.

1. The executive traveled to London in December 1961.   True   False
2. The executive invited the band to London.   True   False
3. The band went to London and played on New Year's Eve.   True   False
4. The company didn't call the band immediately.   True   False
5. The band signed a contract with another company.   True   False

C Notice Answer the questions. Use the article to help you.

1. Can you find the past forms of these verbs in the article?

Present	travel	invite	play	wait	sign
Simple Past	traveled		play	waited	sign

2. What do the simple past verbs in question 1 have in common?

3. Can you find the past forms of these verbs in the article?

Base Form	go	think	have	tell	become
Simple Past					

4. How are these simple past verbs different from the verbs in question 1?

2 | Simple Past Statements: Regular Verbs

▶ Grammar Presentation

The simple past describes events that started and ended before now.	In 1961, he **traveled** to Liverpool. The band **played** for two hours. They **didn't hear** any news for weeks.

2.1 Affirmative Statements

Subject	Simple Past Verb	
I You We They He / She / It	**started**	in 1962.

2.2 Negative Statements

Subject	Did + Not	Base Form of Verb	
I You We They He / She / It	**did not** **didn't**	**sign**	a contract.

2.3 Using Simple Past Statements

a. Use the simple past for events that started and ended in the past.	the past now
It can be one event or repeated events.	*He **traveled** to Liverpool.* *The band **played** in clubs every week.* *They **didn't hear** any news.*
b. You can use the simple past to describe a feeling in the past.	*He **didn't like** the band.*

2.4 Spelling: Regular Simple Past Verbs

a. For most verbs, add *-ed*.	work → work**ed**
b. For verbs ending in *e*, add *-d*.	live → liv**ed**
c. For verbs ending in consonant + *y*, change *y* to *i* and add *-ed*.	study → stud**ied**
d. For verbs ending in vowel + *y*, add *-ed*.	play → play**ed**
e. For one-syllable verbs ending in consonant-vowel-consonant, double the consonant.	plan → pla**nned**
f. Do not double the consonant if the verb ends in *-x* or *-w*.	show → show**ed**
g. For two-syllable verbs ending in consonant-vowel-consonant and stressed on the first syllable, do not double the consonant.	travel → trave**led**
h. For two-syllable verbs ending in consonant-vowel-consonant and stressed on the second syllable, double the consonant.	control → contro**lled**
Here are some of the most common regular simple past verbs.	called wanted started happened worked lived tried moved looked talked liked decided

▶▶ Spelling and Pronunciation Rules for Regular Verbs in Simple Past: See page A21.
▶▶ Common Regular and Irregular Verbs: See page A15.

▶ Grammar Application

Exercise 2.1 Affirmative Simple Past Statements: Regular Verbs

Complete the sentences about The Beatles. Use the simple past form of the verbs in parentheses.

1. The Beatles first _visited_ (visit) the United States in 1964.

2. They _landed_ (land) in New York on February 7, 1964.

3. The door of the plane _opened_ (open).

4. The Beatles _appeared_ (appear).

5. The fans _cheered_ (cheer) and _shouted_ (shout).

6. Some fans _screamed_ (scream) and others _cried_ (cry).

7. The Beatles _played_ (play) on *The Ed Sullivan Show* on TV.

8. About 74 million people (over 40 percent of the country) _watched_ (watch) the show.

9. Their long hair _shocked_ (shock) the country.

10. They _changed_ (change) popular music forever.

Exercise 2.2 Negative Simple Past Statements: Regular Verbs

A Complete the first paragraph of this biography with negative simple past verbs. Use the full form *did not*.

This child _did not talk_ (talk) before the age of
(1)
four. He _did not learn_ (learn) to read before the age
(2)
of seven. He _did not like_ (like) his high school, and
(3)
he _did not pass_ (pass) the entrance exam for the
(4)
Swiss Federal Polytechnic School, a university in Zurich.
One teacher _did not believe_ (believe) that he was
(5)
intelligent at all. However, this boy _did not stop_
(6)
(stop) working hard. His teachers _did not recognize_
(7)
(recognize) his genius, but he _did not listen_ (listen)
(8)
to their discouraging words.

B Complete the rest of the biography with simple past forms of the verbs in the box.

~~enjoy~~   explain   ~~not perform~~   ~~study~~
~~enter~~   ~~graduate~~   show   ~~work~~

He _did not perform_ well in school, but he _showed_ an interest in
(1)   (2)
science, and he _did not enjoyed_ math. He _did not studied_ for a high school
(3)   (4)
diploma, and finally he _entered_ the university. He _graduated_ four
(5)   (6)
years later and then _worked_ on a Ph.D. He later _did explained_ the laws
(7)   (8)
of the universe. Who is he? _Albert Instein_ [The answer is on page 144.]

Exercise 2.3 🔊 Pronunciation Focus: Saying Simple Past Verbs

When the verb ends in /t/ or /d/, say -ed as an extra syllable /ɪd/ or /əd/.	**/ɪd/ or /əd/** /t/ wai**t** → waited /d/ deci**de** → decided
When the verb ends in /f/, /k/, /p/, /s/, /ʃ/, and /tʃ/, say -ed as /t/.	**/t/** /f/ lau**gh** → laughed /s/ mi**ss** → missed /k/ loo**k** → looked /ʃ/ fini**sh** → finished /p/ sto**p** → stopped /tʃ/ wat**ch** → watched
For verbs that end in other consonant and vowel sounds, say -ed as /d/.	**/d/** list**en** → listened pl**ay** → played cha**nge** → changed agr**ee** → agreed li**ve** → lived borr**ow** → borrowed

A 🔊 Listen and repeat the verbs in the chart above.

B *Pair Work* Add simple past endings to the verbs below. Then read the sentences aloud with a partner. Do the verbs have an extra syllable? Check (✔) *Yes* or *No*.

	Yes	No
1. A friend **call**ed__ me last night.		✔
2. I **invite**d___ her to dinner.	✔	
3. We **talk**_t_ about music.		✔
4. She **want**_ed_ to get an old album from the 1960s for her grandfather.		✔
5. We **surf**_ed_ the Internet.		✔
6. We **look**_ed_ for the album.		✔
7. I **download**_ed_ the music files.		✔
8. We **play**_ed_ them.		✔
9. They **sound**_ed_ funny.		✔
10. We **forward**_ed_ the music files to her grandfather.		✔
11. He **listen**_ed_ to the songs.		✔
12. Then he **delete**_ed_ them. Not all music from the 1960s is good.		✔

C *Over to You* Tell a partner about four things you did last night. Use some of the verbs in A.

I watched TV last night.

Exercise 2.4 Vocabulary Focus: Time Expressions

[handwritten: in the eighties]
[handwritten: in the]

yesterday	last ...	...ago	Prepositions
yesterday	last night	two days ago	in 2007
yesterday morning	last week / month / year	six weeks ago	on June 19
yesterday evening		10 months / years ago	at 7:30
	last Friday / June / spring	a long time ago	before / after the audition

Time expressions usually come at the end of a sentence.	*I listened to a Beatles album **last night**.* *The Beatles became famous **in 1962**.*
Time expressions can also come at the start of a sentence when they are very important.	***After the audition**, they went home and waited.* ***In 1961**, a record company executive traveled to Liverpool.*

Complete the sentences about a famous poet. Use the words from the box. Some words are used more than once.

after	ago	in	last	on

1. I borrowed a book of poems from the library __*last*__ week.

2. The poet lived in Massachusetts over 100 years ___*ago*___.

3. She published only seven poems ___*in*___ her lifetime.

4. She died at the age of 55 ___*on*___ May 15, 1886.

5. ___*after*___ the poet's death, her sister discovered over 1,800 poems in her room.

6. Her first book of poems appeared four years after she died, ___*after*___ 1890.

7. T. H. Johnson published a complete collection of her poems ___*in*___ 1955.

8. I prepared a presentation about her for class ___*last*___ night.

Collected Poems of
EMILY DICKINSON

1830–1886

Exercise 2.5 Time Expressions

Pair Work When was the last time you or a friend did these things? Ask and answer questions with a partner. Write sentences about your partner.

1. borrow a book from the library *Marie borrowed a book from the library three weeks ago.*
2. listen to an MP3 player *Mario listened to MP3 player yesterday*
3. laugh or cry at a movie *Are laughed or cry at a movie two days ag*
4. move to another apartment or house *Alejandro move to another apartment six w*
5. try really hard to do something *Carlos tried really hard to do something agn*
6. travel to another city *I travel to another city in six weeks ago shop*

Exercise 2.6 *Did Not* and *Didn't* in Writing

Data from the Real World

Didn't or *Did Not*?		*Didn't* and *Did Not* Compared
People use *didn't* in speaking and informal writing.	*Hey! You **didn't** call yesterday!*	**Academic Writing** didn't ▪ did not ▬▬▬ **Conversation** didn't ▬▬▬▬▬▬▬▬▬ did not ▪
They use *did not* in formal writing.	*The audition **did not** go well.*	

Rewrite these sentences about the famous poet Emily Dickinson for academic writing. Change the contractions.

1. Emily Dickinson didn't publish a lot of poems in her lifetime.

   Emily Dickinson did not publish a lot of poems in her lifetime.

2. Even her family didn't know about the 1,800 poems in her room.

   _____

3. In the nineteenth century, some critics didn't like her work, but she continued to write for herself.

   _____

4. She didn't write like other poets.

   _____

5. She didn't use correct punctuation.

   _____

6. In the 1950s, poetry experts published her work again. This time, they didn't edit it.

   _____

3 | Simple Past Statements: Irregular Verbs

▶ Grammar Presentation

Irregular simple past verbs don't end in *-ed*.	In 1961, he **went** to Liverpool. The company **made** a big mistake.

3.1 Irregular Verbs

AFFIRMATIVE STATEMENTS

Subject	Simple Past Irregular Verb	
I You We They He / She / It	**became**	popular.

NEGATIVE STATEMENTS

Subject	*Did* + *Not*	Base Form of Verb	
I You We They He / She / It	**did not** **didn't**	**become**	popular.

3.2 Using Irregular Simple Past Verbs

a. 🌐 Here are the most common irregular verbs.	come → came make → made do → did put → put get → got read → read go → went say → said have → had see → saw
b. Be careful with the verb *do*.	I **did** my homework last night. I **didn't do** my homework this morning.

▸▸ Irregular Verbs: See page A16.

▶ Grammar Application

Exercise 3.1 Simple Past Statements with Irregular Verbs

A Make guesses about things your partner did yesterday. Use the verbs in parentheses. Write affirmative and negative sentences.

1. You _____*didn't do*_____ (do) your homework last night.
2. You _____*didn't read*_____ (read) your e-mail after dinner.
3. You ___*didn't get up*___ (get up) late yesterday morning.
4. You ___*didn't come*___ (come) to school early today.
5. You ___*didn't go*___ (go) to work last night.
6. You ___*didn't make*___ (make) a wonderful dinner yesterday.
7. You ___*didn't see*___ (see) a movie in a theater last weekend.
8. You ___*didn't read*___ (read) a newspaper this morning.
9. You ___*didn't have*___ (have) breakfast this morning.
10. You ___*didn't see*___ (see) the weather report on TV this morning.

B *Pair Work* Read the sentences to your partner. Are your guesses correct?

A *You didn't do your homework last night.*
B *That's true. I did my homework this morning! / That's not true. I did my homework after dinner.*

Exercise 3.2 ◀》Pronunciation Focus: Saying Irregular Simple Past Verbs

Sometimes the spelling of two verbs is the same, or similar, but the pronunciation is different.	read → read say → said BUT pay → paid hear → heard
Sometimes the letters *gh* are not pronounced.	buy → bought think → thought

When you learn an irregular verb, learn the pronunciation, too.

A ◀》 Listen and repeat the verbs in the chart above. Notice the pronunciation of the irregular past forms.

B Tell a partner about something...

1. you bought last week.
2. you read recently.
3. your teacher said in the last class.
4. you thought about today.
5. you paid a lot of money for years ago.
6. you heard on the news today.

Exercise 3.3 More Irregular Simple Past Verbs

A Complete the descriptions with the verbs below. Can you match the pictures to the texts?

Vincent van Gogh

J. K. Rowling

Marilyn Monroe

Abraham Lincoln

1. see   not get   come

    In 1944, Norma Jean Baker _came_ to see the director of a modeling agency for a job
    interview. Unfortunately, Baker ___didn't get___ the job. The next time the director
    ___saw___ her, she had a different name and was a famous movie star. Who was
    she? ___marilyn mon___

2. buy   make   pay

    This artist ___mad___ over 800 paintings, but only one person
    ___bought___ one in his lifetime. The sister of a friend ___paid___
    400 francs (about $1,600 today) for it. Who was he? ___vicent var gog___

3. become   go   read   lose   not have

    This man ___didn't have___ a lot of money as a child. He ___went___ to
    school for only 18 months, but he ___read___ hundreds of books. As a politician, he
    ___lost___ his first election. Later, he ___become___ an important president
    in U.S. history. Who was he? ___Abraha lick___

4. become   say   write   tell   buy

    This single mother ___wrot___ her first book in a café. Twenty publishers
    ___tell___ her they didn't want it. Finally, one publisher ___told___
    "Yes." Millions of people ___writer___ ___bought___ the book, and it ___beca___ a
    successful movie. Who is she? ___she row___ J K Rowlin

B *Group Work* Discuss the famous people in this unit. Who is the most interesting to
you? Why?

Answer to Exercise 2.2B, p. 138: Albert Einstein

4 | Avoid Common Mistakes ⚠️

1. Use simple past verbs to write or talk about the past.

     started
He ~~starts~~ his career in 2002.

     ate
I ~~eat~~ at a restaurant last night.

2. After *did not / didn't*, use the base form of the verb. Do <u>not</u> use the past form.

     earn
They didn't ~~earned~~ a lot of money.

3. For the negative, write *did not* as two words.

     did not
She ~~didnot~~ get the job.

4. Use the correct spelling for simple past verbs.

bought	*took*	*read*	*studied*	*dropped*	*paid*
~~buyed~~	~~taked~~	~~red~~	~~studyed~~	~~droped~~	~~payed~~

5. The simple past negative of *have* is *did not / didn't have*. The simple past negative of *do* is *did not / didn't do*.

     didn't have
He ~~had not~~ a successful career.

     did not do
She ~~did not~~ her homework last night.

Editing Task

Find and correct ten more mistakes in this paragraph about the inventor of the lightbulb.

    Thomas Edison was born in 1847 in Milan, Ohio. He ~~had not~~ *did not have* very

much education in school. His mother taught him reading, writing, and

math. Like many children at the time, he ~~droped~~ *dropped* out of school and got a

job. At age 13, he ~~sells~~ *sold* newspapers and candy at a railroad station. Thomas

5 continue to learn about science by reading. At age 16, he ~~become~~ *became* a telegraph

operator.[1] Later he ~~start~~ *started* to invent things. In 1869, he moved to New York City.

One of his inventions earned him $40,000, so he opened his first research

laboratory[2] in New Jersey. He tried hundreds of times to make the first lightbulb, but he ~~had not~~ *didn't have*

success. However, Thomas Edison ~~didnot~~ *did not* give up. He ~~learn~~ *learned* from his mistakes. In 1879, he introduced

10 his greatest invention, the electric light for the home. He told a reporter, "I didn't fail 1,000 times.

The lightbulb was an invention with 1,000 steps."

[1]**telegraph operator:** a person who worked with a communication device that sent and received signals | [2]**research laboratory:** a building with equipment for doing scientific tests

5 | Grammar for Writing ✎

Writing About People in the Past

Writers use the simple past to describe specific events and repeated events in a person's life. Remember:

- **Use the simple past with time expressions to tell the order of events in stories.**
  Twenty-five years ago, Jenna wrote an important letter. She waited a long time, but after six months, she got an answer to her letter.

- **Many verbs are irregular, and there are many ways to spell irregular verbs.**
  He had three different jobs one year.   They went to school at night.

Pre-writing Task

1 Read the paragraph about an immigrant from Vietnam. How was he successful?

A Success Story

In 1996, Tam left Vietnam and came to the United States. Life was difficult in the beginning because he didn't speak English. He took English classes at night and looked for jobs during the day. He did not find a job at first, but after
5 several months, he found a good job at a local grocery store. Tam was very hardworking, and he learned the business very quickly. After a few years, the store owners gave Tam the job of manager. In 2002, the owners retired. Tam bought the store. The store is a very popular place in our neighborhood.
10 Tam's story is a good success story.

2 Read the paragraph again. Circle the regular past tense verbs and underline the irregular past tense verbs. Then double underline the time phrases. Notice how the time expressions tell the order of events in the story.

Writing Task

1 *Write* Use the paragraph in the Pre-writing Task to help you write a paragraph about a success story you know. What happened in this person's life? Use time expressions to tell the order of the events. Explain why the person is successful. You can write about a person you know or about the life of someone well known on the Internet. Use time expressions such as:

- In (year), he / she _____.
- Later, he / she _____.
- After (period of time), he / she _____.

2 *Self-Edit* Use the editing tips below to improve your sentences. Make any necessary changes.

1. Did you use the simple past to describe the person's success story?
2. Did you use time expressions to explain the order of events in the story?
3. Did you check the form and spelling of the simple past forms of your verbs?
4. Did you avoid the mistakes in the Avoid Common Mistakes chart on page 145?

1 Grammar in the Real World

A Do you know a business owner? Read the conversation between two students below. What is unusual about Blake Mycoskie's business?

Greg Hey, Liliana. **Did you finish** your report for class tomorrow?

Liliana No, but I found a really interesting businessman, Blake Mycoskie. Do you remember him from that
5   reality TV show, *The Amazing Race*?

Greg No, not really. **Did he win?**

Liliana No, he didn't, but that's not important. My report is on his *business*. It's really unusual.

Greg Why? **What did he do?** Let me guess. . . . He started
10   a cool company, and he made millions from his idea.

Liliana He started a cool company, and it helps fight poverty. He sells shoes, and . . .

Greg **Did you say** "shoes"?

Liliana Yes, he started TOMS Shoes in 2006. For every pair of shoes he sells, he donates
15   a pair to a child in need.[1] By the end of September 2010, he distributed[2] his one millionth pair.

Greg Hmm. Interesting. But **why did he decide to sell shoes?**

Liliana During *The Amazing Race*, he traveled with his sister all over the world. He saw a lot of very poor people and lots of children without shoes. A lot of these children
20   had diseases because they walked barefoot.[3] The schools did not allow children to attend without shoes. So he came up with this concept[4] of selling and donating shoes. In the future, he plans to expand[5] his business and make other products, too.

Greg Oh, I see. He's a social entrepreneur. He wants to make money, but he also wants to help people.

[1]**in need:** not having enough money | [2]**distribute:** give something to many people | [3]**barefoot:** not wearing any shoes or socks | [4]**concept:** idea | [5]**expand:** make something bigger

B *Comprehension Check* Answer the questions.

1. Did Blake Mycoskie win *The Amazing Race* on TV? _____

2. When did he start TOMS Shoes? _____

3. How many pairs of shoes did he distribute by the end of September 2010? _____

4. What are two problems for children without shoes? _____

C *Notice* Find the questions in the conversation. Complete the questions.

1. Did you _____ your report for class tomorrow?

2. What did he _____ ?

3. Did you _____ "shoes"?

4. Why did he _____ to sell shoes?

What form of the verb did you use to complete the questions?

2 | Simple Past *Yes / No* Questions

▶ Grammar Presentation

Simple past *Yes / No* questions ask about actions and events that happened before now.	***Did** you **finish** your report?* ***Did** he **win** the competition?*

2.1 *Yes / No* Questions

Did	Subject	Base Form of Verb	
Did	I you we they he / she / it	**finish**	the report?

2.2 Short Answers

AFFIRMATIVE				NEGATIVE		
Yes	Subject	*Did*		*No*	Subject	*Did + Not*
Yes,	I you we they he / she / it	**did.**		**No,**	I you we they he / she / it	**did not.** **didn't.**

2.3 Using Simple Past *Yes* / *No* Questions

a. Questions in the simple past often use definite past-time expressions.	*Did Blake go to college **in the 1990s**?* *Did he start his company **11 years ago**?*
b. Use the contraction *didn't* in negative short answers. The full form *did not* is very formal.	*"Did Blake win The Amazing Race?"* *"No, he **didn't**."*
c. Use pronouns in short answers.	*"Did Blake start a shoe company?"* *"Yes, **he** did."*
To give extra information, you can also answer *Yes* / *No* questions with long answers.	*"Yes, **he started TOMS shoes in 2006**."*

▶ ## Grammar Application

Exercise 2.1 Simple Past *Yes* / *No* Questions

Liliana heard about Blake Mycoskie and then went to a trade show[1] for entrepreneurs. Complete the questions in the simple past. Use the words in parentheses.

Liliana ___Did you have___ (you / have) a
(1)
good weekend?

Simon Yeah, pretty good. How about you?

Liliana Yes, very good.

Simon _Did you go out_ (you / go out)?
(2)

Liliana Yeah. I went out with Aisha on Saturday.

Simon Oh, _Did you go_ (you / go)
(3)
somewhere interesting?

Liliana Yeah. We went to a trade show. There were lots of exhibits[2] from new companies.

Simon A trade show? I didn't know you were interested in business!

Liliana Yes, I'm very interested in it. _Did I tell_ (I / tell) you about my
(4)
grandmother's company?

Simon No.

Liliana My grandmother had her own clothing design company, so I want to do

something like that.

[1]**trade show:** a large event at which companies show and sell their products and try to increase their business
[2]**exhibit:** a collection of things people can see in public

Simon   Really? __did you see__ (you / see) any design companies there?
(5)

Liliana Yeah. We saw some. A lot of the companies' owners are young entrepreneurs.

Simon   __did you speak__ (you / speak) with any interesting people?
(6)

Liliana Yeah. I spoke with the owner of a men's tie company. He designs his own fabric.[3]

Simon   Hmm. __did he have__ (he / have) any good ideas for you?
(7)

Liliana Yes. He told me one thing: find a good business partner. What do you say?

         Do you want to be my business partner?

[3]**fabric:** cloth or material

Exercise 2.2 Simple Past Yes/No Questions and Answers

A Read Liliana's notes for her report on Blake Mycoskie. Then write the questions.

> ### Questions About Blake Mycoskie
>
> 1. Second in "The Amazing Race"?
> 2. Other businesses before TOMS?
> 3. Sister – start the business with him?
> 4. Any experience in fashion?
> 5. Company – difficulties at the beginning?

1. he / finish   _Did he finish second in "The Amazing Race"?_
2. he / have   Did he have other businesses before Toms
3. his sister / start   Did his sister start sister,
4. he / have   Did he have Any experience in fashio?
5. the company / have   Did the company have company difficulties in the beginning

B Read some more information about Blake. Then answer the questions in A. First, write one short answer, and then write one long answer with extra information for each question.

When Blake Mycoskie competed in *The Amazing Race* with his sister Paige, they finished third. They lost the race by only four minutes. His sister helped him with the concept of TOMS Shoes, but he started the business by himself. He had previous experience in business, but he didn't have any experience in fashion. But he liked to design things. Before TOMS shoes, he started five other businesses, including a college laundry business and a reality TV channel. When he started TOMS, he had a lot of problems with the shoe factory.[1] Now the factory runs well, and a lot of people work for him.

[1]**factory:** a building where people use machines to produce things

1. a. _No, he didn't._
   b. _No, he finished third._
2. a. Yes, he did
   b. yes, re started busnsses
3. a. yes, She did
   b. yes, She helped him
4. a. No, he didn't
   b. No, he had experience in foshion
5. a. yes, he did
   b. yes, he had problems the shoe factory

C *Pair Work* Ask and answer the questions about Blake with a partner.

Exercise 2.3 More Simple Past Yes/No Questions and Answers

A *Over to You* Write questions to ask a partner about last weekend. For question 5, use your own verb.

1. (do) _Did you do anything interesting?_
2. (work) Did you Working in Austin?
3. (have) Did you have breakfast old toys?
4. (go out) Did go out you familyn
5. Did you do start homework?

B *Pair Work* Ask and answer the questions with your partner. Give your partner additional information.

A *Did you do anything interesting?*   A *Did you go out on Saturday?*
B *No, not really. I stayed home.*   B *Yes, I went to ..../No, I worked all day.*

3 | Simple Past Information Questions

▶ Grammar Presentation

Simple past information questions ask about people, things, times, places, etc., that happened before now.	***What did*** he ***do***? ***Why did*** he ***decide*** to make shoes?

3.1 Information Questions

Wh-Word	Did	Subject	Base Form of Verb	
Who			**write**	about?
What		I	**do**	yesterday?
When		you	**finish**	our report?
What time	**did**	we they	**begin**	writing?
Where		he	**visit**	on vacation?
Why		she it	**start**	a company?
How			**save**	enough money?

3.2 Using Simple Past Information Questions

a. Use simple past information questions to ask for specific information about something that happened in the past.	*"**Where did** she **study** business?"* *"She studied at Florida State."* *"**When did** she **graduate**?"* *"She graduated in 2012."*
b. Use *Wh-* words with *did* to ask about habits and regular activities.	*"**What did** she **do** every summer?"* *"She worked at a restaurant."*

3.3 Using *Wh-* Words in Simple Past Information Questions

a. Use *Who* to ask about people.	***Who*** did you start your company with?	*My sister.*
b. Use *What* to ask about things.	***What*** did you make?	*Shoes.*
c. Use *When* to ask about time (days, months, years, seasons, parts of the day).	***When*** did you have this idea?	*Last week.*

3.3 Using *Wh-* Words in Simple Past Information Questions *(continued)*

d. Use *What time* to ask about clock time.	***What time*** *did you start work today?*	*At seven o'clock.*
e. Use *Where* to ask about places.	***Where*** *did you go to business school?*	*In Boston.*
f. Use *Why* to ask about reasons.	***Why*** *did you open a restaurant?*	*Because I love food.*
g. Use *How* to ask about manner.	***How*** *did you save enough money?*	*I saved some every month.*

▶ Grammar Application

Exercise 3.1 Simple Past Information Questions and Answers

A Shelly Hwang, an entrepreneur, started a chain of frozen yogurt stores called Pinkberry. Unscramble the words to make questions about her.

Shelly Hwang, founder of Pinkberry

1. Why / she / to / move / did / the United States?
   Why did she move to the United States?

2. What / after / she / did / college? / do
   whot did she after college?

3. Who / she / with? / develop / the concept / did
   who did she the concept develop with?

4. When / open / store? / she / did / her first
   when did she first open store

5. What / have? / the store / did / flavors
   what did the store flavors have?

B 🔊 Listen to an instructor talk about Hwang. Then write short answers to the questions in A.

1. _To study business._
2. _____
3. _____
4. _____
5. _____

4 Avoid Common Mistakes ⚠️

1. Use *did* + subject + base form of the verb.

    did   *graduate*
When you ~~graduated~~ from business school?

2. In information questions, use *did* and the base form of the main verb. Do <u>not</u> use the past form.

    open   *become*
Where did you ~~opened~~ the first store? Did it ~~became~~ a success?

3. When *do* is the main verb, use *did* + subject + *do* (base form of verb).

    do
What did you at the company?

Editing Task

Find and correct the mistakes in these questions about your work experience.

    work
1. Did you ~~worked~~ for a relative?
2. Who did you ~~worked~~ for?
3. What did you? do?
4. How many hours did you ~~worked~~ each week?
5. How much money did you ~~earned~~ each week?
6. You did enjoy ~~enjoyed~~ your job?
7. What did you learned ~~learned~~ from this job?
8. Why did you ~~stopped~~ working?

5 | Grammar for Writing ✐

Writing Questions About People's Activities in the Past

Writers use questions in the simple past to get specific information about the topic or person they want to write about. They use *Yes / No* and information questions together to help them get all the information they need.

Remember:

Question word order for *Yes / No* questions and for information questions is similar.

<u>Did Mira work</u> at her organization at night?

<u>Where did Mira work</u> during the daytime? (at which organization?)

Pre-writing Task

1 Read the interview questions and answers about Aunt Liz. Then read the paragraph a student wrote about her. Why does the student admire Aunt Liz?

1. *A* (What) did you <u>do</u>?

   B I took care of my parents – your grandparents – when they were sick.

2. *A* Why did you do this?

   B I helped them because they needed help. They were too sick to cook or even go to their doctors' appointments.

3. *A* When did you do this?

   B This happened last year when they had the flu.

4. *A* How did you do this?

   B I went to their house every day and did what they needed.

5. *A* Did you work at the same time?

   B Yes. I went to their house after my own work.

6. *A* Did you ever complain?

   B No, I didn't. Why should I complain? I am healthy and they're my parents.

Amazing Aunt Liz

My Aunt Liz is an outstanding person. She cares about people a lot, and she always helps people. Last year, both my grandparents got sick, and Aunt Liz took care of them. The whole family helped, but my Aunt Liz did most of the work. She went to their house every day after work. She cooked their meals, and she cleaned their house. She often drove my grandparents to doctors' appointments. She got very tired, but she didn't complain. My grandparents are well now because of Aunt Liz.

2 Read the interview questions again. Circle the question words and underline the main verb.

Writing Task

1 *Write* Use the questions and paragraph in the Pre-writing Task to help you write interview questions about a person you admire or who did something important. Ask for specific information about the person. You can write about a person you know or find out about a famous person on the Internet.

2 *Self-Edit* Use the editing tips below to improve your sentences. Make any necessary changes.

1. Did you use *Yes / No* and information questions to get specific information about the person you admire?
2. Did you use the correct word order for *Yes / No* and information questions?
3. Did you avoid the mistakes in the Avoid Common Mistakes chart on page 155?

Simple Past of *Be*

Life Stories

1 | Grammar in the Real World

A What were you like as a child? Read the magazine article about Bill Gates. What was he like as a child?

Bill Gates

Bill Gates started the software[1] company Microsoft, and it is now one of the computer giants[2] of the world. However, Bill started his life in an ordinary family. He **was** born in Seattle,
5 Washington, in 1955. His father **was** a lawyer. His mother did volunteer work in the community. Bill **was** the second of three children in the Gates family: Bill, his sister Kristianne, and his sister Libby. They **were** all very intelligent children.

10   When Bill **was** about 12 years old, his parents began to worry about him. He **was** a good student, but life **was** not perfect at home. Bill **was** bored, and he often argued with his family. Eventually, his parents sent him to a new school. This **was** an important step for Bill because in this new school, there **were** some computers. Bill began to learn about computers, and he loved them. He and his
15 friends spent many hours on them. Bill also began to write software programs. In the new school, he **was** active and busy, and he **was** happy.

    After high school, Bill went to Harvard University, but he **was** in the computer lab a lot and didn't go to class all the time. After one year, he left Harvard and formed a software company with his friend Paul Allen. Their
20 company later became Microsoft.

[1]**software:** computer programs | [2]**giant:** a very large or powerful organization

B *Comprehension Check* Do these words describe Bill Gates as a child or as an adult? Check (✓) the correct answers. Some words describe both. Use the article to help you.

	As a Child	As an Adult
1. head of a computer giant	☐	☑
2. bored	☑	☐
3. intelligent	☐	☑
4. a good student	☑	☐

C *Notice* Read the sentences. Circle *was* or *were*. Use the article to help you.

1. His father **was** / **were** a lawyer.
2. They **was** / **were** all very intelligent children.
3. This **was** / **were** an important step for Bill.
4. Bill **was** / **were** the second of three children.
5. There **was** / **were** some computers.
6. Life **was** / **were** not perfect at home.

When do you use *was*? When do you use *were*?

2 Simple Past of *Be*: Affirmative and Negative Statements

▶ Grammar Presentation

The simple past of *be* describes people, places, or things in the past.	*His home **was** in Seattle, Washington.* *He and his sisters **were** good students.*

2.1 Statements

AFFIRMATIVE			NEGATIVE		
Subject	*Was / Were*		**Subject**	*Was / Were + Not*	
I He She It	was	in the computer lab.	I He She It	was not wasn't	in class.
We You They	were		We You They	were not weren't	

2.2 Using Simple Past of *Be*

a. Use the simple past of *be* to talk or write about people, places, or things in the past. *Be* has two past forms: *was* and *were*.	He **was** a lawyer. The students **were** in their class. I **was not** in the computer lab. They **were not** bored.
b. Use *was* / *were* + *born* to say when or where someone was born.	He **was born** in Seattle, Washington, in 1955.
c. *Not* comes after *be* in negative statements.	He was a good student, but life **was not** perfect at home.
d. In speaking, you can use the contractions *wasn't* and *weren't* in negative statements.	Bill **wasn't** interested in school. They **weren't** wealthy.
e. We often use past time expressions with the simple past of *be*: *ten years ago / yesterday / this morning / last week / in the past*	**In 1973**, Bill **was** a student at Harvard. We **were** in Seattle **last week**.
Past time expressions can go either at the beginning of a sentence or at the end of a sentence.	

▶ Grammar Application

Exercise 2.1 Simple Past of *Be*: Affirmative and Negative Statements

A Read the descriptions of three famous women. Complete the sentences with *was* / *wasn't* or *were* / *weren't*. Write the names on the lines.

Oprah Winfrey	Taylor Swift	Penélope Cruz

1. _penelope Cruz_

She __was__ born in Madrid, Spain, in 1974. Her father
                (1)
__was__ an auto mechanic[1] and her mother __was__
  (2)   (3)
a hairdresser.[2] She studied ballet and jazz dance as a child.

When she __was__ a teenager, she started acting. At 17,
            (4)
she __was__ in her first film.
      (5)

[1]**auto mechanic:** someone who repairs cars | [2]**hairdresser:** a person who cuts and styles hair (usually women's hair)

2. ___Oprah Winfrey___

She ___was___ born in Mississippi in 1954. Her mother
(6)
and father ___were___ very poor. Her father ___was___ a
(7)   (8)
barber.[3] When she ___was___ in high school, she got her
(9)
first radio job. She ___was___ a student at Tennessee State
(10)
University for several years. She got her first TV job in 1972.
By age 32, she ___was___ a millionaire.
(11)

[3] **barber:** a person who cuts men's hair

3. ___Taylor Swift___

She ___was___ born in Pennsylvania in 1989. As a child,
(12)
she loved to write and wrote in her diary every day. When she
___was___ in the fourth grade, she won a poetry contest.[4] She
(13)
began to write songs, and she sang at festivals and contests.
She ___wasn't___ (not) shy, and she liked to perform. In high
(14)
school, she ___wasn't___ (not) very popular. Other students
(15)
___wasn't___ (not) friendly with her. Now she's very popular.
(16)

[4] **contest:** a competition to win a prize

B Complete the sentences with *was* and *wasn't*. Use the information in A to help you.

1. Penélope Cruz ___wasn't___ born in the United States.
2. As a child, Taylor Swift ___wasn't___ a songwriter.
3. Oprah Winfrey's family ___wasn't___ wealthy.
4. As a child, Penélope Cruz ___wasn't___ a dancer.
5. By age 32, Oprah Winfrey ___wasn't___ poor.
6. Oprah Winfrey's father ___wasn't___ a TV star.
7. Penélope Cruz ___was___ a teenager when she started acting.

Exercise 2.2 Simple Past of *Be*: More Affirmative and Negative Statements

A *Over to You* What were you like as a child? Write six sentences about you and your family members. Write three sentences with *was / were* and three sentences with *wasn't / weren't*. Use the words in the box and your own ideas.

~~a bad student~~	active	~~busy~~	funny	~~intelligent~~	short	talkative
~~a good student~~	bored	friendly	happy	quiet	shy	tall

I was very shy. I wasn't a good student. My father was a mechanic.

was / were

1. I was a good student
2. I was active
3. I was busy

wasn't / weren't

1. I wasn't intelligent o bad student
2. I wasn't bored
3. I wasn't friendly

B *Pair Work* Tell your partner what you were like as a child and about your family members.

A *I was very shy. I wasn't very talkative.*
B *Really? That's surprising. What about your brothers and sisters?*
A *They weren't shy at all.*

3 Simple Past of *Be*: Questions and Answers

▶ Grammar Presentation

> *Yes / No* questions and information questions with the simple past of *be* ask about people, places, and things in the past.

> "**Were** you in college last year?"
> "No, I **wasn't**."
>
> "When **were** you in college?"
> "I **was** in college three years ago."

3.1 *Yes / No* Questions

Was / Were	Subject	
Was	I he she it	very smart?
Were	we you they	in college?

3.2 Short Answers

AFFIRMATIVE				NEGATIVE		
Yes	Subject	*Was / Were*		*No*	Subject	*Was / Were + Not*
Yes,	I he she it	**was.**		**No,**	I he she it	**was not.** **wasn't.**
	we you they	**were.**			we you they	**were not.** **weren't.**

3.3 Using *Yes / No* Questions with Simple Past of *Be*

a. We often use past time expressions in *Yes / No* questions with the simple past of *be*: *ten years ago / yesterday / this morning / last week* Past time expressions go at the end of a question.	***Were*** you in college ***last year***? ***Was*** Bill famous ***in 1955***? ***Was*** she born ***in 1972***?
b. Use the contractions *wasn't / weren't* in negative short answers.	"Was she a dancer?" "No, she **wasn't**." "Were they wealthy?" "No, they **weren't**."
c. You can also answer with additional information.	"Was she a dancer?" "No, **she was a songwriter**." "Were they wealthy?" "No, **they were very poor**."

(handwritten in margin: Feid terxxo)

3.4 Information Questions

Wh- Word	Was / Were	Subject	
Who		your best friend	as a child?
What	**was**	your favorite class	last semester?
When		her birthday party?	
What time		the meeting	on Monday?
Where		his partners?	
Why	**were**	they	successful?
How		the concerts	the other night?
How old		their cars	in 2010?

(handwritten in margin: Creed 3)

3.5 Using *Wh-* Words with Simple Past of *Be*

a. Use *Who* to ask about people.	***Who*** were the founders of Microsoft?	*Bill Gates and Paul Allen.*
b. Use *What* to ask about things.	***What*** was your favorite class last semester?	*English.*
c. Use *When* to ask about time (days, months, years, seasons, parts of the day).	***When*** was your sister born?	*In April.*
d. Use *What time* to ask about clock time.	***What time*** was your class?	*At eight o'clock.*

e. Use *Where* to ask about places.	***Where*** *were you born?*	*In Tokyo.*
f. Use *Why* to ask about reasons.	***Why*** *were they excited?*	*Because they won the game.*
g. Use *How* to ask what something was like.	***How*** *was the play?*	*It was great.*
h. Use *How old* to ask about age.	***How old*** *was your brother last year?*	*He was 18.*

▶ # Grammar Application

Exercise 3.1 Simple Past of *Be*: Yes / No Questions

A Tanya's class assignment is to interview her grandfather. Complete her questions with *Was* or *Were*.

1. ____Were____ you born in New York City?
2. ____was____ your family large?
3. ____was____ your brother a good student?
4. ____were____ you and your brother good friends?
5. ____were____ your sisters nice to you?
6. ____were____ you and your sisters the same age?
7. ____was____ your father's store near the house?

B ◀)) ***Pair Work*** Listen to the conversation between Tanya and her grandfather. Write short answers about the grandfather's life to the questions in A. Then compare your answers with a partner.

1. _No, he wasn't._
2. _____
3. _____
4. _____
5. _____
6. _____
7. _____

Exercise 3.2 Simple Past of *Be*: Yes / No Questions and Information Questions

A Read the paragraph about a childhood photograph. Then write information questions and answers about the photograph.

My great-grandmother was born in 1901 in Wisconsin. She was born at 12:10 in the morning. She was the first of two children. Her father was a store owner, and her mother was a teacher. They lived in a small town. I once saw a
5 photograph of her house. The house had two floors, and it was very simple. There was no paint on the house, but it was well built. There was a nice front porch with several chairs and some flowers. My great-grandmother and her father were in the photo. Her father was happy, but she was angry
10 because she hated sitting for pictures. She was about three years old in the photo. She was upset but very cute.

1. (When / she born)

   When was she born?   She was born in 1901.

2. (Where / she born)

   where was sno born   She was born in wisconsin
                         She was both at 12:10 in the morning

3. (What time / she born)

   what time was se born   She was born 12:10

4. (What / her father's job)

   what was her father's jo   She was father's job store owner

5. (What / her mother's job)

   what was her mother's job   She was mothers job teacher

6. (Who / in the photo)

   who was in the photo   She was photo in house

7. (What / on the porch)

   what on the porch   She was several chairs

8. (Why / she angry)

   why was she angry   _____

9. (How old / she in the photo)

   How old She in the photo   _____

B Over to You Write questions to ask a partner about his or her childhood. Write *Yes / No* questions and information questions. Use *was / were* and the words in the box or your own ideas.

born	favorite family activity	school
brothers	favorite games	sisters
chores[1]	favorite room in your house	your bedroom
father's / mother's job	favorite toys	

Where were you born?

1. _____
2. _____
3. _____
4. _____
5. _____
6. _____
7. _____
8. _____

[1]**chore:** a job that is often boring but that is important, like washing the dishes

C Pair Work Ask and answer the questions about childhood from B. Take turns.

A *Were you born in the United States?*
B *No, I was born in Thailand.*

Tareas domesticos

4 Avoid Common Mistakes ⚠

1. With *I / he / she / it* or a singular noun, use *was*.
      was
    He ~~were~~ a famous artist.

2. With *you / we / they* or a plural noun, use *were*.
        were
    My brothers ~~was~~ usually nice to me.

3. Use the correct form with *born*.
    were you born   *was born*
    When ~~was you born~~?   I ~~born~~ in 1980.

Editing Task

Find and correct seven more mistakes in the questions and answers about Yo-Yo Ma.

          was
A When ~~were~~ Yo-Yo Ma born?

B He born in 1955.

A He born in the United States?

B No, he wasn't. He was born in France.

5 *A* Were his parents French?

B No, they was not. They was Chinese.

A Were his parents musicians?

B Yes, they was talented musicians.

A How old was he when he first played

10   the cello?

B He was four.

A How old were he when he moved to

    New York City?

B He were five.

15 *A* How many albums does he have?

B Currently, he has more than 75 albums.

Yo-Yo Ma, cellist

5 Grammar for Writing

Writing About Childhood Memories

Writers often use the simple past of *be* to describe people, places, and things in the past. They use other verbs to explain what happened.

Remember:

- **Use the simple past of *be* for your descriptions of the past.**
  Jai and her brother <u>were</u> very smart. They <u>were</u> good students.

- **Use *There was / There were* to show what things or places were like.**
  <u>There was</u> always a lot to do in their neighborhood. <u>There were</u> always other neighborhood children around to play with.

Pre-writing Task

1 Read the paragraph from a student. What did the writer's mother do, and why was it difficult for her?

A Difficult Moment

My mother <u>was</u> always a great singer. When she was 12, (there was) a talent competition at her school. My mother <u><u>registered</u></u> to sing in the show. She <u>was</u> very nervous because it <u>was</u> her first concert. The room <u>was</u>

5 very hot. There <u>were</u> no open windows, and there <u>were</u> many people in the room. My mother did not want to sing because she was <u><u>scared</u></u>. Her throat <u>was</u> very dry. Then she saw her parents. They <u><u>smiled</u></u> at her, and that helped her. She sang her song. It <u>was</u> great! My mother

10 often talks about this memory.

2 Read the paragraph again. Circle all the examples of *there was / there were*. Underline the past forms of *be* verbs, and <u>double underline</u> the other past forms of verbs.

Writing Task

1 *Write* Use the paragraph in the Pre-writing Task to help you write a paragraph about a childhood experience of another person in your class. Ask a partner to think of a happy, sad, exciting, scary, or proud moment. Then ask that person to tell you about this moment. Ask questions.

Use sentences in your paragraph such as:

- When she / he was _____ years old, she / he _____.
- There were / was _____.
- He / She was very nervous / happy / sad because _____.

2 *Self-Edit* Use the editing tips below to improve your sentences. Make any necessary changes.

1. Did you use the simple past of *be* to describe things and other simple past verbs to tell the story of a special childhood memory?
2. Did you use the simple past of *be* in your descriptions?
3. Did you use *there was / there were* in your descriptions?
4. Did you avoid the mistakes in the Avoid Common Mistakes chart on page 167?

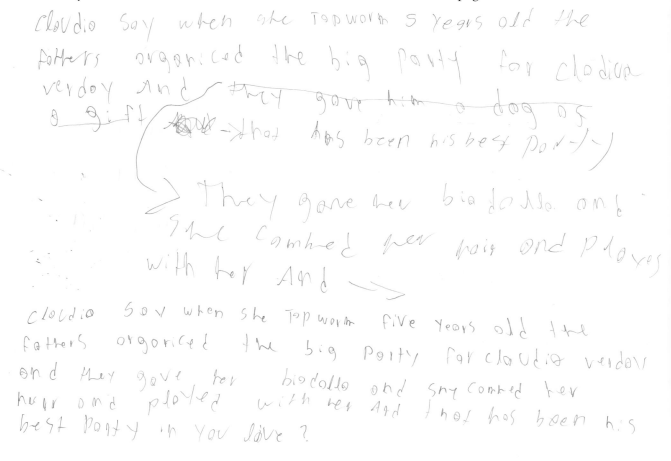

Claudio say when she Top worm 5 years old the fathers organiced the big party for claudia verdoy and they gave him a dog as gift that has been his best party

They gave her big dollo and she combed her hair and played with her And

Claudio sov when she Top worm five years old the fathers orgoriced the big party for claudia verdov and they gove her bio dollo and shy combed her hair and ployed with her And that has been his best party in you love?

Past Time Clauses with *When, Before*, and *After*

Luck and Loss

1 | Grammar in the Real World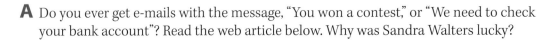

A Do you ever get e-mails with the message, "You won a contest," or "We need to check your bank account"? Read the web article below. Why was Sandra Walters lucky?

Internet Lottery Scam[1]

When Sandra Walters opened her e-mail one day at work last year, she was surprised. One message said, "Congratulations. You are the lucky winner of $2.5 million in the National Millionaire's Contest. Call
5 this number." **When Sandra got home**, she called the number and spoke to a man who seemed very nice. The man told her to send a $1,000 fee[2] to a bank outside the United States. **When Sandra said she didn't have $1,000**, the man said, "No problem. I can
10 charge your credit card." She gave him her credit card number, her bank account number, and her address. The man promised to send her a check for $2.5 million the next day. Then he hung up. **After Sandra put the phone down**, she began to think. What was this
15 contest? She didn't remember entering any contest. How did she win?

Unfortunately, it's a common story. There is no National Millionaire's Contest. In a real contest, you never pay a fee **before you receive your prize**. Sandra wasn't a winner. She was the victim[3] of a scam . . . almost. Luckily, Sandra realized her mistake
20 and called her credit card company. They canceled[4] the card **before the criminals[5] used it**.

Don't fall for[6] this scam. An e-mail message that asks for personal information is probably a scam. Just delete it!

[1]**scam:** a dishonest way of making money | [2]**fee:** money you pay for a service | [3]**victim:** someone who suffers from violence, illness, or bad luck | [4]**cancel:** stop something from working | [5]**criminal:** a person who has done something illegal | [6]**fall for:** believe something is true when it's not

B Comprehension Check Circle the correct answers.

1. Where did Sandra receive the e-mail?
   a. at home   b. at work   c. at the bank

2. How much money did the man ask her to send to a bank outside the United States?
   a. $1,000   b. $2.5 million   c. $25

3. Why did Sandra give her credit card number to the man?
   a. because she didn't have a bank   b. because it was quick   c. to pay the fee

4. When did she realize it was a scam?
   a. when she got home   b. after she finished the call   c. when she called her credit card company

C Notice What did Sandra do first? For each pair of sentences, write *1* and *2*. Use the article to help you.

1. _____ Sandra was surprised.   _____ Sandra read her e-mail.

2. _____ She called the number.   _____ She went home.

3. _____ She said she didn't have $1,000.   _____ The man asked for her credit card number.

4. _____ She began to think.   _____ She put the phone down.

5. _____ She realized her mistake.   _____ She called her credit card company.

2 | Past Time Clauses with *When*, *Before*, and *After*

▶ Grammar Presentation

Time clauses show the order of events in the past. They can begin with *when*, *before*, and *after*.	FIRST EVENT SECOND EVENT **After Sandra put the phone down,** *she began to think.*

2.1 Time Clauses

Time Clause		Main Clause	Main Clause	Time Clause	
When **Before** **After**	**I get to work,**	I check my e-mail.	I check my e-mail	**when** **before** **after**	**I get to work.**

2.2 Main Clauses and Time Clauses

a. A clause has a subject and a verb.

SUBJECT VERB
She was surprised.

SUBJECT   VERB
When **Sandra opened** her e-mail, . . .

b. A main clause is a complete sentence. It has a subject and a verb.

SUBJECT   VERB
Sandra called the number.

SUBJECT VERB
She began to think.

c. A time clause can begin with *when*, *before*, or *after*. It has a subject and a verb. However, it is <u>not</u> a complete sentence. A time clause always goes with a main clause.

SUBJECT VERB   SUBJECT VERB
When **she got** home, she called the number.

SUBJECT   VERB   SUBJECT VERB
After **Sandra put** the phone down, she began to think.

d. You can add a time clause to a main clause to say when something happened.

MAIN CLAUSE   TIME CLAUSE
Sandra called the number **when she got home**.

TIME CLAUSE   MAIN CLAUSE
After Sandra put the phone down, she began to think.

e. A time clause can go before or after the main clause.
When the time clause comes first, use a comma after it.

TIME CLAUSE   MAIN CLAUSE
When Sandra opened her e-mail, she was surprised.

TIME CLAUSE   MAIN CLAUSE
After Sandra put the phone down, she began to think.

When the time clause comes second, do not use a comma.

MAIN CLAUSE   TIME CLAUSE
Sandra was surprised **when she opened her e-mail**.

MAIN CLAUSE   TIME CLAUSE
Sandra began to think **after she put the phone down**.

Time clauses are more common after the main clause.

MAIN CLAUSE   TIME CLAUSE
They canceled the card **before the criminals used it**.

2.3 Ordering Events

a. *When* means "at almost the same time." Use *when* to introduce the first event.	FIRST EVENT SECOND EVENT **When** *Sandra opened her e-mail, she was surprised.* SECOND EVENT FIRST EVENT *Sandra called the number* **when** *she got home.*
b. Use *after* to introduce the first event.	FIRST EVENT SECOND EVENT **After** *Sandra put the phone down, she began to think.* SECOND EVENT FIRST EVENT *She felt much better* **after** *she called the bank.*
c. Use *before* to introduce the second event.	FIRST EVENT SECOND EVENT *She canceled the card* **before** *they used it.* SECOND EVENT FIRST EVENT **Before** *they sent her prize, they asked her to pay a fee.*
d. *Before* and *after* are also prepositions. You can use them before nouns that do not have verbs after them.	**After work**, *she went home.* *She was so excited* **before the phone call**.

▶ Grammar Application

Exercise 2.1 *When*, *Before*, or *After*?

A Choose the correct words to complete the sentences about the article.

1. Sandra opened her e-mail (**when**)/ **before** she got to work.

2. **When / Before** she read the e-mail, Sandra was surprised.

3. She called the number **after / before** she got home.

4. The man and Sandra talked **before / after** he had her personal bank information.

5. **When / Before** Sandra said she didn't have $1,000, the man asked for her credit card number.

6. She gave him her address **after / before** she read out her credit card number.

7. **After / Before** she put the phone down, Sandra realized her mistake.

8. She called her credit card company **before / after** she spoke to the man.

B *Pair Work* Compare your answers with a partner. Which sentences can use both words?

Exercise 2.2 Ordering Events

A 🔊 Listen to the story about another scam. Number the pictures in the order the events happened.

a. _____

He bought a
newspaper.

b. _____

_____

c. _____

_____

d. _____

_____

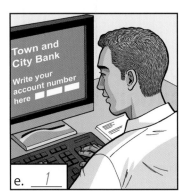

e. _1_

_____

f. _____

_____

B Write the sentences under the correct pictures in A.

~~He bought a newspaper.~~   He left for work.

He read an e-mail from the bank.   He wrote a note to his wife.

He met a co-worker on the train.   He called his wife.

C 🔊)) Complete the story with *when*, *before*, and *after*. Then listen again to check your answers.

   About a year ago, my friend Leo was almost a scam victim. One morning, he saw an e-mail from his bank _before_ he went
(1)
to work. _____ he opened the
(2)
e-mail, it said, "You have a new account number. Write your old account number here so we can check your identity." He didn't have time to reply _____ he left home.
(3)
_____ he left for work, he wrote a
(4)
note to his wife, "Please reply to the bank's e-mail." Then he left for work.

   _____ he got to the subway station, he bought a newspaper.
(5)
_____ he got on the train, he met a co-worker and they talked.
(6)
_____ he read the newspaper at lunchtime, he read an article about a bank
(7)
Internet scam. He realized the e-mail from the bank was that scam. _____
(8)
he read the article, he called his wife. Luckily, _____ his wife read the
(9)
e-mail, she realized it was a scam and deleted the e-mail.

Exercise 2.3 Writing Main Clauses and Time Clauses

A *Over to You* What did you do yesterday? Complete each sentence by adding a main clause with a subject and a verb. For sentences with the time clause first, use a comma.

1. _____ before I left home yesterday morning.

2. After I ate lunch _____ .

3. Before I went home last night _____ .

4. _____ when I got home last night.

5. _____ after I ate dinner.

6. Before I went to bed _____ .

B *Over to You* What did you do today? Complete each sentence by adding a time clause with *when*, *before*, or *after*. For sentences with the time clause first, use a comma.

1. I got dressed _____ .

2. _____ I brushed my teeth.

3. I left the house / apartment _____ .

4. I got to school _____ .

5. _____ I went to the classroom.

6. _____ my English class started.

C *Pair Work* Share your sentences with a partner. Did you do any of the same things?

Exercise 2.4 More Main Clauses and Time Clauses

Pair Work Tell a story about a scam from this unit or use your own ideas. First make notes to help you. Then share your story with a partner. Ask questions about your partner's scam story.

A *This happened to a friend last year. When she checked her e-mail, she saw a message from a stranger.*

B *What did it say?*

3 | Avoid Common Mistakes ⚠

1. Check the spelling of *when*, *before*, and *after*.

~~Whin~~ *When* she read the e-mail, she got excited.   They canceled the card ~~befor~~ *before* the criminals used it.

She thought about it ~~afther~~ *after* she put the phone down.

2. When the time clause comes first, use a comma. Don't use a comma when the main clause comes first.

When she got home,she called the company.   She called the company/when she got home.

3. Don't forget the subject in the main clause and the time clause.

Before Ana called the company, *she* checked the address.

Before *Ana* called the company, she checked the address.

Editing Task

Find and correct 13 more mistakes in this story about a scam.

When I got home one night two months ago I had a voice-mail message. When I
listened to the message, got excited. The message said, "Congratulations. You are a
winner in our contest." Befor I made dinner, called the number. A woman said, "We
called you two weeks ago, but you didn't answer. Please hold." After waited for an
5 hour, I put the phone down.

Whin my wife got home I asked her, "Did you get a message about a prize
drawing?" She said, "Yes, but afther heard it, I deleted it. It's a scam." When she said that
I didn't say anything.

I realized my mistake, when we got the phone bill four days later. When read
10 the bill I didn't believe it. That one-hour call cost $5,000!

4 | Grammar for Writing ✎

Telling Stories

Writers often use time clauses with *when*, *before*, and *after* when they tell a story or write about something that happened. Time clauses help the reader understand the order of events. Remember:

- **Use *when* to introduce an event that happened at the same time as another event, *before* to introduce an event that happened after another event, and *after* to introduce the first event that happened.**

  Milton looked up <u>when</u> Heidi walked in the room.
  <u>Before</u> she spoke to Milton, Heidi sat down. <u>After</u> she sat down, Milton said hello to her.

- **When you use a time clause, always use a main clause.**

  TIME CLAUSE   MAIN CLAUSE
  When he opened his messages, he got a big surprise.

Pre-writing Task

1 Read the paragraph below. What was so bad about the writer's morning?

A Terrible Morning

    I had a terrible morning last week. Many things went wrong. I grabbed my coffee
(before) I left to catch the bus. When I got on the bus, I didn't have my bus pass. I paid
the driver with cash and sat down. After I put my backpack down, I took a sip of coffee.
When I took a sip, the bus went over a bump in the road, and the coffee spilled on me. I
ran to the restroom to clean up before I went to class. Then I ran to class because I was
late. When I sat down, I noticed that the room was empty. There was no class that day
because my teacher was sick.

2 Read the paragraph again. Underline all the time clauses and circle all the time words. Number the two clauses in the sentences with time clauses. Put a *1* over the event that happened first, a *2* over the event that happened second, and a check (✓) over the events that happened at the same time.

Writing Task

1 *Write* Use the paragraph in the Pre-writing Task to help you write a paragraph about an interesting or unusual story that you or someone you know experienced. What happened first? What happened second? What happened at the same time? Use time clauses beginning with *when*, *before*, and *after*.

2 *Self-Edit* Use the editing tips below to improve your sentences. Make any necessary changes.

1. Did you use time clauses with *when*, *before*, and *after* to show the order of events in a story?
2. Did you use *when* to talk about two events that happened at the same time, *before* to introduce the second event in a sentence, and *after* to introduce the first event in a sentence?
3. Did you use time clauses with main clauses?
4. Did you avoid the mistakes in the Avoid Common Mistakes chart on page 177?

16

Count and Noncount Nouns
Eating Habits

1 | Grammar in the Real World

A Do you think your diet is healthy? Read the article from a college website. What kinds of food are part of a healthy diet?

Santos Community College

HOME   CONTACT   NEWS   HEALTH

Food for Health

When you turn on a television or read a **newspaper**, you often find **information** about healthy eating. **Food** and **health** get a lot of **attention** in the **news** these **days**. Researchers seem to find new **things** about how our **diet** affects us every day.

5   Everyone knows it is important to eat **fruit** and **vegetables**. Did you know that eating **fruit** and **vegetables** with different colors is especially good for your **health**? Green, red, blue, and orange **fruit** and **vegetables** all have different **vitamins**[1] to help hydrate you, and they help prevent different **diseases**.

Did you know that dark **chocolate** is good for you, too? Research shows that a
10 little **chocolate** helps your **heart** and your **mood**.[2]

How about **fat**?[3] Maybe you think **fat** is bad for you, but people need a little **fat** in their diet. One type of healthy **fat** is omega-3 **oil**.[4] It comes from **fish** and helps your **heart**, **skin**, and **brain** stay healthy. For **vegetarians** or non-fish eaters, many **seeds**[5] and
15 **nuts** also contain omega-3 **oil**. Omega-3 **oil** comes in **pills**, too.

Finally, **water** is an important part of a healthy **diet**. Try to drink at least six **glasses** of **water** a day, and you don't need to buy it. In most places, tap
20 **water** from the kitchen **faucet** is just fine and tastes great!

It is a **challenge** to change your **diet**, but even small **changes** can help you stay healthy and happy.

[1]**vitamin:** a natural substance in food that is important for good health | [2]**mood:** the way someone feels at a particular time | [3]**fat:** a substance in plants and animals, often used for cooking | [4]**omega-3 oil:** a kind of healthy fat | [5]**seed:** a small hard part of a plant from which new plants can grow

B *Comprehension Check* Answer the questions. Use the article to help you.

1. How do colorful fruit and vegetables help your health?
2. Why is a little dark chocolate good for you?
3. What type of oil is good for you?
4. How much water is good to drink each day?

C *Notice* Find the sentences in the web article, and complete them with *a* or *an* or Ø for no article.

1. When you turn on ___ television or read _____ newspaper, you often find _____ information about healthy eating.

2. _____ food and _____ health get a lot of attention in the news these days.

3. Maybe you think _____ fat is bad for you, but people need a little fat in their diet.

4. It is _____ challenge to change your diet, but even small changes can help you stay healthy and happy.

Look at the noun after each space. Which of the nouns are things you can count? Which are things you cannot count?

2 Count and Noncount Nouns

▶ Grammar Presentation

Nouns are words for people, places, and things.	**Count nouns** name things you can count. *peas, vegetables, eggs, cookies*
There are two types of nouns: count nouns and noncount nouns.	**Noncount nouns** name things you cannot count. *spinach, water, cheese, sugar*

2.1 Count Nouns

A/An	Singular Count Noun	Singular Verb	
A	**vegetarian**	has	a meatless diet.
An	**apple**	is	a healthy snack.

Plural Count Noun	Plural Verb	
Vegetables	have	different vitamins.
Nuts	contain	healthy substances.

2.2 Noncount Nouns

Noncount Noun	Singular Verb	
Health	gets	a lot of attention in the news.
Water	is	an important part of a healthy diet.

▸▎ Noncount Nouns and Containers: See page A17.

2.3 Using Count Nouns

a. Count nouns are things that you can count. You can use numbers with count nouns.	*one egg, six eggs* *one banana, two bananas*	
b. You can use *a/an* with singular count nouns.	*Did you have a banana or a cookie?*	
Remember: Use *an* with words that start with a vowel sound.	*I eat an apple and an orange every day.*	
c. Count nouns can be plural. They can end in *-s.*	*Vegetables are good for you.* *Vitamins keep you healthy.*	
Remember: Some plural nouns are irregular.	*People need good food.* *Some children don't like vegetables.*	
d. A singular count noun takes a singular verb.	*A banana is good on cereal.* *My diet isn't very healthy.*	
e. A plural count noun takes a plural verb.	*Nuts contain oil.* *Vegetarians don't eat meat.*	

2.4 Using Noncount Nouns

a. Noncount nouns are things you cannot count. Don't use numbers with count nouns.	*milk, rice, sugar, cheese, spinach, tea, coffee* NOT ~~one milk, one rice~~
You can use numbers with drinks in a restaurant when you mean a cup of the drink.	*Can we have **three coffees**, please?*
b. Don't use *a/an* with noncount nouns.	*Eat **spinach**. Drink **water**. Cook **shrimp**.* NOT ~~a spinach, a water, a shrimp~~
c. Noncount nouns don't have a plural form. Don't add *-s*.	***Spinach** is good for you.* NOT ~~Spinaches are~~ *good for you.*
d. A noncount noun takes a singular verb.	*Fish **is** good for you.* *Fish oil **improves** your memory.*

▶ Grammar Application

Exercise 2.1 Count and Noncount Nouns

Data from the Real World

Research shows that noncount nouns are often the names of food and drink. The charts below show some of the most common food words in English.

A Which words are count nouns? Which are noncount nouns? Check (✓) the correct column.

	Count	Noncount
apples	✓	
beans	✓	✗
beef		✓
bread		✓
butter		✓
cheese		✓
cookies	✓	
fish		✓
garlic	✗	✓
ice cream		✓
meat		✓

	Count	Noncount
milk		✓
potatoes	✓	
rice		✓
sandwiches	✓	
salt		✓
seafood		✓
shrimp		✓
sugar		✓
tomatoes	✓	✓
vegetables	✗ ✓	✗
water		✓

B *Over to You* Complete the lists with words from the chart. Write *count* after count nouns and *noncount* after noncount nouns.

I never eat / drink . . .	I often eat / drink . . .
apples – count *I have eat* papaya – *nacout* *I or ever drink* joguer – *no cout* *I never eat avocado*	*I often eat PIZZa* *I often drink RedBull – count*

Exercise 2.2 *A* and *An*

A Complete the survey questions. Write *a* or *an* before the count nouns. Write Ø before noncount nouns.

1. Do you usually have _*a*_ sandwich for lunch?
2. Do you often have _Ø_ snack at bedtime?
3. Do you put _Ø_ salt on your food?
4. Do you eat _Ø_ garlic before a class?
5. How do you drink your tea or coffee? With _Ø_ milk and _Ø_ sugar?
6. Do you usually have _Ø_ cookie with your tea or coffee?
7. Do you like _Ø_ butter on your potatoes?
8. How often do you eat _Ø_ pasta?
9. Which do you prefer: _Ø_ apple or _Ø_ banana?
10. Do you prefer _Ø_ cereal or _Ø_ bread for breakfast?

B *Pair Work* Ask a partner the survey questions in A.

A Do you usually have a sandwich for lunch?
B No, I usually have an omelet or a Caesar salad.

Exercise 2.3 Count and Noncount Nouns

Read about the eating habits of these people. Change the singular count nouns in bold to plural nouns. Write Ø next to the noncount nouns.

Sean

I'm a vegetarian.
1. I don't eat **meat** _Ø_ .
2. I eat **egg**_s_ , but not every day.
3. I also eat **nut**_s_ , and I love fresh **vegetable**_s_ .
4. I also like **apple**_s_ and **cheese**_×_ a lot.

Isabel

I don't like dairy food.
5. I don't eat **cheese**_Ø_ or **butter**_×_ .
6. I don't drink **milk**_Ø_ .
7. I love **seafood**_Ø_ , but I'm allergic to **shrimp**_×_ .
8. My favorite food is **bean**_s_ .
9. I eat a lot of **pasta**_Ø_ .

Lin

I love fast food.
10. I love potato **chip**_s_ and **cookie**_s_ .
11. I don't eat **vegetable**_s_ very often.
12. I love desserts with **ice cream**____ .
13. I'm allergic to **chocolate**____ !

Exercise 2.4 Singular and Plural Verbs with Nouns

A Complete the sentences from a magazine article about food. Use the correct form of the verbs in parentheses.

Food Facts

Food satisfies hunger, but it does other things, too. Food can have good and bad effects on your body and sometimes your mind. Did you know these facts about these common foods?

- Carrots _are_ (be) good for your eyes.
  (1)
- Pasta ___makes___ (make) some people sleepy.
  (2)
- Bananas ___give___ (give) you energy.
  (3)
- Garlic ___is___ (be) good for your heart.
  (4)
- Ice ___gives___ (give) some people a headache.
  (5)
- Ice cream ___makes___ (make) some people thirsty.
  (6)
- Spinach ___contain___ (contain) vitamin C.
  (7)
- Fish ___is___ (be) good for your brain.
  (8)
- Some people say green tea ___keeps___ (keep) you thin.
  (9)
- Some people say cheese ___gives___ (give) them nightmares.
  (10)
- Some people say milk ___helps___ (help) them sleep.
  (11)

B *Over to You* Write four sentences about how different kinds of foods affect you.

Ice cream makes me thirsty.
Soda gives me a headache.

1. _____
2. _____
3. _____
4. _____

3 Units of Measure; *How Many . . . ?* and *How Much . . . ?*

▶ Grammar Presentation

Units of measure help us to tell how much or how many of a noun.	I bought **a cup of** coffee in the cafeteria. We had **a bowl of** soup with lunch.
Questions with *How much . . . ?* and *How many . . . ?* ask about quantities.	**How many** vegetables did you use? **How much** rice do you eat each week?

3.1 Units of Measure

Unit of Measure	Noncount or Plural Count Noun
a cup of	coffee
a bag of	rice
a piece of	cheese
a bottle of	water
a bowl of	soup
two bags of	potato chips
a carton of	eggs
a bunch of	bananas
a pound of	apples
three boxes of	cookies
a loaf of	bread

▶◀ Noncount Nouns and Containers: See page A17.

3.2 Using Units of Measure with Count and Noncount Nouns

a. You can use units of measure to count some noncount nouns.	My mother gave me **a bottle of** water. She drinks **a cup of** coffee every day. Did you eat **a piece of** cheese?
You can make these expressions plural.	She took **two bottles of** water. I drank **three cups of** coffee today. We served **some pieces of** cheese.
b. You can use units of measure with count nouns.	I bought **a bag of** apples. David ate **a box of** cookies!
You can make these expressions plural.	We collected **some bags of** apples. Lisa sold **six boxes of** cookies.

3.3 How Many...? and How Much...?

How Many	Count Noun		How Much	Noncount Noun	
How many	apples people bags	did you eat? want food? do you have?	How much	coffee sugar money	do you drink every day? do you put in your coffee? do we need?

3.4 Using How Many...? and How Much...?

a. Use *How many...?* to ask about count nouns.	***How many eggs*** *do you eat every week?* ***How many apples*** *do you bring to school every day?*
b. Use *How much...?* to ask about noncount nouns.	***How much milk*** *do you drink a day?* ***How much meat*** *do you eat in a week?*

▶ Grammar Application

Exercise 3.1 Units of Measure

Complete the menu with the units of measure from the box. You can use some units of measure more than once. Sometimes there is more than one correct answer.

a bag of	a bowl of	a glass of	a plate of
a bottle of	a cup of	a piece of	

Welcome to the Class Picnic!
MENU

Drinks

_____*a cup of*_____ coffee or tea
(1)

_____ water or juice
(2)

_____ lemonade or iced tea
(3)

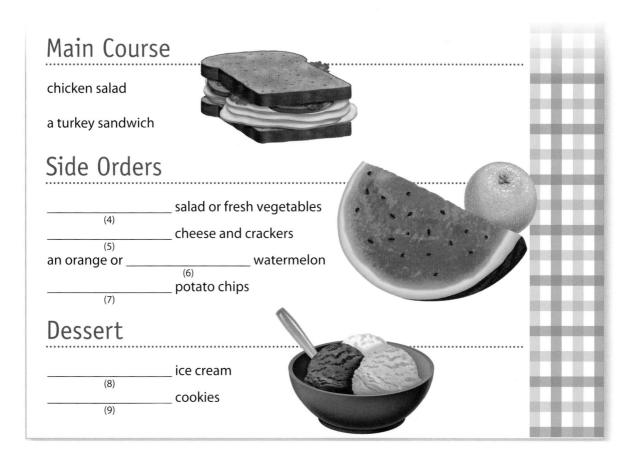

Main Course

chicken salad

a turkey sandwich

Side Orders

_____ salad or fresh vegetables
(4)

_____ cheese and crackers
(5)

an orange or _____ watermelon
(6)

_____ potato chips
(7)

Dessert

_____ ice cream
(8)

_____ cookies
(9)

Exercise 3.2 *How Much . . . ?* and *How Many . . . ?*

A ◀)) Complete each question about the class picnic with *How much* or *How many*. Then listen to the conversation about the picnic and answer the questions.

1. _____*How many*_____ students are there in the class?   ___18___

2. _____ money do they have?   _____

3. _____ people want water?   _____

4. _____ juice do they need?   _____

5. _____ people want sandwiches?   _____

6. _____ bags of potato chips do they need?   _____

7. _____ salad do they need?   _____

8. _____ cheese do people want?   _____

9. _____ people want an orange?   _____

10. _____ watermelon do they need?   _____

B *Pair Work*   Plan a class picnic. Use the menu in Exercise 3.1 and the questions in A to help you.

A How many students are there in our group?

B There are eight. How many people want water?

Data from the Real World

Research shows that these are some of the most common noncount nouns:

equipment	homework	love	music	traffic
fun	information	mail	peace	weather
furniture	insurance	money	software	work

Noncount nouns are of the names of:

materials: *oil, plastic, wood*	**Oil** *costs a lot these days.*
groups of things: *money, cash, furniture, jewelry*	*The* **jewelry** *in this store is expensive.*
subjects: *chemistry, geography, psychology*	**Chemistry** *doesn't interest me at all.*
weather: *snow, ice, fog*	*There's always* **snow** *in the winter here.*

Some noncount nouns end in -s, but they take a singular verb:

subjects: *economics, physics, politics*	**Economics** *was my best subject in high school.*
activities: *aerobics, gymnastics*	**Gymnastics** *is my favorite sport.*
other: *news*	*The* **news** *is really good.*

Students often make mistakes with noncount nouns, especially these:

information	equipment	advice	research	knowledge	furniture
behavior	work	homework	software	damage	training

Exercise 3.3 Categories and Items

A Complete the chart. Use the words in the box.

a check	furniture	a keyboard	music	~~a ring~~
a couch	homework	knowledge	pop	traffic
equipment	information	money	rain	weather
an exercise	~~jewelry~~	motorcycles		

Category: _____jewelry_____
(1)

earrings

a necklace

_____a ring_____
(2)

Category: _____
(3)

a table

a chair

_____
(4)

Category: _____
(5)

a computer

a printer

_____
(6)

Category: _____
(7)

names

dates

_____
(8)

Category: _____
(9)

cars

trucks

_____
(10)

Category: _____
(11)

an essay

a reading

_____
(12)

Category: _____
(13)

classical

hip-hop

_____
(14)

Category: _____
(15)

bills

coins

_____
(16)

Category: _____
(17)

snow

ice

_____
(18)

B *Group Work* Look at the categories in A. How many new words can you add?

4 Avoid Common Mistakes ⚠

1. Do not use *a / an* with noncount nouns.

I'm doing ~~a~~ research on eating habits.

2. Do not make noncount nouns plural or use them with a plural verb.

My teacher gave me some useful ~~advices~~. *advice*

3. Do not use *these* or *those* with noncount nouns.

I hope ~~these informations are~~ useful. *this information is*

4. Use *how much* with noncount nouns, and use *how many* with count nouns.

How ~~many~~ money do you have? *much*   How ~~much~~ classes did you take? *many*

Editing Task

Find and correct the mistakes on this school's website.

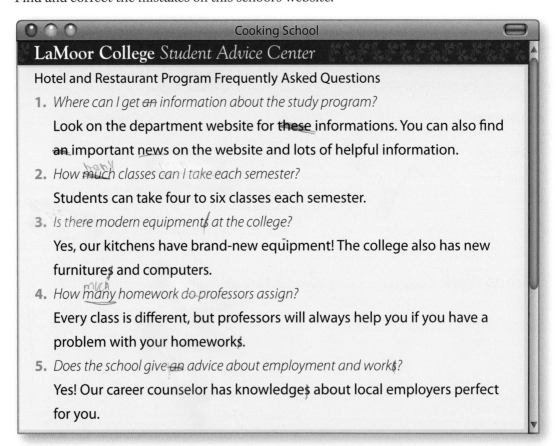

○ ○ ○   Cooking School   ▭

LaMoor College *Student Advice Center*

Hotel and Restaurant Program Frequently Asked Questions

1. Where can I get ~~an~~ information about the study program?

   Look on the department website for ~~these~~ informations. You can also find ~~an~~ important news on the website and lots of helpful information.

2. How ~~much~~ classes can I take each semester?

   Students can take four to six classes each semester.

3. Is there modern equipment~~s~~ at the college?

   Yes, our kitchens have brand-new equipment! The college also has new furniture~~s~~ and computers.

4. How ~~many~~ *much* homework do professors assign?

   Every class is different, but professors will always help you if you have a problem with your homework~~s~~.

5. Does the school give ~~an~~ advice about employment and work~~s~~?

   Yes! Our career counselor has knowledge~~s~~ about local employers perfect for you.

5 | Grammar for Writing ✏

Writing About Meals

Writers use both noncount and count nouns when they write about things such as food. Remember:

- **Use units of measure to show amounts of noncount nouns. Units of measure include count nouns, so you can make them singular or plural.**

	COUNT NOUN	NONCOUNT NOUN
Ignacio used	two pounds of	fish in his fish soup.
I always have	a cup of	strong coffee in the morning.

- **Use singular pronouns to refer to noncount nouns. Use plural or singular pronouns to refer to count nouns.**

There wasn't very much sugar. *It* was also very old. (noncount noun)

The plates are dirty. *They* are all in the dishwasher. (count noun)

Pre-writing Task

1 Read the paragraph below. How many problems did the writer have with his meal?

A Meal with Friends

Last week I cooked a meal for my friends. The food looked good, but it wasn't very tasty. First, I served vegetable soup. It looked beautiful, but it tasted like water. Then I served fish. I gave each person a piece of salmon, but my friends didn't eat very much of it. It was a little dry. We had mashed potatoes, but they were a little salty. For dessert, I gave everyone a piece of apple pie and vanilla ice cream. Fortunately, the pie and the ice cream were delicious. My friends were happy and we had a good time together. I decided to invite my friends for another meal soon.

2 Read the paragraph again. Circle the count nouns and underline the noncount nouns. Double underline the units of measure that go with the noncount nouns.

Writing Task

1 *Write* Use the paragraph in the Pre-writing Task to help you write a paragraph about a meal you cooked or ate recently. What was good? What wasn't good? Describe the food in the meal. Use sentences with units of measure before your noncount nouns.

2 *Self-Edit* Use the editing tips below to improve your sentences. Make any necessary changes.

1. Did you use count and noncount nouns to describe the food?
2. Did you use units of measure to describe the amounts of the noncount food?
3. Did you use the correct pronouns?
4. Did you avoid the mistakes in the Avoid Common Mistakes chart on page 192?

Quantifiers: *Some, Any, A Lot Of, A Little, A Few, Much, Many*

Languages

1 Grammar in the Real World

A Do you know any words that originally come from another language? Read the blog. What languages do some English words come from?

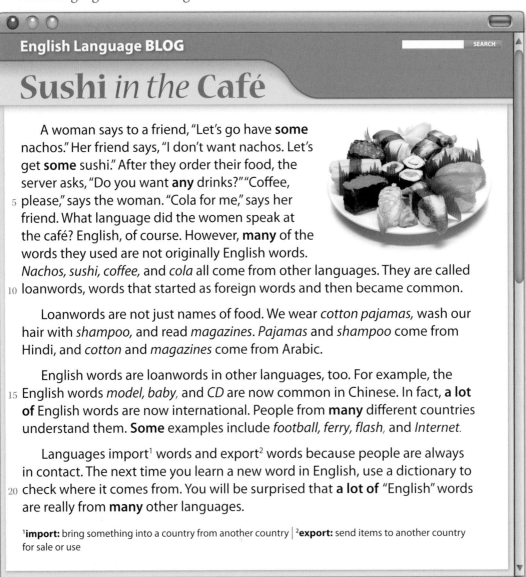

English Language BLOG SEARCH

Sushi *in the* Café

A woman says to a friend, "Let's go have **some** nachos." Her friend says, "I don't want nachos. Let's get **some** sushi." After they order their food, the server asks, "Do you want **any** drinks?" "Coffee,
5 please," says the woman. "Cola for me," says her friend. What language did the women speak at the café? English, of course. However, **many** of the words they used are not originally English words. *Nachos, sushi, coffee,* and *cola* all come from other languages. They are called
10 loanwords, words that started as foreign words and then became common.

Loanwords are not just names of food. We wear *cotton pajamas,* wash our hair with *shampoo,* and read *magazines. Pajamas* and *shampoo* come from Hindi, and *cotton* and *magazines* come from Arabic.

English words are loanwords in other languages, too. For example, the
15 English words *model, baby,* and *CD* are now common in Chinese. In fact, **a lot of** English words are now international. People from **many** different countries understand them. **Some** examples include *football, ferry, flash,* and *Internet.*

Languages import[1] words and export[2] words because people are always in contact. The next time you learn a new word in English, use a dictionary to
20 check where it comes from. You will be surprised that **a lot of** "English" words are really from **many** other languages.

[1]**import:** bring something into a country from another country | [2]**export:** send items to another country for sale or use

B *Comprehension Check* Answer the questions. Use the article to help you.

1. From which language did *pajamas* come? _____

2. Which English words are commonly used in China? _____

3. Is *football* an original English word? _____

4. Which language did *ferry* come from? _____

C *Notice* Find the sentences in the article and complete them with *some* or *any*.

1. Let's go have _____ nachos.

2. Let's get _____ sushi.

3. The server asks, "Do you want _____ drinks?"

Compare the sentences with *some* and *any*. How are they different?

2 | Quantifiers: *Some* and *Any*

▶ Grammar Presentation

We use *some* and *any* to talk about an unknown quantity of something.	*Let's go have **some** sushi.* *Do you want **any** drinks?*

2.1 Affirmative Statements with *Some*

	Some	Noncount Noun
I need		**information.**
Ricardo had	**some**	**sushi.**
We ordered		**food.**

	Some	Plural Noun
Let's have		**nachos.**
I know	**some**	**Italian words.**
Here are		**examples.**

2.2 Negative Statements with *Any*

	Do/Does/Did + Not	Base Form of Verb	Any	Noncount Noun
I	**don't**	**want**		**sushi.**
The book	**doesn't**	**have**	**any**	**information.**
We	**didn't**	**bring**		**food.**

	Do/Does/Did + Not	Base Form of Verb	Any	Plural Noun
I	**don't**	**remember**		**Italian words.**
Yuri	**doesn't**	**want**	**any**	**nachos.**
We	**didn't**	**see**		**examples.**

2.3 Yes/No Questions with *Some* and *Any*

	Some/Any	Noncount Noun	
Can I have	**some**	**sushi**?	
Do you have	**any**	**information**	about the English program?
Did you do	**any**	**research**	on loanwords?

	Some/Any	Plural Noun	
Can you teach me	**some**	**words**	in Italian?
Do you have	**any**	**books**	on loanwords?
Are there	**any**	**examples**	in the book?

2.4 Using *Some* and *Any* in Statements

a. Use *some* with noncount nouns and plural nouns in affirmative statements.	*I found* **some information** *about loanwords in this book.*
In affirmative statements *some* refers to small quantities or unknown quantities.	*There are* **some words** *in English that come from Arabic, but I don't know how many.*
b. Use *some* for small amounts and numbers, not large amounts and numbers.	*There are Latin and Greek words in English.* NOT *There are* **some** *Latin and Greek words in English.* (There are thousands!)
c. Use *any* with noncount nouns and plural nouns in negative statements.	*There isn't* **any food** *in the refrigerator.*
In negative statements *any* refers to a zero quantity.	*I don't remember* **any words** *in Italian.*

2.5 Using *Yes/No* Questions with *Some* and *Any*

a. Use *some* with noncount nouns and plural nouns to ask for something or to offer something that is there.	*Can I get* **some** *information from you about Portuguese, please?* (The person asking knows the other person has information about Portuguese.)
	Do you want to use **some** *words from Russian for your paper about English loanwords?* (The person asking has words to give to the writer.)
b. Use *any* with noncount nouns and plural nouns to ask for unknown quantities.	*Did you make* **any** *progress with your paper?* (The questioner doesn't expect progress.)
	Are there **any** *English words that come from Swahili?* (There may be no English words that come from Swahili. The questioner doesn't know.)

▶ Grammar Application

Exercise 2.1 Statements with *Some* and *Any*

A Julia and her classmates have some questions about loanwords. Complete their conversation with *some* or *any*.

Julia We use __some__ Japanese words in English, for example,
(1)
karaoke and *sushi*.

Simon Yeah, that's true. Do we use _____ Indonesian words in
(2)
English? Do you know, Taufik?

Taufik Yes, there are _____ food words, for example, *satay*.
(3)

Nick Pilar told me _____ Spanish words, for example, *papaya*
(4)
and *Florida*. *Florida* means "a place with flowers."

Julia What about Arabic?

Taufik There aren't _____ Arabic students in the class, so let's
(5)
check online.

Nick Miriam, you lived in Ghana. Tell us _____ words from
(6)
African languages that we use in English.

Miriam Hmm. Yeah, sure. Well, *cola*, *jazz*, and *safari* are from African
languages. There are probably _____ more words, but
(7)
I don't know _____ others.
(8)

Julia Thanks, everyone. Now we know _____ words in English
(9)
that come from other languages. Let's organize them.

B *Over to You* Do you know any other English words that come from other languages? Tell the class.

A I know some Italian words in English.

B Really? I don't know any Italian words. What words do you know?

A I know pesto *and* pizza. *I don't know any others.*

Exercise 2.2 Yes / No Questions with *Some* and *Any*

A Complete the conversations. Write the questions. Use *some* or *any* and the words in parentheses.

Conversation 1

Samantha So, Rafa, I know you're from Spain. You're

from Barcelona, right?

Do you have any friends from Madrid
(1)
(have/friends/from Madrid)?

Rafa Yes, I do. I have some friends who still live there.

And you were born in Canada, right?

_____
(2)
(have/friends/from there)?

Samantha Yes, I have some friends from Toronto and Montreal.

Conversation 2

Rafa How's your English class, Tomoko?

_____
(3)
(have/classmates/from Latin America)?

Tomoko Yes, I do. I have some classmates from Peru, Mexico, and Argentina.

Rafa _____
(4)
(are there/students/from South Asia)?

Tomoko I'm not sure, but I hope so! I want to meet people from all over the world.

Conversation 3

Tara Hey, guys! I made chocolate chip cookies this morning.

_____
(5)
(want/cookies)?

Rafa Oh, yes! Thanks!

_____
(6)
(have/milk)?

Tara Yes, I do. It's in the refrigerator. Help yourself.

Conversation 4

Samantha   Rafa, I like your CD collection.

_____
(7)
(can / I / listen to / music)?

Rafa   Sure! Go ahead. I have a lot of salsa. It's fun to dance to!

Samantha   Oh, I don't know how to dance salsa.

_____
(8)
(are there / salsa clubs / around here)?

Rafa   Yes, there are some clubs downtown. They give dance lessons. Samantha,

_____
(9)
(want / to take / lessons)?

Samantha   Sure!

Rafa   Great! Let's go sometime!

B *Pair Work*   Practice the conversations with a partner.

Exercise 2.3 Statements and Questions

A Write affirmative and negative statements using the verbs in parentheses. Make them true for you. Use *some* for affirmative statements and *any* for negative statements.

1. I *have some / don't have any*_____ books in English at home. (have)
2. I _____ computer equipment. (own)
3. I _____ friends at work. (have)
4. I _____ words in Italian. (know)
5. I _____ people from El Salvador. (know)
6. I _____ TV shows in English. (watch)
7. I _____ podcasts from news websites. (download)
8. I _____ knowledge of French. (have)
9. I _____ e-mails in Portuguese. (write)
10. I _____ online music stores. (use)

B *Pair Work*   Ask and answer questions with a partner based on your sentences in A. Use *any* in your questions.

A *Do you have any books in English at home?*
B *Yes, I have some books in English at home.*

3 | Quantifiers: *A Lot Of, A Little, A Few, Much, Many*

▶ Grammar Presentation

Quantifiers can refer to large or small amounts.	*I know **a lot of** English words.* *I need **a little** extra information for my paper on loanwords.*

3.1 Affirmative Statements

	A Lot Of / A Little	Noncount Noun		*A Lot Of / A Few / Many*	Plural Noun
I found	**a lot of** **a little**	**information.**	She has	**a lot of** **a few** **many**	**friends in Indonesia.**

3.2 *Yes / No* Questions

	A Lot Of / A Little / Much	Noncount Noun
Did you learn	**a lot of** **a little** **much**	English?
Did you need		help?
Do you have		homework?

	A Lot Of / A Few / Many	Plural Noun
Did you meet	**a lot of** **a few** **many**	people?
Do you have		minutes?
Can you speak		languages?

Is There	*A Lot Of / A Little / Much*	Noncount Noun	
Is there	**a lot of** **a little** **much**	information	in the article?

Are There	*A Lot Of / A Few / Many*	Plural Noun	
Are there	**a lot of** **a few** **many**	people	in your class?

3.3 Using Quantifiers

a. In affirmative statements:	
Use *a lot of* for large quantities of plural nouns and noncount nouns.	*I met **a lot of** Russian speakers in North Carolina.* *There is **a lot of** help available for students.*
Use *a little* for small quantities of noncount nouns.	*I understand **a little** Swedish.*
Use *a few* for small quantities of plural nouns.	*Dane has **a few** friends in Asia.*
Use *many* for large quantities of plural nouns.	*There are **many** people that speak Swahili in the neighborhood.*
b. In negative statements:	
Use *not a lot of* for small amounts of plural and noncount nouns.	*There is**n't a lot of** information about some words.* *There are**n't a lot of** students from Denmark at the school.*
Use *not much* for small amounts of noncount nouns.	*Two months is**n't much** time to learn a new language.*
Use *not many* for small amounts of plural nouns.	*There are**n't many** people from Austria in my class.*
c. In questions:	
Use *a lot of* with plural and noncount nouns.	*Do you have **a lot of** relatives in Ireland?* *Is there **a lot of** bad weather in Maine?*
Use *much* in questions with noncount nouns.	*Do you have **much** homework in Spanish class?*
Use *many* with plural nouns.	*Are there **many** Chinese restaurants in Boston?*
d. Don't use *much* in affirmative statements.	*The website had **a lot of** information about Latin.* NOT ~~The website had much information about Latin~~.
e. Use short answers with *a lot*, *a few*, and *not many* to refer to plural nouns.	*"How **many** students did a presentation on loanwords?"* *"**A lot.** / **A few.** / **Not many.**"*
Use short answers with *a lot*, *a little*, and *not much* to refer to noncount nouns.	*"How **much** work did you do on your paper?"* *"**A lot.** / **A little.** / **Not much.**"*

▶ Grammar Application

Exercise 3.1 Count and Noncount Nouns

Write *C* for the count nouns and *NC* for the noncount nouns.

dictionary _C_   homework _____   student _____   song _____   furniture _____

time _____   music _____   knowledge _____   word _____   Korean (language) _____

Exercise 3.2 *A Lot Of, A Little, A Few,* or *Many*

🔊 Listen and complete the paragraph about an English class with *a lot of, a little, a few,* or *many*.

Karina's English class at Dixon College is very international. Her class has
a few Russians: Karina and two others.
(1)
There are _____ students
(2)
from Brazil, perhaps 80 percent. There are
_____ students from Japan,
(3)
but not many. The rest are from other Asian countries like Malaysia, Thailand, and Vietnam.

They come from all over the world and bring interesting stories with them. Rosa is from São Paulo, Brazil, and listens to _____ Brazilian music. She loves it.
(4)
She also has _____ songs from Puerto Rico on her computer, but not many.
(5)

Seri, from Penang, has _____ (6) beautiful furniture from Malaysia in her house.

Keiko, from Japan, taught Karina and Rosa _____ (7) Japanese, but the words are

difficult to remember. Noom, from Bangkok, loves his country's food. Sometimes he makes

_____ (8) Thai food for his classmates, but not much because it's very hot for

them. Linh, who moved from Vietnam, eats _____ (9) spicy food. She loves it!

Sometimes, Karina brings in _____ (10) *borscht*, a Russian soup. Only Keiko and

Noom like it, so she doesn't make a lot of it. The best part of Karina's diverse class is that she

can hear _____ (11) languages besides English every day!

Exercise 3.3 *A Lot Of, A Little, A Few, Much,* or *Many*

A Circle the correct words.

Dustin Hi, Dr. Lanza. Thank you for doing this interview

for *Student Voices*. First, are there **much** /(**many**) (1)

countries in Asia where English is the official

language?

Dr. Lanza Well, there aren't **many / much**, (2) but there are

a little / a few (3) – for example, Pakistan, Singapore,

and the Philippines.

Dustin How **many / much** (4) words are there in English?

Dr. Lanza It's hard to say. Anywhere from 250,000 to 750,000, perhaps! Dictionaries

have **much / a lot of** (5) words, but they don't contain all of them. A big

English dictionary has hundreds of thousands of words.

Dustin Really? That's **many / a lot** (6)! How many words do native English speakers

know? Do they know **a lot of / many** (7) vocabulary?

Dr. Lanza Yes, every native speaker knows **much / a lot of** (8) words. Adults probably

know 20,000 to 30,000 words.

Dustin Very interesting! Thanks for this interview, Dr. Lanza!

B Pair Work Tell a partner what you know about other cultures and languages. Use the
conversation in A as a model. Remember to use *a lot of, a few, a little,* and *many*.

Exercise 3.4 Short Answers

Answer the questions that students in an English class are asking each other before class. Use *a lot, a few, a little, not many,* and *not much.*

1. How much time did you work on your paper?

   <u>A lot</u>. I worked all day on it.

2. I wasn't in class yesterday. How much homework did we have for today?

   _____. The teacher only assigned two exercises in our Workbook.

3. How many classes do you have today?

   _____. I only have two today. Tomorrow I have four!

4. How much time did you spend on homework last night?

   _____. I was very busy, so I didn't have a lot of time.

5. How many minutes do we have before class starts?

   _____. It's going to start in two minutes!

Exercise 3.5 *A Lot Of*, *Much*, and *Many*

Data from the Real World

People often use *a lot of* in speaking. In writing, they often use *much* and *many*.	Say: *"There are a lot of different languages and cultures in South America."* Write: *There are many different languages and cultures in South America.* Say: *"Schools in poorer countries often don't have a lot of modern equipment."* Write: *Schools in poorer countries often do not have much modern equipment.*	
Use *a lot of* in speaking and writing in affirmative statements with noncount nouns.	*The website has a lot of information about English as a global language.*	

A Change *a lot of* to *much* or *many* in the essay.

Communication Shortage?

many

In the twentieth century, ~~a lot of~~ young people had pen pals[1] from other countries. They wrote letters to them and learned about other countries, cultures, and languages. Traveling was expensive, so they did not have **a lot of** opportunities to meet their pen pals. There was not **a lot**
5 **of** direct contact between people from different countries, so letters were a good way to communicate.

Now there are not **a lot of** traditional pen pals. Instead, there are **a lot of** social networking sites on the Internet. People can send electronic messages across the world from these sites. Most young people are very
10 busy and do not have **a lot of** time to write long messages, so messages are short. Today, friends typically send **a lot of** messages, one after another. However, can people exchange **a lot of** information in very short online messages? Can people learn **a lot of** interesting things about the other person's culture in these short messages? This is a good question
15 for discussion.

[1]**pen pal:** someone you exchange letters with as a hobby, especially someone from another country

B *Pair Work* Discuss the essay in A with a partner. Ask each other these questions.
1. Do you have friends you communicate with electronically?
2. Do you think social networking sites are a good way to learn about other countries and cultures? Can you learn a lot from them?
3. What kinds of information do people exchange on social networking sites?

4 Avoid Common Mistakes ⚠

1. Use *many* with plural nouns.

many
Do you write ~~much~~ essays?

2. Use *much* with noncount nouns in <u>negative</u> statements and questions. In affirmative statements with noncount nouns, use *a lot of*, not *much*.

much
The students don't have ~~many~~ work in the lab today.

a lot of
There is ~~much~~ information on loanwords online.

3. For quantities, use *some* with noncount nouns. Do not use *a / an* with noncount nouns.

some
I need ~~an~~ information about Korea.

4. Use *any* with negative statements, and use *some* with affirmative statements.

any
I don't have ~~some~~ dictionaries to use.

some
I learned ~~any~~ Japanese words from a Japanese friend.

Editing Task

Find and correct 11 more mistakes in this interview with Dr. Matthew Sutton, Director of the Language Center at Marsland College.

    Roberto Hello, Dr. Sutton. My name is Roberto

              Ferrer and I'm a student here at the

                                    some
              college. I'd like to ask you ~~any~~ questions

              about the Language Center for our

5   college paper. How does the Language

              Center help language students?

  Dr. Sutton Thanks for asking, Roberto. The center

              is very important. We give students

              much information about foreign

10   languages and cultures, and we have much learning material for 30

              different languages.

    Roberto Wow, that sounds like much information on different languages that

              students can find here.

Dr. Sutton It is, Roberto. Much students find the center really helpful. You see,

15   much students work and do not have many time to study. They can

                come to the center before or after class. They can spend a few minutes

                or one or two hours here. They can do any exercises, or use our CDs and

                DVDs, or read, or just meet friends.

Roberto That sounds great. Do much students use the center?

20 **Dr. Sutton** Right now, about 100 students use the center every day.

Roberto Does the center have modern equipment?

Dr. Sutton Yes, it does. Every year, we buy a new equipment, for example,

                computers and DVD players. We also spend much money to make the

                center a comfortable place. For example, we recently bought a new

25   furniture. Please come and visit! We are open every day.

Roberto All right. Thanks for your time, Dr. Sutton!

5 | Grammar for Writing

Writing About Indefinite Quantities of Things

Writers use the quantifiers *some, any, a lot of, a little, a few, much,* and *many* with nouns when they write about indefinite amounts of things.

Remember:

- **Use *a lot of, much,* and *many* to talk about big quantities, and use *a little* and *a few* to talk about small quantities.**

  Gabe knows a lot of Spanish, but he knows only a little Portuguese.

  Nimita cooks many Indian dishes, but she cooks only a few Mexican dishes.

- **Use *some* to write about plural count and noncount nouns when the exact amount of the noun isn't important or isn't known. Use *not any* when there is none of a plural count or noncount noun.**

  Soraida plays some great Mexican songs on the guitar. She does not play any Mexican songs on the piano.

Pre-writing Task

1 Read the paragraph below. What types of English loanwords does Arabic use, and which Arabic loanwords does the writer write about?

English and Arabic Loanwords

I am from Oman. In Oman we speak Arabic. We have a lot of English words in our language. Classical Arabic does not have any English loanwords, but modern Arabic has a lot. We use a few clothing words. For example, we say *jeans, jacket,* and *T-shirt.* We also use many English computer words, such as *format, save,* and *file.* There are a few English words for food in our language, such as *hot dog, hamburger,* and *ice cream.* A lot of young people use the word *cool.* There are many Arabic words in other languages, too. Some Arabic words in English are *coffee* and *sofa.* Not many people know that these words originally came from Arabic.

2 Read the paragraph again. Circle the quantifiers for big quantities of things and underline the quantifiers for small quantities of things.

Writing Task

1 *Write* Use the paragraph in the Pre-writing Task to help you write a paragraph about something that you have or use that comes from a different country or culture. Write about the amount of this thing in your culture. Is there some of it, a lot of it, or a little of it? You can write about:

- cars
- clothing
- food
- jewelry
- music
- restaurants
- tourists
- words
- your ideas

Use sentences with quantifiers such as:

- We use a lot of _____.
- We don't have much _____.
- They have some _____.
- They don't have any _____.

2 *Self-Edit* Use the editing tips below to improve your sentences. Make any necessary changes.

1. Did you use indefinite quantifiers to write about things in your culture or from another culture?
2. Did you use *a lot of*, *much*, and *many* to talk about big quantities, and *a little* and *a few* to talk about small quantities?
3. Did you use *some* to write about unknown or unimportant amounts, and *not any* to write about nouns that there are none of?
4. Did you avoid the mistakes in the Avoid Common Mistakes chart on page 206?

Articles: *A/An* and *The*

Changes and Risks

1 Grammar in the Real World

A Do you like to take risks?[1] Read the magazine article about how people respond to risk. When you make a decision, what steps do you take?

Decisions in **Risky Times**

In uncertain or difficult times, it's sometimes hard for people to make 5 decisions. For example, when **the** economy is bad, people worry about money and their jobs. Some take risks 10 to try to make things better. Others don't take any risks and hope to stay safe. Guy Burgess, of **the** University of Colorado, says people 15 deal with difficult times differently.

Some people become *ostriches*.[2] **An** ostrich does not like risks. For example, Connor is nervous about **the** economy. He doesn't buy anything 20 expensive, like **a** car, since **the** car he has still works. He doesn't look for **a** new job even though he hates **the** job he has. He knows **the** job he has now is stable.[3]

Others become 25 *rock climbers*. They love taking risks. For example, Kala found a new job and makes a lot more money. But 30 **the** job does not have good health insurance, and it's short-term.[4] She isn't worried because she enjoys 35 taking risks.

Finally, some become *analysts*.[5] For example, Lorena looks carefully at her choices before she makes **an** important decision. She decides to sell her house 40 and put **the** money into a business. She knows she can make a lot of money with **the** business.

Some risks are worth taking and others are dangerous. It's important to 45 know which type of risk taker you are before you make big decisions.

---

[1]**take a risk:** do something where there is a possibility of being hurt or of a loss or defeat | [2]**ostrich:** here, a person who ignores reality or does not accept the truth | [3]**stable:** safe, not likely to change | [4]**short-term:** not for a long time | [5]**analyst:** someone who studies or examines something in detail, such as finances, computer systems, or the economy

B *Comprehension Check* Circle the correct answers from the magazine article.

1. Making decisions during difficult times is
   a. different for everyone.   b. always hard.   c. easy for everyone.

2. If you are an *ostrich*, you
   a. like to take risks.   b. do not like to take risks.   c. look at your choices before you make a decision.

3. If you are a *rock climber*, you
   a. like to take risks.   b. do not like to take risks.   c. look at your choices before you make a decision.

4. If you are an *analyst*, you
   a. like to take risks.   b. do not like to take risks.   c. look at your choices before you make a decision.

C *Notice* Which article (*a* or *an*) comes before these words the first time they appear? Find the words in the text and check the correct article.

	a	*an*
1. ostrich		
2. car		
3. new job		
4. important decision		
5. business		

Compare the words that come after *a* with the words that come after *an*. Look at the beginning sounds of the words. How are they different?

2 | Articles: *A / An* and *The*

▶ Grammar Presentation

Articles are used with nouns. *A / An* is the indefinite article. *The* is the definite article.	Claire is **an** analyst. She thinks carefully before she makes **a** decision, especially when **the** decision is **an** important one.

2.1 Indefinite Article: *A / An*

a. Use *a / an* with singular count nouns.	*She made **a decision** about her job.* ***An analyst** examines something in detail.*
b. Use *a* when the noun begins with a consonant sound.	*She made **a decision** about her job.*
c. Use *an* when the noun begins with a vowel sound.	***An analyst** examines something in detail.*
d. Use *a* before words such as adjectives or adverbs that begin with a consonant sound.	*Tony found **a great** apartment in Chicago.*
e. Use *a* before words that begin with *u* when the *u* makes a "you" sound.	*James went to **a university** in Boston.* *The economy is **a universal** concern.*

2.2 Definite Article: *The*

You can use *the* before singular or plural count nouns, and before noncount nouns.	***The job** is a good one.* ***The choices** were interesting.* ***The information** is very useful.*

▶◀ Indefinite and Definite Articles: See page A19.

2.3 Using *A / An* and *The*

a. Use *a / an* to introduce a person or thing for the first time to a listener. When you mention the person or thing again, use *the*.	*Tom bought **a car**.* (The listener does not know about this car.) ***The car** was not very expensive.* (Now the listener knows about this car.)
b. Use *the* to talk about specific people or things that both the listener and speaker know about.	***The president** discussed **the plan**.* (Everyone knows the president and the plan.) ***The moon** and **the stars** were beautiful last night.* (Everyone knows the moon and the stars.) *"**The game** was interesting." "I agree."* (The speaker and listener are thinking of the same game.)

▶ Grammar Application

Exercise 2.1 Sentences with *A/An*

A Complete the sentences with *a* or *an*.

1. A rock climber takes _*a*_ risk easily.

2. _____ analyst thinks about choices before he / she decides.

3. _____ ostrich doesn't like to take risks and wants to be safe.

4. Connor doesn't look for _____ job because he already has one.

5. Kala was glad she got _____ interview.

6. Lorena owns _____ business.

7. She made _____ decision about the business.

8. She decided to sell her house and rent _____ apartment.

9. I hope to go to _____ university in Europe.

10. I want to go to _____ information session and talk to _____ academic adviser.

B *Over to You* Which kind of risk taker are you? Discuss with a partner and explain your choice.

A *I'm a rock climber because I love to take risks. I left a good job to go back to college.*

B *Oh, I'm an ostrich. I don't like to take risks at all.*

Exercise 2.2 🔊 Pronunciation Focus: Pronouncing *A* and *An*

We pronounce *a* and *an* with a weak sound, /ə/ or /ən/, because we don't stress the articles.	*a decision* *a business* *a risk*	*an analyst* *an ostrich* *an opinion*

A 🔊 Listen and repeat the phrases in the chart above.

B Read the interview and complete the sentences with *a* or *an*.

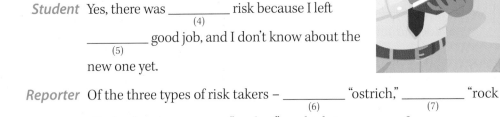

Reporter Hi, my name is Steve. I'm a reporter with the *New Times*, and I have some questions for you about taking risks. Can you describe _a_ decision that was really difficult for you?

(1)

Student Yes, I made _____ decision to leave my job.

(2)

Reporter Do you think there was _____ risk in that decision?

(3)

Student Yes, there was _____ risk because I left _____ good job, and I don't know about the new one yet.

(4) (5)

Reporter Of the three types of risk takers – _____ "ostrich," _____ "rock climber," and _____ "analyst" – which type are you?

(6) (7) (8)

Student Oh, I'm _____ analyst!

(9)

Reporter Do you think analysts always make good decisions?

Student Yes, because _____ analyst looks at all of the choices carefully.

(10)

Reporter How do you think _____ ostrich manages stress?

(11)

Student Well, _____ ostrich makes sure everything in his or her life is stable.

(12)

Reporter Do you know someone who is _____ rock climber?

(13)

Student I do! My sister is _____ rock climber. She always takes risks!

(14)

C *Pair Work* Practice the interview with a partner.

Exercise 2.3 *A / An* or *The*?

A Complete the conversation with *a*, *an*, or *the*.

Emma Guess what, Isabella? I want to start _*a*_ catering business![1]
(1)

Isabella That's great! I know you love to cook!

Emma I went to _____ exciting class for new female entrepreneurs.
(2)

_____ teacher for the class taught us a lot of things. For example, now
(3)

I know how to get _____ loan[2] from a bank. When I get it, _____
(4)   (5)

loan can help me buy the equipment I need to start _____ business.
(6)

Isabella Are you nervous? Isn't it risky to start your own business?

Emma Of course! There is definitely _____ risk in starting your own business.
(7)

When you know _____ risks, you can plan well. _____ class also
(8)   (9)

taught me to write _____ marketing plan. _____ plan can guide
(10)   (11)

my sales[3] of my catering services. I need

to design _____ menu and make
(12)

_____ website for my business.
(13)

When _____ menu is ready and
(14)

_____ website is up, I'll be ready to
(15)

go!

Isabella Wow, that all sounds great! Do you need

my help? I'm in _____ web design
(16)

course right now. I can design something

really great for your new business!

Emma Thanks! I'd like that.

[1]**catering business:** a business that provides and serves food and drinks for a particular event, such as a wedding or party | [2]**loan:** money that you can borrow but you have to pay back with interest (extra money) | [3]**sales:** the number of items sold

B Complete the story with *a*, *an*, or *the*.

Martin moved to New York City from Bogotá, Colombia, a year ago. He lives in _*a*_ neighborhood (1) on the Upper West Side. He was worried because _____ neighborhood is expensive. He found (2) _____ entry-level[1] job at _____ bank, but (3) (4) he did not make enough money. This made him uncomfortable because he does not like to take risks. His friends told him he could always get _____ (5) second job. He took their advice and got _____ (6) interesting job as a server at _____ coffee shop. (7) _____ job is great! _____ coffee shop is near (8) (9) his apartment, so he can walk to work. _____ (10) job is much more relaxing than _____ bank job. (11) Martin gets to chat with _____ customers who (12) come in as he fills their orders. He makes a lot of new friends there, too. Also, _____ second (13) job allows him to save money. Now he feels much better and enjoys life in New York City!

[1]**entry-level:** starting level

C *Pair Work* Talk to a partner about Emma in A and Martin in B. Is one of them an ostrich? An analyst? A rock climber? Why?

3 | Article or No Article?

▶ Grammar Presentation

We sometimes do not use an article before plural count and noncount nouns.	Rock climbers love taking **risks**. I have **homework** to do.

3.1 No Article

Use no article before plural count and noncount nouns when the nouns have a general meaning.	*Analysts* do not make quick decisions. I need **money** to buy that car! *Insurance* is very expensive.

3.2 *The* and No Article with Geographical Places and Languages

a. Use *the* before the names of: • mountain ranges • regions • famous places and buildings • rivers • seas and oceans • deserts	*the Andes, the Himalayas, the Rocky Mountains* *the Midwest, the Arctic, the Great Lakes* *the Grand Canyon, the Eiffel Tower, the White House* *the Amazon, the Nile, the Mississippi River* *the Mediterranean, the Atlantic, the South China Sea* *the Sahara, the Mojave Desert*
b. Use no article before the names of: • most countries • continents • individual mountains • individual lakes	*Canada, Colombia, Japan* *Europe, Asia, Africa* *Mount Everest, Mount Kilimanjaro, Mount Fuji* *Lake Michigan, Lake Tahoe, Lake Victoria*
c. Some countries have *the* in their names.	*the United States, the United Kingdom, the United Arab Emirates, the Netherlands, the Philippines*
d. Use no article before the name of a language.	*Can you speak Japanese?* *Chinese is a difficult language for English speakers.*

▶ Grammar Application

Exercise 3.1 *The* or No Article?

A Complete the conversation with *the* or ∅ for no article.

Mi-Young You know, life as an international student is very stressful. We took a big risk to come to this new country!

Adriana You think so? I like taking risks. I think it's exciting. I don't worry about things. What do you worry about?

Mi-Young Oh, everything! I worry about __*the*__ future. I
(1)
worry about _____ money. I worry about
(2)
_____ life in general.
(3)

Adriana Yeah, I guess it is a little stressful. We work and we study long hours. We also have to use _____ English all the time!
(4)

Mi-Young True. We're at work or in class all day, and we never see _____ sun.
(5)
_____ teachers are good, and our classmates are fun, but _____
(6)   (7)
courses are really difficult. All I think about is _____ home – there
(8)
was no risk there!

Adriana I think _____ risks are important, though. They sometimes help you
(9)
succeed. Right now, _____ education is important. That's what I
(10)
worry about.

Mi-Young Aha! So you worry about something! You're just the same as everyone else!

Adriana I guess so. Well, everybody worries – _____ life is like that!
(11)

B *Pair Work* Practice the conversation with a partner.

Exercise 3.2 More Practice with *The* and No Article

A Complete the professor's welcome speech with *the* or ∅ for no article.

Welcome, ∅ international students! We're so excited to have you here. Be ready for
　　　　(1)
a fun and busy year! We at _____ university understand many of you are far away from
　　　　　　　　　　　(2)
_____ home. We know that can be scary. You all took _____ risks in coming here,
　(3)　　　　　　　　　　　　　　　　　　　　　(4)
and you're all very brave.

In your packets, there's _____ information on housing. There are _____ maps
　　　　　　　　　　　(5)　　　　　　　　　　　　　　　　　(6)
of _____ entire campus and this part of _____ city. You're all invited to _____
　(7)　　　　　　　　　　　　　　　　(8)　　　　　　　　　　　　(9)
weekly socials[1] where you can share _____ information about what you learn. It's also
　　　　　　　　　　　　　　　(10)
a time to meet _____ friends, both old
　　　　　　(11)
and new!

We also assigned _____
　　　　　　　　(12)
"language buddies." _____ buddies are
　　　　　　　　(13)
other students who help with _____
　　　　　　　　　　　　(14)
English practice every day. When you
need _____ help with anything, please
　　(15)
contact me! We want you to feel like this
is your home away from _____ home.
　　　　　　　　　(16)
Once again, welcome!

[1]**socials:** get-togethers, or parties

B *Over to You* Talk to a partner about a time when you took a risk like the one in A.
Did other people help you? What was helpful for you?

　A I enrolled in night classes. The college helped me find a part-time job during the day.

　B How did the college help you do that?

　*A They gave me some information about local businesses. These companies needed
　part-time workers.*

Exercise 3.3 *The* and No Article with Languages and Geographic Places

Complete the blog with *the* or ∅ for no article.

Jenna's Travels

People usually have strong reasons for doing volunteer work: They care about other people and worry about __*the*__ world in general.
(1)

I grew up in _____ United States, in _____ Midwest, near _____
(2)   (3)   (4)
Mississippi River. But there is a different world on the other side of _____ Atlantic.
(5)

I was always interested in _____ Africa, so I volunteered to work in _____
(6)   (7)
Namibia. Even though it was scary to go to _____ Africa, I was glad to take the risk.
(8)

I really wanted to help _____ people in a different part of the world.
(9)

I worked in a village school, teaching _____ English to young children. I
(10)
loved it. I also traveled a lot and saw some great places. I went to _____ Namib
(11)
Desert, I saw _____ Lake Victoria, and I climbed _____ Table Mountain in
(12)   (13)
_____ South Africa.
(14)

Best of all, volunteers make a difference and help other people. It's not enough to just worry about the world or be anxious about the future. Taking risks to help others is rewarding.[1] Volunteer work is a great way to do something to help _____ world.
(15)

[1] **rewarding:** satisfying, something that makes you happy

---

220 Unit 18 Articles: *A / An* and *The*

4 Avoid Common Mistakes ⚠

1. Do not use *a / an* with a noncount noun.

I'm making ~~a~~ progress with my English.

I have ~~a~~ homework tonight.

2. Do not use *the* to talk about things or people in general.

Life

~~The life~~ is often difficult for ~~the~~ students.

Students get ~~the~~ homework every night.

3. Do not use *the* with the names of languages, most countries, or continents.

~~The~~ Japanese is a beautiful language.

I want to go to ~~the~~ Australia.

4. Use *a* before consonant sounds. Use *an* before vowel sounds.

a

I have to make ~~an~~ decision quickly!

an

There is ~~a~~ online university in Caracas.

Editing Task

Find and correct 10 more mistakes in these sentences about risk taking.

1. I read an interesting article about how ~~the~~ people manage risk.

2. The professor gave us an lecture on economics.

3. A ostrich worries about getting a good job when he or she finishes college.

4. Analysts hope they have an insurance at work but will find an new job if they need to.

5. Some people feel a fear when they have to move to a new country.

6. I hope to become an volunteer in the South America after the college.

7. I don't speak the Spanish, so that's an risk. But maybe it can be fun!

5 | Grammar for Writing ✎

Writing About Risks and Challenges

Writers use articles in many types of writing and with many different topics, including when they write about taking risks and challenges.

Remember:

- **Use *a / an* before a singular count noun when you introduce it. Use *the* before the noun after the first time.**

  Maya took <u>a</u> big risk last year with her job. <u>The</u> risk turned out very well for her.

- **Use no article for noncount nouns with a general meaning.**

  Trevor doesn't have money to buy insurance.

- **Use no article with languages.**

  He speaks Japanese.

- **Use *the* or no article before geographical locations.**

  He worked in <u>the</u> United Arab Emirates and Turkey.

Pre-writing Task

1 Read the paragraph below. What kind of person is the writer's friend? What example does the writer use to show this?

Stressful Risks

My friend Dara is ⓐ rock climber. <u>Risks</u> and stress excite her. Life is not fun for her without risks. She says that they help her feel alive. For example, Dara often has large dinner parties. She invites new friends to her dinner parties, and she always cooks new dishes. My dinner parties are always with old friends. I prefer to cook for people I know. I never cook new things. It's too stressful. Sometimes Dara's parties are fun, and sometimes they are disasters. <u>The</u> last dinner party was a disaster. The guests did not like each other, and the food wasn't very good, but Dara doesn't care. She already has plans for another dinner party.

2 Read the paragraph again. Circle the indefinite articles, underline the nouns without articles, and <u>double underline</u> the definite articles.

Writing Task

1 *Write* Use the paragraph in the Pre-writing Task to help you write a paragraph about someone you know who is an ostrich or a rock climber. What does your friend do that shows he or she is an ostrich or a rock climber? Give examples from this person's daily life.

2 *Self-Edit* Use the editing tips below to improve your sentences. Make any necessary changes.

1. Did you use nouns with indefinite articles, definite articles, and no article to talk about someone who is an ostrich or a rock climber?
2. Did you use *a / an* when you wrote about a singular count noun for the first time and *the* after that?
3. Did you use no article for noncount nouns with a general meaning?
4. Did you avoid the mistakes in the Avoid Common Mistakes chart on page 221?

Possessive Pronouns and Indefinite Pronouns

Meals Around the World

1 | Grammar in the Real World

A What is your favorite breakfast food? Read the conversation between three college roommates as they discuss typical breakfasts in their countries. What do people in your country usually eat for breakfast?

What's for Breakfast?

Kyla Is that all you eat for breakfast? It's so little!

Sara Well, it's typical in Mexico to have coffee and a nice *bolillo*, or crusty French bread. It's all I want most days, but on weekends, I have a big breakfast with my family.

5 *Mei-li* We do that in our family, too. In Hong Kong, we used to have *dim sum* every Saturday.

Sara What's that?

Mei-li It's a lot of small, light dishes: dumplings – steamed or fried dough filled with meat, seafood, or vegetables – rice noodle rolls, *congee* –
10 a sort of rice soup, thick like oatmeal – and tea, of course. What do you have at your family brunches?[1]

Sara We have *huevos rancheros* – fried eggs with a spicy sauce and a *tortilla* – beans, a lot of fresh fruit, sometimes fish that my father catches on his boat. We always drink coffee or hot chocolate. My father loves strong
15 coffee, and **his** is very sweet!

Mei-li Our breakfast is pretty good, Sara, but I want to try **yours**! How about breakfast in the United States, Kyla?

Kyla Well, some people here say breakfast is the most important meal of their day. I have cereal, milk, fruit, yogurt, sometimes eggs – and
20 always coffee. It's a lot of food, but it's not a heavy meal. It's not like the meals people had in the past. For example, my grandparents always had coffee, juice, potatoes, a big plate of eggs with ham and cheese, and pancakes or donuts! They put cheese in their eggs, but I don't put it in **mine**.

25 *Sara* Your grandparents ate a large breakfast! I'd like to try **theirs**. Did **everybody** eat like that?

Kyla Many did, I think. People did hard physical work and needed a big meal in the morning. Today, some people still eat like that, and some don't have time to eat **anything** at all!

[1]**brunch:** a meal you sometimes eat in the late morning that combines breakfast and lunch

B *Comprehension Check* Complete the chart. Check (✓) the box next to the food people eat for breakfast in each place. Use the conversation in A to help you.

United States	Hong Kong	Mexico
☐ cereal	☐ cereal	☐ cereal
☐ coffee	☐ coffee	☐ coffee
☐ dumplings	☐ dumplings	☐ dumplings
☐ tea	☐ tea	☐ tea
☐ French bread	☐ French bread	☐ French bread

C *Notice* Circle the correct answer. Use the conversation to help you.

1. We always drink coffee or hot chocolate. My father loves strong coffee, and **his** is very sweet!

   What noun does the pronoun **_his_** replace?   a. my father   b. my father's coffee

2. They put cheese in their eggs, but I don't put it in **mine**.

   What noun does the pronoun **_mine_** replace?   a. cheese   b. eggs

3. Your grandparents ate a large breakfast! I'd like to try **theirs**.

   What noun does the pronoun **_theirs_** replace?   a. breakfast   b. grandparents

2 | Possessive Pronouns

▶ Grammar Presentation

Possessive pronouns tell us who something belongs to.	*That coffee is* **mine**. *I think this one is* **yours**. **Hers** *is still in the kitchen.*

2.1 Possessive Pronouns

Personal Pronouns	Possessive Determiners	Possessive Pronouns
I	**my** + noun **My** *apples are sweet.*	**mine** *Mine are sweet.*
you	**your** + noun **Your** *apples are sweet.*	**yours** *Yours are sweet.*
he	**his** + noun **His** *apples are sweet.*	**his** *His are sweet.*
she	**her** + noun **Her** *apples are sweet.*	**hers** *Hers are sweet.*
it	**its** + noun **Its** *apples are sweet.*	**Its** cannot be a pronoun. *Its are sweet.*
we	**our** + noun **Our** *apples are sweet.*	**ours** *Ours are sweet.*
they	**their** + noun **Their** *apples are sweet.*	**theirs** *Theirs are sweet.*

▶▎ Subject and Object Pronouns: See page A18.

2.2 Using Possessive Pronouns

a. Possessive pronouns show who or what a noun belongs to.	*This is my sister's cereal. The cereal is* **hers***.*
b. When you use a possessive pronoun, don't repeat the noun or noun phrase.	*Those apples are* **mine***.* NOT *Those are* **mine** *apples.*
c. Possessive pronouns have one form. They do not change when the noun is plural.	*This apple isn't* **mine***.* **Mine** *is on the table.* *These apples aren't* **mine***.* **Mine** *are on the table.* NOT *These apples aren't* **mines***.* **Mines** *are on the table.*
The verb changes when the replaced noun is plural.	*My apples are on the table.* **Mine are** *on the table.* *Mine is replacing* my apples, *so we need to use a plural verb.*
d. There is no possessive pronoun for *it*.	*That tree's apples are juicy.* **Its** *apples are juicy.* NOT **Its** *are juicy.*

Data from the Real World

Research shows that possessive determiners are much more common in writing.

I eat breakfast every day. **My** *breakfast is always delicious!*

Possessive pronouns are much more common in conversation.

"My breakfast is good. How is **yours***?"*
*"****Mine*** *is delicious!"*

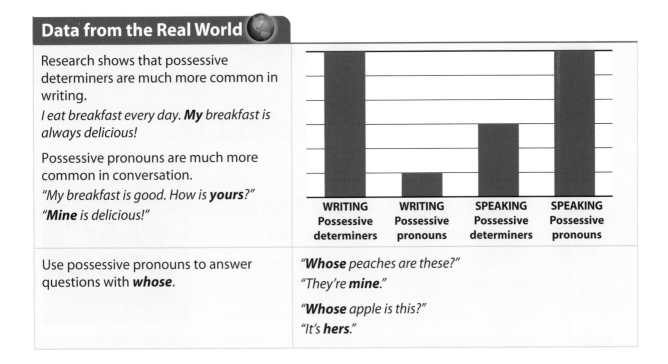

Use possessive pronouns to answer questions with **whose**.

*"****Whose*** *peaches are these?"*
"They're **mine***."*

*"****Whose*** *apple is this?"*
"It's **hers***."*

▶ Grammar Application

Exercise 2.1 Possessive Pronouns

Rewrite each sentence. Replace the possessive determiner and noun in bold with a possessive pronoun.

1. That is **my coffee**.

   That is mine.

2. Did you finish **your breakfast**?

   _____

3. **Their breakfast** tasted delicious.

   _____

4. John didn't take **my donut**; he took **her donut**!

   _____

5. Oh, you can have **our pancakes**.

   _____

6. **His hot chocolate** is probably the best.

   _____

7. I like fruit with **my breakfast**.

   _____

Exercise 2.2 More Possessive Pronouns

A Complete the sentences with *theirs*, *yours*, *his*, or *hers*.

Meal Times Around the World

People from all around the world eat their main meal at different times. Mexicans eat _theirs_ in the afternoon. They eat between 2:00 and 4:00 p.m.
₍₁₎

People in Spain have their main meal in the afternoon, too. Dinner in Spain is late. They usually eat _____ at 10:00 p.m.! Some visitors don't like that
₍₂₎
custom. While in Spain, you can eat _____ early
₍₃₎
because restaurants are open for travelers like you!

In Thailand, dinner is the main meal. Thais usually eat _____ early in the evening.
₍₄₎

In the United States, dinner is also the main meal. You might notice that families don't eat together all the time. For example, sometimes the father works late and misses dinner. In cases like this, he has _____ when
₍₅₎
he gets home. Sometimes the daughter has soccer practice in the evening. These evenings, her parents make her an early dinner. She often eats _____ at
₍₆₎
5:00 p.m., before the rest of the family.

B *Over to You* Tell a partner about the eating habits in your country. What time do people eat their main meal? What do they eat?

Exercise 2.3 Possessive Pronouns, Possessive Determiners, and Verbs

A 🔊 Complete the sentences with the correct words. Then listen and check your answers.

Sara Kyla, let's cook dinner!

Kyla Wow, your kitchen is complicated. Look at all the shelves!

Sara Well, that's Franny's shelf. She eats a lot of junk food. Those bags of chips

is / are **her / hers**. As you can see, **her / hers** shelf is full of chips and candy.
  (1)   (2)   (3)

Kyla It looks like Su's shelf is full of healthy things.

Sara Yes. Those vitamins **is / are** **her / hers**. **Her / Hers** shelf is always very neat,
           (4)   (5)   (6)

too. Su and Mari share one shelf. That top shelf is **their / theirs**. It always has
                                              (7)

baskets of fruit on it.

Kyla Which shelf is **your / yours**?
                   (8)

Sara This one **is / are** **my / mine**.
          (9)   (10)

Kyla Oh, so are those your bowls?

Sara Yes, those are **yours / mine**. They're from Japan.
                   (11)

Kyla They're very pretty. **Who's / Whose** things are on this shelf?
                        (12)

Sara Oh, those are **ours / our**. We all share that shelf. OK. Well, let's start cooking.
                  (13)

Kyla Right. So, **who's / whose** coming for dinner tonight?
                (14)

Sara Our families. We have a lot of cooking to do.

B *Pair Work* Practice the conversation in A with a partner.

Exercise 2.4 Vocabulary Focus: *Theirs and There's*

Theirs and *there's* (*there is*) sound the same but mean different things. Be careful with the spelling of these two words.	*I ate my lunch in the office, but they ate **theirs** in the park.* NOT *I ate my lunch in the office, but they ate **there's** in the park.* *Near the café **there's** a park.* NOT *Near the café **theirs** a park.*

Read the blog. Choose the correct words.

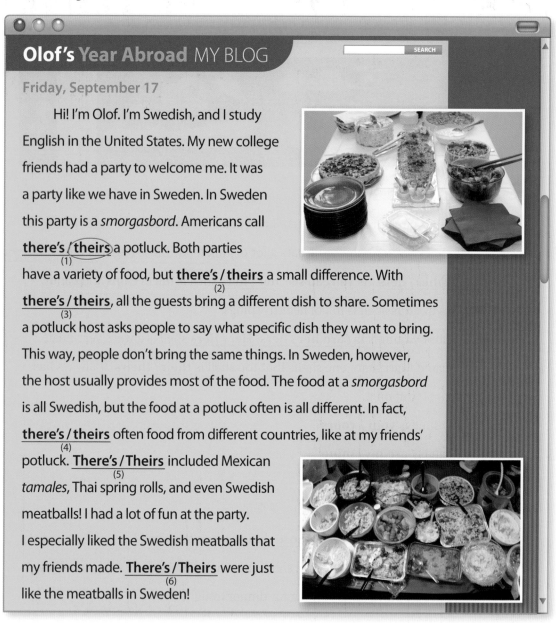

Olof's Year Abroad MY BLOG

SEARCH

Friday, September 17

Hi! I'm Olof. I'm Swedish, and I study English in the United States. My new college friends had a party to welcome me. It was a party like we have in Sweden. In Sweden this party is a *smorgasbord*. Americans call **there's / theirs** a potluck. Both parties
(1)
have a variety of food, but **there's / theirs** a small difference. With
(2)
there's / theirs, all the guests bring a different dish to share. Sometimes
(3)
a potluck host asks people to say what specific dish they want to bring. This way, people don't bring the same things. In Sweden, however, the host usually provides most of the food. The food at a *smorgasbord* is all Swedish, but the food at a potluck often is all different. In fact, **there's / theirs** often food from different countries, like at my friends'
(4)
potluck. **There's / Theirs** included Mexican
(5)
tamales, Thai spring rolls, and even Swedish meatballs! I had a lot of fun at the party. I especially liked the Swedish meatballs that my friends made. **There's / Theirs** were just
(6)
like the meatballs in Sweden!

3 | Indefinite Pronouns

▶ Grammar Presentation

Indefinite pronouns refer to people or things that are not specific, not known, or not the focus of the sentence.	***Everyone*** *loved the food at the party.* ***Somebody*** *made dinner.* *Does **anyone** want breakfast?*

3.1 Indefinite Pronouns

	-one	*-body*	*-thing*
some +	**someone**	**somebody**	**something**
any +	**anyone**	**anybody**	**anything**
every +	**everyone**	**everybody**	**everything**
no +	**no one**	**nobody**	**nothing**

3.2 Using Indefinite Pronouns

a. Use an indefinite pronoun with *-one* or *-body* to refer to a person or a group of people.	***Everyone*** *knows fruit is good for you.* ***Somebody*** *brought this delicious salad.*
b. Use an indefinite pronoun with *-thing* to refer to things (not people).	*I know **something** about healthy food choices.* ***Everything** I eat is from my garden.*
c. Use a third-person singular verb when the subject is an indefinite pronoun.	SUBJECT VERB ***Something smells*** *good!* SUBJECT VERB ***Everyone eats*** *food.*
d. Use indefinite pronouns with *some +*, *every +*, and *no +* in affirmative statements.	***Someone*** *ate all the apples.* ***Everyone*** *eats vegetables.* ***No one*** *eats junk food in my family.*
e. Use indefinite pronouns with *any +* in negative statements.	*She **doesn't** eat lunch with **anybody**.* *I **don't** see **anything** healthy about junk food.* *He **doesn't** think **anyone** should eat fast food.*
Don't use indefinite pronouns with *no +* in negative sentences.	NOT ~~She **doesn't** eat lunch with **nobody**.~~ NOT ~~I **don't** want **nothing** for dessert.~~

3.2 Using Indefinite Pronouns *(continued)*

f. In *Yes/No* questions, use indefinite pronouns with *some* +, *any* +, or *every* +.	*Is **someone** home?* *Does **anyone** eat apples?* *Is **everyone** here?*
You can use indefinite pronouns with *no* + in *Yes/No* questions, but it's very formal.	*Is **nobody** home?*

3.3 Types of Statements That Use Indefinite Pronouns

	Affirmative Statements	Negative Statements	Yes/No Questions
anyone, anybody, anything	no	yes	yes
someone, somebody, something	yes	no	yes
everyone, everybody, everything	yes	no	yes
no one, nobody, nothing	yes	no	no

▶ # Grammar Application

Exercise 3.1 Indefinite Pronouns with *-one*, *-body*, or *-thing*

A Complete the words with *-one*, *-body*, or *-thing*. Sometimes there is more than one correct answer.

1. We sent **every**<u>*one*</u> in our class an invitation to our international dinner party last night.

2. Gladi wanted to bring dessert. She brought **some**_____ from Laos.

3. I didn't know **any**_____ about Laotian food before the party.

4. **Some**_____ brought some delicious Mexican *enchiladas*.

5. **No**_____ brought any Chinese food.

6. Maybe that's because our class doesn't have **any**_____ from China in it.

7. **Every**_____ was delicious, so people ate a lot.

8. By 10:00, there was **no**_____ left to eat, so we played games and danced instead!

B *Pair Work* Compare your answers with a partner. Which sentences can have more than one answer?

Exercise 3.2 *Yes / No* Questions with Indefinite Pronouns

A Complete the questions with an indefinite pronoun. Sometimes there is more than one correct answer.

1. Do you know *anyone / anybody* who eats rice for breakfast?
2. Does _____ eat dinner after 9:00 p.m.?
3. Do you know _____ in your neighborhood?
4. Do you know _____ about cooking?
5. Does _____ cook for you?
6. Can you tell me _____ about food in your country?

B *Pair Work* Ask and answer the questions in A with a partner.

A *Do you know anyone who eats rice for breakfast?*
B *Yes! I usually eat rice in the mornings.*

Exercise 3.3 Indefinite Pronouns

A Complete the sentences. Choose the correct indefinite pronoun.

Yuki Hello?

Lisa Yuki? Hi, it's Lisa. Did you get my message about coming

over to my house for dinner?

Yuki Hi, Lisa. No, I didn't get your message. **Anybody / Nobody**
(1)
told me you called! Sure, I can come for dinner. What time?

Lisa Come at 7:00. What do you want to eat?

Yuki I don't know **anybody / anything** about cooking, and I like
(2)
everyone / everything, so you decide.
(3)

Lisa Well, OK. I don't really cook either. How about sushi from Matsuri Restaurant? I

know the owner. I can have **something / someone** there make us a special dinner.
(4)

Yuki That sounds great. So you don't mind calling? I don't know **no one / anyone** at
(5)
that restaurant.

Lisa Sure. Do you want me to call Roberto? **Something / Someone** told me he loves sushi.
(6)

Yuki Oh, yes, I know. I can call him. Do you want to invite **anybody / anything** else?
(7)

Lisa I'm not sure if **no one / anyone** else is around tonight, but that's OK.
(8)
See you tonight!

B *Pair Work* Practice the conversation in A with a partner.

Exercise 3.4 Indefinite Pronouns with *-one* and *-body*

Data from the Real World

We use indefinite pronouns with *-one* more often in writing and formal speaking.	If **anyone** likes pizza, it's college students. **Everyone** needs to eat the right foods.	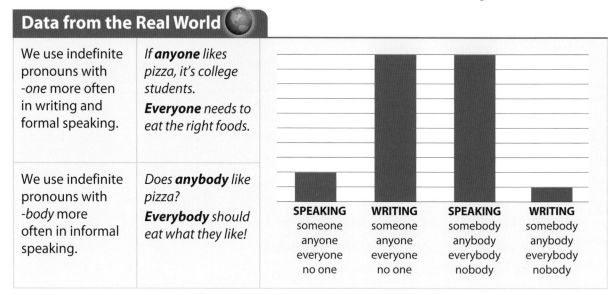
We use indefinite pronouns with *-body* more often in informal speaking.	Does **anybody** like pizza? **Everybody** should eat what they like!	

Check (✔) the box if the indefinite pronoun is more common in speaking or writing.

	Speaking	Writing
someone	☐	✓
everybody	☐	☐
anybody	☐	☐
anyone	☐	☐
no one	☐	☐
everyone	☐	☐
somebody	☐	☐
nobody	☐	☐

4 | Avoid Common Mistakes ⚠️

1. Don't repeat the noun after the possessive pronoun.

That's not your apple. It's mine ~~apple~~.

2. Don't confuse *theirs* with *there's*.

The apple is not mine. It's ~~there's~~. *[theirs]*

3. Possessive pronouns have one form. They do not change when the noun is plural.

The apples are ~~mines~~. *[mine]*

4. In negative statements use indefinite pronouns with *any* +.

I don't want to eat ~~nothing~~. *[anything]*

Editing Task

Find and correct six more errors in this blog about a favorite place to eat.

Jessie's Snack **BLOG** Tuesday, March 8   SEARCH

Best Sandwiches in Town

Everyone has a favorite sandwich shop in town, and the Snack Stop is definitely mine ~~favorite~~. I eat sandwiches a lot, and there's are the best. What do you think? Please leave a comment and let me know!

5 <u>**Comments:**</u>

Richard: I ate there once with my brother and sister, but I didn't like it. Everyone says the sandwiches are delicious, but ours sandwiches weren't good at all. Plus, my sister ordered dessert, but the server didn't bring her nothing. We had to remind him of our order. Then

10   he charged my brother for French fries, but the fries were mines.

Jeff: Wow. I remember the first time I ate at the Snack Stop. It was with my cousin. My sandwich was delicious, and so was hers sandwich. In fact, there wasn't nothing wrong with the whole meal.

5 | Grammar for Writing

Writing About an Event

Writers use indefinite pronouns to write about what people generally do and what things usually happen at an event or in a situation.
Remember:

- **Use the third-person singular verb form with indefinite pronouns.**
  Everyone helps with cleanup after our dinner parties.

- **Use *-one* to refer to people and *-thing* to refer to things.**
  Everyone brings something to a potluck dinner.

Pre-writing Task

1 Read the paragraph below. When is this writer's special event, and who comes to it?

My Parents' Potluck Dinners

On the first Sunday of every month, we
have a big potluck dinner party at my parents'
house. At about 5:00 p.m., everyone starts
to arrive. My cousins and my aunts and
5 uncles always come. In addition, some of
us bring friends as guests. My parents often
invite someone from work. Everyone brings
something to eat. There is always a lot of
excellent food. No one leaves our dinner
10 parties hungry! Everyone always goes home
full. Usually everyone takes something home
with them for lunch the next day. Cleanup
is always a big job, but everyone helps do
something. I always enjoy those Sunday
dinners!

2 Read the paragraph again. Circle the indefinite pronouns that refer to people and underline the indefinite pronouns that refer to things. <u>Double underline</u> the verbs that follow the indefinite pronouns that are subjects. Are the verbs singular or plural?

Writing Task

1 *Write*   Use the paragraph in the Pre-writing Task to help you write a paragraph about a regular event or celebration in your life. Who attends? What do people do? What does no one do? Use indefinite pronouns.

2 *Self-Edit*   Use the editing tips below to improve your sentences. Make any necessary changes.

1. Did you use indefinite pronouns to tell what people generally do at the event and what things usually happen?
2. Did you use the third-person singular verb form for the verb following an indefinite subject pronoun?
3. Did you use *-one* to write about people and *-thing* to write about things?
4. Did you avoid the mistakes in the Avoid Common Mistakes chart on page 235?

Imperatives
Social Customs

1 | Grammar in the Real World

A What do people do on the first day of a new job? Read part of a web article below. What are two good things to do at a new job?

HOME   JOBS   CONTACT   [   ] **SEARCH**

Dos and *Don'ts* at a New Job

It's easy to make mistakes when you go to work at a new job. There are unspoken[1] rules that people don't tell you. Here are some tips to help you avoid some common
5 mistakes.

- **Be** friendly. When you arrive at your new job, **smile** and **introduce** yourself to people. **Say** "Good morning" or "Hi" and the person's name (if you know it).

10 - **Look** at people when you talk to them. It isn't polite to look down, but you shouldn't stare,[2] either.

- **Don't interrupt**[3] people who are very busy.

- When people at work know each other well, they sometimes talk about their families or their lives at home. **Don't do** this in the beginning. **Wait** until you know people a little.
15 **Don't assume** that people want to talk about private things immediately, or at all.

   In some workplaces, there are uniforms[4] or rules about clothes. If there are no rules, **notice** what other people wear. If they wear jeans or other casual clothes, then you can wear jeans, too.
   Above all, **smile** and **be** helpful. **Show** that you want to learn and work hard.

[1]**unspoken:** not said, even though somebody thinks or understands it | [2]**stare:** look directly at someone for a long time | [3]**interrupt:** stop something from happening for a short period, or start talking when someone else is already talking | [4]**uniform:** special clothing that shows you are part of an organization or job

B *Comprehension Check* Complete the chart. Use the article to help you. Check (✓) Yes or No.

When you're at a new job, . . .	Yes	No
1. smile and introduce yourself to people.	☐	☐
2. interrupt people who are busy.	☐	☐
3. ask about your co-workers' families on your first day.	☐	☐
4. look down when you talk with people.	☐	☐
5. smile and be helpful.	☐	☐

C *Notice* Find these sentences in the article. Complete the sentences.

1. _____ "Good morning" or "Hi" and the person's name.

2. _____ at people when you talk to them.

3. _____ people who are very busy.

4. _____ and be helpful.

What do the verbs in 1–4 do? Circle the correct answers.

a. describe people's habits   c. describe the past

b. give advice   d. tell you what to do

2 Imperatives

▶ Grammar Presentation

Imperatives tell people to do things. They can give instructions, directions, or advice.	**Be** *friendly.* **Don't interrupt** *people who are very busy.*

2.1 Statements

AFFIRMATIVE		NEGATIVE		
Base Form of Verb		Do + Not	Base Form of Verb	
Smile	and be helpful.	**Don't /** **Do not**	**interrupt**	people who are very busy.
Look	at people when you talk to them.		**do**	this in the beginning.

2.2 Using Imperatives in Writing

Imperatives are common in texts that tell people what to do and what not to do. They appear:

• on public signs and advertisements	*Do not enter.* *Stand behind the yellow line.* *Buy now and save $4.99.*
• on forms and websites	*Please write in CAPITAL LETTERS.* *Log in. Enter your password. Search.* *Restart your computer after you install a new program.*
• in texts with instructions (like manuals, recipes, and labels)	*Add hot water and stir.* *Lift here to open.*
• in texts with advice (e.g., magazine articles, leaflets)	*Wait until you know people a little.* *Show that you want to learn and work hard.*

2.3 Using Imperatives in Speaking

a. Imperatives are common in classrooms and demonstrations.	*Listen to the conversation.* *Don't open your books.* *Turn on the computer and enter the password.*
b. You can use imperatives to give directions.	*Make a left at the next traffic light.* *Don't turn right.*
c. You can use imperatives in common social expressions or offers.	*Have a good day!* *Take care.* *Have a cookie.*
d. You can use imperatives to warn people about dangers.	*Watch out!* *Be careful! There's a step there.*
e. When you know people well, you can use imperatives in everyday situations to ask for things or to give instructions or advice.	*Call me later.* *Don't forget your keys.* *Don't worry.*

When you don't know people well, don't use imperatives to tell them to do something. Even if you say *please,* you can sound rude.

f. 🌐 *Do not* is very strong and is not common in conversation. It is common to write it in formal situations, but do not use it in informal conversation.

▶ Grammar Application

Exercise 2.1 Imperatives: Advice

A Give some advice about work. Use the negative or affirmative forms of the verbs in parentheses.

1. ___*Don't ask*___ (ask) about co-workers' lives at home when you are new.

2. _____ (take) a lunch break every day.

3. _____ (enjoy) long coffee breaks in the morning and afternoon.

4. _____ (eat) lunch with your co-workers.

5. _____ (socialize) with your co-workers after work if they invite you.

6. _____ (talk) about vacations or your weekend plans at work.

7. _____ (talk) about money or politics.

8. _____ (learn) from your mistakes.

B *Pair Work* Compare your answers with a partner. Are your imperatives the same? Discuss which advice is different.

C *Over to You* Write six sentences about work in a culture you know well. Use the imperative.

Don't ask about your co-workers' families.
Don't take too many breaks.
Have lunch with your boss when she invites you.

Exercise 2.2 Imperatives: Social Customs

A Jane is taking a work trip to Japan and India. Use the verbs in the box to give her some advice. You need to make the verb negative two times.

eat	give	take	wear
forget	keep	~~take off~~	wrap

1. _____*Take off*_____ your shoes.

2. _____ a small gift.

3. _____ your gift nicely.

4. _____ food with your left hand.

5. Also, _____ things to people with your left hand.

6. _____ your feet on the ground when you sit.

7. _____ nice clothes.

8. _____ to write a thank-you note later.

Do you take off your shoes?

Or wipe your feet?

B *Over to You* What are some social dinner customs you know? Write four imperatives about social dinner customs in a country you know well.

In the United States, bring flowers to the host(ess). Don't take your shoes off.

1. _____

2. _____

3. _____

4. _____

Exercise 2.3 Imperatives: Signs

A Look at the signs and complete the imperatives in the chart. Use the verbs from the box.
Sometimes you need to make the verb negative. Then compare your answers with a partner.

bring   drink   feed   ride   ~~throw~~   turn   use   wear

Throw your trash here.
(1)

_____ the animals.
(2)

_____ your bicycle here.
(3)

_____ the water.
(4)

_____ food or drink into the museum.
(5)

_____ left here.
(6)

_____ your cell phone.
(7)

_____ your helmet.
(8)

B *Pair Work* With a partner, write a list of six signs you see every day. How many use imperatives?

Do not use elevators in case of fire.

1. _____
2. _____
3. _____
4. _____
5. _____
6. _____

C *Over to You* Write six signs for doors in your home and one for your classroom door. Make them funny. Then read your signs to a partner.

refrigerator door	
bedroom door	
front door	
living room door	
closet door	
kitchen door	
classroom door	

My sign for the refrigerator says, "Do not drink my soda!" What does your sign say?

Exercise 2.4 Imperatives: Directions

A Look at the map. Write down directions from Rogers College to Bob's Cafe. Use some of the imperative directions in the box below.

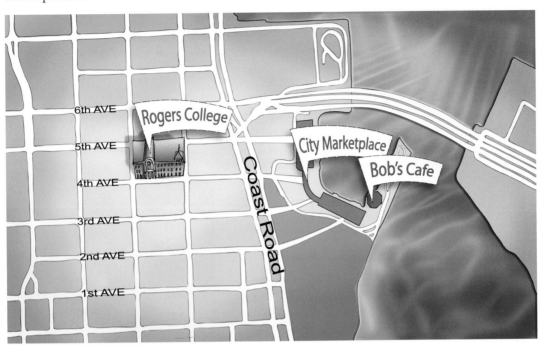

Common Directions				
Take a right on . . .	Go straight on . . .	Go around the corner.	Cross the street.	Walk up the street two blocks.
Go past City Marketplace.	Cross Second Avenue.	Cross Coast Road.	Be careful!	Watch for cars!

Go straight on 4th Avenue.

_____

_____

_____

_____

B *Pair Work* Write directions to a place in the neighborhood you are in. Read them to a partner. Switch roles. Guess your partner's place.

Exercise 2.5 Imperatives with *Always* and *Never*

Data from the Real World

Research shows that people often use *always* and *never* in writing to make imperatives stronger. This is not common in conversation.	**Always shake** hands when you meet someone new. **Never wear** shoes in someone's house. NOT ~~Never do not wear~~ shoes in someone's house.

A ◀)) Complete the sentences from a brochure about visiting Brazil with *always* or *never*. Then listen to the student podcast.

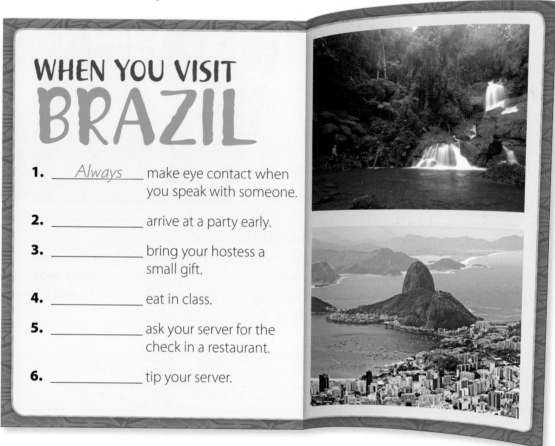

WHEN YOU VISIT
BRAZIL

1. ___*Always*___ make eye contact when you speak with someone.

2. _____ arrive at a party early.

3. _____ bring your hostess a small gift.

4. _____ eat in class.

5. _____ ask your server for the check in a restaurant.

6. _____ tip your server.

B *Over to You* For each topic, write three pieces of advice for visitors to the country you are in now. Use *always* and *never* for strong advice. Read your sentences to a partner.

Advice for eating in restaurants:

1. _____

2. _____

3. _____

Advice for talking to people:

1. _____

2. _____

3. _____

Advice for going to a new college:

1. _____

2. _____

3. _____

3 Avoid Common Mistakes ⚠

1. Use *don't* to form negative imperatives.

   Don't
   ~~No~~ forget to do your homework.

2. Remember to write *do not* as two words.

   Do not   *Do not*
   ~~Donot~~ be late for class.   ~~Do n't~~ be late for class.

3. Use an apostrophe to write *don't*. Put the apostrophe between the *n* and *t*.

   Don't   *Don't*
   ~~Dont~~ send text messages during class. ~~Do'nt~~ eat in the computer lab.
   Don't
   ~~D'ont~~ forget to save your work.

Editing Task

Find and correct nine more mistakes in these sentences about advice for college students in different countries.

   Don't
1. ~~Dont~~ be late for class.

2. No stand up when the teacher walks into the classroom.

3. Donot use the teacher's first name.

4. No forget to write the date your assignment is due.

5. Dont forget your homework assignment.

6. Don't copy another student's homework.

7. Donot buy or download essays on the Internet.

8. D'ont listen to your MP3 player in class.

9. No answer your cell phone in class.

10. Do n't send or read text messages in class.

4 Grammar for Writing ✏

Writing Travel Tips

Travel writers use imperatives to give people advice or travel tips. Often writers add sentences to explain these tips.

Remember:

- **Use the base form of the verb without *to*. Also, use *don't* instead of *do not*, but use *do not* for formal writing.**

Affirmative imperative	*Stand in line to get on the bus.*
Negative imperative	*Don't talk loudly on the bus.*
Imperative with a time clause	*When you sit down, put your bags on your lap. Don't put them on the floor of the bus.*

Pre-writing Task

1 Read the Hawaii travel tips below. Are any of the tips helpful for a traveler to a place that you know well?

Tips for Travelers to Hawaii

Hawaii is a wonderful place to visit. Here are some useful travel tips.

- Before you leave your home, (pack) carefully. Pack clothes that are light and don't weigh a lot. Also,
5   pack a raincoat. It often rains in Hawaii.

- Don't go outside without sunscreen. The sun is very strong.

- Learn some words in Hawaiian. *Mahalo* means "thank you." When you meet someone, say *Aloha*.
10   Say *Aloha* again when you leave.

- When you are in the water, don't turn away from the ocean. Small waves can change to big waves very quickly.

- Don't leave Hawaii without a *lei*. A *lei* is a necklace
15   of flowers. You wear it around your neck. Hang it over your door after you get home for good luck.

2 Underline the tips. Circle the imperatives with time clauses. Double underline the sentences that explain the tips.

Writing Task

1 *Write* Use the travel tips in the Pre-writing Task to help you write tips for visitors to a place you know. Write at least four tips. Use time clauses to begin or end some of your tips. Add sentences that explain the tip.

2 *Self-Edit* Use the editing tips below to help you improve your sentences. Make any necessary changes.

1. Did you start your list of tips with a sentence or two about your place?
2. Did you write negative and affirmative tips?
3. Did you start or end some imperatives with time clauses?
4. Did you avoid the mistakes in the Avoid Common Mistakes chart on page 247?

Ability and Possibility
Making Connections

1 | Grammar in the Real World

A How do you stay in touch with friends and family? Read the web article. Does technology help you stay in touch?

TECHNOLOGY FOR MAKING CONNECTIONS

Technology helps us do many things that we **could not** do even a few years ago. Here is one way that technology changes our lives: It helps us keep in touch[1] – in touch with the world and with our friends and family.

For example, because of the Internet, we **are able to** get information about
5 almost any topic at any time. The Internet **can** provide us with up-to-date news, music, movies, and even television shows.

The Internet also helps us connect with other people. We **can** share pictures, we **can** make our own websites and blogs, and we **can** communicate by e-mail and texting.[2]

10 One of the most popular ways we **are able to** connect with people is through social networking websites. On these websites, people **can** share their news and pictures. Then family and friends **can** post[3] comments. They **can** also read each other's comments. In the past, we **could not** communicate on websites
15 like these. They did not exist. Most people **could** only communicate by phone, letters, and e-mail. But now even children **know how to** use social networking sites to keep in touch with their friends.

20 Because of technology, we **can** get information and connect with others whenever we want. All of that is just a click away.

[1]**keep in touch:** communicate with someone regularly | [2]**text:** send a short message to someone's cell phone by pushing buttons for letters on your phone; short for *text messaging* | [3]**post:** write a note or message or information on a website

B Comprehension Check Answer the questions. Use the article to help you.

1. What is a popular way the Internet helps us connect with people?
2. Name two things friends can share on social networking sites.
3. What can we do with technology that we couldn't do in the past?

C Notice Find these sentences in the article. Complete the sentences with *can*, *could*, or *could not*.

1. Technology helps us do many things that we _____ do even a few years ago.

2. On these websites, people _____ share their news and pictures.

3. They _____ also read each other's comments.

4. Most people _____ only communicate by phone, letters, and e-mail.

What form of the verb comes after *can*, *could*, or *could not*?

2 | *Can* and *Could* for Ability and Possibility

▶ Grammar Presentation

Can and *could* express ability or possibility.	The Internet **can** provide us with music, movies, and even television shows. Fifteen years ago, most people **could not** communicate by texting.

2.1 Statements

AFFIRMATIVE

Subject	*Can / Could*	Base Form of Verb	
I You We They He / She / It	**can** **could**	**use**	e-mail.

NEGATIVE

Subject	*Can / Could + Not*	Base Form of Verb	
I You We They He / She / It	**cannot** **can't** **could not** **couldn't**	**use**	e-mail.

2.2 *Yes / No* Questions and Answers

Can / Could	Subject	Base Form of Verb	
Can **Could**	I you we they he / she / it	**use**	the computer?

AFFIRMATIVE ANSWERS				NEGATIVE ANSWERS		
Yes	Subject	*Can / Could*		*No*	Subject	*Can / Could + Not*
Yes,	I you we they he / she / it	**can.** **could.**		**No,**	I you we they he / she / it	**cannot.** **can't.** **could not.** **couldn't.**

2.3 Information Questions

Wh- Word	*Can / Could*	Subject	Base Form of Verb	
Who			**ask**	about the program?
What	**can** **could**	I you we they he / she / it	**do**	on that website?
When			**read**	the e-mail message?
Where			**use**	our cell phones?
How			**communicate**	with each other?

2.4 Using *Can* and *Could*

a. Use *can* to talk about ability or possibility in the present.

> I **can** use the Internet at the school library.
> Friends **can** post comments to each other.

b. Use *could* to talk about ability or possibility in the past.

> I **could** use the Internet at my old school.
> My grandparents **could** only get the news through radio and television when they were young.

c. You can spell *cannot* as one word or as two words (*can not*), but it is usually spelled as one word (*cannot*). Spell *could not* as two words.

> I **cannot** remember my password.
> I **can not** remember my password.
>
> I **could not** read the e-mail.
> NOT I ~~couldnot~~ read the e-mail.

d. Use the contractions *can't* or *couldn't* in speaking, e-mails, and conversations but not in formal writing.

> They **can't** remember the password.
> I **couldn't** read your e-mail.
> People **could not** communicate quickly and easily before the Internet.

▸◂ Modal Verbs and Modal-like Expressions: See page A25.

▶ Grammar Application

Exercise 2.1 *Can* and *Could* for Ability and Possibility

A Complete the sentences in the blog. Circle the correct words.

Serena's Blog: *My New Life in the United States*

Last year I moved from Chile to San Diego, California. I am a student at the local community college, and I am learning many new things. When I was a student in Chile, I **cannot /** (**could not**) use a computer. However,
(1)
my new roommate in San Diego **can / could**
(2)
use computers really well. In fact, she is teaching me many new things.

A few months ago, I **can't / couldn't** even surf the Internet, but now
(3)
I **can / could** send e-mails to my friends in Chile, and I **can / could** share
(4)   (5)
photos on a social networking site. In Chile, my friends and I wanted to chat on the Internet, but we **can't / couldn't** because we didn't know how.
(6)
I learned how to chat online here in San Diego, and many of my friends in Chile learned, too. Now we **can / could** chat all the time.
(7)
At the beginning of the semester, many students **can't / couldn't** create
(8)
a blog, but now we all **can / could**. This means that now I **can / could** write
(9)   (10)
this blog, and my family in Chile **can / could** read about my everyday life.
(11)
There's one more thing I want to learn about computers. A lot of my friends here **can / could** use their computers to call family members in other
(12)
countries. I still **can't / couldn't** do that, but I want to learn.
(13)

B Unscramble the words to make *Yes / No* questions and information questions with *can* and *could*.

1. Can / photos / receive / you / on your cell phone / ?

   Can you receive photos on your cell phone?

2. Can / from your phone / you / send / an e-mail / ?

   _____

3. check / your e-mail / can / When / you / ?

   _____

4. can / buy / I / a good computer / Where / ?

   _____

5. How / learn / I / to design websites / can / ?

   _____

6. five years ago / you / send / an e-mail / Could / ?

   _____

7. your parents / e-mail / use / Can / ?

   _____

8. to the Internet / five years ago / Could / connect / your parents / ?

   _____

9. text messages / Who / 10 years ago / could / send / ?

   _____

10. send / you / Could / an attachment / five years ago / ?

    _____

11. you / Can / text / quickly / ?

    _____

12. How / communicate / could / people / 20 years ago / ?

    _____

C *Pair Work* Ask and answer the questions in B with a partner.

Exercise 2.2 🔊 Pronunciation Focus: Saying *Can* and *Can't*

Sometimes it's hard to hear the difference between *can* and *can't*.

People usually do not pronounce the *a* in *can* very clearly.	*I can use a laptop* usually sounds like *I c'n use a laptop.* *Can I use your phone?* usually sounds like *C'n I use your phone?*
People always say the *a* in *can't* very clearly.	*I can't use an e-reader.*[1] *He can't find his phone.*
In short answers, people always say the *a* in *can* and *can't* clearly.	*Yes, I can.* *No, I can't.*

[1] **e-reader:** electronic reading device

A 🔊 Listen and repeat the sentences.

1. I **can** use a laptop.
2. I **can't** use a laptop.
3. I **can** design a blog.
4. I **can't** design a blog.
5. He **can** find his phone.
6. He **can't** find his phone.

B 🔊 Listen. Complete the chart. Check (✓) all the things you can do on the *Gen 5* and *Linkage* websites. Write an ✗ for everything you can't do.

	Gen 5 website	*Linkage* website
1. chat	✓	✗
2. join interest groups		
3. download songs		
4. send songs to friends		
5. find a job		
6. post pictures		

C *Pair Work* Look at the chart in B. Choose the website that is best for you. Share your reasons with a partner.

I like Gen 5. You can chat with Gen 5, but you can't chat with Linkage.

3 | *Be Able To* and *Know How To* for Ability

▶ Grammar Presentation

Be able to expresses ability. *Know how to* expresses things we learned to do in the past.	Warren **is able to** watch movies on his phone. I **know how to** post videos on the Internet. *Someone taught me.*

3.1 *Be Able To*: Affirmative Statements

Subject	*Be*	*Able To*	Base Form of Verb	
I	am / was			
You We They	are / were	able to	send	text messages.
He She It	is / was			

3.2 *Be Able To*: Negative Statements

Subject	*Be + Not*	*Able To*	Base Form of Verb	
I	am not / 'm not was not / wasn't			
You We They	are not / aren't were not / weren't	able to	send	text messages.
He She It	is not / isn't was not / wasn't			

3.3 *Be Able To*: *Yes / No* Questions

Be	Subject	*Able To*	Base Form of Verb	
Am / Was	I			
Are / Were	you we they	**able to**	send	text messages?
Is / Was	he / she / it			

3.4 *Know How To*: Affirmative Statements

Subject	*Know*	*How To*	Base Form of Verb	
I You We They	**know**	**how to**	design	a website.
He / She / It	**knows**			

3.5 *Know How To*: Negative Statements

Subject	*Do + Not*	*Know How To*	Base Form of Verb	
I You We They	**do not / don't**	**know how to**	design	a website.
He / She / It	**does not / doesn't**			

3.6 *Know How To*: *Yes / No* Questions

Do	Subject	*Know How To*	Base Form of Verb	
Do	I you we they	**know how to**	design	a website?
Does	he / she / it			

3.7 Using *Be Able To* and *Know How To*

a. You use *be able to* to express ability. It has the same meaning as *can / could*.	They **are able to** send photos with their phones. Mariko **wasn't able to** send a photo with her phone.
b. You use *know how to* to talk about things you learned to do.	Suri **knows how to** create a web page. My grandmother **didn't know how to** send e-mail until I taught her.

▸◁ Modal Verbs and Modal-like Expressions: See page A25.

▶ Grammar Application

Exercise 3.1 Expressing Ability with *Be Able To* and *Know How To*

Complete the questions and answers about a class survey. Circle the correct words.

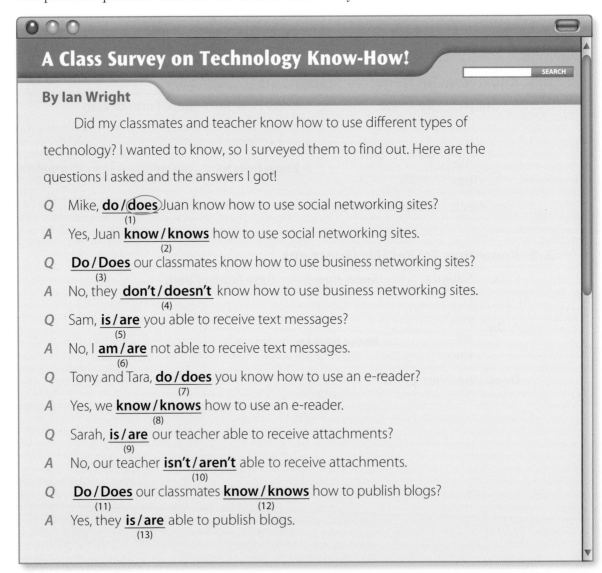

A Class Survey on Technology Know-How!

SEARCH

By Ian Wright

Did my classmates and teacher know how to use different types of technology? I wanted to know, so I surveyed them to find out. Here are the questions I asked and the answers I got!

Q   Mike, **do /(does)** Juan know how to use social networking sites?
           (1)

A   Yes, Juan **know / knows** how to use social networking sites.
                (2)

Q   **Do / Does** our classmates know how to use business networking sites?
    (3)

A   No, they **don't / doesn't** know how to use business networking sites.
            (4)

Q   Sam, **is / are** you able to receive text messages?
         (5)

A   No, I **am / are** not able to receive text messages.
         (6)

Q   Tony and Tara, **do / does** you know how to use an e-reader?
               (7)

A   Yes, we **know / knows** how to use an e-reader.
          (8)

Q   Sarah, **is / are** our teacher able to receive attachments?
         (9)

A   No, our teacher **isn't / aren't** able to receive attachments.
            (10)

Q   **Do / Does** our classmates **know / knows** how to publish blogs?
    (11)   (12)

A   Yes, they **is / are** able to publish blogs.
          (13)

Exercise 3.2 Expressing Ability with *Be Able To* and *Know How To*

A Complete the sentences with the correct form of *be able to* or *know how to*. Use the words in parentheses.

Queta and her husband, Marco, live in Texas, but right now Marco has a new job in Nigeria. For Marco, phone calls to Queta and their daughter, Daniela, are very expensive. Queta _knows how to_ (know how to) use a free Internet phone service, but Marco

_____ (not know how to) use it.
(2)

Also, Marco _____ (not be able to) talk to his family on his computer because his computer

is at work. He _____ (be able to) talk to Queta and Daniela at night only. However,

Queta and Daniela _____ (not be able to) talk at that time. That's because Marco's nighttime is their daytime. They _____ (not be able to) leave work or school at that time. Queta and Marco _____ (not know how to) solve this problem. Living so far apart is difficult! But they

_____ (be able to) send e-mails. For now, this is an easy solution to their problem.

B Complete the conversation with the correct form of *can* (*not*), *be* (*not*) *able to*, or (*not*) *know how to*. Sometimes there is more than one correct answer.

Jerry My phone bill is so expensive!

Mark Do you __*know how to*__ use a computer for
          (1)
         phone calls?

Jerry No, do you?

Mark Yes. I _____ use TalkNow.
                      (2)
         I _____ talk with anyone,
                (3)
         anywhere in the world for free!

Jerry Wow, is it very hard?

Mark No, it's really easy. Anyone _____ do it.
                                          (4)
         I learned how to use it after only 15 minutes.

Jerry _____ you _____ use a webcam with TalkNow?
              (5)   (5)

Mark No. There's no video with TalkNow, so you _____ see the other
                                                        (6)
         person. The sound is very clear, though, so you _____ hear
                                                                (7)
         them very well.

Jerry You're sure it's free?

Mark Yes, it's free. Absolutely free!

Jerry That's great! When _____ you teach me?
                                  (8)

Mark How about right now?

C *Pair Work* Work with a partner. Ask each other about some popular technology. Use
      Yes / *No* questions with *can, could, be able to,* and *know how to.*

      A Do you know how to take videos on your phone?
      B Yes, I do.
      A Are you able to use e-mail on your phone?

4 Avoid Common Mistakes ⚠️

1. There is only one form of *can* and *could*.

can
He ~~cans~~ send e-mail.

could
Ten years ago, she ~~coulds~~ only use a computer for typing reports.

2. Use the base form of the verb with *can* and *could*.

listen
Sue can ~~listens~~ to her MP3 player on the bus.

listen
Yesterday Sue could ~~listened~~ to music all day.

3. Do not use *to* with the base form of the verb.

I can ~~to~~ read a text message from my phone.

4. Use *could* to talk about ability in the past.

could not
Yesterday I ~~cannot~~ send an attachment.

Editing Task

Find and correct six more mistakes on Jenny's *Connected* page.

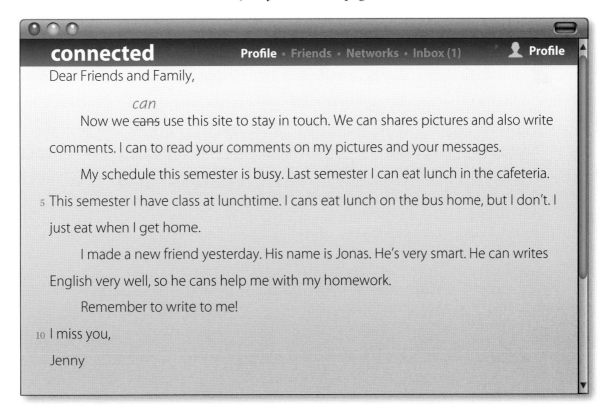

connected   Profile · Friends · Networks · Inbox (1)   👤 **Profile**

Dear Friends and Family,

can
    Now we ~~cans~~ use this site to stay in touch. We can shares pictures and also write comments. I can to read your comments on my pictures and your messages.

    My schedule this semester is busy. Last semester I can eat lunch in the cafeteria.
5 This semester I have class at lunchtime. I cans eat lunch on the bus home, but I don't. I just eat when I get home.

    I made a new friend yesterday. His name is Jonas. He's very smart. He can writes English very well, so he cans help me with my homework.

    Remember to write to me!

10 I miss you,

Jenny

5 | Grammar for Writing

Writing About Abilities

Writers use *can, could, be able to,* and *know how to* to write about present and past abilities. Remember:

- **Use *can (not)* for the present and *could (not)* for the past. Use *be (not) able to* and *(not) know how to* for the present or the past.**

  PRESENT   *He <u>can</u> use Excel. He <u>knows how to</u> use Word. He <u>is able to</u> make PowerPoint presentations.*

  PAST   *They <u>could not</u> use Excel last year. They <u>did not know how to</u> use Word before this semester. They <u>were not able to</u> make PowerPoint presentations last semester.*

Pre-writing Task

1 Read the paragraph below about students' new skills and abilities. What are some of the new skills it mentions?

New Skills and Abilities

First-year students learned English and other skills at school this year. Before entering school, many students could not understand much English. Now, after one year, they can understand their teachers and they are able to reply in English. Before school, many students didn't know how to register for classes, but now everyone knows how to choose classes, and they can even register for their classes online. Many students were not able to use computers. Now they know how to use computers. They know how to use different programs on the computers in the lab. Also, they can write their homework with Word, and they are able to e-mail their homework to their teachers. All of these skills are important to learn because they help students be successful in school.

2 Reread the paragraph and complete the chart with what the students learned for each skill. Include the verbs *can / could*, *are / were able to*, and *know how to*.

Skills	Before entering school, students...	After one year, students...
1. English	*could not understand much English.*	*can understand their teachers.* *are able to reply in English.*
2. Registering for classes		
3. Using computers		

Writing Task

1 *Write* Use the paragraph in the Pre-writing Task to help you write a paragraph about your own new skills or the new skills of other people. Compare the things you or others can do now with things you could do in the past. You can talk about new skills in:

- English
- school
- work
- home
- new technology

Use *can, could, be able to,* and *know how to.*

2 *Self-Edit* Use the editing tips below to help you improve your sentences. Make any necessary changes.

1. Did you start your paragraph with a general sentence about the place where you or the other people learned these skills?
2. Did you use all four ways to talk about abilities (*can, could, be able to, know how to*) in your paragraph?
3. Did you use the base form of the verb after *can, could, be able to,* and *know how to*?
4. Did you avoid the mistakes in the Avoid Common Mistakes chart on page 261?

1 | Grammar in the Real World

A Do you have an academic adviser? Read the academic adviser's web page. What are some things an academic adviser can help you with?

Department of Languages

SEARCH

Hello,

My name is Henry Driscoll, and I am one of the academic advisers for the Department of Languages. My job is to help you with your educational and career goals. Students often come to my office to ask questions. Here are some typical questions:

5
- **Can** you help me choose the right classes for my major?

- I want to take some courses in another department. **Could** you give me some advice, please?

10
- I need a tutor to help me with my English. **Can** you give me information about tutors, please?

- **May** I come to your office to talk with you about a problem I have?

- I have a financial problem. **Can** you help me?

15
- I have a problem with my classes. **Can** you help me with it?

Often my answer is, "Sure! No problem. Of course I can help." But sometimes I have to say, "Sorry, I **can't** help you with that" or "I'm sorry, I **can't** discuss that." For example, I **cannot** discuss questions about very personal issues, such as health or family problems. However, I **can** always refer[1] you to a person who can help you.

20
Here is my favorite question: "**Would** you come to our class and talk about your work as an academic adviser, please?" For that question, the answer is always YES!

For more information and FAQs,[2] go to the school's home page at www.DCweb. cambridge.org.

[1]**refer:** send you to a different place or to a person who knows more about or can help more with a subject
[2]**FAQs:** frequently asked questions

B Comprehension Check Answer the questions. Circle *Yes* or *No*. Use the article to help you.

1. Do students ask Henry different kinds of questions?   Yes   No
2. Does Henry discuss very personal problems?   Yes   No
3. Does Henry go to students' classes to talk about his work?   Yes   No
4. Can students find more common questions on the school's home page?   Yes   No

C Notice Find the student questions in the article. Complete the sentences.

1. _____ you help me choose the right classes for my major?
2. _____ you give me some advice, please?
3. _____ you give me information about tutors, please?
4. _____ you come to our class and talk about your work as an academic adviser, please?

What is the purpose of all these questions?

2 | *Can*, *Could*, and *Would* for Requests

▶ Grammar Presentation

We use *can*, *could*, and *would* to ask people to do things.	**Can** you help me, please? **Could** you give me some advice? **Would** you please help me with my paper?

2.1 *Can*, *Could*, and *Would* for Requests

Can / Could / Would	Subject	Base Form of Verb	
Can **Could** **Would**	you	advise	me about the program?
		open	the door for me, please?
		come	to our class and talk about your work, please?

2.2 Using *Can, Could,* and *Would* to Make Requests

a. Use *can*, *could*, and *would* to ask people to do something.	***Can*** you meet me at 2:00 p.m. today? ***Could*** you give me some advice? ***Would*** you reserve a seat for me, please?
b. *Could* and *would* are more polite than *can*. Use *could* and *would* in formal situations.	***Can*** you give me a call tonight? ***Could*** you advise me about my project, please? ***Would*** you help me write my résumé, please?
c. Use *please* when you ask a person you do not know well to do something.	*Excuse me. Can you tell me the way to Mason Street,* ***please****?*
Use *please* in formal situations.	*Would you* ***please*** *come this way?*
You can use *please* at the end of the sentence or after the subject.	*Could you sign this document,* ***please****?* *Could you* ***please*** *sign this document?*

▸▸ Modal Verbs and Modal-like Expressions: See page A25.

2.3 Answering Requests

a. When you agree to a request, you can give a short answer.	*"Can you come tonight?"* *"**Yes.**" / "**Yes, I can.**"*
You can include the request in your answer.	*"Can you help me?"* *"Yes, **I can help you.**"*
Often we say other words of agreement instead of *yes*. Informal Responses: *OK, sure, no problem* Formal Responses: *of course, certainly*	*"Could you please help me find the career adviser's office?"* *"**Sure** I can."* *"**Certainly**. Just follow that corridor. First door on the left."*

2.3 Answering Requests *(continued)*

b. We use *cannot* or *can't* in negative answers to requests, even when the request uses *could* or *would*.	*"Could you please give me your book?"* *"No, I **can't**. I don't have it with me."* *"Would you come to the meeting with us?"* *"No, I **can't**. Sorry, I'm busy."*
Can't is informal.	*"Can you help me with this vocabulary word?"* *"No, I **can't**. I don't know what it means."*
Cannot is more formal.	*"Could you help me with my health issues, please?"* *"No, I **cannot** discuss health problems with you."*
We often use *sorry* instead of *no*.	*"Would you like to go out tonight?"* *"**Sorry**, I can't. I have a lot of homework."*
I'm sorry is more formal than *sorry*.	*"Could you please tell me the time?"* *"**I'm sorry**. I **can't**. I don't have a watch."* *"Can you pass the dictionary?"* *"**Sorry**, I **can't** reach it."*
We often give a reason when we give a negative response to a request.	*"Would you speak to our class tomorrow?"* *"No, I'm sorry. **I can't. I'm in a conference all day**."* *"Can you help me tonight?"* *"Sorry, **I can't. I have to work**."*

▶ Grammar Application

Exercise 2.1 Using *Can*, *Could*, and *Would* in Requests and Answers

A 🔊 Complete the sentences with *can*, *could*, *would*, or *can't*. Then listen to the conversations. Check your answers.

Elena I need to talk to Professor Baker.

___*Can*___ you tell me what building
(1)
he's in?

Freda Yeah, sure. He's in the Ross Building.
I'm going there now. Come on! So,
what's up?

Elena Oh, it's just a problem about the
exams. _____ you come with me
(2)
to Professor Baker's office? Do you
know where it is?

Freda Yeah, sure. I met with him last
semester.

Elena When I finish with the professor,
_____ we meet up again later?
(3)

Freda Yeah, good idea!

Elena Just one problem. I don't know what
time the meeting finishes. _____
(4)
you wait for me in the cafeteria?

Freda No problem. I can do my homework.

Elena Hello, Professor Baker. Do you
have a minute?

Prof. Baker Certainly. _____ you close
(5)
the door, please?

Elena Of course. _____ you help
(6)
me, please? I have an exam next
Tuesday, and I have a family
wedding on that day. _____
(7)
you write a letter to the exam
professor about this?

Prof. Baker Oh, I'm sorry. I _____. A
(8)
family wedding is not an excuse
to miss an exam. That's the
college's policy.

Elena Oh! Really?

Prof. Baker I'm very sorry. Those are the
rules.

Elena Oh, well, OK. Thank you for your
time.

B *Pair Work* Practice the conversations in A with a partner.

Exercise 2.2 Making and Answering Requests

A Change the imperatives to questions. Use *can*, *could*, or *would*. Sometimes there is more than one correct answer.

1. Help me write my résumé.

   Can you help me write my résumé?

2. Meet me at the cafeteria after class today.

   _____

3. Tell me the things that I need to put in the résumé.

   _____

4. Show me your résumé.

   _____

5. Advise me on the correct style for a résumé.

   _____

6. Correct my mistakes.

   _____

7. Help me arrange my résumé so it looks good.

   _____

8. Read my résumé and make sure it's OK.

   _____

B *Pair Work* Work with a partner. Ask and answer the questions in A. First, agree to the requests. Use *sure*, *no problem*, and *of course*. Then give negative answers. Use *sorry* and *I'm sorry*. Give a good reason for your negative answers. Take turns.

A *Can you help me write my résumé?*	A *Can you help me write my résumé?*
B *Sure!*	B *Sorry, I can't help you. I'm really busy today.*

3 | *Can*, *Could*, and *May* for Permission

▶ Grammar Presentation

We use *can*, *could*, and *may* to ask for permission to do things.	**Can** I make an appointment for tomorrow? **May** I please come in? **Could** I ask you a question?

3.1 *Can*, *Could*, and *May* for Permission

Can / Could / May	Subject	Base Form of Verb	
Can **Could** **May**	I	use	this pencil?
		leave	early today?
		ask	a question?

3.2 Using *Can*, *Could*, and *May* for Permission

a. Use *can* in most situations.	**Can** I borrow your pen? **Can** I take a picture with your camera?
b. *Could* is more polite than *can*.	**Could** we use Room 208 for our student meeting?
Use *could* with strangers and people you do not know well.	**Could** I study with you for the exam?
Use *could* in formal situations.	**Could** I talk to you for a moment?
c. *May* is very polite.	Professor Wodak, **may** I interview you for the student newspaper, please?
Use *may* with people you do not know well in very formal situations.	**May** I use your pen for a moment?
d. *Please* can make a request for permission more polite.	
Use *please* when you ask a person you do not know well for permission.	Can I use this telephone, **please**?
Use *please* in formal situations.	May I use your pen for a moment, **please**?
Use *please* at the end of the request or after the subject.	Doctor Takano, may I **please** ask a question about my project? May I ask a question about my project, **please**?

▸ Modal Verbs and Modal-like Expressions: See page A25.

3.3 Answering Requests for Permission

a. When you agree to a request for permission, you can give a short answer.	*"Can I sit in this chair?"* **"Yes."**
You can include the request in your answer.	*"Could I work in your group?"* **"Sure**, *you can work in our group!"*
Often we say other words of agreement instead of *yes*. Informal responses: *sure, no problem, go ahead* Formal responses: *of course, certainly*	*"Can I see your homework?"* **"No problem**!*"* *"May I contact you by e-mail?"* **"Of course."**
b. We often use *sorry* when we give a negative answer to a request for permission. People do not usually say *no*. They say *sorry* and give a reason.	*"Could I see that?"* **"Sorry**. *It's not mine."*
I'm sorry is more formal than *sorry*.	*"Can I speak to you for a moment?"* **"I'm sorry**. *I'm very busy. Maybe after class?"*

▶ # Grammar Application

Exercise 3.1 Requests for Permission with *Can*, *Could*, and *May*

A Complete the requests. Circle the best answer.

1. To a friend: (Can) / **May** I call you later?

2. To a professor: **May** / **Could** I leave early today?

3. To a stranger: **Can** / **May** I look at your bus schedule for a moment?

4. To a friend: **Could** / **May** I see your phone?

5. To a boss: **May** / **Could** I speak to you for a moment?

6. To a friend: **May** / **Can** we finish this tomorrow?

B *Pair Work* Practice saying and answering the requests in A with a partner. Give some affirmative answers and some negative answers.

A *Can I call you later?*   A *Can I call you later?*
B *Sure. Call me anytime.*   B *Sorry, I'm busy tonight. I can call you tomorrow.*

Exercise 3.2 More Requests for Permission

A Complete the chart. Who is the speaker? Where does the request take place? Use your own ideas.

A student	A professor	A boss	A co-worker	Who?	Where?
1. Can I sit next to you, Joanna?				*student*	*in class/ in a café*
2. Could I please leave early today, Professor?					
3. May I have next Monday off, please? It's my birthday.					
4. Could I use your office for an hour today?					
5. May I use your telephone, please?					
6. Could I please make two copies of my report?					
7. Can I have one of your French fries?					
8. May I please talk to you about my schedule?					
9. Can I look at your project? There are problems with mine.					

B *Pair Work* With a partner, write answers to the requests in A. Practice saying and answering the requests.

A *Can I sit next to you, Joanna?*
B *Sure!*

A *Could I leave early today, Professor?*
B *I'm sorry. You left early yesterday.*

Exercise 3.3 Formal Requests for Permission

Complete the sentences with the words in parentheses. Reorder the words to make requests for permission.

---

send **attach** **save draft** **forward** **close**

To: Professor Machado

Subject: Interview for *English Now* Newsletter

Dear Professor Machado,

My name is Ricardo Yaka. I am the editor of the *English Now* newsletter.

May I interview you (I/interview/may/you) for about 15 minutes for this
(1)
month's newsletter? _____ (come/could/I/to
(2)
your office/please) for the interview?

The newsletter often has articles about the lives of faculty members. We
know that students like to read about their professors' college experiences.

_____ (ask/I/may/you) about your
(3)
college days? To make it easy for you, _____
(4)
(can/you/I/please/send) a list of my questions?

The articles in our newsletters are informal, and many have photographs.

_____ (please/I/could/take) your
(5)
picture? You can see a copy of the newsletter before the interview.

_____ (e-mail/I/may) it to you?
(6)
The newsletter is very popular. About 200 students read the interviews
every month, and more students read the newsletter on the Internet.

_____ (I/may/please/put) your interview on
(7)
our website, too?

After you have read the questions, _____
(8)
(visit/I/could/please) you at your office sometime this week?

Thank you very much. I look forward to your reply.

Kind regards,

Ricardo Yaka

Exercise 3.4 More Requests for Permission

Write a request for permission based on each situation.

1. You want to come in late for work tomorrow. Ask your boss.
   Could I come in late tomorrow, please? / May I
   please come in late tomorrow?

2. You want to use your best friend's pen. Ask him/her.

   _____

3. You want to change the channel on the TV at home. Ask a family member.

   _____

4. You want to hand in your homework one day late. Ask your teacher.

   _____

5. You want to speak to your boss after work today. Ask him/her.

   _____

6. You want to borrow your classmate's electronic dictionary. Ask him/her.

   _____

7. You want to charge your cell phone in the school office. Ask the secretary.

   _____

8. You want to use the atlas behind the reference desk in the library. Ask the librarian.

   _____

9. You want to borrow your roommate's bicycle. Ask him/her.

   _____

10. You want to get your professor's e-mail address. Ask him/her.

   _____

4 Avoid Common Mistakes ⚠️

1. **Use the correct word order for making requests.**

   Can you
   ~~You can~~ help me?

2. **Use the base form of the verb after *can*, *could*, *may*, or *would*.**

   help
   Can you ~~to help~~ me?

3. **Use *can*, *could*, or *would* to ask people to do something. Do not use *do*.**

   Would
   ~~Do~~ you come to my office, please?

4. **Use *can*, *could*, or *would* to ask people to do something. Do not use *may*.**

   Could
   ~~May~~ you reserve a place for me, please?

Editing Task

Find and correct eight more mistakes in this e-mail about a college music show.

| send | attach | save draft | forward | close |

To: Dance Club

Subject: End-of-Semester Music Show

Hi Everyone,

    The show is next week!

        Can you
- Everyone: ~~You can~~ please make a list of the equipment you need?

- Gregori: You can tell me how many microphones we need?

5 • Jason: Could we to borrow your microphone, please? Thanks!

- Anna: We need a laptop from the computer lab. Can you to pick it up today?

- Jessie: May you contact Mr. Sparks about the lights?

- Hector: Your job is to get the chairs. You can please arrange that?

- Mari: Mr. Sanchez has the music CDs. Do you please contact him?

10 • Hong-yin: May we to borrow your projector, please?

    Finally, may you all please come to the meeting at 2:00 p.m. tomorrow in Room 305?

Thanks!
Kazuo

5 | Grammar for Writing ✎

Writing to Ask for Permission and to Make Requests

Writers use *can*, *could*, *may*, and *would* to make requests and to ask permission for something in letters or e-mails.
Remember:

- **Use different request and permission words for different situations.**

  To make a request or to ask permission, use *can* with friends and in informal situations.

REQUEST	PERMISSION
Can you give me a ride to school?	*Can I use your cell phone?*

  To be polite, use *could*, *may*, and *would* to make a request or to ask permission.

REQUEST	PERMISSION
Would you help me fill out this form?	*Could you please e-mail me the newsletter?*

Pre-writing Task

1 Read the e-mail. What is the purpose of the e-mail? Circle one.

a. to ask permission
b. to request help
c. both a and b

Dear Professor Harper:

Could I miss my grammar tutoring appointment today? I'm very sorry, but my boss called me this morning. He needs me at work this afternoon because a co-worker is sick and she can't go to work. Would you have time for an appointment tomorrow morning? I am at school every Wednesday from 8:00 a.m. until noon. Also, may I bring a paper for my writing class to our appointment, too? The paper is due on Thursday. Would you be able to help me with my grammar mistakes on that paper?

Sincerely,

Clara Marcos

2 Reread the e-mail and underline the request and permission words. Is this e-mail formal or informal?

Writing Task

1 *Write* Use the e-mail in the Pre-writing Task to help you write a letter or an e-mail. In your letter or e-mail, make a request and ask permission for something. Use one of the situations below.

- Write to your boss to make a request, like a change in your work hours.
- Reply to a job advertisement.
- Write to a teacher to make a request or ask permission for something, such as help with an assignment.
- Write to a school you want to go to, and ask for information.
- Write to a landlord to ask him/her to fix something in your house or apartment.
- Your own idea

Use the base form of the verb after *can, could, may,* and *would.*

2 *Self-Edit* Use the editing tips below to help you improve your sentences. Make any necessary changes.

1. Did you use *can, could,* and/or *would* to make requests?
2. Did you use *can, could,* or *may* to ask permission?
3. Did you write sentences to explain your requests or your requests for permission?
4. Did you avoid the mistakes in the Avoid Common Mistakes chart on page 275?

Present Progressive

Body Language

1 | Grammar in the Real World

A What do you do during a conversation? Do you smile? Do you cross your arms? Do you nod your head? Do you make eye contact? Read the article below about body language. Why is it important?

Understanding Body Language

Body language is a crucial[1] part of face-to-face communication. Some experts[2] say that 93 percent of communication is nonverbal.[3] Of course, the meaning of body language varies from culture to culture. Even in one culture, experts do not always agree on the meaning of every gesture.[4] However, here are some things to remember
5 for your next conversation, meeting, or interview. They apply mostly to communication in North America.

How **Are** You **Sitting**?

Lean[5] toward the other person to show you are interested in what he or she **is saying**. Nod to
10 show **you are listening**.

Are You **Crossing** Your Arms?

Crossing your arms can seem defensive.[6] In an argument, it can mean you don't agree.

What **Are** Your Hands **Doing**?

15   Keep your hands out and open. Some experts say that when you keep your hands under the table, it can mean you **are not telling** the truth. However, a hand on the chin can just mean you **are thinking**.

20 ### Where **Are** You **Looking**?

Make eye contact. When you **are talking** to someone face-to-face, it is important to look at them. This shows that you **are listening** to them.

Learn to use positive body language. After all, what you *do* may communicate more than 90 percent of your message.

[1]**crucial:** extremely important | [2]**expert:** a person with a high level of knowledge or skill about a subject | [3]**nonverbal:** not spoken | [4]**gesture:** a movement of the body, hands, arms, or head to express an idea or feeling | [5]**lean:** move your body so it's bent forward | [6]**defensive:** wanting to protect or defend oneself

B *Comprehension Check* What can these gestures mean? Use the article to help you. Circle *a* or *b*.

1. A person is leaning toward you in a conversation.

   a. He doesn't like what you are saying.   b. He is interested.

2. Your friend is crossing her arms during an argument.

   a. She doesn't agree with you.   b. She is thinking about something else.

3. A person is touching her chin a lot during a discussion.

   a. She is thinking.   b. Maybe she's lying.

C *Notice* Complete these sentences. Use the forms of the verbs from the article.

1. Nod to show you _____ (listen).

2. Some experts say that when you keep your hands under the table, it can mean you _____ not _____ (tell) the truth.

3. However, a hand on the chin can just mean you _____ (think).

Look at the verb forms. How many parts does each verb have? What do they have in common?

2 Present Progressive Statements

▶ Grammar Presentation

The present progressive describes actions and events that are in progress now and around the present time. "In progress" means the action started before now but is not finished or complete.	*He **is not listening** to the professor.* *We **are studying** body language in my psychology class.*

2.1 Affirmative Statements

Subject	*Be*	Verb + *-ing*	Contractions
I	am		I am → I'm
You We They	are	talking.	You are → You're We are → We're They are → They're He is → He's She is → She's It is → It's
He She It	is		

2.2 Negative Statements

Subject	*Be + Not*	Verb + *-ing*	Contractions		
I	**am not**		I am not → **I'm not**		
You We They	**are not**	**talking**.	You are not → You**'re not** We are not → We**'re not** They are not → They**'re not**	You **aren't** We **aren't** They **aren't**	
He She It	**is not**		He is not → He**'s not** She is not → She**'s not** It is not → It**'s not**	He **isn't** She **isn't** It **isn't**	

2.3 Spelling *-ing* Forms

a. For most verbs, add *-ing*.

talk → talk**ing**
say → say**ing**
go → go**ing**

b. If the verb ends in a silent *-e*, delete *e* and add *-ing*.

liv**e** → liv**ing**
mak**e** → mak**ing**
writ**e** → writ**ing**

c. For *be* and *see,* don't <u>drop</u> the *e* because it is not silent.

be → be**ing**
see → see**ing**

d. If the verb ends in *-ie*, change the *ie* to *y* and add *-ing*.

l**ie** → l**ying**

e. If the verb has one syllable and follows the pattern consonant – vowel – consonant (CVC), double the last letter and add *-ing*.

sit → sit**ting**
put → put**ting**
get → get**ting**

f. Do not double the consonant if the verb ends in *-w, -x,* or *-y*.

gro**w** → grow**ing**
fi**x** → fix**ing**
sa**y** → say**ing**

g. If the verb has two syllables, ends in the pattern CVC, and is stressed on the last syllable, double the last letter and add *-ing*.

begin → begin**ning**

h. If the verb has two syllables and is stressed on the first syllable, do not double the last letter before adding *-ing*.

listen → listen**ing**
travel → travel**ing**
visit → visit**ing**

▸▪ Spelling Rules for Verbs Ending in *-ing*: See page A20.

2.4 Using Present Progressive

a. Use the present progressive for actions in progress as you write or speak. The action is not finished.	*I **am writing** for information about . . . (in a letter)* *Look at that man. He**'s talking** to that woman, but he**'s** not **smiling**.*
b. You can also use the present progressive for actions in progress "around now," at the present time.	*I **am studying** psychology this semester.* *This week we**'re looking** at body language.*
c. Use contractions in speaking.	*He**'s taking** psychology this semester.*
Do not use contractions in very formal writing.	*I **am writing** to express my interest in this job. . . . (in a letter)*
d. You can use the present progressive with present time expressions like *now, right now, at the moment, this week / month, these days.*	*Sorry, I can't talk. I**'m going** into class **right now**.* *I**'m working** two jobs **at the moment**.*

▶ # Grammar Application

Exercise 2.1 Present Progressive Verb Forms

A Complete the sentences below using the present progressive. Use contractions when possible.

1. The woman _is talking_ (talk).
2. She _____ (lean) toward the man.
3. He _____ (smile).
4. The man _____ (listen) to her.
5. They _____ (make) eye contact.
6. They _____ (get) along.

7. The man and woman _____ (not get along).
8. They _____ (not smile).
9. The woman _____ (not look) at the man.
10. She _____ (lean) away from him.
11. She _____ (not talk).
12. Maybe they _____ (have) an argument.

B *Pair Work* With a partner, describe some more things the people in A are doing. Use these verbs or your own ideas. Write affirmative and negative sentences for each picture.

drink   eat   laugh   look   sit   talk

Exercise 2.2 Statements

A What are the people doing before class? Use the words to write sentences about them. Use the present progressive.

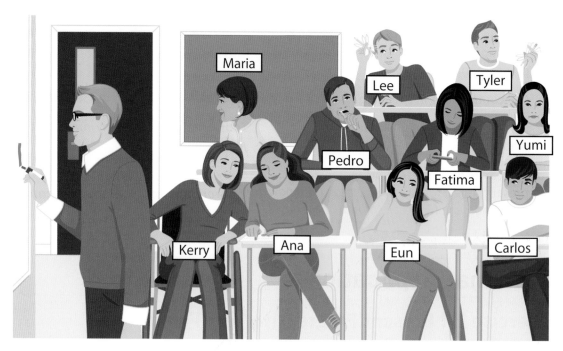

1. Fatima / text her friend   _Fatima is texting her friend._

2. Pedro / chew his pen _____

3. Carlos and Eun / not sit up straight _____

4. Ana and Kerry / talk _____

5. Lee and Tyler / not look each other in the eye _____

6. Yumi / not smile _____

7. Maria / stare at the door _____

8. The teacher / write on the board _____

B *Over to You* Look around your classroom. What are people doing? Write three affirmative sentences and three negative sentences about your classmates. Then compare your sentences with a partner.

Exercise 2.3 Vocabulary Focus: Time Expressions

There are many time expressions you can use with the present progressive. These are some:

| (right) now | at the moment | tonight | today | this morning / afternoon / evening |
| this week | this semester | this month | this year | |

| You can put a time expression at the beginning or at the end of a sentence. You usually put a comma after the time expression if it is at the beginning of a sentence. If the time expression is just one word, you don't have to use a comma. | **Right now,** I'm typing a letter.

Julia is listening to her professor **at the moment**.

Today I'm studying for an exam. |

Complete the e-mail. Use the present progressive form of the verbs in parentheses and an appropriate time expression (TE) from the box. More than one time expression can be correct.

---

send   attach   save draft   forward   close

To: Josh

From: Alex

Subject: How's it going?

Hi Josh,

How are you? How's college? I'm fine. I _'m sitting_ (sit) in a classroom _right now_ (TE).
(1)   (2)
I _____ (wait) for class to start. _____ (TE), we
           (3)   (4)
_____ (study) communication. I _____ (enjoy) it.
        (5)   (6)
_____ (TE), I _____ (write) a paper on nonverbal
        (7)   (8)
communication. I _____ (take) a marketing class _____ (TE), too.
                          (9)   (10)

I _____ (not play) a lot of sports _____ (TE). I'm too busy!
         (11)   (12)
I _____ (work) in a grocery store. My parents _____ (plan) a trip
         (13)   (14)
to Mexico in the summer, and I _____ (save) some money to go with them.
                                         (15)

What else is new? Oh, my cousin _____ (stay)
                                          (16)
with us. I think he _____ (enjoy) his time with us.
                 (17)

OK. That's all for now. Class _____ (start).
                                        (18)
Write to me soon,

Alex

Exercise 2.4 Negative Contractions

Research shows that in speaking, people usually use the negative forms *'s not* and *'re not*, especially after pronouns.	He / She / It's not . . . ing / You / We / They're not . . . ing He / She / It isn't . . . ing / You / We / They aren't . . . ing
People often say *isn't* and *aren't* with names and nouns when it is difficult to add *'s not* and *'re not*.	*Marcos **isn't** working.* (names and nouns) *He**'s not** working.* (pronouns)

Complete the conversation with negative contractions. Then listen and check your answers.

Carla Hey, Rod. You<u>'re not studying</u> (study) today?
(1)

Rod No, Chris _____ (come) to class today.
(2)

Carla You're doing a project together, right?

Rod Yes, with Jon, Lisa, and Cristina . . . but it _____ (go) well.
(3)

We _____ (get) along well, either.
(4)

Carla Really? Why not?

Rod Well, Chris _____ (do) his share of the work. He
(5)

_____ (read) the books, and he _____ (come)
(6)   (7)

to meetings with the group.

Carla What do the others in the group think?

Rod They _____ (feel) too happy with him. In fact, they
(8)

_____ (speak) to him. We wrote a letter to the teacher about him.
(9)

Carla Maybe it's time to talk to him about it. I know he _____ (do)
(10)

a good job, but maybe there's a reason for it.

Rod I guess we _____ (give) him a chance to explain.
(11)

3 | Present Progressive Questions

▶ Grammar Presentation

Present progressive questions ask about actions and events that are in progress now and around the present time.

Are you crossing your arms?
What are your hands doing?
What are you studying?

3.1 *Yes / No* Questions

Be	Subject	Verb + *-ing*
Am	I	
Are	you we they	**working**?
Is	he / she / it	

3.2 Short Answers

AFFIRMATIVE	NEGATIVE	
Yes, I **am**.	No, I**'m not**.	
Yes, you **are**.	No, you**'re not**.	No, you **aren't**.
Yes, we **are**.	No, we**'re not**.	No, we **aren't**.
Yes, they **are**.	No, they**'re not**.	No, they **aren't**.
Yes, he / she / it **is**.	No, he / she / it**'s not**.	No, he / she / it **isn't**.

3.3 Information Questions

Wh- Word	*Be*	Subject	Verb + *-ing*
Who	**am**	I	**hearing**?
What			**feeling**?
When	**are**	you we they	**leaving**?
Where			**studying**?
Why			**laughing**?
How	**is**	he / she / it	**going**?

Wh- Word as Subject	*Be*	Verb + *-ing*
Who	**is**	**talking**?
What		**happening**?

3.4 Using Present Progressive Questions

a. Use the present progressive to ask questions about actions in progress as you write or speak. The action is not finished.

Look at that man. **Is** *he* **talking** *to that woman?*

b. Use the present progressive to ask questions about actions in progress at the present time (now) or "around now."

" **Are** *you* **studying** *for an exam?" "Yes."*
"What **are** *you* **doing***?" "I'm studying."*

c. The *Wh-* word is sometimes the subject.

" **Who***'s studying in the library now?"*
"Jo and Marta."
" **What***'s going on?" "We're studying."*

d. You can use the present progressive with present time expressions like *now, right now, at the moment, this week / month,* and *these days* to ask questions.

Are you going into class **right now***?*
Are you working two jobs **at the moment***?*

e. Time expressions always come at the end of the question, not at the beginning.

What are they talking about **right now***?*
Is she crossing her arms **at the moment***?*

▶ ## Grammar Application

Exercise 3.1 Yes / No Questions and Answers

Write the questions and answers. Use the correct form of the verbs in parentheses.

Ashley Hi, Jack. <u>Am</u> I <u>disturbing</u> (disturb) you?
                   (1)   (1)

Jack No, _____ . Not at all.
           (2)

Ashley _____ you _____ (study)?
         (3)   (3)

Jack Yes, _____ . Well, kind of.
              (4)

Ashley Oh, _____ you _____ (watch) a movie?
          (5)   (5)

Jack No, _____ . It's a video for my French class.
            (6)

Ashley _____ the actors _____ (speak) French?
         (7)   (7)

Jack Yes, _____ . I think that guy _____ (say), "I love you."
           (8)   (9)

Ashley _____ you _____ (tell) me you can't understand it?
         (10)   (10)

Jack Well, yes. I only started my French class last week!

Exercise 3.2 Forming Questions and Answers

A Unscramble the words to make present progressive questions.

1. notes? / you / are / taking

   Are you taking notes?

2. doing / what / your classmates / are / right now?

   _____

3. is / your teacher / what / saying?

   _____

4. to the teacher? / listening / who / is

   _____

5. right now? / happening / is / what / in class

   _____

6. are / up straight? / you / sitting

   _____

B *Pair Work* Ask and answer the questions in A with a partner.

4 | Present Progressive and Simple Present

▶ Grammar Presentation

The present progressive describes actions and events that are in progress now and around the present time. The simple present describes things that happen repeatedly or all the time.	I'm *studying* psychology right now. I **take** four classes every semester.

4.1 Present Progressive and Simple Present

a. Use the present progressive for actions and events in progress now.	I'm **writing** an essay about body language. Sorry, I can't talk. I'm **going** into class.
Use the simple present for repeated actions and events.	I **write** one essay every month. I **go** to school on Mondays and Wednesdays.

4.1 Present Progressive and Simple Present *(continued)*

b. Use the present progressive for temporary events.	A friend **is visiting** this week. She**'s staying** with me.
Use the simple present for permanent situations.	I **come** from Ohio, but my family **lives** in Texas.
c. Use the present progressive with present time expressions like *right now*, *at the moment*, and *today*.	I'm riding the train **at the moment**. (on the phone) **Right now,** I'm going to work.
Use the simple present with frequency adverbs like *often*, *never*, *every week*, etc.	I **often** look at people on the subway and **watch** their behavior. Do you **usually** smile when you **meet** new people?

4.2 Non-active or Stative Verbs

a. Stative verbs describe states, not actions.	I **don't like** rude people. NOT I'm not liking rude people.
These are some stative verbs: *love, know, want, need, seem, mean,* and *agree*. Use the simple present with stative verbs, not the present progressive.	What **do** you **know** about this? NOT What are you knowing? They **seem** upset. NOT They are seeming upset. Experts **don't agree** on the meaning of some gestures. NOT Experts are not agreeing on the meaning of some gestures.
b. Some verbs have a stative meaning and an action meaning.	STATIVE I **think** grammar is fun. (= an opinion) ACTION I**'m thinking** about my homework. (= using my mind) STATIVE The book **looks** interesting. (= appears) ACTION We**'re looking** at the book right now. (= using our eyes) STATIVE **Do** you **have** a dog? (= own) ACTION **Are** you **having** a good time? (= experiencing)
c. You can use *feel* with the same meaning in the simple present and the present progressive.	I **feel** tired today. OR I**'m feeling** tired today. How **do** you **feel**? OR How **are** you **feeling**?

▶▶ Stative (Non-Action) Verbs: See page A26.

▶ Grammar Application

Exercise 4.1 Statements

Complete the sentences about students in an English class with the present progressive or the simple present. Use the verbs in parentheses.

1. In our English class, I normally _sit_ (sit) up straight.
2. Right now, my friend José _____ (relax) in a comfortable chair.
3. Our classmate Maria _____ (cross) her arms a lot when she listens.
4. In conversations, I usually _____ (make) eye contact with my partner, Sara.
5. Sara often _____ (chew) on her pens and pencils when she's nervous.
6. Three other students _____ (chew) gum at the moment.
7. No one _____ (sit) quietly in class right now!
8. Our teacher usually _____ (stand) in class when she lectures.

Exercise 4.2 Vocabulary Focus: Some Common Stative Verbs

Possession	have, own
Feelings, wants, and needs	be, feel, hate, like, love, mind, need, want
Senses	hear, look (= seem), seem, sound, feel
Thought	agree, believe, know, mean, remember, think, understand

A Complete the questions with the present progressive or the simple present.

1. __Do__ you _____own_____ (own) a car?
2. _____ you _____ (look) for a new car right now?
3. _____ your voice _____ (sound) soft or loud?
4. _____ your last name _____ (mean) anything?
5. _____ you usually _____ (understand) movies in English?
6. _____ you _____ (read) anything interesting at the moment?
7. _____ you _____ (like) English grammar?
8. _____ you _____ (mind) working late on weekends?
9. _____ you _____ (feel) tired after school?

B *Pair Work* Ask and answer the questions in A with a partner.

Exercise 4.3 Present Progressive or Simple Present?

A professor is showing a video to the class. Complete the sentences using the present progressive or the simple present form of the verbs. Some sentences are negative.

Children and Body Language

The children in this video _are playing_ (play).
(1)

They _____ (not know) that we
(2)

_____ (film) them. They _____
(3)   (4)

(look) busy, don't they?

These little girls _____ (not sit) on
(5)

the floor. They _____ (look) at each other.
(6)

They _____ (make) eye contact. They
(7)

_____ (talk) about their friends. They
(8)

_____ (seem) very happy together.
(9)

_____ you _____ (agree)?
(10)   (10)

It _____ (seem) that little girls often
(11)

_____ (talk) about their friends. They often
(12)

_____ (tell) secrets, too. When little girls talk,
(13)

they _____ (like) to look at their friends. On
(14)

the other hand, little boys usually _____ (play)
(15)

games. In general, they _____ (not look) at their
(16)

friends. They often _____ (sit) side by side.
(17)

5 | Avoid Common Mistakes

1. **To form the present progressive, use *be* and verb + *-ing*.**

   am
   I living in a dorm this semester.

   studying
   I am ~~study~~ business administration.

2. **Check the spelling of the *-ing* verb form.**

   writing
   I'm ~~writeing~~ a paper on psychology.

3. **Use present progressive for temporary and ongoing activities at the present time.**

   am writing
   Right now, I ~~write~~ an essay on reality shows.

Editing Task

Find and correct nine more mistakes in this student's essay and progress report.

Talent Shows

are
Talent shows becoming a very popular form of entertainment these days. The

contestants[1] in the shows trying to be famous. They sing every week. Millions of people

watch these shows every week.

People like the shows for a number of reasons. First, the shows have good music.

5 For example, this season they are includeing a woman who sings opera. Second, viewers

can vote for the winners every week. Third, the contestants in the shows come from

ordinary backgrounds.

[1]**contestant:** someone who competes in a game show

Progress Report—Psychology 111

In my group, we study one talent show this semester called *Have You Got

It?* We are look at the body language of the contestants. We are try to see how it

changes. I looking at hand gestures, and I am writeing a paper about the hand

gestures of the losers. The paper goes well. I finding some interesting things to

write about.

6 Grammar for Writing ✎

Writing About What You See

> Writers often use the present progressive and the simple present together when they write about their lives at the moment.
> Remember:
>
> - **Use the present progressive to describe what is happening around you and for temporary activities in your life or in others' lives.**
>   *Everyone is working hard on their homework.*   *We are taking three classes this semester.*
> - **Use the simple present with stative verbs.**
>   *We have a couple of hours of homework every night.*

Pre-writing Task

1 Read the e-mail. Where is Caitlin, and what is she doing?

Hi Mei,

I'm in the lab at school at the moment. There are a lot of students here. All the computers are busy. It's very noisy and crowded. Marc is sitting next to me. He's not working, though. He is e-mailing someone. He looks angry because he is sitting with his
5 arms crossed. I wonder who he is writing to! Our teacher is walking around. Some of the students are raising their hands for help. There are a lot of students who need help! I don't need help. My class seems easy this semester. I understand everything. I'm doing research for a paper on weather changes. It's pretty interesting. The weather is very nice here right now. How's the weather there these days? I'm looking for more ideas for my paper.

10 That's all from me for the moment,

Caitlin

2 Read the e-mail again. Underline the present progressive verbs and circle the simple present stative verbs.

Writing Task

1 *Write* Use the e-mail in the Pre-writing Task to help you write an e-mail to a friend about what you are doing at the moment. Imagine you are sitting in a room with other people. Describe the people around you. What are those people doing? Describe someone's body language. What feelings does it show? Use the present progressive and the simple present with stative verbs. Use some time expressions with your present progressive verbs.

2 *Self-Edit* Use the editing tips below to improve your sentences. Make any necessary changes.

1. Did you use the present progressive and the simple present to write an e-mail about your life at the moment?
2. Did you use the present progressive to describe what you and other people around you are doing?
3. Did you use the simple present with stative verbs to write about your life?
4. Did you avoid the mistakes in the Avoid Common Mistakes chart on page 291?

Past Progressive and Simple Past

Inventions and Discoveries

1 | Grammar in the Real World

A Can you think of an accidental invention or discovery? Read the magazine article below about the invention of Post-its. Who had the idea of using glue with bookmarks?

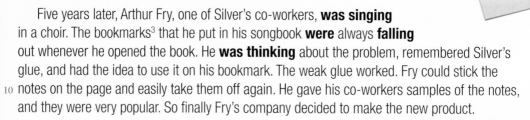

A Great Invention

In 1968, Spencer Silver, a researcher[1] for the company 3M, **was trying** to make a strong glue, but he actually invented a very weak glue. The glue stuck[2] things together, but they could separate easily. Silver showed the invention to his company's management,
5 but they weren't interested. They didn't see a use for it.

Five years later, Arthur Fry, one of Silver's co-workers, **was singing** in a choir. The bookmarks[3] that he put in his songbook **were** always **falling** out whenever he opened the book. He **was thinking** about the problem, remembered Silver's glue, and had the idea to use it on his bookmark. The weak glue worked. Fry could stick the
10 notes on the page and easily take them off again. He gave his co-workers samples of the notes, and they were very popular. So finally Fry's company decided to make the new product.

In 1980, Post-its were in stores nationwide. Marketing of the invention was easy. Everyone wanted to buy the small sticky notes. Today the whole world uses Post-it notes. Most people do not realize that this invention was just a lucky accident: Silver and Fry **were trying** to solve two
15 different problems, and Fry saw the connection. Thanks to Fry, we now have a product that we can't live without!

[1]**researcher:** a person who studies a subject in order to discover new information about it │ [2]**stuck:** simple past of *stick* │ [3]**bookmark:** something you can put between pages in a book to show where you stopped reading

B *Comprehension Check* Answer the questions. Use the article to help you.

1. In 1968, what was Spencer Silver's job?
2. What did he make?
3. What did Arthur Fry use Silver's invention for?
4. What product did the company make based on Silver's and Fry's ideas?

C *Notice* Find the sentences in the article. Write the missing verbs. Notice that there are two lines for the verbs.

1. In 1968, Spencer Silver, a researcher for the company 3M, _____ _____ to make a strong glue.

2. Five years later, Arthur Fry, one of Silver's coworkers, _____ _____ in a choir.

3. He _____ _____ about the problem.

4. Silver and Fry _____ _____ to solve two different problems.

What are the first words in each verb? What ending is on the second word in each verb?

2 | Past Progressive

▶ Grammar Presentation

The past progressive describes things that were in progress at a specific time in the past.	*Arthur Fry **was singing** in a choir.* *I **was studying** psychology last semester.*

2.1 Statements

AFFIRMATIVE				NEGATIVE			
Subject	**Past of *Be***	**Verb + *-ing***		**Subject**	**Past of *Be* + *Not***	**Verb + *-ing***	
I He She It	**was**	**working**.		I He She It	**was not / wasn't**	**working**.	
You We They	**were**			You We They	**were not / weren't**		

2.2 *Yes / No* Questions

Past of *Be*	Subject	Verb + *-ing*
Was	I he she it	**working**?
Were	you we they	

Short Answers

AFFIRMATIVE				NEGATIVE		
	Subject	Past of *Be*			Subject	Past of *Be* + *Not*
Yes,	I he she it	**was**.	No,		I he she it	**was not.** **wasn't.**
	you we they	**were**.			you we they	**were not.** **weren't.**

2.3 Information Questions

Wh- Word	Past of Be	Subject	Verb + -ing
Who		I	**studying**?
What	**was**	he	**doing**?
When		she it	**researching**?
Where			**working**?
Why	**were**	you we they	**experimenting**?
How			**feeling**?

Wh- Word as Subject	Past of Be	Verb + -ing
Who	was	**talking**?
What	was	**happening**?

▶▶I Spelling Rules for Verbs Ending in -ing: See page A20.

2.4 Using Past Progressive

a. Use the past progressive to talk about an event in progress at a specific time in the past.

In 2010, I **was working** in a science lab.
"**Were** you **studying** in the cafeteria at lunchtime?"   "No. I **was studying** in the library."

b. Use information questions to ask about events in progress at a specific time in the past.

Why were the researchers **working** all night?
What was Lucy **wearing** at the party?
Who were you **talking** to this morning?

c. Use the full negative forms when writing in class.

The machine **was not working**.

Use negative contractions in everyday speaking.

I **wasn't working** yesterday afternoon.

▶ Grammar Application

Exercise 2.1 Past Progressive Statements

A Complete the sentences with the past progressive form of the verb in parentheses.

1. I ____was surfing____ (surf) the Web the other day, and I found out some interesting information about inventions.

2. In 1968, another scientist, Spencer Silver, __was trying__ (try) to make a strong glue, but he made a very good weak glue. Arthur Fry, a co-worker, put the glue on small pieces of paper and used the sticky papers at work. Soon the other co-workers

were using (use) the sticky papers, too. The sticky papers became Post-its.

3. In 1945, a scientist named Percy Spencer _was experimenting_ (experiment) with microwave energy. He _was standing_ (stand) too close to a machine when it melted a peanut candy bar in his pocket. The machine became the first microwave oven.

4. In 1930, Ruth Wakefield _was making_ (make) cookies for customers at her restaurant. She put small pieces of chocolate in the cookies and called them chocolate chip cookies. Soon Wakefield's customers _was asking_ (ask) her for the cookie recipe, and it is now on bags of chocolate chips.

5. In 1853, George Crum, a chef at a New York restaurant, _was feeling_ (feel) unhappy with a customer. The customer _was refusing_ (refuse) to eat his potatoes because they were too thick. So Crum cut the potatoes into thin slices and fried them, and they became the first potato chips.

B *Pair Work* Ask and answer *Wh-* questions with *Who* as the subject about the inventors in A. Use the past progressive.

A *Who was feeling unhappy with a customer?*

B *George Crum was feeling unhappy because a customer wasn't eating his food.*

Data from the Real World

The past progressive is used most commonly with verbs of speaking and thinking, such as *talk, think, say, wonder,* and *ask*.	What **were** you **talking** about at breakfast? Fry **was thinking** about bookmarks. He **was wondering** how to keep them inside his songbook. They **were asking** about the accident last night.
The past progressive is also used with verbs that describe everyday actions, such as *do, try, look, get, come, work, sit, walk, take, watch, read, make, drive,* and *wear*.	Silver **was trying** to invent a strong glue. He **was working** all day Thursday, so he missed class. **Were** you **watching** TV at 8 o'clock last night? Ruth Wakefield **was making** cookies.

Exercise 2.2 Commonly Used Verbs

Write sentences with the commonly used verbs to describe what the people were doing at 7:15 p.m. yesterday evening.

1. José *was driving home from school.*
   (drive / home from school)

2. Thomas _____
   (think / about his children)

3. Lorna _____
   (watch / TV)

4. Gabi and Jim _____
   (sit / in a restaurant)

5. Liz _____
   (try / to park her car)

6. Kevin and Selena _____
   (look / at some photos)

7. Peter _____
   (work / at his computer)

8. Clara _____
   (talk / to a friend on the phone)

Exercise 2.3 Yes / No Questions and Information Questions

A Read Joe's schedule for yesterday. Write questions about him. Use the words in parentheses with the verbs in the past progressive.

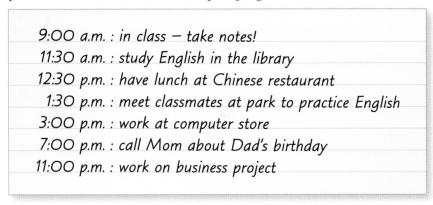

> 9:00 a.m. : in class — take notes!
> 11:30 a.m. : study English in the library
> 12:30 p.m. : have lunch at Chinese restaurant
> 1:30 p.m. : meet classmates at park to practice English
> 3:00 p.m. : work at computer store
> 7:00 p.m. : call Mom about Dad's birthday
> 11:00 p.m. : work on business project

1. (what / Joe / do / at 9:00 a.m.?)   _What was Joe doing at 9:00 a.m.?_

2. (he / eat / lunch at 11:30 a.m.?)   _Was he eating lunch at 11:30 a.m.?_

3. (what / he / study?) _____

4. (his friends / meet / him at 12:30 p.m. for lunch?) _____

_____

5. (where / his classmates / meet / him?) _____

6. (what / he / do / at 3:00 p.m.?) _____

7. (what / he / do / at 7:00 p.m.?) _____

8. (who / he / talk / to last night?) _____

9. (he / work / on his project / at 11:00 p.m.?) _____

_____

B *Pair Work* With a partner, practice asking and answering the questions in A. Then write and ask two more questions.

   A What was Joe doing at 9:00 a.m.?   *A* Where was Joe having lunch?
   B He was taking notes in class.   *B* He was having lunch at a Chinese restaurant.

C *Pair Work* Create your own schedules for a day last week. Do not show your partner. Ask and answer questions to find out what your partner was doing.

   A Were you working in the afternoon?   *A* What were you doing at 7:00 p.m.?
   B Yes, I was.   *B* I was doing my homework.

3 | Time Clauses with Past Progressive and Simple Past

▶ Grammar Presentation

A time clause tells when the main clause happened.	MAIN CLAUSE *He called me on his cell phone* TIME CLAUSE ***while he was walking home yesterday***.

3.1 *When* or *While* + Event in Progress

a. *When* refers to a particular time or period that something was in progress.

I met Joanna.
↓
—— I was living in Houston. ——→
I met Joanna **when I was living** in Houston.

b. *While* means at the same time that, or during the time that, an event was in progress.

The phone rang three times.
↓   ↓   ↓
—— We were having dinner. ——→
The phone rang three times **while we were having** dinner.

3.2 Time Clauses with Past Progressive

	Time Clause (with Past Progressive)	Main Clause (Simple Past)
When **While**	**he was working**,	he discovered the cure.

Main Clause (Simple Past)	Time Clause (with Past Progressive)	
He discovered the cure	**when** **while**	**he was working**.

3.3 Time Clauses with Simple Past

	Time Clause (with Simple Past)	Main Clause (Past Progressive)	Main Clause (Past Progressive)	Time Clause (with Simple Past)	
When	**he discovered the cure**,	he was working.	He was working	**when**	**he discovered the cure**.

3.4 Using Time Clauses with Past Progressive or Simple Past

a. You can use a time clause with *when* or *while* and the past progressive to talk about an event that was in progress when a second event happened.

EVENT IN PROGRESS   SECOND EVENT
***While Tim was thinking about the problem**, he had an idea.*

SECOND EVENT   EVENT IN PROGRESS
*Mr. Crum invented chips **while he was working in a restaurant**.*

Use the simple past for the second event in the main clause.

EVENT IN PROGRESS   SECOND EVENT
*When we were sitting in the library, **the alarm went off**.*

SECOND EVENT   EVENT IN PROGRESS
***I met an old friend** when I was walking home.*

b. You can also use a time clause with *when* and the simple past to talk about a second event that happened while another event was already in progress.

EVENT IN PROGRESS   SECOND EVENT
*She was driving home **when she saw the accident**.*

Use the past progressive for the event that was already in progress (in the main clause).

SECOND EVENT   EVENT IN PROGRESS
*When my friend arrived, **I was watching TV**.*

c. Don't forget to use a pronoun in the second clause if the subject is the same in both clauses.

***Marie** was talking about her problem when **she** thought of a solution.*

*When **Marie** thought of a solution, **she** was talking about her problem.*

d. Remember that a time clause can come before or after the main clause.

MAIN CLAUSE   TIME CLAUSE
*It started to rain **while we were walking in the park**.*

MAIN CLAUSE   TIME CLAUSE
*José was taking a test **when his cell phone rang**.*

Use a comma when the time clause comes first.

TIME CLAUSE   MAIN CLAUSE
***While we were walking in the park**, it started to rain.*

TIME CLAUSE   MAIN CLAUSE
***When his cell phone rang**, José was taking a test.*

▶ Grammar Application

Exercise 3.1 Past Progressive and Simple Past

A Complete the sentences from a magazine article. Use the past progressive or the simple past form of the verbs in parentheses.

Accidental Discoveries!

Sometimes unexpected things happen, and someone invents or discovers something. The discovery of gravity – the force that pulls all the stars and planets to each other in the universe – is an example of this. In 1666, Isaac Newton, an English scientist, _was sitting_ (sit)
(1)
in his garden when an apple _____ (fall) from an apple
(2)
tree. Newton got the idea of gravity from that one moment.

Another story is about James Watt, who was born in 1736. Some people say that while James Watt _____ (look) at a
(3)
boiling tea kettle, he _____ (get) the idea for a steam
(4)
engine.[1]

In 1799, French soldiers _____ (work) in Egypt
(5)
when they _____ (find) a stone with writing on it. This
(6)
was the famous Rosetta Stone. The stone helped people learn how to read Egyptian writing.

In 1908, while a German woman _____ (make) a
(7)
cup of coffee, she _____ (discover) that paper worked
(8)
as an excellent filter for coffee and water. She invented coffee filters.

In 1895, a German scientist _____ (experiment)
(9)
with electricity when he _____ (notice) that one piece
(10)
of equipment _____ (create) some strange green
(11)
light around some objects. While he _____ (work), he
(12)
noticed that the stripes of light – or rays – _____ (go)
(13)

[1]**steam engine:** an engine that makes something move because steam goes through it

through paper but not thicker objects, and through humans but not through bones. By 1900, scientists everywhere _____ (work) with the new rays, and doctors
(14)
_____ (use) X-rays to take pictures of people's bones.
(15)

It's amazing that all these inventions and discoveries _____ (happen)
(16)
by accident!

B 🔊 Now listen and check your answers.

C *Pair Work*   Ask three questions using *What was / were . . . doing?* about the events in A. Ask and answer the questions with a partner.

A *What was the German woman doing?*
B *She was making a cup of coffee.*

Exercise 3.2 Past Progressive and Simple Past with *When* and *While*

A Combine the ideas in the stories about unexpected events using the past progressive and simple past. Circle *when* or *while*.

Alice needed some money. She didn't

know where she could get some. One day,

she _was walking_ (walk) down the street
(1)
when / while she _____ (find) a
(2)   (3)
$100 bill. She was able to pay her phone bill and

buy groceries at the supermarket.

When / While Eric _____
(4)   (5)
(write) a paper for school, he _____
(6)
(receive) an e-mail from a stranger in France

with the same last name. **When / While** Eric
(7)
_____ (read) the e-mail and
(8)
_____ (learn) about the man's
(9)
family history, he _____ (realize)
(10)
that they were cousins.

Julia and Susan went to a party. They _____ (look around) to
(11)
see who they knew **when / while** they _____ (see) their co-worker
(12)   (13)
John. They _____ (smile) and _____ (wave) at him,
(14)   (15)
but he _____ (not wave) back. The next day, **when / while** they
(16)   (17)
_____ (work), they _____ (see) him walk into the office.
(18)   (19)
He said he wasn't at the party. It was his twin brother!

B *Pair Work* With a partner, tell stories about unexpected events. Take turns. Use *when*
and *while* with the simple past and past progressive.

    A *What were you doing when it started to rain yesterday?*
    B *I was waiting for the bus.*

4 Avoid Common Mistakes ⚠

1. Form the past progressive by using *was* / *were* + verb + *-ing*.

    were
Some strange things happening in the laboratory.
               ^

                  studying
    We were ~~study~~ in the library.

2. With the subjects *I, he, she, it*, or a singular noun, use *was* in the past progressive.

            was
The professor ~~were~~ asking some questions about the experiment.

3. With the subjects *you, we, they*, a plural noun, or a compound subject, use *were* in the past progressive.

         were
The scientists ~~was~~ trying to find a solution to
the problem.

               were
Diana and I ~~was~~ working in
the library.

4. In information questions, use question word order after the *Wh-* word in the past progressive.

         were you
What ~~you were~~ doing at 5 o'clock yesterday?

Editing Task

What were you doing when . . . ? We asked some people to remember what they were doing on special days. Find and correct ten more mistakes in the questions and answers.

Person	Question	Answer
Juno (30 years old)	What ~~you were~~ *were you* doing when Barack Obama became president?	I watching TV all day.
Elsa (71 years old)	What was you doing when the first men landed on the moon?	I was listen to the radio, and I talking to a friend on the phone.
Pamela (18 years old)	What you doing at 2:00 p.m. on your birthday?	I were having lunch with some friends.
Andrea (37 years old)	What was you and your husband doing at midnight last New Year's Eve?	We dancing at a party at a friend's house.
Helen (52 years old)	What you were doing at 4:00 p.m. last 4th of July?	My family and I was having a picnic.

5 | Grammar for Writing

Writing About a Past Event

Writers often use the past progressive and the simple past together to explain when things happened during a story or situation.

Remember:

- **Use the past progressive to describe an event in progress when something else happened.**

  Joe <u>was getting</u> ready to go to bed when the telephone rang.

- **Use a comma when the time clause comes first.**

  <u>While he was experimenting</u> with light, he discovered X-rays.

- **A time clause without a main clause is a fragment.**

  Berlin, she
  When she was working in ~~Berlin. She~~ met a famous German scientist.

Pre-writing Task

1 Read the paragraph. How did Susannah and Peter meet? Why was it strange?

A Happy Coincidence

A strange coincidence (happened) last year. My friend Leslie and I <u>were having</u> lunch <u>when</u> we started talking about my cousin Susannah. Susannah was looking for someone special on Internet dating sites because she was single. Leslie told me about her friend Peter. Peter was also looking for someone special. I talked to Susannah about Peter. She was interested. Then, a little later, Susannah was looking on an Internet dating site when she got a message from a man named Peter. It was Leslie's friend. While I was telling Leslie about my cousin, Peter was looking at my cousin's profile on the site. They met a few days later, and they started dating.

2 Read the paragraph again. Underline the past progressive verb forms and circle the simple past verbs. <u>Double underline</u> the examples of *when* and *while*. Which events happened at the same time? Which events interrupted other events?

Writing Task

1 *Write* Use the paragraph in the Pre-writing Task to help you write a paragraph about something that you discovered or something that happened in your life. Use the past progressive to describe the event in progress when something else happened. You could write about:

- a place or thing you discovered
- something you once invented
- a coincidence that happened to you or someone else
- your own idea

2 *Self-Edit* Use the editing tips below to improve your sentences. Make any necessary changes.

1. Did you use the past progressive and the simple past to write about something that happened in your life or in someone else's life?
2. Did you use the past progressive to describe the event in progress when something else happened?
3. Did you use a comma when the time clause came first?
4. Did you avoid the mistakes in the Avoid Common Mistakes chart on page 304?

Subject and Object Pronouns; Questions About Subjects and Objects

Fast Food or Slow Food

1 | Grammar in the Real World

A How many times a week do you eat dinner at home? Read the article below. What do you eat when you are in a hurry?

Should You Change the Way You Eat?

Eating habits in the United States are now different from what **they** were 40 years ago. Nowadays, Americans are eating more unhealthy food, and **they** are getting heavier because of **it**. Also, because their

5 schedules are busy, Americans do less cooking at home, and many of **them** often eat at fast-food restaurants. The food at these restaurants can be high in fat and calories,[1] and some of **it** is made from processed,[2] or pre-cooked, ingredients.[3] This means that many

10 Americans are eating less natural, less healthy food.

Some chefs are not happy about these new eating habits, and **they**'re working to change **them**. **They** are promoting healthy food and encouraging Americans to be more careful about what **they** eat. For example, one chef recently wrote a new healthy-eating cookbook. **He** adapted the recipes[4] for popular high-calorie dishes and made **them** healthier. This means

15 that now people can cook their favorite meals, and **they** get only half the calories. Another chef is visiting towns in the United States to help people think about their diets.[5] **She** wants the people in these towns to change the way **they** eat. **She** also wants children to eat healthy food, so **she** is encouraging schools to create healthy lunch plans for **them**.

[1]**calorie:** a unit for measuring the amount of energy food provides | [2]**processed:** treated with chemicals that preserve or give food extra taste or color | [3]**ingredient:** one part of a mixture | [4]**recipe:** a set of instructions for how to prepare and cook a kind of food | [5]**diet:** the food and drink a person has every day

B *Comprehension Check* Answer the questions. Use the article to help you.

1. What is different about American eating habits today?
2. Why are Americans cooking less at home?
3. What changes is one chef making to recipes?
4. Why is another chef visiting American towns?

C *Notice* Read the sentences from the article. Answer the questions about the words in bold.

1. "Nowadays, Americans are eating more unhealthy food, and **they** are getting heavier because of **it**."
   Who does *they* refer to? What does *it* refer to?

2. "For example, one chef recently wrote a new healthy-eating cookbook. **He** adapted the recipes for popular high-calorie dishes and made **them** healthier."
   Who does *he* refer to? What does *them* refer to?

3. "Another chef is visiting towns in the United States to help people think about their diets. **She** wants the people in these towns to change the way **they** eat."
   Who does *she* refer to? Who does *they* refer to?

2 | Subject and Object Pronouns

▶ Grammar Presentation

Pronouns refer to nouns. There are different pronouns for subjects and objects.	*Rachel* usually makes lunch for *Diego*. (= RACHEL) (= DIEGO) *However, yesterday **she** decided to take **him** to a restaurant.*

2.1 Subject and Object Pronouns

Subject Pronouns	Object Pronouns
I	me
you	you
he	him
she	her
it	it
we	us
they	them

▶▶◄ Subject and Object Pronouns: See page A18.

2.2 Using Subject and Object Pronouns

a. The subject in a sentence is the person or thing doing the action. Subject pronouns replace nouns that are the subject of a sentence.

SUBJECT   SUBJECT PRONOUN

Our chef *wrote a cookbook.* ***He*** *included many new recipes.*

SUBJECT   SUBJECT PRONOUN

Americans *cook less at home.* ***They*** *often eat at restaurants.*

b. The object in a sentence is the person or thing receiving the action. Object pronouns replace nouns that are the object in a sentence or the object of a prepositional phrase.

OBJECT   OBJECT PRONOUN

I remember ***James***. *I met* ***him*** *in the cafeteria.*

OBJECT   OBJECT PRONOUN

My sister loves ***hamburgers***. *My mom often makes* ***them***.
She wants ***children*** *to eat healthy food. She is making healthy lunch plans for* ***them***.

c. A pronoun can refer to one or more noun phrases.

I grow ***carrots and tomatoes***.

They *taste good.*

d. When talking about yourself and another person, put yourself last. Use the correct pronoun. (SUBJECT = *I*; OBJECT = *me*)

Eric and I *eat vegetables.*
Martha told ***Eric and me*** *about the new store.*

e. Use a pronoun <u>after</u> the noun is introduced.

My brother *eats fast food.* ***He*** *likes fries.*
NOT ***He*** *eats fast food.* ~~***My brother***~~ *likes fries.*

▶ Grammar Application

Exercise 2.1 Choosing Pronouns

A Complete the sentences with the correct subject or object pronoun for the underlined words.

1. These days, many <u>people</u> are eating better. **(They)** / **Them** are choosing healthy foods.

2. For example, instead of ice cream, some people order frozen <u>yogurt</u>. **It** / **He** doesn't have as many calories.

3. <u>My friends and I</u> love hamburgers, but **we** / **us** make <u>turkey burgers</u> because **they** / **them** are healthier!

4. I really don't like <u>vegetables</u>, but **they** / **them** are good for **I** / **me**.

5. My friend <u>Marco</u> loves pizza. I made one for **he** / **him** with just a little cheese and a lot of vegetables. **He** / **Him** loved it!

6. <u>Marco and I</u> ate <u>vegetable pizza</u> twice last week. **It** / **They** tasted great and made **we** / **us** happy!

B *Pair Work* Discuss these questions with a partner.

1. What food do you like to eat?
2. What food is good for you?
3. What food isn't good for you?

A I love to eat pasta. How about you?
B I love it, too, but I need to eat more vegetables.

Exercise 2.2 Using Subject and Object Pronouns

A Complete the sentences using the correct subject pronoun or object pronoun for the underlined words. Use some of the pronouns in the chart.

Subject	I	you	he	she	it	we	they
Object	me	you	him	her	it	us	them

COLLEGE NEWS

Cobalt University Cafeteria: Now Serving . . . Vegetables!

By Yuki Tanaka

The university cafeteria is offering a new menu to give students healthy options for their meals. <u>Students</u> often eat unhealthy food. __*They*__ (1) don't usually have time to cook, so _____ (2) eat in either fast-food restaurants or in the cafeteria. To help _____ (3) eat healthier food, the school asked nutritionists[1] to create a healthy menu for the cafeteria. <u>Nutritionists</u> found that if _____ (4) can offer quick <u>food</u> that is both healthy and tasty, students will enjoy eating _____ (5). Nutritionists also know that <u>students</u> perform better if _____ (6) eat healthy <u>food</u> because _____ (7) gives _____ (8) energy and nutrients[2] – two things that are very important to a busy student.

I surveyed some students about the new menu yesterday. One student said, "My <u>roommates and I</u> just had <u>breakfast</u> here, and _____ (9) loved _____ (10)." Another student reported, "<u>We</u> asked for better food in the cafeteria, and the school listened to _____ (11). This is great news for everyone."

Check out the new <u>menu</u> as soon as you can! It's long, and you can order many things from _____ (12). For example, there are all kinds of salads, sandwiches, vegetarian choices, and smoothies. Students can even order <u>sushi</u>. _____ (13) is delicious!

[1]**nutritionist:** an expert on the subject of how the body uses food | [2]**nutrient:** something that plants, animals, and people need to grow

B *Pair Work* Compare your answers with a partner. Discuss any differences in the pronouns you chose.

3 Questions About the Subject and the Object

▶ Grammar Presentation

Subjects are the people or things that do the action in a sentence. Objects receive the action in a sentence. *Wh-* questions with *who* or *what* can ask about the subject or the object.

*"**Who** made this sandwich?"*
SUBJECT
*"**Rachel** made it."*

*"**What** did you eat?"*
OBJECT
*"I ate **a salad**."*

3.1 Questions and Answers About the Subject

QUESTIONS			ANSWERS			SHORT ANSWERS	
Who / What	Verb		Subject	Verb		Subject	Form of *Do*
Who	eats ate	fast food?	**My sister**	eats ate	fast food.	**My sister**	does. did.
What	makes made	the food good?	**The spices**	make made	it good.	**The spices**	do. did.

3.2 Questions and Answers About the Object

Who / What	Form of *Do*	Subject	Verb		Subject	Verb	Object
Who	does did	James	see	in the cafeteria?	**He**	sees saw	**Rachel**.
What	do did	the students	eat	for lunch?	**They**	eat ate	**tacos**.

3.3 Asking and Answering Questions About Subjects and Objects

a. Use *who* to ask about people.

*"**Who** ate lunch with you?"*   *"Kevin did."*
*"**Who** did you take to lunch?"*   *"I took Kevin."*

b. Use *what* to ask about things.

*"**What** smells good?"*   *"The food does."*
*"**What** did you eat for lunch?"*   *"I ate a sandwich."*

c. Answer questions about the subject with the subject and *do / does / did*.

"Who wants dessert?"   *"I **do**."*
"Who likes sushi?"   *"Carla **does**."*
"Who went with you?"   *"Su-bin **did**."*

d. You can answer questions about the object with just the object.

"Who did you see in the cafeteria?" *"Carla."*
"What did you eat for lunch?" *"A sandwich."*

e. Use *who* in object questions.

"Who did you eat with?" "I ate with my mom."

Whom is rarely used nowadays and is very formal.

~~With whom~~ did you eat?

f. 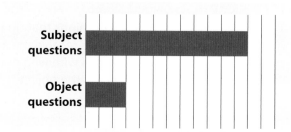 In conversation, subject questions are four times more common than object questions.

▶ Grammar Application

Exercise 3.1 Using *Who* and *What*

A Complete the questions using *Who* or *What*.

Ana Maria is a writer for the university e-newsletter. She is curious about the eating habits of students. She interviewed several students on campus.

Ana Maria Hi! My name is Ana Maria. __*What*__ did you eat
                                         (1)
for lunch today?

Philip I ate a garden salad.

Ana Maria _____ did you eat with?
                   (2)

Philip I ate with my roommate here, Mike.

Ana Maria Hi! _____ did you have for lunch?
                       (3)

Mike I had a chicken sandwich and fresh tomato soup.

Ana Maria Thanks! Excuse me, can I ask you some questions?

_____ usually cooks your dinner?
      (4)

Maya My mom usually does.

Ana Maria _____ is your favorite dish?
                   (5)

Maya It's definitely my mom's orange chicken. It's great.

Ana Maria Thanks so much!

B 🔊 Listen to the interviews in A. In each answer, underline the subject or object that Ana Maria's question asks about. Some questions may ask about more than one subject or object.

Ana Maria   *Hi! My name is Ana Maria. What did you eat for lunch today?*
Philip   *I ate a <u>garden salad</u>.*

Exercise 3.2 Forming Questions About Subjects and Objects

A Look at the restaurant receipts below for these students' lunches. Write questions about them. Use the underlined words in the answers to help you.

Ricardo's Lunch

Bill's Burger Bar

1 cola	$2.50
1 large fries	$3.25
1 double cheeseburger with tomatoes and mushrooms	$6.00
1 large chocolate milkshake	$3.75
Subtotal	$15.50
Tax	$1.55
Total	**$17.05**

Kai Lin and Clara's Lunch

The Garden Room

1 hot tea	$2.00
1 bottle of water	$1.50
2 large garden salads	$12.00
1 baked potato	$6.00
Subtotal	$21.50
Tax	$2.15
Total	**$23.65**

1. *Who ate fast food?* _____   Ricardo ate fast food.

2. _____   He ate a double cheeseburger.

3. _____   Kai Lin ate with Clara.

4. _____   He drank a milkshake.

5. _____   Clara had a baked potato.

6. _____   Kai Lin had a bottle of water.

7. _____   Kai Lin and Clara had a healthier lunch.

8. _____   Ricardo spent less money.

B *Pair Work* Write three more questions about the receipts. Then ask and answer the questions with a partner.

A *Who drank a cola?*
B *Ricardo did.*

C Group Work Think about your last meal. Ask four classmates about their last meals, and tell them about your meal. Then enter their information in the chart and report to the class.

A *What did you have for lunch, Paulo?*
B *I had a chicken sandwich and some chips.*
A *Who did you eat with?*
B *I ate lunch alone.*

Who	What
1. *Paulo*	1. *chicken sandwich and chips*
2.	2.
3.	3.
4.	4.

Paulo had a chicken sandwich and chips. He ate alone. He said his lunch was great!

4 Avoid Common Mistakes ⚠

1. Do not confuse subject and object pronouns.

My friends and ~~me~~ eat together at school. (*I*)
~~Her~~ never eats breakfast. (*She*)

2. Use the correct gender in pronouns: *he / him* for males, and *she / her* for females.

Mr. Jack eats salad for lunch. ~~She~~ is concerned about his health. (*He*)

3. Use a pronoun after the noun is introduced.

~~He~~ makes a tasty vegetable pot pie. ~~Henry~~ uses sweet potato, mushrooms, carrots, and cheese. (*Henry*) (*He*)

Editing Task

Find and correct the mistakes in Nicole and Alison's blog about fast food.

Fast Food Blog

Hi! Welcome to our Fast Food Blog!

Who eats fast food? So many of ~~we~~ *us* do.

My sister and me started this blog because a lot of our friends and family members had unhealthy diets. We wanted to help they make
5 healthier choices. We also wanted to give other people information to help they make better choices about their diet.

Alison had the idea to start a blog. He told me about her idea, and I liked it. Then my
10 friend James helped Alison and I design the site. Thanks, James!

If you have questions about fast food or about healthy eating, just post your question or e-mail it to we. Alison and me read the
15 questions every day and try to answer them.

He sent us our first question. John wrote this: "Why do so many Americans eat fast food?" Well, John, some people eat it because them have very busy schedules. Other people eat it because it's affordable. But, of course, lots of people just eat fast food because them like it! We do, too! Alison and me just want to remind people
20 that TOO MUCH fast food is not a good idea!

We hope that helps.

5 | Grammar for Writing ✒

Writing About Healthy Living

Writers often use subject and object pronouns to help connect sentences and avoid repeating nouns and noun phrases. This is useful when writing about people and their healthy living and food habits.

Remember:

- **Replace nouns and noun phrases with the correct pronoun.**

  Marie and her children called their grandfather last night. <u>They</u> *told* <u>him</u> *about a new health food restaurant in their neighborhood.*

- **Don't use pronouns too many times. Only use pronouns when it is clear what they are replacing.**

  Natalie and Chito went to the new health food restaurant with Chito's parents. <u>They</u> *liked* <u>it</u> *a*
      Chito's parents
  lot, but ~~they~~ *did not like it.*

Pre-writing Task

1 Read the paragraphs below.

My Family's Food Habits

<u>My family</u> tries to eat healthy food, but this is sometimes difficult. <u>We</u> are often busy. Sometimes we eat in fast-food restaurants. They do not have many healthy choices on their menus, but they are changing. Now, many hamburger restaurants have salads on the menu. My sister and I try to eat (them) more often. We try

5 to be careful with any extras. They can be very unhealthy, too. My mother does not like to eat burgers and fries. She never eats them when we eat at these places. But my father eats them. He eats almost anything! My brother likes to eat hamburgers. He and his friends eat them

10 all the time.

At home, when we have time, we make traditional dishes. Most of the food is healthy. It has a lot of vegetables. Sometimes the food has some fat, but it is delicious. We try not to eat too much of it.

15   One problem is the desserts. My sister and I love to make them. Our mother and
grandmother taught us. When we bake, we have a lot of fun. I think our mother is proud
of us, too. We do not have perfect habits, but we enjoy our food.

2 Read the paragraphs again. Underline three of the subject pronouns and circle three
of the object pronouns. <u>Double underline</u> the nouns or noun phrases the pronouns
replace and draw arrows from the pronouns to the nouns or noun phrases.

Writing Task

1 *Write* Use the paragraphs in the Pre-writing Task to help you write a paragraph
about healthy or unhealthy habits. What healthy or unhealthy things do you do?
What healthy or unhealthy food do you eat? Are any of your habits changing?
Use subject and object pronouns to replace nouns and noun phrases.

2 *Self-Edit* Use the editing tips below to improve your sentences. Make any
necessary changes.

1. Did you use subject and object pronouns to write about healthy living habits?
2. Did you use subject and object pronouns to replace nouns and noun phrases?
3. Did you use subject and object pronouns only when it was very clear what they
   were replacing?
4. Did you avoid the mistakes in the Avoid Common Mistakes chart on page 316?

Infinitives and Gerunds

Do What You Enjoy Doing

1 | Grammar in the Real World

A What kinds of things do you use a computer for? Read this article from a magazine for business owners. How did Ashley's interest in computers change her life?

An Interest in Computers Leads to Success

Ashley Qualls

A lot of children **like to play** on their computers. However, Ashley Qualls's interest in computers went beyond just a hobby. Her interest helped her become
5 a millionaire by the time she was 17 years old!

At the age of nine, Ashley **started to play** with website design programs. She **enjoyed making** pictures and designs and
10 **wanted to share** them with her friends. Then she **learned to design** pages for the social networking site MySpace.

In 2004, when she was just 14, she borrowed $8.00 from her mother and
15 started her website, WhateverLife.com. It offered free MySpace layouts[1], design help, and activities for teens. Her classmates and other young people loved it. Then business owners saw the site and **wanted**
20 **to advertise** on it. They paid a lot for the advertising space.

Ashley came from an average working-class[2] family. She never **expected to make** money from her hobby, but she soon had a monthly paycheck of over $70,000. In 2006, 25 someone **wanted to buy** the company for $1.5 million, but she **refused**[3] **to sell**. She dropped out[4] of high school because she **wanted to develop**[5] the business. She also found a business adviser to help her. 30

Ashley's hobby became a successful business. She is a remarkable young woman with a bright future and an amazing past.

[1]**layout:** the way something is designed or arranged | [2]**working class:** the group of people in society who use physical skills in their jobs and are usually paid by the hour (e.g., electrician, factory worker, plumber) | [3]**refuse:** say no | [4]**drop out:** leave school before graduation | [5]**develop:** grow, build, make

B *Comprehension Check* Match Ashley's age with the event that took place in her life.

1. Ashley became a millionaire. _____   a. age 9
2. She started playing with website design programs. _____   b. age 14
3. She borrowed $8.00 to start her website. _____   c. age 17

C *Notice* Find similar sentences in the article. Complete the sentences with the verb in parentheses. Use the article to help you with the form of the verb.

1. A lot of children like _____ (play) on their computers.
2. At the age of nine, Ashley started _____ (play) with website design programs.
3. Then business owners saw the site and wanted _____ (advertise) on it.
4. Ashley never expected _____ (make) money from her hobby.
5. She wanted _____ (develop) the business.

2 | Infinitives

▶ Grammar Presentation

An infinitive is *to* + the base form of the verb: *to design, to play, to do, to be.* Infinitives follow some verbs.

She *learned* **to design** pages for the site.
She *wanted* **to develop** the business.

2.1 Verb + Infinitive

Subject	Verb	Infinitive	
Children	like	to play	on computers.
Ashley	loves	to design	web pages.
People	started	to pay	for advertising.
Someone	wanted	to buy	her company.
Ashley	refused	to sell	it.

2.2 Using Infinitives

a. You can use an infinitive after these verbs: *want, need, like, love, hate, prefer*	Ashley **wanted to develop** her business. She **didn't need to borrow** much from her mother. Children **like to play** on computers. Ashley **loved to design** pictures. Some people **hate to work** on computers. I **prefer to make** phone calls.
b. You can use an infinitive after these verbs: *plan, decide, expect, hope*	How does she **plan to develop** her business? She **decided not to sell** her business. She never **expected to make** money from her hobby. She **hopes to employ** more people.
c. You can use an infinitive after these verbs: *begin, start, continue*	She **began to make** money from her idea. Ashley **started to play** with website design programs when she was nine. The website **continued to grow**.
d. You can use an infinitive after these verbs: *learn, refuse, try*	She **learned to create** layouts. She **refused to sell** her business. Someone **tried to buy** her company in 2006.

▸▸ Verbs + Gerunds and Infinitives: See page A26.

2.3 Using Infinitives with *Would Like*

a. *Would like* is a polite way to say *want*.	Ashley **would like to keep** her life private. (= She wants to . . .)
Use an infinitive after *would like*.	They **would like to design** a website.
b. People usually use *I'd like, she'd like*, or *they'd like* in speaking.	**I'd like to learn** more about business, too.
c. Notice the difference between *I'd like to* and *I like to*.	**I'd like to play** chess online. (Person doesn't play yet.) Sometimes **I like to play** chess online. (Person plays sometimes.)
d. To ask someone if they would like to do something, say or write, "*Would you like + infinitive . . . ?*"	"**Would you like to read** more about Ashley?" "Yes, I'd like to know more."

▶ Grammar Application

Exercise 2.1 Infinitives

A It's the first day of computer class, and Professor Sullivan asked how his students and their friends use technology. Complete the sentences with infinitives from the boxes.

buy   chat   ~~check~~   reply   spend   write

Jaime   I like __to check__ my e-mail before class.
            (1)

Ana   My friend Paulo refuses _____
                                              (2)
          clothes in stores. He only shops online.

Rosa   My friends and I don't like _____
                                                (3)
           to e-mail. We prefer _____ on
                                      (4)
           social networking sites.

Clarissa   I love _____ time on the Internet.
                           (5)

Alejandro   I recently started _____ a blog.
                                        (6)

do   miss   send   surf   watch

Sam   I love _____ text messages to friends.
                      (7)

Rafael   I watch TV on my cell phone on the bus. I don't want

             _____ my favorite shows. I can watch them online
                  (8)
             anytime.

Sun-mi   I like _____ the Web. I bookmark all my favorite sites.
                          (9)

Susan   I try _____ the latest videos on YouTube when I have
                       (10)
            time.

Hiroshi   I like _____ everything my classmates said. I'm on my
                          (11)
              computer 24/7!

B *Over to You*   Make the sentences in A true for you. Then compare with a partner.

   A *I like to check my e-mail before class. How about you?*
   B *Well, I like to check my e-mail in the evenings.*

Exercise 2.2 🔊 Pronunciation Focus: Saying *To*: *Want To, Would Like To*

In natural speech, people say *to* quickly. It can sound like /ta/ or /tə/.	*Children like to play on computers.* *She wanted to share her pictures.*
Want to often sounds like "wanna."	CONVERSATION *What do you want to do?* *Do you want to go?*
Do not use "wanna" in writing and formal speaking.	FORMAL SPEAKING *In this presentation, I want to talk about three problems.*
People say *'d* softly in *I'd like to.*	*I'd like to join that new social networking site.*

A 🔊 Listen and repeat the sentences in the chart above.

B 🔊 Listen to the conversation. Check (✓) the topics they talk about.

☐ careers   ☐ family   ☐ hobbies   ☐ teaching

☐ computers   ☐ friends   ☐ school   ☐ working with children

C 🔊 Complete the conversation with the verbs + infinitives from the box. Then listen to the conversation and check your answers.

'd like to be	hope to have	like to work	need to stay	want to have
'd like to work	like to spend	need to do	~~want to do~~	want to teach

Vic What do you _want to do_ as a career?
(1)

Bryan I _____ a teacher. You know, I really _____
(2)   (3)
elementary school. I _____ with children. How about you?
(4)

Vic Well, I _____ my own business one day.
(5)

Bryan Really? So, what kind of business do you _____?
(6)

Vic Well, I _____ with computers somehow. Computers are my
(7)
hobby right now. I actually _____ time in front of a screen.
(8)

Bryan So, how do you do that? I mean, what do you _____?
(9)

Vic I guess I _____ in college another year and develop my
(10)
computer skills.

D *Pair Work* With a partner, talk about what you would like to do or want to do on the Internet this week. Use these verbs: *chat, download, listen to, look for, read, reply, send, watch, write.* Say *to* quickly.

3 Gerunds

▶ Grammar Presentation

A gerund is the base form of the verb + *-ing*: *going, watching, working.*
Gerunds follow some verbs.

She enjoyed **making** *things.*
She kept **learning** *about web design.*

3.1 Verb + Gerund

Subject	Verb	Gerund	
I	**stopped**	**taking**	a web design course.
They	**finished**	**reading**	the new blog posts.
Ashley	**enjoyed**	**working**	on the computer.
She	**keeps**	**making**	great designs.

3.2 Using Gerunds

a. You can use a gerund after these verbs:
enjoy, stop, avoid, miss, finish, keep, imagine

Ashley **enjoyed making** *designs on the computer.*
She **stopped going** *to school.*
Sal **avoided taking** *computer classes because he was afraid of computers!*
I **miss listening** *to music on my MP3 player.*
They **finished working** *on the new design yesterday.*
She **kept developing** *her website every day.*
Can you **imagine being** *a millionaire at 17?*

b. Don't confuse the present progressive with verb + gerund. The present progressive uses the verb *be* + base form of verb + *-ing*.

VERB + GERUND
She **enjoys developing** *the website.*

PRESENT PROGRESSIVE
She **is developing** *a website right now.*

3.3 Verbs + Gerund or Infinitive

You can use either a gerund or an infinitive after these verbs:
like, love, hate, prefer, begin, continue, start
The meaning is exactly the same.

She **started to play** *with web designs.*
She **started playing** *with web designs.*

▶▶ Verbs + Gerunds and Infinitives: See page A26.

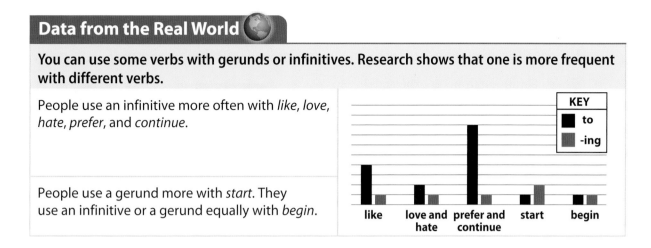

Data from the Real World

You can use some verbs with gerunds or infinitives. Research shows that one is more frequent with different verbs.

People use an infinitive more often with *like*, *love*, *hate*, *prefer*, and *continue*.

People use a gerund more with *start*. They use an infinitive or a gerund equally with *begin*.

KEY
■ to
■ -ing

like   love and   prefer and   start   begin
        hate   continue

▶ Grammar Application

Exercise 3.1 Gerunds

A Complete the questions with gerunds. Use the verbs in the box. Sometimes more than one answer is correct.

do   e-mail   learn   play   read   ~~use~~   visit   write

Chad is writing an essay on students and their computer use. He created this online survey for students around campus to complete. He hopes to get some useful information.

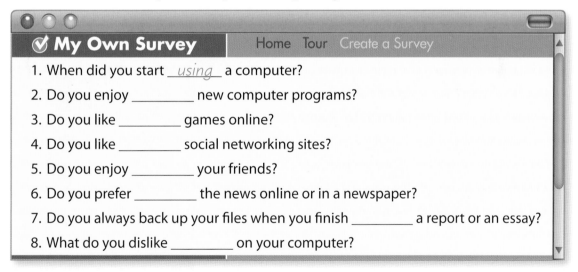

☑ **My Own Survey**   Home   Tour   Create a Survey

1. When did you start _*using*_ a computer?
2. Do you enjoy _____ new computer programs?
3. Do you like _____ games online?
4. Do you like _____ social networking sites?
5. Do you enjoy _____ your friends?
6. Do you prefer _____ the news online or in a newspaper?
7. Do you always back up your files when you finish _____ a report or an essay?
8. What do you dislike _____ on your computer?

B *Pair Work* With a partner, ask and answer the questions from Chad's survey. You can add extra information.

A *When did you start using a computer?*
B *Only about two years ago.*
A *What did you start using it for?*
B *I needed to write papers for school.*

Exercise 3.2 Gerunds or Infinitives

A Circle the correct form of the verbs in this article. Sometimes both are correct.

Sarah Amari never expected
(**to make**)/ **making** money from her hobby, but
(1)
now she runs a successful business. Sarah always
enjoyed **to take** / **taking** photographs. She also
(2)
liked **to edit** / **editing** them on her computer.
(3)
She continued **to work** / **working** on her
(4)
photographs until she liked the result. She never

expected **to give** / **giving** them to people. Then one day a friend said she wanted
(5)
to use / **using** one of Sarah's photographs. She planned **to put** / **putting** it on a
(6)   (7)
birthday card. This gave Sarah an idea. She decided **to make** / **making** greeting cards
(8)
with her photographs. She learned **to design** / **designing** her own website, and then
(9)
she started **to sell** / **selling** her cards online. She kept **to add** / **adding** new cards for
(10)   (11)
different holidays and celebrations. The business continues **to grow** / **growing**. Sarah
(12)
is doing something she loves.

B Complete the sentences with a gerund or an infinitive. Sometimes both are possible.

Monica and Jenna are new community college friends
and are getting to know each other.

Monica   Jenna, how do you stay in touch with your

friends? Do you like _to text_ (text) them?
(1)

Jenna   Not really. I prefer _____ (chat)
(2)
on a social networking site. I like

_____ (read) their news and
(3)
I enjoy _____ (check) out all
(4)
their photos.

Monica   I like that, too. I also enjoy _____ (read) my friends' updates
(5)
on my phone. I have a great cell phone plan, so I can text as much as

I want.

Jenna   Cool. But can you imagine _____ (live) without computers?
                                            (6)

Monica   No! I'm a huge Internet fan, too. I miss _____ (surf) when
                                                        (7)

I'm in class or at work.

Jenna   Hey, I hear there's a new social networking site called *Hands Around the*

World. Do you want _____ (join) it?
                        (8)

Monica   Not really. I can't continue _____ (check) all those sites.
                                            (9)

I have too many friends online already.

Jenna   I do, too. But I love _____ (meet) new people. There's a
                                    (10)

big world out there, and you never know what interesting people you

can meet.

Monica   Be careful, Jenna. Don't start _____ (give) people too much
                                                (11)

information about yourself.

Jenna   Don't worry. I avoid _____ (say) too much about
                                    (12)

myself online.

Monica   Good. You have to be careful these days. Let's meet again after class so we

can start _____ (study).
            (13)

Jenna   OK. See you then.

C *Pair Work* Ask and answer these questions with a partner.

1. What Internet sites do you like visiting?

2. What social networking site do you prefer to go on? Why?

3. Do you enjoy texting? How often do you text?

4. Do you like meeting new friends online?

Exercise 3.3 Vocabulary Focus: Go + Gerund

You can use *go* + a gerund for some sports and leisure activities.	I **go dancing** every weekend. I **went dancing** last week. I would like to **go swimming** soon.

go bowling	*go fishing*	*go running*	*go skating*
go camping	*go hiking*	*go shopping*	*go skiing*
go dancing	*go jogging*	~~*go sightseeing*~~	*go swimming*

Pair Work Complete the questions with the verbs + gerunds from the box above.
(You do not need to use all the verbs + gerunds above.) Then ask and answer the
questions with a partner. Make the questions true for you.

1. Do you usually _go sightseeing_ on vacation?

2. Do you and your friends ever _____ ?

3. Do you like to _____ on the weekend?

4. How often do you and your friends _____ ?

5. Did your family _____ last year?

6. Do you or your friends _____ every week?

7. Would you like to _____ with your friends or family?

8. Would you like to _____ ?

4 Avoid Common Mistakes ⚠

1. Don't use a base form when you need an infinitive or gerund.

to
Eliza hopes ⌃finish college soon.

meeting
I enjoyed ~~meet~~ you.

2. Learn which verbs take an infinitive.

to have
I want ~~having~~ my own business.

to take
Joe needs ~~taking~~ one more computer class.

3. Learn which verbs take a gerund.

learning
I enjoyed ~~to learn~~ about website design.

working
Ashley keeps ~~to work~~ hard on her business.

4. *I would like to* / *I'd like to* means "I want to do this." *I like to* means "I do this now and I enjoy it."

I'd like to
~~I like to~~ go to college next year.

5. In writing, use *want to*. Never write *wanna*.

want to
I ~~wanna~~ work in the summer.

Editing Task

Find and correct six more mistakes in this student's e-mail to her professor.

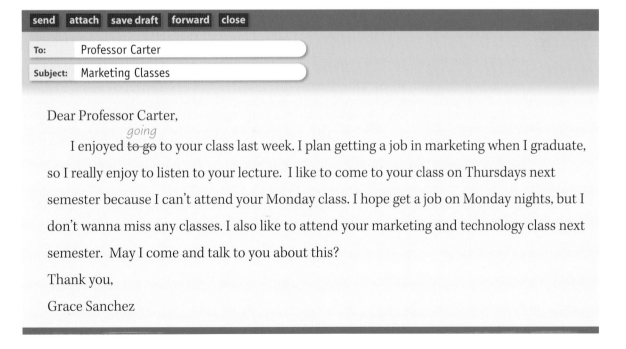

| send | attach | save draft | forward | close |

To: Professor Carter

Subject: Marketing Classes

Dear Professor Carter,

going
I enjoyed ~~to go~~ to your class last week. I plan getting a job in marketing when I graduate, so I really enjoy to listen to your lecture. I like to come to your class on Thursdays next semester because I can't attend your Monday class. I hope get a job on Monday nights, but I don't wanna miss any classes. I also like to attend your marketing and technology class next semester. May I come and talk to you about this?

Thank you,

Grace Sanchez

5 | Grammar for Writing ✏

Writing About Things People Like to Do

Writers use infinitives and gerunds when writing about things they enjoy doing, would like to do, or want to do.

Remember:

- Use *to* + the base form of the verb to form an infinitive, and the base form of the verb + *-ing* to form the gerund.

- Gerunds follow some verbs; infinitives follow other verbs. Check the verb lists in the unit to make sure you are using the correct form – gerund or infinitive – after verbs.

  He hopes to be an engineer one day.
  She wanted to study Japanese in college.
  They like working at home. OR *They like to work at home.*

Pre-writing Task

1 Read the paragraph below. Why does the writer want to work with children?

Working with Children

I would like to work with children. I enjoy being with them a lot. They always make me smile. I started babysitting for our neighbors when I was 12. Then two years ago, I started working for a family. I take care of a three-year-old boy and a four-year-old girl. I like the family very much. The children are fun and well behaved. I often play music and sing with them. They love to sing and dance. They also enjoy going to the park and seeing friends. I would like to be a kindergarten teacher or a child-care worker one day. I think education is important for young children, and I think that I am a good teacher. I plan to take early childhood education classes at my community college.

2 Read the paragraph again. Circle the gerunds and underline the infinitives. Find the use of *like* without a gerund or infinitive after it. What follows it?

Writing Task

1 *Write* Use the paragraph in the Pre-writing Task to help you write a paragraph about a hobby or job you would like to do. Why would you like to do this hobby or job? What do you need to do to have this job or hobby? Use sentences such as:

- I enjoy _____.
- I would like to _____.
- I plan / intend to _____.

2 *Self-Edit* Use the editing tips below to improve your sentences. Make any necessary changes.

1. Did you use infinitives and gerunds to write about something you would like to do?
2. Did you use the correct infinitive or gerund form after verbs?
3. Did you use *to* to form the infinitive and *-ing* to form the gerund correctly?
4. Did you avoid the mistakes in the Avoid Common Mistakes chart on page 331?

27 Future with *Be Going To*, Present Progressive, and *Will*

The Years Ahead

1 | Grammar in the Real World

A What are your plans after graduation? Read this article from a college newsletter. Are any of these students doing something you would like to do?

 GREENLOUGH COLLEGE CAREER CENTER NEWSLETTER

What's Next?

Every June, thousands of students graduate from college. What are these new graduates' plans and hopes for their future? Several graduates recently shared their plans with us.

5   Sarah Woodley, who is getting a degree in English, **is moving** to Chile to teach English. "I really want to experience living in a different culture. I**'m going to enjoy** learning Spanish while I teach English. I'm also **going to** really **enjoy** helping people!"

10   Tara Stout **is joining** the Teach for America program. It's a program that places new college graduates in city schools across the country to teach for two years. Tara says, "I know I **will be** nervous teaching kids for the first time, but teaching is my dream. This is a perfect way to begin!"

    José Marquez **is graduating** with an associate's degree in graphic design.[1] "I used the
15 career center here at Greenlough, and I found a job at an advertising company as a junior designer. I**'m starting** right after graduation. I **will certainly put** all of my training in this field to good use! I'm expecting terrific results."

    Finally, George Guzmán, also an English major, **is going to take** a special course in publishing[2] this summer. "I really want to become an editor[3]. Meeting people in publishing
20 **will help** a lot. I'm sure I**'ll find** a good job."

    We are so excited for all of these graduates and their classmates. Congratulations and good luck, graduates!

[1]**graphic design:** using pictures and diagrams, especially made by a computer, to make advertisements, posters, logos, etc. | [2]**publishing:** the business of making books, magazines, and newspapers | [3]**editor:** a person who corrects and makes changes to texts such as books and magazines

B *Comprehension Check* Answer the questions. Use the newsletter to help you.

1. What are three different things the students at Greenlough College plan to do after graduation?
2. What is one reason Sarah Woodley is going to Chile to teach English?
3. What does the Teach for America program do?
4. How did José Marquez get his new job?

C *Notice* Read the sentences. Look at the underlined verb in each sentence. Is the sentence about something now or in the future? Check (✓) the correct box.

	Now	Future
1. Sarah Woodley <u>is moving</u> to Chile to teach English.	☐	☐
2. George Guzmán <u>is going to</u> take a special course.	☐	☐
3. I <u>will be</u> nervous teaching kids for the first time.	☐	☐

2 Future with *Be Going To* or Present Progressive

▶ Grammar Presentation

We can talk about the future using *be going to* or the present progressive.	Sarah **is going to enjoy** learning Spanish. José **is starting** his new job right after graduation.

2.1 Statements with *Be Going To*

AFFIRMATIVE					NEGATIVE				
Subject	Be	Going To	Base Form of Verb		Subject	Be + Not	Going To	Base Form of Verb	
I	am				I	am not			
You We They	are	going to	get	a job.	You We They	are not	going to	get	a job.
He She It	is				He She It	is not			

2.2 Yes / No Questions with *Be Going To*

Be	Subject	Going To	Base Form of Verb	
Am	I			
Are	you we they	**going to**	get	a job?
Is	he / she / it			

▸▸ Short Answers with *Be Going To*: See page A13.

2.3 Information Questions with *Be Going To*

Wh- Word	Be	Subject	Going To	Base Form of Verb	
Who	**am**	I		interview	tomorrow?
What		you we they		do	after graduation?
When	**are**			leave	for New York?
Where			**going to**	work	after college?
Why	**is**	he she it		move	to Canada?
How				pay	his loans?

Wh- Word as Subject	Be	Going To	Base Form of Verb	
Who	**is**	**going to**	get	a job after college?
What			happen	after school?

2.4 Statements with Present Progressive

AFFIRMATIVE				NEGATIVE			
Subject	Be	Verb + *-ing*		Subject	Be + Not	Verb + *-ing*	
I	**am**			I	**am not**		
You We They	**are**	**moving**	next week.	You We They	**are not**	**moving**	next week.
He / She / It	**is**			He / She / It	**is not**		

▸▸ Spelling Rules for Verbs Ending in *-ing*: See page A20.
▸▸ Present Progressive (Contractions): See page A8.

2.5 *Yes / No* Questions with Present Progressive

Be	Subject	Verb + *-ing*		Short Answers	
Am	I			Yes, you **are**.	No, you**'re** not.
Are	you we they	**moving**	tomorrow?	Yes, we **are**. Yes, they **are**.	No, we**'re** not. No, they**'re** not.
Is	he / she / it			Yes, he / she / it **is**.	No, he**'s** / she**'s** / it**'s** not.

2.6 Information Questions with Present Progressive

Wh- Word	*Be*	Subject	Verb + *-ing*	
Who	**am**	I	**interviewing**	tomorrow?
What		you we they	**doing**	after graduation?
When	**are**		**leaving**	for New York?
Where			**working**	after college?
Why	**is**	he she it	**moving**	to Canada?
How			**paying**	his loans?

Wh- Word as Subject	*Be*	Verb + *-ing*	
Who	**is**	**getting**	a job after college?
What		**happening**	after school?

2.7 Using *Be Going To* and Present Progressive

a. Use *be going to* when you talk about plans or intentions for the future.

She's going to apply for a job in a software company. (intention)

b. Use the present progressive for arrangements already made for the near future.

She's applying for a job in a software company tomorrow. (arrangement already made)

c. Use *be going to* when you feel certain about something in the future based on evidence in the present.

The sky is very dark. It's going to rain.
I love my classmates. I'm going to miss them.

d. Use full forms when writing in class.

They are graduating next week.

e. Use contracted forms in everyday speaking and informal writing.

I'm going to rewrite my résumé.

▶ Grammar Application

Exercise 2.1 *Be Going To*

A A group of college students is talking about summer plans. Complete the conversation with *be going to* + the verb in parentheses. Use contractions when possible.

Laurie I <u>'m going to travel</u> (travel) around Europe with my
(1)
backpack for the summer!

Daniela Great! My sister and I <u>are goin to join</u> (join) a
(2)
volunteer group to help city kids. What about you, Luke?

Luke I <u>'m goin to look</u> (look) for a job right away.
(3)

Imelda Laurie, you <u>are going to do</u> (do) the same thing
(4)
as me! I <u>'m goin to go</u> (go) to Europe, too.
(5)

Matthew It sounds like all of you <u>are gona to do</u> (do) some
(6)
fun things. Not me. I <u>am going to work</u> (work) at the
(7)
bakery all summer. How about you, Fiona?

Fiona My mother <u>is going to be</u> (be) here from Ireland
(8)
next month. She <u>is going to take</u> (take) me to
(9)
San Francisco! I can't wait.

Ruth Hey, maybe we can see you in San Francisco,
Fiona. My friend Anna and I <u>are going to rent</u> (rent)
(10)
a camper and drive across the United States.

Yolanda I wish I could join you! I <u>'m going go</u> (not go)
(11)
anywhere! I <u>an going to stay</u> (stay) home and relax!
(12)
It all sounds great!

B *Pair Work* Write information questions about the friends in A. Then ask a partner for the answers. Write the answers.

A *Where's Laurie going to travel this summer?*   **B** *She's going to go to Europe.*

1. <u>is mother going to have fun this summer</u> _____
2. <u>Where is Ruth goin to travel this</u> _____
3. <u>is luke going do share words</u>
   <u>summer</u> _____

Exercise 2.2 Future Use of Present Progressive

A Complete the sentences using the present progressive form of the verbs.

Ruth and Anna are in Arizona. Fiona is in New York waiting for her mother to arrive. Ruth and Fiona are texting each other. They want to meet up in San Francisco.

> **Option** 🔋📶
>
> *Ruth* How are you? __Is__ your mom _coming_ (come) today?
> (1)   (1)

> **Option** 🔋📶
>
> *Fiona* I'm fine. She ____ar̶r̶i̶v̶i̶n̶g____ (arrive) this evening.
> (2)

> **Option** 🔋📶
>
> *Ruth* We're in Arizona. We ____is̶ ̶g̶o̶i̶n̶g̶____ (go) to the Grand
> (3)
> Canyon tomorrow. The weather is going to be beautiful,
> so we ____meeting____ (meet) the tour group at 7:00 a.m.
> (4)

> **Option** 🔋📶
>
> *Fiona* Have a great time! Mom and I ____are leaving____
> (5)
> (leave) for San Francisco on Friday. When
> ____are____ you ____getting____ (get) there?
> (6)   (6)

> **Option** 🔋📶
>
> *Ruth* Probably by Saturday afternoon. Where
> ____are____ you ____staying____ (stay)?
> (7)   (7)

> **Option** 🔋📶
>
> *Fiona* At the Golden Gate Bridge Hotel. Call us when you arrive.
> We ____are going____ (go) to the aquarium early on Sunday.
> (8)
> I hope you can join us.

B *Pair Work* Ask *Yes* / *No* and information questions to find out your partner's plans for the next few weeks. Use the time expressions in the box. Use the present progressive in your questions.

| at (5:00 p.m.) | at lunchtime | next (Monday) | this weekend | tomorrow | tonight |

A Are you staying in town this weekend?   *A What are you doing tonight?*
B No, I'm going to New Jersey.   *B I'm playing basketball with some friends.*

Exercise 2.3 *Be Going To* or Present Progressive

A 🔊 Listen to the speech and complete the sentences with *be going to* or the present progressive form of the verb in parentheses.

Welcome, students, and thank you for coming today! As you know, we're all here because of your efforts to help Redview Community College become a better place of learning! With your help, we now have enough money to begin improvements.

First, we _'re replacing_ (replace) all the old
(1)
computers in the library with new ones. The technician
are coming (come) in on Monday to begin work.
(2)
The librarian _are ordering_ (order) new reference
(3)
materials. They _are _____ (be) here by
(4)
next semester.

We _are expanding_ (expand) our recycling
(5)
program. I _am meeting_ (meet) with some people
(6)
from the environmental studies program this afternoon to
finalize the details.

The biggest news is that we _are building_ (build) a new student center.
(7)
It _are is having_ (have) a food court, a large bookstore, and conference rooms for
(8)
student groups to meet in. We think that the builders _are starting_ (start) next week.
(9)
Unfortunately, it _____ (not be) ready until next year.
(10)
I hope you're looking forward to the great new services on campus! Thank you, once
again, for all of your help!

B *Pair Work* Look at the speech again with a partner. Discuss which items in the speech are (a) plans or intentions for the future, or (b) definite plans already made for the near future.

> *A I think that replacing the old computers is a definite plan.*
>
> *B I agree. It says, "The technician is coming on Monday." That's also definite.*

C *Group Work* Write three information questions about the speech. Use present progressive and *be going to* + verb. Ask your group. Write the answers.

> *A What is the librarian ordering for the library?*   *B She's ordering new reference materials.*

1. _____   _____
2. _____   _____
3. _____   _____

3 | Future with *Will*

▶ Grammar Presentation

We can use *will* to talk about facts in the future or to make predictions.	*I will be 25 next year.* *The economy will grow next year.*

3.1 Statements

AFFIRMATIVE				NEGATIVE			
Subject	*Will*	Base Form of Verb		Subject	*Will* + *Not*	Base Form of Verb	
I You We They He / She / It	**will** **'ll**	**have**	a healthy life.	I You We They He / She / It	**will not** **won't**	**have**	a healthy life.

3.2 *Yes / No* Questions

Will	Subject	Base Form of Verb		Short Answers			
Will	I you we they he / she / it	**have**	a healthy life?	Yes, I Yes, you Yes, we Yes, they Yes, he / she / it	**will**.	No, I No, you No, we No, they No, he / she / it	**won't**.

3.3 Information Questions

Wh- Word	Will	Subject	Base Form of Verb	
Who			meet	at the interview tomorrow?
What		I you	do	in your training program?
When	will	we they	return	your documents?
Where		he	find	information about careers?
Why		she it	travel	to South America?
How			build	new apartments?

3.4 Using *Will* to Talk About the Future

a. Use *will* for predictions and expectations about the future.

The economy **will grow** next year.

b. Use *will* for things that are certain in the future. You could also use *be going to*, but *will* is more common in academic writing.

Next year **will be** the city's 150th anniversary.
Next year **is going to be** the city's 150th anniversary.

c. Use *will* for an immediate decision about a future action, often with *I'll* or *we'll*.

(to a server in a restaurant) I**'ll have** the chicken salad, please.
I have to go. I**'ll call** you this evening. Bye.

d. Do not use *will* for arrangements already made in the near future. Use the present progressive.

I'm sorry, I'm busy this evening. I**'m meeting** Andrea.
NOT ~~I'll meet Andrea~~.

e. Do not use *will* for plans and intentions. Use *be going to*.

I**'m going to** buy a new laptop, so I'm looking at prices on the Web.
NOT ~~I'll buy a new laptop~~.

f. We often use *I think, I suppose,* and *I guess* before statements with *will*. *I guess* is informal.

I think it **will cost** about $250.
I guess it **won't happen** until next year.

g. Use full forms when writing in class.

The building **will not be** ready until 2020.

h. Use contracted forms in everyday speaking and informal writing.

She**'ll be** 28 on her next birthday.

▶ Grammar Application

Exercise 3.1 *Will* and *Will Not* for Predictions

A Complete the sentences about life in 2025 using *will* or *will not* and the verb in parentheses.

○ ○ ○

Science Tomorrow By Scott Lupine

One of my favorite things to do is to think about how life will be in the future. Here are some of my ideas about a "green" future in the year 2025.

1. Cars and trucks _will run_ (run) on clean hydrogen[1] power.
2. All used products __will be__ (be) recycled.
3. People _will make_ (make) energy in their homes.
4. People _will_ (grow) their own fruit and vegetables.
5. We _will_ (not use) oil for energy.
6. We _will st_ (store) body heat to warm a building.
7. We _will_ (get) all our power from the sun, wind, and water.
8. We _will change_ (change) garbage into energy.
9. We _____ (not pay) high prices for alternative energy.[2]

[1]hydrogen: a very light gas that is one of the chemical elements │ **[2]alternative energy:** energy from a natural source, like wind, water, and the sun, that doesn't hurt the environment

B *Over to You* How many of the predictions in A do you think will be true? If you think the statements will *not* be true, change them. Explain your answers.

I think we will continue to use oil. There will still be some in the world.

Exercise 3.2 *Be Going To* and *Will*

A Write sentences with *be going to* or *will*. In one sentence, either one is possible.

Mia I / move to a new apartment. (going to)

1. *I'm going to move to a new apartment.*

Debra When / that be? (will)

2. _____

Mia Next week. The landlady / give me the key soon. (going to)

3. _____

Debra I / help you move. (will)

4. _____

Mia Great. I / need all the help I can get. (will / be going to)

5. _____

Debra Then I think I / call Roberto and Ivan to help you, too. (will)

6. _____

Mia That / make it much easier for me. Thanks. (will)

7. _____

Debra Let's celebrate then. You / love having your own place! (going to)

8. _____

B *Over to You* Moving is a big change in life. Are you going to make any changes in the near future? Write sentences about the change. Then tell a partner about it.

I'm going to quit my job soon. Then I'll look for another one.

Exercise 3.3 ◀)) Pronunciation Focus: Information Questions with *Will*

When people speak quickly and informally, they often use the contraction *'ll* instead of *will* after a *Wh-* word.	**Who'll** turn garbage into energy? **What'll** we do without oil? **How'll** we use body heat to warm a building? **When'll** we have cleaner cars and trucks?

◀)) Listen and repeat the questions in the chart above.

4 Avoid Common Mistakes

1. **Use the present progressive for arrangements already made for the near future. Do not use *will*.**

   is meeting
   Trudy is busy this evening. She ~~will meet~~ Alex.

2. **Use *be going to* for plans and intentions. Do not use *will*.**

   am going to
   I ~~will~~ apply to graduate school. Can you give me any advice?

3. **The form in *be going to* statements is *am / is / are* and the *-ing* form of the verb *go*.**

   is
   She ∧ going to do volunteer work.

4. **Use *will*, not the simple present, for predictions.**

   will
   Many more countries ∧ have a female president in the next 10 years.

   will become
   The earth ~~becomes~~ warmer over the next 30 years.

5. **Use question word order in information questions about the object.**

   are you
   What ~~you are~~ going to do during the vacation?

Editing Task

Find and correct eight more mistakes in this e-mail.

| send | attach | save draft | forward | close |

To: nuala@cambridge.org

From: fandi@cambridge.org

Subject: RE: Meeting with Career Adviser

Hi Nuala,

    am meeting
I ~~will meet~~ with a career adviser next week, and I going to discuss my future. What can I tell him? My dream is to work in television or the movies. I think I going to apply to a media studies program. I going to take a special course or something. I going to talk to some people who know about *career* careers in TV soon. I think they give me some good advice.

    Can we talk about this? What *are you* you are doing on Monday? I go away on the weekend, but I be back Monday morning. I call you then.
               I'm calling

Thanks,

Fandi

5 | Grammar for Writing

Writing About Future Plans

Writers use the present progressive, *be going to*, and *will* to explain their plans for the future and other things that they want to do but may not do.
Remember:

- **Use the present progressive for plans and arrangements that are already made, and *be going to* for possible plans and intentions.**

  The students are registering for the fall semester tomorrow.

  He is going to buy an online reading device soon.

- **Use *will* for things that are certain or that will happen as a result of other things.**

  I will not have enough money to take summer classes. I will need to work.

Pre-writing Task

1 Read the paragraph below. What two specific benefits of the change does the writer mention?

My Plans to Finish My English Classes

I am going to finish my English classes in three semesters. I'm taking a grammar class this summer. I registered for it last week. I'm taking only one class this summer. In the fall, I'm going to take reading and conversation classes. I'm also going to take another grammar class. Three classes will be a lot of work, so I am not going to work full-time. That will give me time for my homework at night. I'm also going to save all my money this summer. That will help. There will be an online writing class in the spring. I hope to take that class. It will be my first online class. I will also need to take one more reading class. That will be my last English class!

2 Read the paragraph again. Underline all the uses of the present progressive forms, circle all the *be going to* forms, and double underline all the uses of *will* and the verbs that follow. Which plans is the writer the most certain of? Which plans are a result of other possibilities?

Writing Task

1 *Write* Use the paragraph in the Pre-writing Task to help you write a paragraph about your current plans and your future plans and intentions. Include some things that will happen in the future. You can write about your plans using the ideas below or your own ideas:

- to finish English
- for the next weekend or your next vacation
- to take other classes
- to get a job

Use the present progressive, *be going to*, and *will*.

2 *Self-Edit* Use the editing tips below to improve your sentences. Make any necessary changes.

1. Did you use future forms to write about your future plans?
2. Did you use present progressive to write about definite plans and *be going to* to write about intentions?
3. Did you use *will* to write about things you are sure will happen or things that will happen as a result of other things that happen?
4. Did you avoid the mistakes in the Avoid Common Mistakes chart on page 345?

Will, *May*, and *Might* for Future Possibility; *Will* for Offers and Promises

Will We Need Teachers?

1 | Grammar in the Real World

A How do you think schools will be different in 20 years? Read this article from an education magazine. How many of your ideas are in the article? How much of this is happening already in your school?

Virtual¹ Education

Imagine this. On Monday morning, you log on to an online school from home. Your work is in an online folder. You do an activity and e-mail it to your teacher. He promises he **will** check it and send it back in three hours. After lunch, you discuss the
5 next assignment with classmates in Asia, Africa, and North America. Then your teacher calls through the computer, and you discuss your work.

For millions of students, this is already a reality. Soon it **might** be the way that everyone learns. More and more
10 students **will** work in virtual classrooms from their home computers. Class materials **will** be online, so students **may not** need to buy books, pens, or paper.

Will students still need teachers? The answer is yes, but the teacher's job **will** probably change. The teacher **may** become
15 a "learning manager" or coach.² Teachers in the future **may** look different, too. By 2050, some teachers **might not** even be human. They **might** be robots³ or virtual teachers who only exist online.

Online learning probably **won't** replace the classroom
20 completely. People **will** always enjoy going to class. However, most education in the future **will** likely continue to combine both classroom and online learning.

¹**virtual:** through the use of a computer | ²**coach:** a person who trains a person or a team, usually in sports | ³**robot:** a mechanical device that works automatically or by computer control

B *Comprehension Check* Answer the questions about the article.

1. What is a virtual classroom? *Com Puted*
2. Why can students in virtual classrooms live in different countries? *will*
3. How will the teacher's job probably change? *Will yes*
4. Will online learning replace classrooms completely? Why or why not?
   NO   NO is the same

C *Notice* Find these sentences in the article. Complete the missing part of the verbs.

1. More and more students _____will_____ work in virtual classrooms from their home computers.

2. Class materials will be online, so students ___may not___ need to buy books, pens, or paper.

3. By 2050, some teachers ___might to___ even be human.

4. People ___will___ always enjoy going to class.

2 | *May* and *Might*; Adverbs with *Will*

▶ Grammar Presentation

You can use *may* or *might* and a base form of a verb to talk and write about what is possible in the future.	*Students **may** not need to buy books.* *Everyone **might** take classes online.*

2.1 Statements with *May* and *Might*

Subject	May/Might	Not	Base Form of Verb	
I You We They He She	**may** **might**	(not)	go talk	to a different kind of school in the future. to classmates all over the world.
It			be	the future of education.

2.2 Using *Will, May,* and *Might*

a. You can use *will* when you are 100 percent certain about something.

By 2050, there **will** be new ways to learn.

b. Use *may* or *might* when you are less than 100 percent certain.
They have a similar meaning, but *may* sounds a little more certain than *might*.

Students **may** do all of their work online.
Computers **might** become teachers.

c. You can use *may* or *might* to answer questions with *be going to* or *will*.

"Are you going to enroll in an online course?"
"I **might**. I **might not**. I'm not sure yet."

d. You can use *might*, but not *may*, with *Wh-* words to ask questions about possibility. These questions are not very common.

What **might** computers be able to do in 2050?

e. Use the full negative forms *might not* and *may not*. Don't use contractions.

Students **may not** have to sit in classrooms at all.
Teachers **might not** be human.

f. Don't confuse the adverb *maybe* and *may be*. *Maybe* usually comes before the subject.

I **may** be in college this time next year.
Maybe I'll go to college next year.

▶▎ Modal Verbs and Modal-like Expressions: See page A25.

Data from the Real World

You can use *may* and *might* in speaking and writing. *Might* is more common in conversation. *May* is more common in writing. *May* sounds more formal.

2.3 Using Adverbs with *Will* for Levels of Certainty

a. You can use these adverbs **after** *will*, **between** *will* and *not*, or **before** *won't*.

100% certain	certainly, definitely, surely
less than 100% certain	likely, probably
	possibly

Online learning **certainly won't** replace the classroom.
They **will surely** do all of their work online for most classes.
Class materials **will likely** be online.
Students **will probably not** use books.
Some teachers **will possibly** be robots.

b. *Probably* is the most frequent of these adverbs. You can also use it in writing, but it is more common in speaking.

I'**ll probably** take the online course next term.
Jake **probably won't** because his computer broke.

▶ Grammar Application

Exercise 2.1 *Will*, *May*, and *Might*

A 🔊 Listen to the conversation. Complete the text with *will* (*not*/*won't*), *may* (*not*), or *might* (*not*). Use contractions when possible.

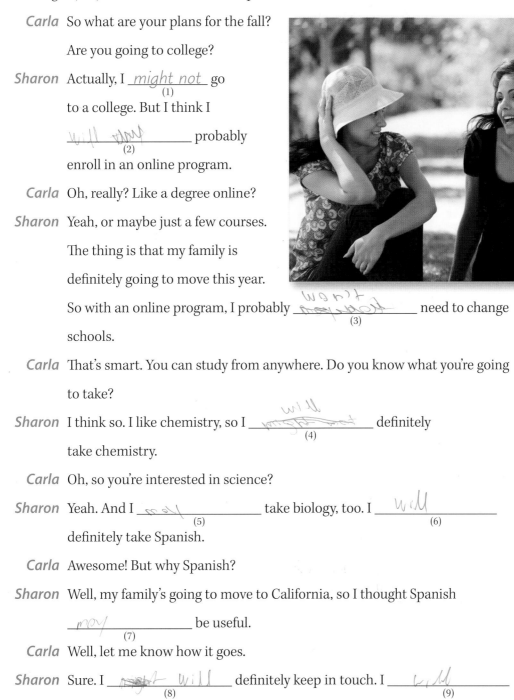

Carla So what are your plans for the fall? Are you going to college?

Sharon Actually, I <u>*might not*</u> go
(1)
to a college. But I think I

<u>will ~~may~~</u> probably
(2)
enroll in an online program.

Carla Oh, really? Like a degree online?

Sharon Yeah, or maybe just a few courses. The thing is that my family is definitely going to move this year. So with an online program, I probably <u>~~may not~~ won't</u> need to change
(3)
schools.

Carla That's smart. You can study from anywhere. Do you know what you're going to take?

Sharon I think so. I like chemistry, so I <u>~~might~~ will ~~not~~</u> definitely
(4)
take chemistry.

Carla Oh, so you're interested in science?

Sharon Yeah. And I <u>may</u> take biology, too. I <u>will</u>
(5)   (6)
definitely take Spanish.

Carla Awesome! But why Spanish?

Sharon Well, my family's going to move to California, so I thought Spanish

<u>may</u> be useful.
(7)

Carla Well, let me know how it goes.

Sharon Sure. I <u>~~might~~ will</u> definitely keep in touch. I <u>will</u>
(8)   (9)
be online all the time!

B *Pair Work* Answer the questions. Compare your answers with a partner.

1. What are Sharon's plans?

_____

2. Why is she making these plans?

_____

3. What is she going to study?

_____

4. How certain or sure is Sharon about her plans? Write her plans in the correct section of the chart.

Sharon's Plans	
Certain	**Not Sure**
	attend a college

Exercise 2.2 More *Will*, *May*, and *Might*

A Complete the sentences with *will* (*not*) / *won't*, *may* (*not*), or *might* (*not*). Give your own opinion. Sometimes there is more than one correct answer.

Classrooms of the Future

What do you think classrooms of the future will look like?

1. Students __*may*__ go to class one or two days a week.
2. They ___might___ not sit in classrooms.
3. The classrooms ___may___ not have desks.
4. They ___might___ just have computers.
5. Every student ___will___ own a computer.
6. The students' computers ___might___ look like cell phones.
7. Students ___will___ spend more time talking to their teacher.
8. The teachers ___might___ live in a different country.

B *Pair Work* Discuss your sentences about classrooms of the future with a partner. Do you agree?

> A *I wrote, "Students may go to class one or two days a week."*
>
> B *I don't agree. I think we won't go to class at all.*

C *Over to You* Complete the sentences with *will* (*not*) / *won't*, *may* (*not*), or *might* (*not*). Give your own opinion. Then discuss with a partner.

Schoolwork and Exams

What do you think schoolwork and exams will be like in the future?

1. Students _will not_ need to take handwritten notes in lectures.
2. Students _____ do more activities online.
3. They _____ write in books.
4. They _____ go to libraries.
5. Exams _____ be different.
6. Students _____ need to memorize facts for exams.
7. People _____ need to write at all in 2050.
8. Computers _____ teach and grade students' work.
9. Teachers _____ be in the same classroom as the students.
10. Students _____ have paper books.
11. Computers _____ be very small and light.
12. Students _____ only speak with other students online.

Exercise 2.3 Adverbs with *Will*

A Write sentences about your opinion with the words below. Use *will* or *will not/won't* and an adverb of certainty from the box.

certainly	definitely	likely	possibly	probably	surely
certainly not	definitely not	likely not	possibly not	probably not	surely not

1. Teachers / give all their classes from home.

   Teachers will probably not give all their classes from home. / Teachers
   probably won't give all their classes from home.

2. Teachers / be robots.

   Teachers will possibly be robots.

3. Teachers / need to prepare for their classes.

   Teachers will surely need to prepare for their classes

4. They / check exercises.

   They will definitely not check exercises

5. Computer software / check students' work.

   Computer software will probably not check student's work

6. Teachers / spend more time with each student.

   Teachers will certainly spend more time with each student

7. They / need to speak English.

   They will likely not need to speak English

8. Computer software / translate from any language.

   computer software will probably translate from any language

B *Pair Work* Compare your sentences with a partner. Do you have the same ideas? What other ideas do you have about teachers in the future? Think of three more ideas.

   A I think teachers probably won't teach all their classes from home.
   B Well, I think some teachers will. Some teachers will probably give classes in classrooms, too.

C *Over to You* Write sentences about your future. Use *may*, *will*, or *might* with an adverb (*certainly*, *definitely*, *surely*, *likely*, *probably*, *possibly*). Give specific information about the topics below.

1. school plans

   I'll probably enroll in an online degree program.

2. place to live

   I'll possibly live with my family

3. subject of study

   I'll probably study math or in university

4. learn another language

   I'll definitely continue to learn English

5. start a business or find a job

   I definit will continue the same job, so I definitely won/orts

6. your own idea

   I'll probably choose myown idea

D *Pair Work* Ask and answer questions with a partner about your plans.

A *Are you going to go to a four-year college next year?*

B *I might. I'll definitely study somewhere.*

3 | Offers and Promises

▶ Grammar Presentation

This is an offer:	This is a promise:
*I'll **help** you with your homework tonight.*	*I'll **call** you. **I won't forget.***

3.1 Making Offers

a. You can use *I'll* to make an offer.

"Where is the cafeteria?"
*"**I'll** show you. **I'll** take you there."*

b. You can also offer other people's help using *will*.

"My computer's not working."
*"My sister **will** help you. She knows all about computers."*

3.2 Making Promises

You can use *I'll, I will,* or *I won't* to make promises.

*I'll send my comments on your assignment today. I **won't** forget.*

"Will you marry me?"
*"Yes, **I will**!"*

▶ Grammar Application

Exercise 3.1 Offers and Promises

A Complete the conversation. Use Pat's offers of help and Chris's promises. Add *I'll*.

Pat's Offers
~~lend you $10~~
look at the homework with you
drive you home
show you

Chris's Promises
help you with your math homework
~~pay you back~~
make you dinner

Chris I don't have any money for lunch.

Pat *I'll lend you $10.*
(1)

Chris Thanks! _____ I'll pay you back _____ tomorrow.
(2)

Chris Where's the computer room? I'm lost.

Pat _____ I'll show y? _____
(3)

Chris I can't carry all my books home. They're so heavy.

Pat I'll help you with your math ho
(4)

Chris Great! Are you hungry? It's already 6:00 p.m. make you dinner
(5)

356 Unit 28 *Will, May,* and *Might* for Future Possibility; *Will* for Offers and Promises

Chris   I'm having trouble with my English homework.

Pat   I'll look at the homework with yo
(6)

Chris   How can I thank you? I know.   I'll drive yo home
(7)

B *Pair Work*   Practice the conversation in A with a partner. Add more details.

   A   *I don't have any money for lunch. I left my wallet at home. I was in a hurry this morning.*

   B   *I'll lend you $10 for lunch. Would you like to have lunch together?*

   A   *Sure, thanks. I'll pay you back tomorrow.*

4 Avoid Common Mistakes ⚠

1. ***Maybe*** **and** ***may be*** **have different meanings.**
   May be **is the verb** ***may*** **+ base form of the verb** ***be.*** ***Maybe*** **is an adverb. Use it before the subject.**

   may be
   Books ~~maybe~~ rare in the future.

   Maybe
   ~~May be~~ people will stop using books.

2. **Use** ***might*** **or** ***may*** **to talk about possibility in the future. Avoid using** ***can*** **for predictions about the future.**

   may / might
   Some students ~~can~~ prefer to go to a regular class.

3. **Use** ***will*** **to talk about certainty in the future. Avoid using** ***can.***

   will
   Everyone ~~can~~ study in a virtual classroom in the future.

Editing Task

Find and correct 10 more mistakes in this education article.

The Future of Education

will
The Internet ~~can~~ change education completely in the future.

maybe
May be colleges will not be buildings with people and furniture, but complex websites. Teachers

may be
maybe characters in virtual worlds like *Second Life*. In the future, students

might
can

migh
"travel" to different countries using their computers. They can walk around the

maybe
world's famous museums without leaving home. May be students will go back

in time. They ~~can~~ *will* possibly "talk to" famous people from the past, like George
Washington. History students ~~can~~ *might* watch or be part of historic events. We ~~can~~ *might*
buy artificial brains so we won't have to go to school at all! There ~~maybe~~ *may be* many
changes to education, but learning can ~~definitely~~ *will* never stop.

5 | Grammar for Writing

Writing About Future Predictions and Possibilities

Writers use *will*, *may*, and *might* to write about future predictions and possibilities. They
use these forms to show how their predictions can solve certain problems.
Remember:

- **Use *will (not)* + base form of the verb for predictions about possible future changes
  that you are very sure of and *may (not)* and *might (not)* + base form of the verb for
  future possibilities that you are less certain of.**
  Many classes <u>will be</u> online in the future.
  There <u>might not be</u> any classrooms with desks in the future.
  Students <u>may take</u> tests from their home computers in the future.

- **You can also use adverbs with *will* to show your level of certainty about a prediction.**
  Online classes <u>will certainly be</u> different from traditional classroom classes.

Pre-writing Task

1 Read the paragraph below. What does the writer believe will happen to future
universities? What problem will this solve?

Future Universities

I believe that universities <u>will be</u> completely online in the future. This will <u>certainly</u>
be very good for the environment. There (may not be) any physical libraries in the future
because all the books might be in online libraries. That way, people will not have to cut
down as many forests. Students might meet with their teachers on their computers.
Universities will surely need fewer buildings and parking lots. The current university
buildings may become apartment buildings. Students and teachers will not need cars and
buses to get to school. This will definitely help the pollution problem. It may also help
housing problems in some communities. I believe that online universities will be a very
good thing.

2 Read the paragraph again. Underline all the uses of *will* and the verbs that follow. Circle the uses of *may* and *might* and the verbs that follow. <u>Double underline</u> the adverbs of certainty the writer uses with *will*. Which predictions is the writer the most sure of?

Writing Task

1 *Write* Use the paragraph in the Pre-writing Task to help you write a paragraph about future predictions and a problem those changes might solve. You can write about your predictions for:

- education
- food
- homes
- transportation
- the workplace
- your own idea

Use *will* (*not*), *may* (*not*), and *might* (*not*). Use adverbs such as *certainly, surely, likely, probably,* and *possibly.* Begin and end your paragraph with sentences such as:

- I believe that _____.
- I don't think that _____.

2 *Self-Edit* Use the editing tips below to improve your sentences. Make any necessary changes.

1. Did you use *will* (*not*)/*won't, may* (*not*), and *might* (*not*) to write about future predictions that might solve a problem?
2. Did you use *will* (*not*)/*won't* + base form of the verb to write about predictions you are sure of?
3. Did you use *may* (*not*) and *might* (*not*) + base form of the verb for predictions you are less certain of?
4. Did you use adverbs with *will* to show your level of certainty?
5. Did you avoid the mistakes in the Avoid Common Mistakes chart on page 357?

29 Suggestions and Advice

Study Habits

1 | Grammar in the Real World

A What are two ways that you study? Read the web article about study tips. How many different suggestions does the writer give?

Study to Learn, Learn to Study
By Amy Chin, Communications Major

By the time we get to college, we think we know how to study. Then the first time we get a test back with a low grade, we wonder what happened. Research shows that many students
5 study ineffectively.¹ Here are a few suggestions about how to study more effectively.

First, it's important to find the right place to study. You **ought to** study in a quiet place. If you live with other people, you **should** probably try to study when no one else is at home. If your roommates are noisy, you **might want to** go to the library to study. If
10 you have to study in a noisy place, try listening to soft music with earphones.

Once you find a quiet place, you **should** make sure you're not hungry. You **might want to** eat a small snack before you study so you can concentrate better.

Next, set a study goal. Look at your task and decide how much you want to accomplish² during this study session. For example, **should** you read all four chapters
15 now? Maybe you **ought to** read two now and the other two later. You **should** set a realistic goal and work to reach it. Setting a study goal will help you focus on the task you need to do, but it's easy to get distracted.³ You **should** not check e-mail, text, or surf the Web while you study.

If you have to learn a lot of facts or study for a math test, you **might want to** study
20 with a friend. Just say, "**Let's** meet after class and review our notes."

Why don't you try these suggestions for a month? You will definitely see results!

¹**ineffectively:** in a way that doesn't get the results you want; not effectively | ²**accomplish:** do or finish something successfully | ³**distracted:** when someone's attention is taken away from what they are doing or should be doing

B Comprehension Check Answer the questions.

1. What should you do if you live in a noisy place and need to study?
2. Why might you want to eat a snack before you study?
3. How do you set a study goal?
4. Should you check your e-mail while you study? Why or why not?
5. How could you ask a friend to study with you?

C Notice Answer the questions. Use the article to help you.

1. Write the two verbs that come after the bold words in the third paragraph.

   a. _____make_____   b. _____eat_____

2. What verb form are the words in item 1? _____base form_____

3. Which is used most in the text: *should, might,* or *ought to*? _____should_____

   Why don't you

4. Find the form *"why don't you . . . "* in the last paragraph. Is it asking for a reason or making a suggestion? _____

2 | Suggestions and Advice

▶ Grammar Presentation

You can make suggestions or give advice with *should, ought to, might want to, why don't,* and *let's.*	You **should** probably write new words in a vocabulary journal. You **ought to** listen to these suggestions! You **might want to** write sentences with each new word. *"***Why don't we** study together?"* *"Yes!* **Let's** *study math first."*

2.1 Statements with *Should, Ought To, Might Want To,* and *Let's*

AFFIRMATIVE			
Subject	**Modal /** *Might Want To*	**Base Form of Verb**	
I You We They It He She	**should** **ought to** **might want to**	stay	inside in this weather. late.

2.1 Statements with *Should, Ought To, Might Want To,* and *Let's* (continued)

NEGATIVE			
Subject	**Modal/*Might Not Want To***	**Base Form of Verb**	
I You We They It He She	**should not** **ought not** **might not want to**	stay	outside in this weather.
			late.

LET'S			
Let's (Let + us)	**(Not)**	**Base Form of Verb**	
Let's	not	read	the chapter together.
		study	alone tonight.

2.2 Questions with *Why Don't You / We*

Why Don't	**Subject**	**Base Form of Verb**		**Answers**
Why don't	**you** **we**	study	in your room?	OK. That's a good idea.
		go	to the library now?	I can't.

2.3 Using *Should, Ought To, Might Want To, Why Don't You / We,* and *Let's*

a. *Might want to* is softer and more polite than *should* or *ought to.*

You **might want to** take Ms. Novak's writing class.

b. Use *maybe, probably,* or *I think* with *should* and *ought to* to soften the suggestion or advice.

Maybe we **should not** listen to loud music while we study.

In affirmative statements, *probably* can come before or after *should.*

We **should probably** study together.
We **probably should** study together.

In negative statements, *probably* comes before *should not.*

We **probably should not** study together.

Maybe and *probably* always come before *ought to.*

We **probably ought to** go to the movies later.
Maybe we **ought to** go to the movies later.

c. Use the expression *Why don't you / we . . .* to make suggestions or give advice in a soft, polite way.

(SUGGESTION) **Why don't we** study together on Tuesday night?
(ADVICE) **Why don't you** keep a vocabulary journal?

d. Use the expression *Let's . . .* to make suggestions that include you and the listener.
Let's = Let us

Let's study at the library.
Let's not stay up late the night before our test.

▸▸◄ Modal Verbs and Modal-like Expressions: See page A25.

Data from the Real World

We and *you* are the most common subjects for suggestions and advice.	*We* should keep a vocabulary journal. *You* ought to study for the test.
Should is the most common form used for suggestions and advice. *Ought to* is very rare. *Ought not to* is also very rare.	You **should** learn a new word every day.
Might is usually followed by *want to* when making suggestions or giving advice.	You **might want to** review for the vocabulary test.

▶ Grammar Application

Exercise 2.1 Suggestions and Advice

A The students in an English class are having some vocabulary problems. Give advice for each student. Use the words in parentheses and *should* (*not*), *might want to*, or *ought to*. Sometimes there is more than one correct answer.

Problem	**Advice**
1. Marissa doesn't read well because she doesn't know a lot of words.	*She ought to read more.* (she / read more)
2. Veronica wants to learn lots of new words quickly.	should (she / practice new words every day)
3. Petra wants to remember how to use new words.	ought to (she / write sentences with the new words)
4. Ricardo is afraid to try new words.	_____ (he / practice using the words with a friend)
5. Eniko and Irina want a fun way to practice vocabulary.	_____ (they / do crossword puzzles)
6. The whole class wants a good way to learn new words.	_____ (they / create a picture in their minds that shows the meaning of each word)

B *Pair Work* With a partner, write three suggestions for learning new words. Use your own experience or ideas from the unit. Then share your ideas with the class.

A *Let's write new words on cards and practice them.*
B *We might want to tape the cards on a wall to practice.*

Exercise 2.2 More Suggestions and Advice

A 🔊 Listen. Complete the class discussion with the missing words.

Professor Taking good notes is an important part of being a successful student. Let's hear some advice from students about how they take notes.

Teresa Some teachers speak very quickly. You __should__ ask these teachers if you can
(1)
record the class. Then you can listen to the notes again in your home. You _____ record the class
(2)
without the teacher's permission.

Amadou You _____ attend a workshop on note taking. That can be
(3)
very helpful. I know it helped me.

Alex Find a student with good notes, and ask him or her if you can copy the notes. You _____ offer to buy that student coffee or a
(4)
snack. _____ you _____ suggest a time to
(5)   (5)
meet once a week to trade notes. If you aren't sure how to suggest this,
here are some ways: "_____ we get together on Thursdays
(6)
to trade notes?" or "_____ meet in the student union."
(7)

Professor Thank you for your suggestions. I _____ add here that
(8)
you _____ just copy the notes. You _____
(9)   (10)
compare their notes with yours. Try to figure out what's different.

B *Pair Work* Use the information in A to give your partner suggestions or advice about taking notes. Take turns.

A *Why don't you ask the teacher's permission to record the class?*
B *That's a good idea.*

A *You should attend a workshop on note taking.*
B *I'll look for one.*

C *Over to You* Many people give us advice and suggestions. What is some advice that you received recently? Was it helpful?

3 | Asking for and Responding to Suggestions and Advice

▶ Grammar Presentation

Use *Yes / No* and information questions to ask for suggestions and advice.	*"**Should** I register for a writing class?"* *"**That's a good idea.**"* *"**When should** I register for class?"* *"**Why don't you** register next week?"*

3.1 *Yes / No* Questions to Ask for Suggestions and Advice

Should	Subject	Base Form of Verb		Answers
Should	I we	take	a math class?	That's a good idea.
		meet	you in the student union?	I think it's closed.

3.2 Information Questions to Ask for Suggestions and Advice

Wh- Word	*Should*	Subject	Base Form of Verb		Answers
What			bring	to class?	I don't know.
Where		I you we they he she it	meet	you?	Let's meet at the library.
Who			ask	for help?	Ask Professor Li.
When	**should**		tell	the boss?	As soon as possible.
How			study	for the test?	She ought to study one chapter at a time.
Why			be	difficult?	Because the teacher gives hard tests.

3.3 Responding to Questions for Suggestions and Advice

a. For a strong, <u>positive</u> response to a Yes/No question for suggestions or advice, use:
Yes./That sounds great./Definitely./Absolutely.

"***Should** we eat lunch before our class?*"
"*Yes. **That sounds great!***"
"***Definitely!***"
"*Oh, **absolutely!***"

b. If you are <u>uncertain</u> about the answer to a Yes/No question, use:
Maybe./Probably./I'm not sure.

"***Should** we eat lunch before our class?*"
"***Maybe.***"
"***Probably**. Let's check my schedule.*"
"*Oh. **I'm not sure.***"

c. For a strong, <u>negative</u> response to a Yes/No question for suggestions or advice, use:
That's not a good idea.
Why don't we + different idea
I'd like to, but + reason

"***Should** we eat lunch before our class?*"
"***That's not a good idea.** We don't have enough time.*"
"***Why don't we** eat after class?*"
"***I'd like to, but** I have to study.*"

d. Respond to information questions with:
probably/maybe/why don't you

Using ***should*** alone is stronger.

"*What class **should** I take next semester?*"
"*You should **probably** take a writing class.*"
"***Maybe** you should take a writing class.*"
"***Why don't you** take a writing class?*"

Data from the Real World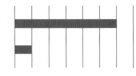

What should I/we...? and *Where should we...?* are the most common information questions used to ask for suggestions/advice.

What should I/we...?
Where should I/we...?

▶ Grammar Application

Exercise 3.1 Responding to Questions for Advice

A Complete the conversation. Use the cues to help you.

Jill Hi, Sandra! I'm so glad to see you! Could you help me with something? I need to find an apartment. I know you know a lot about the area. ___*Should*___ (Yes/No question) I rent a
(1)
place near school?

Sandra ___*Yes. Absolutely!*___ (a strong positive response) It's so much easier to live near school.
(2)

368 – 369

Jill _____Where should_____ (3) (*Wh-* questions) I look to find an apartment for rent? Can I look in the local paper?

Sandra Yes. You _____should probably_____ (4) (uncertain answer) look in the paper or online. That's a good place to start.

Jill Great! Do you have any other advice?

Sandra Yes, you _____should definitely_____ (5) (strong response) ask about utilities. Sometimes things like electricity, heat, and air-conditioning are included in the rent.

Jill Oh, right. _____Should I_____ (6) (*Yes/No* question) I also ask about deposits?

Sandra _____Ab definitely_____ (7) (strong positive response)!

Jill Thanks, Sandra. You're a great friend!

B *Pair Work* Write a conversation with suggestions/advice for <u>one</u> of the situations below. Use the conversation in A to help you. Then share with another pair.

1. **Two Classmates:** One classmate just started college in the United States and needs advice on study habits.

2. **Graduating Student and Job Coach:** A student is looking for advice on how to begin a job search / get a job.

3. **College Freshman and College Senior:** A freshman wants advice on courses, restaurants, bookstores, etc.

Situation 1

A *My English is not very strong. What should I do to improve my vocabulary?*

B *Well, first you should definitely keep a vocabulary journal....*

noti

I should habts to study habits in united states

chatGPT

A. KYUN

Exercise 3.2 Asking for and Giving Advice

A Respond to the situations below. Ask for advice or give advice.

1. You want to ask your friend for advice about how to fix your computer.

   What should I do first?

2. You are not sure which movie to go to. Ask a friend for advice.

   what shall moviee go to

3. A friend asks for advice on how to take notes. What do you say?

   what Shoul la take not

4. You are not sure where to buy school supplies. Ask a friend for advice.

   where should buy school suppli

5. Your teacher asks for advice on what cell phone to buy. What do you say?

   what shoul cell phone to buy

6. A classmate is about to do something that is not a good idea. What advice do you give?

   what shoul that is not good idea

7. A classmate needs help with his math homework. What advice do you give?

   what should help with his math hor work

8. You want to learn more English vocabulary. Ask your teacher for advice.

   you should more Fralsi vocabulare

B *Pair Work* Compare your answers with a partner. Did you use any of the same expressions to ask for or give advice?

C *Over to You* Think of two problems or situations this week that you will need advice on. Write your questions here, asking for advice.

1. _____

2. _____

4 Avoid Common Mistakes ⚠

1. Use the base form of the main verb after *should*.

He should ~~eats~~ *eat* lunch before class.

We should ~~to~~ study after class.

2. After *ought*, use *to* + the base form of the main verb.

He ought *to* eat lunch.

3. The subject comes after *should* and *might* in information questions.

Where *I* should meet you?

4. Put *probably* and *maybe* before *ought to*.

We *probably* ought to ~~probably~~ go to the library.

5. In negative statements, *probably* comes before *should not*.

Tim *probably* should not ~~probably~~ call tonight.

Editing Task

Find and correct the mistakes in this conversation between two classmates.

Julia Monica, I need help studying! How ~~I~~ should *I* tell the professor?

Monica Don't worry. I can help. First, we should shares class notes.

Julia When we should meet at the library? After class today?

Monica Sure, but we ought to probably meet in the cafeteria. I'll want to

5   eat something.

Julia OK. We should eats dinner while we study. What I should bring?

Monica Just your notebook. You should not probably bring the big textbook –
           I don't think we'll need it.

Julia You should to be ready for a lot of questions from me! I have so many!

10 **Monica** As long as you are ready to learn, I'm happy to help! When we're done, we
           ought see a movie!

Julie That sounds great! See you later!

Monica See you then, Julie. We should to study together more often!

5 | Grammar for Writing

Making Suggestions and Giving Advice

Writers can use *should, ought to,* and *might want to* when they give suggestions or advice about studying, work, or relationships.

Remember:

- **Use *should (not)* + base form of the verb or *ought to* + base form of the verb for strong suggestions or advice. Use *maybe, probably,* or *I think* before *should* or *ought to* to make your strong suggestions and advice more polite.**

  You *should* register for classes today before the classes fill up.

  The project is due next week. *Maybe* you *ought to* get started on it.

- **You can also use *might want to* for polite suggestions or advice.**

  We *might want to* find another student for our group project.

Pre-writing Task

1 Read the paragraph below. Why does the writer suggest studying in the library? How many study tips does the writer suggest?

Using the Library to Study

You may find it hard to study in your room because family and roommates can be very distracting. The library is a great place to study. Here are some suggestions for studying in the library. If possible, you should go to the library at the same time every day. That will help you create good study habits. When you are in the library, you should not sit near your friends. Instead, you should find a quiet place to work. You ought to turn your cell phone off. Every text or call is a distraction. When you are working with other students, you should use a study room for groups. You might want to reserve a study room in advance, especially around exam time.

2 Read the paragraph again. Underline all the uses of *should* and *should not*. Circle the suggestion with *might want to*. Double underline the suggestion with *ought to*. Could you replace *should* with *ought to* for all the sentences? Why or why not?

Writing Task

1 *Write* Use the paragraph in the Pre-writing Task to help you write a paragraph for an English department newsletter with suggestions and advice about a common problem. You can give advice about:

- creating vocabulary-learning tips
- finding someone to study with
- making an appointment with a teacher

- finding a tutor
- improving computer skills
- your own idea

Use *should / ought to* and *might want to*. Also use *maybe, probably,* or *I think*. Explain the common problem in your first sentence.

2 *Self-Edit* Use the editing tips below to improve your sentences. Make any necessary changes.

1. Did you use *should (not), ought to*, and *might want to* to give suggestions or advice about a problem?
2. Did you use *maybe, probably,* or *I think* before *should* to make your suggestion more polite?
3. Did you also use *might want to* to give polite suggestions and advice?
4. Did you avoid the mistakes in the Avoid Common Mistakes chart on page 369?

Necessity and Conclusions
Getting What You Want

1 Grammar in the Real World

A How much does your school cost each year? How do you pay for it? Read the web article below about scholarships.

Scholarship Review	College Scholarships News Help

Applying for a Scholarship[1]

As a student, you **must** agree that college is expensive in the United States. Many students **need to** apply for scholarships to lower their education costs. Here are a few
5 tips on how to complete a good scholarship application.

There are many scholarships available every year, but students **have to** search for them. Search online with keywords like
10 *scholarship* or *grant*.[2] There are also scholarships for people with specific skills, backgrounds, and ethnicities.[3] Eligible[4] students **must** search for scholarships that are appropriate for them.

You **need to** ask your adviser for help. He or she knows a lot about scholarships and can help you complete your application. Ask your
15 adviser to help you create a schedule for each step in the application. Think of a time line for when you **must** finish each step. Try to have everything ready one week before you send your application.

You should start your scholarship applications early, about six months before they are due. Your application will take time to complete because
20 you will **need to** request letters of recommendation[5] from teachers and a transcript[6] from your school. Your school will need time to send the transcript

[1]**scholarship:** money given to a person to help pay for his or her education | [2]**grant:** a sum of money that a university, government, or an organization gives to someone for a purpose, such as to do research or study | [3]**ethnicity:** shared national, racial, or cultural origins of a group, often with the same language | [4]**eligible:** having the necessary qualities | [5]**recommendation:** a letter or statement saying someone is good or suitable for something, like a job, school, or scholarship | [6]**transcript:** an official, written copy of someone's grades at an institution

to the scholarship organization, and your teachers will need time to write the recommendations. When you ask a teacher for a recommendation, give him or her a deadline. All students **must** send their applications out on time, so be
25 persistent and remind your teachers of the due dates.

You **don't have to** feel stressed about being able to complete a good application. With a little hard work and care, you can send out a good scholarship application and lower your school costs.

B *Comprehension Check* Answer the questions. Use the article to help you.

1. Is college expensive in the United States?
2. Are there many scholarships available for students?
3. How early should you start your applications?
4. Who can help you with your application?
5. What do you need to give your teachers for their recommendations?

C *Notice* Read the sentences. Decide if the actions are *necessary* or *not necessary*. Circle *necessary* or *not necessary*.

1. Many students **need to** apply for scholarships to lower their education costs.   necessary   not necessary
2. You **don't have to** feel stressed about being able to complete a good application.   necessary   not necessary
3. Eligible students **must** search for scholarships that are appropriate for them.   necessary   not necessary
4. You **need** to ask your adviser for help.   necessary   not necessary

2 | Necessity and Conclusions with *Have To, Need To, Must*

▶ Grammar Presentation

Have to, *need to*, and *must* express an obligation or necessity. *Must* also expresses a conclusion we can make about something.	Students **need to** apply for scholarships. (= It is necessary.) Students **do not have to** feel stressed about completing their application. (= It is not necessary.) As a student, you **must** know that college is expensive in the United States. (CONCLUSION Students know that college is expensive in the United States.)

2.1 Statements with *Have To* and *Need To*

AFFIRMATIVE				NEGATIVE				
Subject		Base Form of Verb		Subject			Base Form of Verb	
I You We They	**have to need to**	write	an essay.	I You We They	**do not don't**	**have to need to**	write	an essay.
He She It	**has to needs to**	search	online.	He She It	**does not doesn't**		search	online.

2.2 Statements with *Must*

AFFIRMATIVE				NEGATIVE			
Subject		Base Form of Verb		Subject			Base Form of Verb
I You He / She / It We They	**must**	know.		I You He / She / It We They	**must**	**not**	know.

2.3 Using *Have To*, *Need To*, and *Must*

a. *Have to*, *need to*, and *must* talk about things that are important or necessary to do.

Students **need to** send an application.

b. Using *must* in conversation can seem rude.

She **needs to** make a schedule.
She **must** make a schedule. (Sounds rude.)

c. In conversation, *must* usually expresses conclusions.

Today is Monday, so tomorrow **must** be Tuesday.

d. *Have to* can also express conclusions. *Need to* <u>never</u> expresses conclusions.

Today is Monday, so tomorrow **has to** be Tuesday.
NOT ~~Today is Monday, so tomorrow needs to be Tuesday.~~

e. *Do not have to* or *do not need to* means it is not necessary. There is no obligation.

Tom **doesn't have to** pay for school.
He **does not need to** pay for school.

Must not means it is forbidden.
Mustn't is <u>very</u> rare.

Students **must not** forget to send in their application on time.

▸▸ Modal Verbs and Modal-like Expressions: See page A25.

2.4 Yes / No Questions with *Have To* and *Need To* and Short Answers

Do / Does	Subject	Have to / Need to	Base Form of Verb		Yes / No	Subject	
Do	I you we they	**have to need to**	write	an essay?	Yes,	I you	do.
					No,	we they	do not / don't.
Does	he she it				Yes,	he she	does.
					No,	it	does not / doesn't.

2.5 Information Questions with *Have To* and *Need To* and Responses

Wh- Word	Do / Does	Subject		Base Form of Verb
When	**do**	I you we they	**have to need to**	send the application?
	does	he she it		

Subject	Do / Does (Not)		Base Form of Verb
I You We They	do not / don't	**have to need to**	send the application next month.
He She It	does not / doesn't		

Note: Using *must* in questions is very rare.

▶ Grammar Application

These are some of the most frequent verbs used with *have to*, *need to*, and *must* in speaking and writing:

be	go	get	take	know	talk	give
do	have	make	look	say	come	work

Exercise 2.1 Necessity and Obligation

A Complete the sentences with the correct form of *have to*, *need to*, or *must*.

DRIVER'S LICENSES IN CANADA AND THE UNITED STATES   SEARCH

In the U.S. and Canada, states and provinces have different rules for getting a driver's license.

1. Drivers *have to* (have to) get a license in their state of residence. They can go to their local DMV (Department of Motor Vehicles*).

2. Generally, a person _____ (have to) be 16 to 18 years old to have a license. This depends on the state or province.

3. A driver _____ (need to) show documents to prove his or her identity.

4. An acceptable document _____ (need to) have your name and address.

5. Foreigners can drive in the U.S. and Canada. Drivers _____ (not / have to) be U.S. or Canadian citizens.

6. Foreign drivers _____ (have to) have an international driver's license.

7. Some states require new drivers to take a driving class. In most states in the U.S., new drivers _____ (have to) pass an exam in order to get a license.

8. In some states, people who already drive _____ (not / need to) take any exams to get a new license.

9. However, in other states, people who already drive _____ (have to) take an exam to get a new license.

10. You _____ (not / must) forget to bring the right documents to the DMV. This can save you a lot of time and frustration.

*Note: Not all states and provinces call this the Department of Motor Vehicles. However, everyone in the United States and Canada understands the term *DMV*.

B Unscramble the words to make questions with *have to* and *need to*.

1. have to have / drivers / a driver's license?

   Do drivers have to have a driver's license?

2. a driver / how old / have to be?

   _____

3. have to / what / bring / drivers / to the DMV?

   _____

4. need to say? / what / an acceptable document

   _____

5. have to / be citizens? / drivers

   _____

6. need to take / new drivers / a class?

   _____

7. pass an exam? / have to / new drivers

   _____

8. need to go / drivers / to get their license? / where

   _____

C *Pair Work* Ask and answer the questions in B with a partner. Use the information in A to find the answers.

Exercise 2.2 ◀)) Pronunciation Focus: *Have To* and *Has To*

Have to is usually pronounced "hafta."	I **hafta** win the game. You **hafta** see my new game!
Has to is usually pronounced "hasta."	She **hasta** try harder to win. He **hasta** think quickly when he plays this game!

A ◀)) Listen and repeat the sentences in the chart above.

B ◀)) Listen. Complete the sentences with *have to* or *has to*.

STACK'EM   GAMING   NEWS   CODES

Welcome to the Stack'em game website!
Here are some tips on how to win the game!

1. You don't _*have to*_ know many rules to win the game.

2. A player _____ move around different shapes to make lines.

3. Players _____ turn the pieces to make them fit.

4. The pieces _____ fit together with no spaces to make the line disappear.

5. As players get better, the pieces come more quickly. The player _____ think very quickly.

6. You don't _____ play against someone. You can play by yourself.

7. Players _____ have one of the top five scores for their name to be added to the "champion" list.

8. Stack'em is fantastic! You _____ play a lot to become good, but it's fun!

C *Pair Work* Write three sentences about the rules of a game you know how to play. Then share them with a partner.

In "Go Fish," players have to ask each other for cards.

1. _____

2. _____

3. _____

Exercise 2.3 Necessity and Conclusions

A Complete the sentences with the correct verb combination. Use a verb of necessity or conclusion with the words in parentheses. Then label *N* for necessity and *C* for conclusion. Sometimes more than one answer is possible.

1. Sarah has a lot of work to do in the office, then she goes to school at night. She
   *must work* (work) hard. _N_

2. She always has a lot of homework. She _____ (be) exhausted after
   a long week of work and school. _____

3. He says that when Sarah _____ (take) a quick break,
   she can. _____

4. Sarah wants to have a week off.¹ She _____ (talk) to her boss to
   schedule her time off. _____

5. Her boss _____ (look) at the schedule. _____

6. Her boss _____ (make) sure he has enough workers during the
   time when Sarah is off. _____

7. She _____ (not / do) any work when she is away on vacation. Her
   boss will not let her. _____

8. Sarah says her office is a great place to work. She _____ (like) her
   boss and the people she works with. _____

¹**a week off:** a week without work

B *Pair Work* Write four sentences about some of the things you have to do to get ahead in your life. Share your sentences with a partner. Make conclusions about what they do with *must*.

A *I have to work all day and go to school at night.*
B *You must be exhausted!*

1. _____
2. _____
3. _____
4. _____

3 | Avoid Common Mistakes ⚠

1. Make sure *have to* and *need to* agree with the subject.

    has
She ~~have~~ to be very skilled.

2. Use the base form of the verb after *have to*, *need to*, or *must*.

    have
He needs to ~~has~~ his passport.

3. Do not use *to* after *must*.

I must ~~to~~ follow the rules.

4. Use the base form of *have to* and *need to* in negative statements and in questions.

    need
He doesn't ~~needs~~ to register.

    have
Does she ~~has~~ to write an essay?

5. Use *have to* or *must* to express conclusions. Do not use *need to* for conclusions.

    has to / must
Today is Tuesday. Tomorrow ~~needs to~~ be Wednesday.

Editing Task

Find and correct 10 more mistakes in this conversation about someone trying to break a record.

    Pete   Does Jack ~~needs~~ *need* to have a lot of skill to play the game?

    Jim   No, he has to has a lot of luck.

    Pete   How many times does he has to win to break the record?

    Jim   He have to win three more times.

5 ***Pete***   He won eight times, so the record must to be 10.

    Jim   Yes, the world record needs to be 10.

    Pete   Does he need to has a certain time to win?

    Jim   No, he must to have a certain number of points.

    Pete   Jack also has to wins five games in a row.[1] He must to really like this

10   computer game!

    Jim   Yeah, he loves it. He doesn't needs to play it every day, but he enjoys it.

[1]**in a row:** without interruption

4 Grammar for Writing

Writing About Necessity and Obligation

Writers use *have to*, *need to*, and *must* when writing about things that are necessary or important to have or do.

Remember:

- **Use *have to* and *need to* for things that are necessary or important. Use *must* to show a very strong obligation.**

  Clara <u>has to</u> leave work early today. She has a doctor's appointment.

  Everyone <u>needs to</u> take a break from work or studies from time to time.

  You <u>must</u> get more sleep, or you will get sick.

- **Use *do not have to* and *do not need to* to show that something is not necessary or important.**

  We <u>do not need to</u> know all the rules of the game before starting to play.

  They <u>didn't have to</u> get home before midnight.

- **Use *must not* to show that something is forbidden or not allowed. It is common in legal language and in signs.**

  Drivers <u>must not</u> drive faster than 65 miles per hour.

Pre-writing Task

1 Read the paragraph below. How many people does the writer mention?

Relaxing

Everyone needs to find a way to relax or manage stress. This is particularly important before going to bed. Different people have different ways of relaxing. My aunt Flora needs to do something with her hands. She often knits while watching TV. My brother has a very stressful job. He <u>has to do</u> something to help him forget about his stressful day. He says that he has to play cards or read a magazine after dinner. My uncle Ralph has a lot of problems sleeping. He says he has to go for a bike ride or a walk every night after dinner. He does not need to be out for a long time, but he has to exercise and get some fresh air. I <u>must take</u> a hot shower in the evening. Without a shower, I cannot fall asleep. And I must not go to bed too late, or I'll get sick. I really must try hard to get to sleep early.

2 Read the paragraph again. Underline all the uses of *have to* and the verb that follows, and circle the uses of *need to* and the verb that follows. <u>Double underline</u> the uses of *must* and the verbs that follow. Why do you think the writer uses *must* here?

Writing Task

1 *Write*   Use the paragraph in the Pre-writing Task to help you write a paragraph about the different things you and people you know do to relax or to manage stress. You can write about relaxing before bedtime, on the weekends, or while on vacation. You could also write about managing stress at work, at school, or at home. Use *have to*, *need to*, and *must*. Write at least one negative sentence.

2 *Self-Edit*   Use the editing tips below to improve your sentences. Make any necessary changes.

1. Did you use *have to*, *need to*, and *must* to write about ways people relax or manage stress?
2. Did you use *have to*, *need to*, and *must* correctly?
3. Did you use *do not have to*, *do not need to*, and *must not* correctly?
4. Did you avoid the mistakes in the Avoid Common Mistakes chart on page 380?

Adjectives and Adverbs
Making a Good Impression

1 | Grammar in the Real World

A Do you know how to give a presentation? What do you do to prepare? Read the article. How many of your ideas are in the web article?

How to Be a Successful Presenter

For many people, giving a presentation can be a **scary** experience. If you feel **nervous** about giving presentations, here are some helpful tips.

- Prepare your presentation **carefully**. **Careful** preparation will give you confidence, and this will impress[1] your audience. A **confident**[2] presenter
5   always makes a **good** impression.[3]

- Organize your ideas. Think about what you want to say. Then list your three or four main points on note cards.

- Practice giving your presentation aloud[4] by yourself
10   and with friends, too. Tell your friends to give you **honest** feedback,[5] but make sure they tell you first what you did **well**.

- On the day of the presentation, arrive at the room **early**. Think **positive** thoughts and remember that
15   you can do this.

- Before you start, breathe **deeply** and smile **confidently** at your audience. Speak **slowly** and **clearly**. Make eye contact with people in **different** parts of the room. Look at your notes **quickly** when you need to. Your audience wants you to do **well**. Then relax and do your best.

20   After your presentation, ask people for feedback and advice. Use the ideas in your next presentation. With practice, you will learn to give **good** presentations, and you may even enjoy giving them.

[1]**impress:** cause people to admire and respect you | [2]**confident:** not having a doubt about yourself or your abilities | [3]**impression:** an idea or opinion of what someone is like | [4]**aloud:** in a voice loud enough that people can hear it | [5]**feedback:** response after seeing an activity or performance

B *Comprehension Check* Does the article answer these questions? Write *Yes* or *No*. Then answer the questions.

1. What can give you confidence as a presenter? _____

2. What are some ways that can help you organize your ideas? _____

3. What should you do when you practice? _____

4. What should you do after your presentation? Why? _____

C *Notice* Look at the word in bold in each sentence. Circle the word that it describes. How are the words you circled in item 1 different from the words you circled in item 2?

1. a. A **confident** presenter always makes a good impression.
   b. Think **positive** thoughts.

2. a. Smile **confidently**.
   b. Before you start, breathe **deeply**.

Next, complete the sentence below. How do you know which word to use?

3. He walks _____ .
   a. confident
   b. confidently

2 | Adjectives and Adverbs of Manner

▶ Grammar Presentation

2.1 Adjectives and Adverbs of Manner

a. Adjectives give information about nouns. They often come before a noun or after *be*.

> ADJ.   NOUN
> I want your **honest** feedback.

> BE   ADJ.
> The slides were **clear**.

b. Adverbs give information about verbs.

> VERB   ADV.
> The presenter spoke **clearly**.

> VERB   ADV.
> She prepared her presentation **carefully**.

c. Adverbs of manner usually come after a verb or a verb + object.

> VERB   ADV.
> Dress **nicely**.

> VERB   OBJ.   ADV.
> She looked at the audience **quickly**.

2.1 Adjectives and Adverbs of Manner *(continued)*

d. Don't put an adverb between a verb and an object. Place it after the object.

| VERB | OBJECT | ADVERB |

*Prepare your presentation **carefully**.*

NOT ~~*Prepare carefully your presentation*~~.

2.2 Basic Forms of Adverbs

	Adjective	Adverb
a. For most adverbs of manner, add -*ly* to the adjective form.	*bad* *careful* *clear* *fluent* *loud* *nervous* *quick*	*bad**ly*** *careful**ly*** *clear**ly*** *fluent**ly*** *loud**ly*** *nervous**ly*** *quick**ly***
b. With adjectives ending in -*y*, change *y* to *i* and add -*ly*.	*easy* *happy*	*eas**ily*** *happ**ily***
c. With adjectives ending in -*ic*, add -*ally*.	*automatic* *academic*	*automatic**ally*** *academic**ally***
d. With adjectives ending in a consonant + -*le*, drop *e* and add -*y*.	*gentle* *terrible*	*gent**ly*** *terri**bly***
e. The adverb and adjective form of the following words are the same: *early, fast, hard, late*.	*He is **early**.* *It sounds **fast**.* *It's a **hard** test.* *They're **late**.*	*He went home **early**.* *He talks **fast**.* *He studied **hard**.* *They arrived **late**.*
f. *Well* is the adverb form of the adjective *good*.	*He's **good** at English.*	*He speaks English **well**.*
Well can also be an adjective. It means "healthy."	*He isn't **well**.*	
g. Some adjectives that end in -*ly* do not have an adverb form. Do <u>not</u> use them as adverbs.	*elderly, friendly, lively,* *lonely, lovely, ugly*	

Adverbs with -*ly*: See page A24.

Data from the Real World

These are the most common adverbs of manner:

well	late	easily	carefully	seriously	automatically
hard	fast	clearly	strongly	differently	properly
early	quickly	slowly	closely	badly	

▶ Grammar Application

Exercise 2.1 Adjectives and Adverbs

A Circle the adjectives and draw an arrow to the nouns they describe. Underline the adverbs and draw a line to the verbs they describe.

I'm a (professional) hairstylist, and I'm very good at my job. I'm friendly and polite to my clients, so I make a good impression. But I don't schedule clients early in the day because I'm not in a good mood until noon.

Of course, I don't get an early start to my day. I wake up late and start my day slowly.
5 I can't think clearly without three cups of strong coffee. After breakfast, I take a shower, get dressed, and check my e-mail. I don't talk to anyone in the morning, except for my elderly neighbor when I leave home. He likes to sit on the front porch. I think he's lonely.

I drive to work, but my commute isn't bad. When I get to work, I check my
10 schedule closely and make a few quick phone calls. At 11:55 a.m., I finish my last cup of coffee and smile warmly at my first client at 12:00 noon.

B *Over to You* What is your morning routine? Write four sentences using adjectives and adverbs. Then tell a partner.

A I get up early. I'm awake by 6:00 a.m.
B I sleep late. On the weekends, I sleep until 11:00 a.m.

Exercise 2.2 More Adjectives and Adverbs

A Complete each sentence pair with the adverb or adjective form of the underlined word in the first sentence. The sentences will have a similar meaning. (Remember: Some adjectives do not change form when they are adverbs.)

1. Cindy makes a good impression when she presents in front of a group.

   a. She is <u>careful</u> when she researches her topic. She researches her topic _carefully_ .

   b. Her voice is <u>clear</u> and easy to understand. She speaks _____ .

   c. When she starts to speak, her smile is <u>automatic</u>. When she starts to speak, she _____ smiles.

   d. She <u>strongly</u> argues her points. She makes _____ arguments for her points.

2. Robert made a good impression at the job interview.

   a. He was <u>polite</u>. He talked _politely_ to the interviewer.

   b. He was <u>early</u>. He arrived at the company _____ .

   c. He thought about the questions, and he answered the questions <u>carefully</u>. He was _____ in his answers.

   d. He was <u>good</u> at answering the questions. He answered the questions _____ .

   e. He didn't speak <u>badly</u> about his former employer. He didn't say _____ things about his former employer.

B *Pair Work* Take turns reading the sentences. Identify the adjective and adverb form of the words.

Exercise 2.3 Adverbs of Manner

A Complete the questions about making a good impression at school and at work. Use the adverb forms of the words in parentheses.

Questionnaire

1. Do you get to work or school _early_ (early), or do you arrive _late_ (late)?
2. Do you take your job or your studies _____ (serious)?
3. Do you work _____ (hard), or are you lazy?
4. Do you check your assignments _____ (careful)?
5. Do you try to do every job _____ (proper), or do you do everything _____ (quick)?
6. Do you always dress _____ (appropriate) for work or school?
7. Do you always speak _____ (polite) to your boss or teacher?
8. Do you plan your time _____ (good) and complete your work on time?
9. Do you organize your desk _____ (neat)?
10. Can you give instructions _____ (clear)?
11. Do you like to work _____ (close) with co-workers or classmates?

B *Pair Work* Ask and answer the questions in A. Give more information in your answers.

A Do you get to work early?
B No, I don't. I usually arrive just in time.

C What do you think are the six most important qualities of a good employee? What about a good student? Complete the sentences using ideas from A and your own ideas.

A good employee . . .	A good student . . .
1. _works hard_	1. _studies hard_
2. _____	2. _____
3. _____	3. _____
4. _____	4. _____
5. _____	5. _____
6. _____	6. _____

3 Adjectives with Linking Verbs; Adjectives and Adverbs with *Very* and *Too*

▶ Grammar Presentation

3.1 Adjectives with Linking Verbs

a. Use an adjective, not an adverb, after these linking verbs: *be, get, seem, look, feel, sound, smell, taste*	ADJ. I **get confused** when someone asks difficult questions. ADJ. The presentation **looked interesting**. ADJ. ADJ. You may **feel nervous**, but try to **sound confident**. ADJ. That coffee **smells good**.
b. When *feel* means "have an opinion," use the adverb *strongly*.	FEEL + ADV. (OPINION) I **feel strongly** that people should speak clearly. BUT I felt weak when I had the flu, but I feel **strong** now.

3.2 *Very* and *Too* + Adjective or Adverb

a. You can use *very* and *too* before adjectives or adverbs to make their meaning stronger. *Very* and *too* do not have the same meaning.	VERY + ADJ. VERY + ADV. She is **very serious**. She works **very hard**. TOO + ADJ. TOO + ADV. The talk was **too long**. He spoke **too fast**.
b. *Very* makes an adjective or an adverb stronger.	Her ideas were **very helpful**. He spoke **very fast**. I understood him, but it was difficult.
c. *Too* means "more than necessary." It usually has a negative meaning and means there's a problem.	He spoke **too fast**. I couldn't understand anything that he said. The school is **too expensive**. I can't afford it.
d. You can also use *very* (but not *too*) before an adjective + a noun.	ADJ. + NOUN It's a **very expensive program**. NOT It's a too expensive program.

3.2 *Very* and *Too* + Adjective or Adverb *(continued)*

e. You can use an infinitive after *too* + an adjective or adverb.

*She's **too tired to study**.*
(= She can't study because she's too tired.)
*She spoke **too fast to understand**.*
(= I did not understand her because she spoke too fast.)
*The words on the slides were **too small to read**.*
(= No one could read the words because they were too small.)

▶ Grammar Application

Exercise 3.1 Adjectives with Linking Verbs

A Complete the sentences about how people react in new social situations. Choose the correct adjective or adverb in parentheses. When you finish, check (✓) the statements that are true for you.

1. I often get **nervous** / **shyly** in new social situations. _____

2. I am **confident** / **easily** around new people. _____

3. I often feel **excited** / **nervously** before a party. _____

4. I feel **uncomfortable** / **fast** when I'm nervous. _____

5. I hope other people think I look **attractive** / **confidently**. _____

6. I try to be a **nicely** / **friendly** person. _____

7. I like to tell jokes and make people laugh. I tell jokes **bad** / **well**. _____

8. I get **excited** / **well** when I listen to music and sing along to the songs. _____

9. It's never a problem for me to remember people's names. I do that **easily** / **automatic**. _____

10. I give my opinion when I feel **strong** / **strongly** about something. _____

B *Pair Work* Compare sentences from A. Do you act the same way in new situations?

    A I often get nervous in new social situations. How about you?

    B I don't get nervous. I'm always excited about meeting new people.

Exercise 3.2 Adjectives with *Very* and *Too*

A Complete the sentences about a party. Use *very* or *too*.

1. The party lasted for six hours. The party was ___*very*___ long, so we went home early.

2. The party lasted for an hour. Everyone wanted to stay longer. The party was _____ short.

3. There were 75 people at the party. The living room holds 50. The room was _____ small.

4. There were five people at the table. The table seats 12. The table was _____ big.

5. The party was noisy, and I couldn't hear conversations. The party was _____ noisy.

6. The party was noisy, but I had a great time. The party was _____ noisy.

7. Some people spoke quickly, but I understood most of it. Some people spoke _____ quickly.

8. One man spoke quickly, and I didn't understand a word of it. He spoke _____ quickly.

9. It was 25°F (-4°C) outside on the porch. We had to leave. It was _____ cold.

10. It was 43°F (6°C) outside on the porch. I wore my coat. It was _____ cold.

B 🔊 Now listen and check your answers.

Exercise 3.3 Adjectives with *Too* + Adjective + Infinitive

A *Pair Work* Complete the conversations. Use the word given with *too* + adjective + infinitive (*to* + verb). Then practice with a partner.

1. **A** You passed your exams with straight As.
   B That can't <u>be true</u>.

   (good) It's _too good to be true_ .

2. **A** Do you like your new job?
   B I can't <u>say</u>. I only started today.

   (early) It's _____ .

3. **A** Mom! Dad! We want <u>to get married</u>.
   B You're only 16!

   (young) You're _____ .

4. **A** I want <u>to change programs</u> in school.
   B Well, there's still time.

   (not late) It's _____ .

5. **A** Let's <u>go camping</u> this weekend.
   B Camping? It's 10 below outside!

   (cold) It's _____ .

6. **A** Is your brother <u>going to work</u> today?
   B Well, I think he has the flu.

   (sick) He's _____ .

7. **A** Why don't you <u>ask</u> your boss for help?
   B I can't, I'm afraid of him.

   (scared) I'm _____ .

8. **A** You look really stressed today.
   B Do I? You know, I can't <u>think</u>.

   (busy) I'm _____ .

B *Group Work* Discuss these questions in a group. Which ideas do you share?

1. Do you ever get too tired to think?
2. Are you ever too scared to ask questions?
3. Do you ever feel too embarrassed to apologize for something?
4. Were you ever too sick to go to work or school this year?
5. What is something you feel is too difficult to do?
6. Are 17-year-olds too young to get married?

Data from the Real World

People often use *not very* + adjective or adverb to make negative statements "softer," less critical, or less direct.	*The speaker wasn't very good. He didn't speak very well.* NOT *The speaker was bad. He spoke badly.*

Exercise 3.4 *Not very . . .*

Read the notes that an interviewer wrote about a job candidate. Make them less critical, or direct, and write statements using *not very* and the words in parentheses.

1. unfriendly *He wasn't very friendly.* (friendly)
2. spoke nervously *He didn't speak very confidently.* (confidently)
3. wore a dirty shirt _____ (clean)
4. bad at problem solving _____ (good at)
5. answered questions badly _____ (well)
6. looked dishonest _____ (honest)
7. seemed inexperienced _____ (experienced)
8. acted bored _____ (interested)

4 Avoid Common Mistakes ⚠️

1. **Use an adverb when you give information about most verbs. Some adverbs are irregular and do not end in -ly.**

        efficiently   *hard*

   I work ~~efficient~~.   I work very ~~hardly~~.

2. **Use an adjective after the linking verbs be, feel, get, look, seem, smell, sound, and taste.**

          strange

   He seemed ~~strangely~~.

3. **Be especially careful with *good* and *well*. People often use *good* instead of *well*, especially when they speak, but do not write this.**

           well

   I try to do things ~~good~~.

4. **Do not use an adverb between a verb and its object.**

                carefully

   I always prepare ~~carefully~~ my answers. ∧

5. **Do not use *too* when you mean *very*.**

        very

   My teacher is ~~too~~ good. I'm learning a lot.

Editing Task

Find and correct the mistakes in this article about job interviews.

Preparing for an Interview

    An interview can be a difficult experience. Prepare ~~carefully~~ your responses, *carefully* ∧ and you will make a good impression.

    Before the interview, research thoroughly the company. Find out about its products and services. You should always be truthfully about the things you do

5 good. When you talk about something you do bad, choose a weakness that is not serious. Say that you are too aware of the weakness and that you are working hardly to improve yourself. Say you want a new challenge and that you want to progress in your career. Always sound positively and don't complain about your current job.

    On the day of the interview, dress nice. Shake firmly hands when you meet the

10 interviewer. Try to sound sincerely and look too confident. Follow these steps and you'll do good.

5 | Grammar for Writing ✐

Writing About People's Behavior in Different Situations

Writers use adjectives and adverbs to describe people and the way they do things in situations such as job interviews, presentations, and social situations.
Remember:

- **Use adjectives to talk about people's personalities and adverbs to talk about the way people do things.**

  Eduardo is a very friendly person. He never speaks badly about anyone.

- **Use *very* to strengthen your statements and *not very* in negative statements to be more polite or to sound less negative.**

  Sadie is a very serious student.
  Our neighbors do not speak English very well.

Pre-writing Task

1 Read the paragraph below. What situation is the writer giving tips about? What tip do you think is the most useful?

Meeting People

Do you get nervous meeting new people at parties? Many people are not very comfortable in these situations. Some people are afraid that they are not very interesting. Other people talk too much or too loudly. Here are some tips for making a good impression at parties. Don't worry about finding intelligent things to say. Listen closely to others instead. Many people can talk very happily about themselves for a long time. Listen carefully and then ask questions. Also, when you listen to people, make eye contact with them. People will think you are very nice, and they will want to be your friend. These tips will help you enjoy parties and make new friends very easily.

2 Read the paragraph again. Underline all the adverbs of manner and circle all the adjectives. Draw arrows from the adverbs and adjectives to the verbs and nouns or pronouns they describe. Double underline the uses of *very* and *not very*. Notice how *very* strengthens the statement and *not very* makes it sound less negative.

Writing Task

1 *Write* Use the paragraph in the Pre-writing Task to help you write a paragraph about making a good impression in a new situation. You can write about making a good impression in a new class, in a new job, in a group with students, on a team at work, or in a new social situation.

2 *Self-Edit* Use the editing tips below to improve your sentences. Make any necessary changes.

1. Did you use adjectives and adverbs to write about uncomfortable situations?
2. Did you use adjectives to write about personalities and adverbs to write about the way people do things?
3. Did you use *very* to strengthen your statements and *not very* to "soften" your negative statements?
4. Did you avoid the mistakes in the Avoid Common Mistakes chart on page 395?

32

Comparative Adjectives and Adverbs

Progress

1 | Grammar in the Real World

A How has modern life changed in the last 15 years? Read the question forum from a website. What changes does the forum discuss?

Question Forum[1] Ask your question here.

SEARCH

Dear Question Forum:

My grandmother says that everything got **bigger**, **faster**, and **better** in the twentieth century. Is that true? Did some things get **smaller**, **slower**, or **worse** than in the years before?
–Lorraine, San Diego, CA

5 **Forum Answer:**

It's a matter of opinion, but what your grandmother says is generally true. In the twentieth century, buildings became **taller**. Bridges became **longer** than they were in the nineteenth century, and highways became **wider** and **faster** than the old roads. Cities became **larger** and **more**
10 **crowded** than they had been before. New airplanes were suddenly **larger** and **heavier** than old airplanes. Large companies joined together to make even **bigger** global corporations.[2] Technology in the home got **better**. Home electrical appliances like refrigerators and washing machines became **better**, **cheaper**, and **more efficient**. Computers became **more**
15 **powerful** and **more complicated** but **easier** to use. The Internet gave us **faster** communication and a **smaller** world – what we now call the global village.

Did everything get **larger** and **better**? Not everything. A lot of things did not get **bigger**, and some things got **worse**, like some environmental
20 problems. Some things became **smaller** but **better**. For example, phones became **thinner**, cameras got **lighter**, and modern video cameras became much **smaller** than **older** video cameras. Unfortunately, the ice sheets[3] in the Arctic and Antarctic became **smaller**, too, as the world became **hotter**. Generally, things did not become **slower** – except perhaps traffic in cities, which
25 became **more congested**.[4] The big question is: Are people **happier** now?

[1]**forum:** a place to talk about something of public interest | [2]**corporation:** a large company | [3]**ice sheet:** layer of ice | [4]**congested:** too blocked or crowded

B *Comprehension Check* Complete the sentences. Use the text in the forum answer to help you.

1. Highways became _____wider_____ and _____faster_____.
2. Computers became _____more powerful_____ and _____more ampio_____ but _____easier_____ to use.
3. The Internet gave us _____faster_____ communication and a _____smaller_____ world.

C *Notice* Complete each word or phrase. Use the text to help you.

1. small__er__   3. large_larger_   5. _more_ powerful
2. bigg_er_   4. _more_ efficient   6. _more_ congested

What are the two different ways to change the adjectives?

2 | Comparative Adjectives

▶ Grammar Presentation

You can use comparative adjectives to describe how two people or things are different from one another.	*New airplanes were **larger** and **heavier than** old airplanes.*

2.1 Comparisons with *Be* + Adjective

	Be	Comparative Adjective	*Than*	
I	am	older		my brother.
		more serious		my parents.
You We They	are	happier	than	Elisa.
		more successful		our co-workers.
He She It	is	taller		me.
		more excited		the teachers.

2.2 Comparative Adjective + Noun

	Comparative Adjective	Noun
The Internet gave us	**faster**	communication.
Large companies joined together to make	**bigger**	corporations.
We now have	**more powerful**	computers.

2.3 Comparative of Short Adjectives (One Syllable)

	Adjective	Comparative
a. For one-syllable adjectives, add -er.	low	low**er**
	fast	fast**er**
b. For one-syllable adjectives ending in -e, add -r.	safe	safe**r**
	large	large**r**
c. If the adjective ends with one vowel + one consonant, double the last letter and add -er.	hot	ho**tter**
	big	bi**gger**
d. If the adjective has two syllables and ends in -y, change the y to i and add -er.	heavy	heav**ier**
	easy	eas**ier**

2.4 Comparative of Long Adjectives (Two or More Syllables)

Adjective	Comparative
crowded	**more** crowded
powerful	**more** powerful
economical	**more** economical
efficient	**more** efficient

2.5 Two-Syllable Adjectives That Take -er

Adjective	Comparative
narrow	narrow**er**
quiet	quiet**er**
simple	simpl**er**

2.6 Irregular Adjectives

Adjective	Comparative
good	better
bad	worse
far	further (farther)

 Further is over 10 times more frequent than *farther*.

▶◀ Adjectives and Adverbs: Comparative and Superlative Forms: See page A22.

2.7 Using Comparative Adjectives

a. Use comparative adjectives to show a difference between two people, places, things, or ideas.

*The Sears Tower is **taller than** the Empire State Building.*

b. Use *than* after a comparative and before the second person or thing that you are comparing. Don't use *that* or *then*.

*Jessica is older **than** Denise.*
NOT *older ~~that~~ Denise / older ~~then~~ Denise*

c. You can use a comparative adjective without *than* when the second part of the comparison is obvious.

*I need a **bigger** apartment.*
(= a bigger apartment than the apartment I have now)

d. *Less* is the opposite of *more*. Do not use *less* with one-syllable adjectives.

*The traffic here is **less congested** than in the city.*
*Pennsylvania is **smaller** than California.*
NOT *~~less big~~*

e. You can use a pronoun after *than* instead of a noun.

*Mike's sister is taller **than he is**.* (= than Mike is)
*Sue sings better **than I do**.*

In speaking, you can use an object pronoun. In academic writing, always use a subject pronoun.

*My brother is older **than me**.*
*My brother is older **than I am**.*

Data from the Real World

The 15 most common comparative adjectives ending in *-er* in writing and speaking are:

better	easier	higher	lower	stronger
bigger	further	larger	older	worse
earlier	greater	later	smaller	younger

The 10 most common comparative adjectives with *more* are:

comfortable	efficient	important	powerful	serious
difficult	expensive	interesting	recent	successful

▶ Grammar Application

Exercise 2.1 Comparisons with *Be*

A How do things today compare with 20 years ago? Write the correct forms of the comparative adjectives in parentheses.

1. Home appliances are _cheaper_ (cheap).

2. Laptop computers are _____lighter_____ (light).

3. Desktop computers are _____quieter_____ (quiet).

4. Digital cameras are _____easyer_____ (easy) to use.

5. Bicycles are _____faster_____ (fast).

6. Cars are _____safer_____ (safe).

7. Cell phones are _____smaller_____ (small).

8. Homes are _____bigger_____ (big).

B Compare cell phones from many years ago and now. Use comparative forms of the adjectives in the box.

Early cellular phone

Smartphone

| big | cheap | expensive | fast | ~~heavy~~ | powerful | slow | thin |

1. _Old cell phones were heavier._   5. _New cellphone were faster_

2. _Old cellphones were bigger._   6. _____

3. _New phone was expensier_   7. _____

4. _New phone were powerfull_   8. _____

Exercise 2.2 Comparative Adjectives and Nouns

A Read about a city's problems. How can it become a better place to live? Complete the sentences and make solutions. Use comparative forms of the adjectives in the box and nouns. Use each adjective once.

attractive	clean	energy-efficient	new	~~wide~~
~~cheap~~	clear	frequent	~~safe~~	

Problem	Solution
1. The main highway through the city is narrow.	We should build a _wider highway_ .
2. The bridge over the river is old and dangerous.	We should build a _safer bridge_ .
3. The downtown parking is very expensive.	We should have _cheaper parking_
4. The city parks are not clean.	We should have _clean parks_ ne
5. The city's buses are not energy-efficient.	We should buy _energy-efficient buses_
6. The street signs are confusing.	We should install _new streets_ .
7. The bus service is infrequent.	We should have _freq better bus servis_
8. The city's website is unattractive.	The city should create a _attractive city ps_

B *Pair Work* What changes should happen to improve your town or city? Discuss with a partner.

A *Our city needs a more frequent subway service.*

B *We need nicer department stores downtown. We should have . . .*

C *Group Work* Compare cities and towns that you know. Work in groups. Then tell the class about them. Use the adjectives in parentheses.

1. (modern) _Houston is more modern than San Antonio._
2. (big) _New York has bigger parks than Miami._
3. (traditional) _____
4. (cheap) _____
5. (good / job market) _____
6. (clean) _____
7. (historic) _____
8. (fancy / stores) _____
9. (crowded) _____

3 | Comparative Adverbs

▶ Grammar Presentation

You can use comparative adverbs to describe how two actions or events are different from each other.

*Ashley drives **more slowly** than her brother.*

3.1 Comparisons with Adverbs

	Verb	Comparative Adverb	*Than*	
Joanna	**runs**	**faster**		her brother.
The new printer	**works**	**better**		the old printer.
The population of Italy	**is growing**	**more slowly**	**than**	the population of Canada.
A diesel car	**runs**	**more efficiently**		a gasoline car.

3.2 Comparative of Short Adverbs (One Syllable)

	Adverb	Comparative
For one syllable adverbs, add -er or -r.	fast	fast**er**
	high	high**er**
	late	late**r**
	long	long**er**
	hard	hard**er**

3.3 Comparative of Longer Adverbs (Two or More Syllables)

	Adverb	Comparative
a. For adverbs of two or more syllables, use *more* (or *less*).	often	**more** / **less** often
	carefully	**more** / **less** carefully
	quickly	**more** / **less** quickly
	easily	**more** / **less** easily
b. We say *earlier*, not *more early*.	*This flight arrives **earlier than** the other flight.*	

3.4 Irregular Adverbs

Irregular Adverbs	Comparative
well	better
badly	worse
far	further or farther

▸▎ Adjectives and Adverbs: Comparative and Superlative Forms: See page A22.

3.5 Using Comparative Adverbs

a. You can use comparative adverbs to compare the way two people do the same action.

*Hilda studies **harder than** the other students.*
*My brother drives **more carefully** than my sister.*

b. You can use comparative adverbs to compare the way two actions or events happen.

*Cairo is growing **more rapidly than** London.*

c. You can use comparative adverbs to compare the way an action happened in two different time periods.

*Larissa works **harder** now **than** she did last year.*

d. Use *than* after a comparative adverb and before the second action or event that you are comparing. Don't use *that* or *then*.

*He drives **faster than** his brother.*
NOT *faster ~~that~~ his brother / faster ~~then~~ his brother*

e. You can use a comparative adverb without *than*.

*I can run fast, but Lorna can run **faster**.*

f. *Less* is the opposite of *more*.

*The old car runs **less efficiently** than the new car.*

Do not use *less* with one-syllable adverbs.

*Meryl arrived **earlier than** Patrick.*
NOT ~~less late~~

▶ Grammar Application

Exercise 3.1 Making Comparisons with Adverbs

🔊 Listen to the conversation. Complete the chart with comparative adverbs.

New York, New York	Grant, Florida
1. People walk _more quickly_ .	4. You drive _____ to get to a mall.
2. People work _____ .	5. Joe and Bill go out _____ .
3. Restaurants stay open _____ .	6. You spend money _____ .

Exercise 3.2 More Making Comparisons with Adverbs

A Write the comparative form of the adverb. Then write verbs that go with it from the list. Some verbs can go with more than one adverb.

drive	go to bed	play football	sleep	study
get up	go to the gym	play the guitar	speak English	walk
go out	go to the movies	sing	spend money	work

Adverb, Comparative Adverb	Verb(s)
1. fast *faster*	*run, drive*
2. well	
3. carefully	
4. hard	
5. slowly	
6. early	
7. far	
8. frequently	
9. badly	
10. late	

B *Over to You* How is your lifestyle different from five years ago? In what ways do you do things differently? Use ideas from A.

I speak English better now than I did five years ago.

1. _____
2. _____
3. _____
4. _____
5. _____
6. _____
7. _____

Exercise 3.3 Adverbs and Personal Pronouns

Data from the Real World

Research shows that when people use a personal pronoun after *than*, they use the object forms *me, him, her, us, them*. They do not normally use the subject forms *I, he, she, we, they*.

> You drive better than me / him.
> NOT better than ~~I / he~~

than + object pronoun
than + subject pronoun

People use the subject form of the pronoun with an auxiliary verb (*be, do,* or *have*) or a modal verb (*will, can,* etc.), especially in writing.

> He drives faster than I do. (= faster than I drive)
> She can speak English better than he can. (= better than he can speak English)

A *Over to You* Complete the sentences with the names of people you know. Use a subject pronoun and an auxiliary or modal verb after *than*.

1. _____ gets up earlier than I _do_ .

2. _____ can run faster than I _can_ .

3. _____ eats more slowly than I _____ .

4. _____ exercises more often than I _____ .

5. _____ commutes further than I _____ .

6. _____ studied harder for yesterday's test than I _____ .

7. _____ can speak more fluently than I _____ .

8. _____ did better on the quiz than I _____ .

B *Pair Work* Tell a partner about each person in A. Use object pronouns (*me, him, them,* etc.).

> My friend Charlie gets up earlier than me. He starts work at 7:00 a.m. I get up later than him.

4 Avoid Common Mistakes ⚠

1. Do not use *more* with the *-er* comparative forms of adjectives and adverbs.

She drives ~~more~~ faster than her brother.

This store is ~~more~~ cheaper than the other one.

2. Do not use *more* with one-syllable adjectives and adverbs.

My brother is ~~more~~ *taller* ~~tall~~ than I am.   She speaks ~~more fast~~ *faster* than I do.

3. Do not use the *-er* ending with most adjectives of two or more syllables.

His second movie was ~~excitinger~~ *more exciting* than his first movie.

4. Do not use *more* with *better* or *worse*.

My English is getting ~~more~~ better this year.

5. Use *than* after a comparative, not *that* or *then*.

She works harder ~~then~~ *than* I do.

Editing Task

Progress is change that results in a general improvement in life. Read the ideas about progress. Find and correct eight more mistakes in this blog.

What Is Progress?

It is not easy to answer this question. Here is a list of ideas.

Lisa: Medicines are now more effective and ~~more cheap~~ *cheaper*, so people's health is more better. People expect to live longer then they did 100 years ago.

Dan: There is a more shorter work week for everyone. There are powerfuler machines and computers, so people can be free from manual work.

Sanjay: Children reach a more higher level of education.

Cristina: People have more big houses and a comfortabler life that their parents.

5 | Grammar for Writing ✎

Making Comparisons

Writers use adjectives and adverbs to compare two people, places, animals, or things, or with the way they were at an earlier time.

Remember:

- **Use comparative <u>adjectives</u> to compare the way people, places, animals, and things are.**
  Ignacio is <u>funnier</u> than his brother.
  Santa Barbara is <u>more expensive</u> than it was five years ago.

- **Use comparative <u>adverbs</u> to compare the way people or animals do things.**
  Yoshi talks <u>more quietly</u> than Kim, but he talks <u>more clearly</u> than he did before.
  My dog runs <u>faster</u> than Mariel's dog does.

Pre-writing Task

1 Read the paragraphs below. What two things is the writer comparing? Which of the two things does the writer think is better and which is worse?

Good and Bad Changes

Cars are very different today from cars in the 1990s. A lot of today's cars are <u>smaller</u>. Cars today also run (more) efficiently. They use less gas, so they can go further on one tank of gas. Some cars are easier to park because they have special parking instruments, and some even park themselves! New cars have GPS systems that tell you where you are. Cars
5 are also safer today. Air bags, seat belts, and better brakes that help you stop more quickly make them safer.

I think that one thing that is not better today is the driver. Some drivers drive less carefully these days. The main reason is that people use cell phones. Many drivers still talk on their cell phones while they drive. In many states this is illegal, but people still do it.
10 Cars may be safer today, but the driver must drive safely.

2 Read the paragraphs again. Underline all the comparative adverbs and draw arrows to the verbs they describe. <u>Double underline</u> all the comparative adjectives and draw arrows to the nouns that they describe. Circle *more* and *less* + adjective or adverb.

Writing Task

1 *Write* Use the paragraphs in the Pre-writing Task to help you write a comparative paragraph. You can compare people, places, animals, or things. How are the people, animals, or things different? What do they do differently?

2 *Self-Edit* Use the editing tips below to improve your sentences. Make any necessary changes.

1. Did you use comparative adjectives and adverbs to compare people, animals, or things?
2. Did you use comparative adjectives to compare the way people, animals, or things are?
3. Did you use comparative adverbs to compare the way people, animals, or things act differently?
4. Did you avoid the mistakes in the Avoid Common Mistakes chart on page 409?

Superlative Adjectives and Adverbs
Facts and Opinions

1 | Grammar in the Real World

A What do you know about Vietnam? Read the travel website below. What is the most interesting fact?

Vietnam

Vietnam, in Southeast Asia, shares borders with China, Laos,
5 and Cambodia. It is a long country, and at its **narrowest** point it is only
10 about 50 km (31 miles) wide.

Vietnam's population is about 90 million. The capital is Hanoi. The **biggest** city is Ho Chi Minh City,
15 formerly called Saigon.

Vietnam's **most historic** city is Hue. It was the home of the Nguyen kings, and it has many palaces and monuments.

20 The **most popular** beach is located near the city Nha Trang in the central coast area.

The **most beautiful** area is Ha Long Bay. There are hundreds of small islands and unusual rock formations.[1]

25 Vietnam has a hot and humid climate, with the **hottest** temperatures in April. The **wettest** month is September.
30 The **most important** export[2] is crude oil,[3] and the **most important** crop[4] is rice. The industry that is growing the **most rapidly**
35 is tourism.

[1]**rock formation:** a large area of rock that has characteristics different from the land around it | [2]**export:** an item someone sends to another country for sale or use | [3]**crude oil:** oil from underground that nobody has made into different products yet | [4]**crop:** a plant like a grain, vegetable, or fruit that people grow in large amounts on a farm

B *Comprehension Check* Answer the questions.

1. Where is Vietnam located?
2. What is the climate like?
3. Why is Hue famous?
4. What is Vietnam's most important export?

C *Notice* Find the forms of these common adjectives in the text. Write them in the spaces below.

1. big _____
2. hot _____
3. wet _____
4. narrow _____

5. popular _____
6. historic _____
7. important _____
8. beautiful _____

2 | Superlative Adjectives

▶ Grammar Presentation

You can use superlative adjectives to describe how a person or thing is different from all others.

*The **most historic** city in Vietnam is Hue.*

2.1 Statements

Noun	Be	The	Superlative Adjective	Noun		
Ha Long Bay	is		**most beautiful**	area		Vietnam.
November	isn't	**the**	**wettest**	month	in	the country.
Ho Chi Minh City	is		**biggest**	city		the area.

2.2 Information Questions

Noun	Be	The	Superlative Adjective	Noun		
Which city	is		**most historic**	city		Vietnam?
What	is	**the**	**most important**	export	in	the country?

2.3 Superlative of Short Adjectives (One Syllable)

	Adjective	Superlative
a. For one-syllable adjectives, add -*est*.	*long*	*long**est***
	slow	*slow**est***
b. For one-syllable adjectives ending in -*e*, add -*st*.	*large*	*large**st***
	wide	*wide**st***
c. For adjectives that end in one vowel + one consonant, double the final consonant and add -*est*.	*big*	*bi**ggest***
	hot	*ho**ttest***
d. For two-syllable adjectives ending in -*y*, change *y* to *i* and add -*est*.	*heavy*	*heav**iest***
	tiny	*tin**iest***

2.4 Superlative of Longer Adjectives (Two or More Syllables)

Adjective	Superlative
beautiful	**most** beautiful
historic	**most** historic
important	**most** important
popular	**most** popular

2.5 Two-syllable Adjectives That Take -*est*

Adjective	Superlative
narrow	narrow**est**
quiet	quiet**est**
simple	simpl**est**

2.6 Irregular Adjectives

Adjective	Superlative
good	**best**
bad	**worst**
far	**farthest** or **furthest** (*farthest* is more common)

▶▶ Adjectives and Adverbs: Comparative and Superlative Forms: See page A22.

2.7 Using Superlative Adjectives

a. Use *the* before a superlative adjective followed by a noun.

*Ha Long Bay is **the** most beautiful area in Vietnam.*
NOT *is most beautiful area*

b. Use superlative adjectives to show how one person or thing in a group is different in some way from all the others.

*Orla is **the most intelligent** student in the class.*
*The Nile is **the longest** river in Africa.*

c. You can use a superlative adjective without a noun.

*They have three daughters. Tran is **the youngest**.*

d. You can use a possessive item (*my, your, Patrick's, the world's,* etc.) instead of *the* before a superlative adjective.

*That book is **my most helpful** guide book.*
*Cheetahs are **the world's fastest** animals.*

e. Use *in* + noun after superlative adjectives when you want to talk about a specific group, for example, *in the world, in the class,* etc. Do not use *of*.

*The Nile is the longest river **in** the world.*
NOT *the longest river of the world*

f. *Least* is the opposite of *most*. Do not use *least* with one-syllable adjectives.

*The Royal is the **least expensive** hotel in town.*
*Rhode Island is the **smallest** U.S. state.*
NOT *the least big*

Data from the Real World

The most common superlative adjectives ending in *-est* in writing and speaking are:

biggest	fastest	largest	lowest	strongest
closest	greatest	latest	oldest	youngest
earliest	highest	longest	smallest	

The most common superlative adjectives with *most* in writing and speaking are:

beautiful	difficult	famous	popular	serious
common	effective	important	powerful	significant[1]
dangerous	expensive	interesting	recent	successful

[1]**significant:** a more formal word for *important*

▶ Grammar Application

Exercise 2.1 Superlative Adjectives

A *Pair Work* How good is your geography? Complete the sentences with a partner.
Use superlative adjectives. Then check the answers at the bottom of the exercise.

World Geography Quiz

1. The world's ___smallest___ (small) continent is ___Australia___.
2. The world's _____ (large) continent is _____.
3. The continent with the _____ (more) countries is _____.
4. The _____ (deep) ocean is the _____.
5. The _____ (big) country is _____.
6. The _____ (cold) place in the world is _____.
7. The _____ (high) mountain is _____.
8. The _____ (dry) place on earth is the _____.
9. The _____ (large) city in the United States is _____.
10. The _____ (long) river in the world is _____.
11. The _____ (populated) country in the world is _____.

2. Asia 3. Africa 4. Pacific 5. Russia 6. Antarctica 7. Mount Everest 8. Atacama Desert, Chile 9. New York 10. The Nile 11. China

B Complete the questions with *the* and superlative adjectives. Note that ↑ shows an affirmative two-syllable superlative (with *most*), and ↓ shows a negative two-syllable superlative (with *least*). Then compare your answers with your classmates. You can find the answers at the bottom of the page.

Facts About the United States

What Do You Know About the United States?   **Answers**

1. What is _____*the biggest*_____ (big) waterfall?   ____*Niagara Falls*____
2. What is _____ (long) river?   _____
3. What is _____ (dry) state?   _____
4. What is _____ (wet) state?   _____
5. What is _____ (popular) national park? ↑   _____
6. What is _____ (big) city?   _____
7. What is _____ (wasteful) city? ↓   _____
8. What is _____ (expensive) city to live in? ↑   _____
9. What large city has _____ (bad) air pollution?   _____
10. What is _____ (famous) bridge? ↑   _____
11. What is _____ (busy) airport?   _____
12. What is _____ (populated) state? ↑   _____
13. What is _____ (populated) state? ↓   _____

C *Over to You* Think about your city or town. Complete the sentences. Then compare your answers with your classmates. Take a survey. What are the results?

Best (and Worst) of the Town

1. The _*nicest*_ (nice) neighborhood is _____.
2. The _____ (delicious) pizza is _____.
3. The _____ (crowded) area is _____.
4. The area with the _____ (bad) traffic is _____.
5. The _____ (dangerous) intersection is _____.
6. The _____ (unusual) restaurant is _____.

2. Mississippi 3. Nevada 4. Hawaii 5. Great Smoky Mountains National Park in Tennessee and North Carolina 6. New York 7. San Francisco 8. New York 9. Los Angeles 10. The Golden Gate Bridge, California 11. Atlanta's Hartsfield-Jackson 12. California 13. Wyoming

Exercise 2.2 Superlative Adjectives to Describe People

A Complete the superlative constructions in this conversation. Use *the* when necessary

Claire So, who are _the most important_ (1) (important) people in your life?

Monika Well, I guess my family and my _____ (2) (good) friends.

Claire OK. Tell me about your family.

Monika Well, let's see. My _____ (3) (close) family members all live near me, so I see them often. I have three brothers: Tim, Liam, and Anthony. Anthony is _____ (4) (young). He's just 13. My grandmother is 75. She's my _____ (5) (old) relative. My friends are mostly from my college days. One really special person is Tina.

Claire Tina? Is she your _____ (6) (good) friend?

Monika Yeah. She's _____ (7) (unusual) person I know, and _____ (8) (interesting). She has a pilot's license and a degree in biology! Of all my friends, she definitely has _____ (9) (exciting) job. She works for a tour company that takes people to some of _____ (10) (exotic[1]) places in the world. When we were in college, she always got _____ (11) (high) grades. She's probably _____ (12) (intelligent) person I know, and _____ (13) (successful).

Claire Amazing!

[1]**exotic:** unusual or interesting because of being from a different culture or country

B 🔊 Listen to the conversation and check your answers.

C *Over to You* Answer the questions, and describe your friends or people in your family. Use superlative adjectives. Then share your answers with a partner.

1. Who are the most important people in your life?
2. Who is your best friend?
3. Who is the most successful person you know?
4. Who is the most intelligent? The funniest?

3 | Superlative Adverbs

▶ Grammar Presentation

You can use superlative adverbs to describe how a person's actions or the way something happens is different from all others.	*All the students work hard, but Rosa works **hardest**.*

3.1 Statements

	Verb	*(The)*	Superlative Adverb	
Daniel	ran	(the)	**fastest**	in the men's 100 meters.
This printer	works	(the)	**best**	of all the printers in the office.
Nina	drives	(the)	**most carefully**	of the three women.

3.2 Questions

	Verb	*(The)*	Superlative Adverb	
Who	arrives	(the)	**earliest**	at school every day?
Which industry	is growing	(the)	**most rapidly**	in Vietnam?
What method	works	(the)	**most effectively**	to learn vocabulary?

3.3 Superlative of Short Adverbs (One Syllable)

	Adverb	Superlative
a. For adverbs with one syllable, add *-est*.	*fast*	*fast**est***
	high	*high**est***
	long	*long**est***
	hard	*hard**est***
b. For adverbs with one syllable ending in *-e*, add *-st*	*late*	*late**st***

3.4 Superlative of Longer Adverbs (Two or More Syllables)

Adverb	Superlative
often	**most** often
recently	**most** recently
quickly	**most** quickly
slowly	**most** slowly

We say *earliest,* not *most early.*
*Which flight arrives the **earliest**?*

3.5 Irregular Adverbs

Irregular Adverbs	Superlative
well	**best**
badly	**worst**
far	**farthest** or **furthest** (*farthest* is more common)

▸▸ Adjectives and Adverbs: Comparative and Superlative Forms: See page A22.

3.6 Using Superlative Adverbs

a. You can use superlative adverbs to describe how one action or event is different from all others.

*Hilda studies **the hardest** of all the students in her class.*
*I drive **most carefully** in bad weather or when it's dark.*

b. You can use a phrase with *of* after a superlative adverb.

*The cheetah runs **the fastest** of all the animals.*

c. *Least* is the opposite of *most.*

*Of the three cars, the gasoline car operates **the least efficiently**.*

Data from the Real World

People often use superlative adverbs without *the*, especially in spoken language.	You should wear the colors that suit you **best**. Who do you text **most often**, your family, your classmates, or your friends? Which of the three movies came out **most recently**?
In academic writing, use *the*.	This method works **the most effectively**.

Data from the Real World

Superlative adverbs are much less common than superlative adjectives.

The most common superlative adverbs ending in -*est* in writing and speaking are:	fastest closest longest	hardest nearest lowest	latest earliest highest
The six most common superlative adverbs used with *most* in writing and speaking are:	easily effectively	economically often	recently frequently

▶ Grammar Application

Exercise 3.1 Superlative Adverbs

A Complete the sentences from a student essay. Use the superlative form of the adverbs in parentheses with *the*.

I live in an apartment with three other students: Shinya, Tomas, and Alex. I

arrived _the most recently_ (recently) – in September this year. Shinya has lived
　　　　　　(1)

here _____ (long). He moved into the apartment two years ago. Because
　　　　(2)

we are students, we try to spend as little money as possible. Right now, I think that I live

_____ (economical) because I almost never go out to eat. Tomas eats out
　　(3)

_____ (frequent). Alex probably studies _____ (hard). He
　　(4)　　　　　　　　　　　　　　　　　　　　(5)

always goes to sleep _____ (late). I get up _____ (early)
　　　　　　　　　　　(6)　　　　　　　　　　　(7)

because I travel _____ (far) to school.
　　　　　　　(8)

B *Pair Work*   Complete the sentences with your own ideas. You can use the verbs and adverbs in the boxes to help you. Then share your sentences with a partner.

call	reply	study	work
~~drive~~	speak	text	write

clearly	fast	frequently	hard
early	fluently	good	often

1. Of all my friends, *Hannah drives the fastest* _____.

2. Of all my classmates, _____.

3. Of all the people I know, _____.

4. In this class, _____.

5. Of all my family members, _____.

6. Of all my co-workers (or friends), _____.

7. Of all the people I text, _____.

8. Of all the people I send e-mails to, _____.

4 Avoid Common Mistakes ⚠

1. **Do not use a comparative form instead of a superlative when comparing more than two things.**

   the hottest
   Of all the places we visited, Vietnam in April was ~~hotter~~.

2. **Do not use *most* and *-est* together.**

   My ~~most~~ smallest pet was a goldfish.

3. **Do not use *most* with adjectives and adverbs that take *-est*.**

   cheapest
   The Hollywood Plaza is the ~~most cheap~~ hotel in town.

4. **Do not use *of* instead of *in*.**

   in
   It's the tallest building ~~of~~ the world.

5. **Learn the spelling rules for comparative and superlative adjectives and adverbs.**

   earliest
   Who arrives at school ~~earlyst~~ every day, Joanna or Peter?

   hottest
   June 20 was the ~~hotest~~ day of the year.

Editing Task

Find and correct 10 more mistakes in the magazine article.

Fascinating Facts About Animals

One of the ~~more~~ *most* amazing things of the natural world is the great variety of animal sizes and behaviors. At 200 tons (180 metric tons) and 108 feet (33 meters), the blue whale is the world's heavyest and bigest

5 animal. However, the world's smaller bird weighs less than one ounce (1.8 grams). Giraffes can be 17 feet (5.2 meters) tall, and they are the tallest animals of the world. The cheetah runs the faster of all animals. It can run up to 75 miles per hour (120 kilometers per hour).

10   On the other hand, a sloth is perhaps the world's most slowest animal. It often does not move for hours. The loudest land animal is the howler monkey. You can hear its cry about 10 miles (16 kilometers) away. What is the louder marine animal? The blue whale. Blue

15 whales can hear each other up to 1,000 miles (1,600 kilometers) away. What is the animal that lived the most long? It is a clam from the coast of Iceland. Scientists estimate that it is 405 years old. The gastrotrich, a tiny water animal, has the most short life – three days.

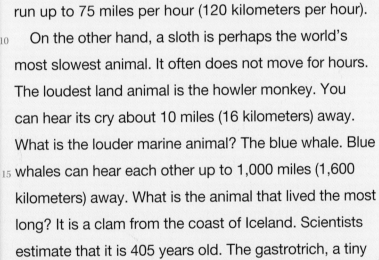

5 | Grammar for Writing ✏

Writing About the Most, Least, Best, and Worst of Things

Writers use superlative adjectives and adverbs when they want to compare the accomplishments or qualities of people. They also use them to compare facts and opinions about places.

Remember:

- **You do not need to identify other members of the group you are comparing if it is clear.**
  Sheila is the most economical person <u>in our family</u>. She spends the least money and saves <u>the most</u>.

- **Use one of these patterns with superlative sentences.**
  a. *Masuma is <u>the best</u> cook in our family.* OR *Masuma cooks <u>the best</u> in our family.*
  b. *Masuma is our family's <u>best</u> cook.* (superlative adjectives only)
  c. *Our family's <u>best</u> cook is Masuma.* (superlative adjectives only)

Pre-writing Task

1 Read the paragraph below. How many people live in the writer's house? Which one of the roommates are you the most similar to?

My Roommates

My roommates and I are all very good friends, but we are all very different. My roommate Sandy is (the most athletic) of us all. She is always outside playing tennis or soccer. We all do those things, but Sandy is the best at them. Shogo is the apartment's most serious person. He works the <u>hardest</u> and does the best. He's going to graduate the earliest. Jess is the most social of all of us. He is always planning fun things to do. He makes friends the easiest and brings home new people the most often. Our apartment's most organized and cleanest person of all the roommates is me! I take care of our apartment the most. It may not sound very interesting, but someone has to do it, and I do not mind.

2 Read the paragraph again. Underline all the superlative adverbs and circle all the superlative adjectives. Match the superlative sentences with the three patterns in the box above. Write *a*, *b*, or *c* over each superlative sentence. Which pattern is the most common?

Writing Task

1 *Write* Use the paragraph in the Pre-writing Task to help you write a paragraph about your friends, family members, or roommates. Talk about who is the best and worst at things or who does the most or least. How is each person different? What does each person do differently?

2 *Self-Edit* Use the editing tips below to improve your sentences. Make any necessary changes.

1. Did you use superlative adjectives and adverbs to show how people you know are all different from all the others in a group?
2. Did you mention the group that you are comparing someone to when necessary?
3. Did you use the different superlative sentence patterns (*a*, *b*, and *c* in the box)?
4. Did you avoid the mistakes in the Avoid Common Mistakes chart on page 422?

Appendices

1. Capitalization and Punctuation Rules

Capitalize	Examples
1. The first letter of the first word of a sentence	*Today is a great day.*
2. The pronoun *I*	*Yesterday I went to hear a new rock band.*
3. Names of people	*Simón Bolívar, Joseph Chung*
4. Names of buildings, streets, geographic locations, and organizations	*Taj Majal, Broadway, Mt. Everest, United Nations*
5. Titles of people	*Dr., Mr., Mrs., Ms.*
6. Days, months, and holidays	*Tuesday, April, Valentine's Day*
7. Names of courses or classes	*Biology 101, English Composition II*
8. Titles of books, movies, and plays	*Crime and Punishment, Avatar, Hamlet*
9. States, countries, languages, and nationalities	*California, Mexico, Spanish, South Korean, Canadian*
10. Names of religions	*Hinduism, Catholicism, Islam, Judaism*

Punctuation	Examples
1. Use a period (.) at the end of a sentence.	*He is Korean.*
2. Use a question mark (?) at the end of a question.	*Do you want to buy a car?*
3. Use an exclamation point (!) to show strong emotion (e.g., surprise, anger, shock).	*Wait! I'm not ready yet. I can't believe it!*

4. Use an apostrophe (') for possessive nouns.
    Add *'s* for singular nouns.
    Add *s'* for plural nouns.
    Add *'s* for irregular plural nouns.
    Use an apostrophe (') for contractions.
	That's Sue's umbrella.
	Those are the students' books. BUT
	Bring me the children's shoes.
	I'll be back next week. He can't drive a car.

5. Use a comma (,):
  • between words in a series of three or more items. (Place *and* before the last item.)
  • before *and, or, but,* and *so* to connect two complete sentences.
	I like fish, chicken, turkey, and mashed potatoes.
	
	You can watch TV, but I have to study for a test.

2. Spelling Rules for Noun Plurals

1. Add -*s* to most singular nouns to form plural nouns.	*a camera – two cameras* *a key – keys*	*a model – two models* *a student – students*
2. Add -*es* to nouns that end in -*ch*, -*sh*, -*ss*, and -*x*.	*watch – watches* *class – classes*	*dish – dishes* *tax – taxes*
3. With nouns that end in a consonant + -*y*, change the *y* to *i* and add -*es*.	*accessory – accessories*	*battery – batteries*
4. With nouns that end in -*ife*, change the ending to -*ives*.	*knife – knives* *wife – wives*	*life – lives*
5. Add -*es* to nouns that end in -*o* after a consonant. **Exception:** Add -*s* only to nouns that end in -*o* and refer to music.	*potato – potatoes* *piano – pianos*	*tomato – tomatoes* *soprano – sopranos*
6. Add -*s* to nouns that end in -*o* after a vowel.	*radio – radios*	*shampoo – shampoos*
7. Some plural nouns have irregular forms. These are the most common irregular plural nouns in academic writing.	*man – men* *child – children* *foot – feet*	*woman – women* *person – people* *tooth – teeth*
8. Some nouns have the same form for singular and plural.	*one deer – two deer* *one fish – two fish*	*one sheep – two sheep*
9. Some nouns are only plural. They do not have a singular form.	*clothes* *glasses* *headphones* *jeans*	*pants* *scissors* *sunglasses*

3. Verb Forms

Present: *Be*
Affirmative Statements

SINGULAR			
Subject	*Be*		
I	**am**	late.	
You	**are**		
He She It	**is**	difficult.	

PLURAL		
Subject	*Be*	
We You They	**are**	from Seoul.

Negative Statements

SINGULAR			
Subject	*Be + Not*		
I	**am not**	in class.	
You	**are not**		
He She It	**is not**		

PLURAL		
Subject	*Be + Not*	
We You They	**are not**	students.

Affirmative Contractions

SINGULAR		
I am	→	I**'m**
You are	→	You**'re**
He is	→	He**'s**
Jun-Ho is	→	Jun-Ho**'s**
She is	→	She**'s**
His mother is	→	His mother**'s**
It is	→	It**'s**
My name is	→	My name**'s**

PLURAL		
We are	→	We**'re**
You are	→	You**'re**
They are	→	They**'re**

Negative Contractions

SINGULAR		
I am not	→	I'm **not**
You are not	→	You**'re not** / You **aren't**
He is not	→	He**'s not** / He **isn't**
She is not	→	She**'s not** / She **isn't**
It is not	→	It**'s not** / It **isn't**

PLURAL		
We are not	→	We**'re not** / We **aren't**
You are not	→	You**'re not** / You **aren't**
They are not	→	They**'re not** / They **aren't**

Singular *Yes / No* Questions

Be	Subject	
Am	I	
Are	you	in class?
Is	he she it	

Singular Short Answers

AFFIRMATIVE		
	Subject	*Be*
Yes,	I	**am**.
	you	**are**.
	he she it	**is**.

NEGATIVE		
	Subject	*Be + Not*
No,	I	**am not**.
	you	**are not**.
	he she it	**is not**.

Plural *Yes / No* Questions

Be	Subject	
Are	we you they	late?

Plural Short Answers

AFFIRMATIVE		
	Subject	*Be*
Yes,	we you they	**are**.

NEGATIVE		
	Subject	*Be + Not*
No,	we you they	**are not**.

Negative Short Answer Contractions

SINGULAR		
No, I am not.	→	No, I**'m not**.
No, you are not.	→	No, you**'re not**. No, you **aren't**.
No, he is not.	→	No, he**'s not**. No, he **isn't**.
No, she is not.	→	No, she**'s not**. No, she **isn't**.
No, it is not.	→	No, it**'s not**. No, it **isn't**.

PLURAL		
No, we are not.	→	No, we**'re not**. No, we **aren't**.
No, you are not.	→	No, you**'re not**. No, you **aren't**.
No, they are not.	→	No, they**'re not**. No, they **aren't**.

Information Questions

SINGULAR SUBJECTS		
Wh- Word	*Be*	Subject
Who		your teacher?
What		your major?
When	is	our exam?
Where		the building?
How		your class?

PLURAL SUBJECTS		
Wh- Word	*Be*	Subject
Who		your teachers?
What		your plans?
When	are	your exams?
Where		your books?
How		your classes?

Contractions with Singular Subjects

Who is	→	**Who's**
What is	→	**What's**
When is	→	**When's**
Where is	→	**Where's**
How is	→	**How's**

There Is / There Are

Affirmative Statements

There	*Be*	Subject	Place / Time
There	**is**	a parking lot a free tour	on Alameda Street. at 10:00.
	are	a lot of little shops free tours	in the area. on most days.

Contraction
There is → There's

Negative Statements

There	*Be + Not / No*	Subject	Place / Time
There	**isn't** **is no**	a bank bank	in Union Station.
	isn't **is no**	a show show	at 8:00.
There	**'s no**	bank	in Union Station.
		show	at 8:00.
There	**aren't** **are no**	any cars cars	on Olvera Street.
	aren't **are no**	any tours tours	in the evening.

Yes / No Questions and Short Answers

Be	*There*	Subject	Place / Time
Is	**there**	a visitor's center	on Olvera Street?
		a performance	at 6:00?
Are		any parking lots	in the area?
		any tours	in the evening?

Short Answers
Yes, **there is**.
No, **there isn't**.
Yes, **there are**.
No, **there aren't**.

Simple Present

Affirmative Statements

SINGULAR		
Subject	**Verb**	
I You	**eat**	vegetables every day.
He She It	**eats**	

PLURAL		
Subject	**Verb**	
We You They	**have**	many friends.

Negative Statements

SINGULAR			
Subject	***Do / Does* + *Not***	**Base Form of Verb**	
I You	**do not** **don't**	**eat**	a lot of meat.
He She It	**does not** **doesn't**		

PLURAL			
Subject	***Do* + *Not***	**Base Form of Verb**	
We You They	**do not** **don't**	**exercise**	in the morning.

Yes / No Questions

Do / Does	**Subject**	**Base Form of Verb**	
Do	I you we they	**fall asleep**	in 30 minutes?
Does	he she it		

Short Answers

AFFIRMATIVE		
Yes	**Subject**	*Do / Does*
Yes,	I you we they	**do**.
	he she it	**does**.

NEGATIVE		
No	**Subject**	*Do / Does* + *Not*
No,	I you we they	**do not**. **don't**.
	he she it	**does not**. **doesn't**.

Information Questions

Wh- word	Do / Does	Subject	Base Form of Verb	
Who		I	see	at school?
What	do	you we they	eat	at parties?
When			celebrate	that holiday?
Where		he	study	for school?
Why	does	she it	live	at home?
How			meet	new people?

Present Progressive

Affirmative Statements

Subject	Be	Verb + -ing	Contractions
I	am		I am → I'm
You We They	are	talking.	You are → You're We are → We're They are → They're
He She It	is		He is → He's She is → She's It is → It's

Negative Statements

Subject	Be + Not	Verb + -ing	Contractions	
I	am not		I am not → I'm not	
You We They	are not	talking.	You are not → You're not We are not → We're not They are not → They're not	You aren't We aren't They aren't
He She It	is not		He is not → He's not She is not → She's not It is not → It's not	He isn't She isn't It isn't

Yes / No Questions

Be	Subject	Verb + -ing
Am	I	
Are	you we they	**working**?
Is	he she it	

Short Answers

AFFIRMATIVE	NEGATIVE	
Yes, I **am**.	No, I**'m not**.	
Yes, you **are**.	No, you**'re not**.	No, you **aren't**.
Yes, we **are**.	No, we**'re not**.	No, we **aren't**.
Yes, they **are**.	No, they**'re not**.	No, they **aren't**.
Yes, he **is**.	No, he**'s not**.	No, he **isn't**.
Yes, she **is**.	No, she**'s not**.	No, she **isn't**.
Yes, it **is**.	No, it**'s not**.	No, it **isn't**.

Information Questions

Wh- Word	Be	Subject	Verb + -ing
Who	am	I	**hearing**?
What	are	you we they	**studying**?
When			**leaving**?
Where			**going**?
Why	is	he she it	**laughing**?
How			**feeling**?

Wh- Word as Subject	Be	Verb + -ing
Who	is	**talking**?
What		**happening**?

Simple Past: *Be*

Statements

AFFIRMATIVE		
Subject	*Was / Were*	
I He She It	**was**	in the computer lab.
We You They	**were**	

NEGATIVE		
Subject	*Was / Were + Not*	
I He She It	**was not** **wasn't**	in class.
We You They	**were not** **weren't**	

Yes / No Questions

Was / Were	Subject	
Was	I he she it	very smart?
Were	we you they	in college?

Short Answers

AFFIRMATIVE			
	Yes	Subject	*Was / Were*
Yes,		I he she it	**was.**
		we you they	**were.**

NEGATIVE			
	No	Subject	*Was / Were + Not*
No,		I he she it	**was not.** **wasn't.**
		we you they	**were not.** **weren't.**

Information Questions

Wh- Word	*Was / Were*	Subject	
Who	**was**	your best friend	as a child?
What		your favorite class	last semester?
When		her birthday party?	
What time		the meeting	on Monday?
Where	**were**	his partners?	
Why		they	successful?
How		the concerts	the other night?
How old		their cars	in 2011?

Simple Past

Statements

AFFIRMATIVE				NEGATIVE			
Subject	Simple Past Verb			Subject	*Did + Not*	Base Form of Verb	
I You We They He She It	started	in 1962.		I You We They He She It	did not didn't	sign	a contract.

Yes / No Questions

Did	Subject	Base Form of Verb	
Did	I you we they he she it	finish	the report?

Short Answers

AFFIRMATIVE				NEGATIVE		
Yes	Subject	*Did*		*No*	Subject	*Did + Not*
Yes,	I you we they he she it	did.		No,	I you we they he she it	did not. didn't.

Information Questions

Wh- Word	*Did*	Subject	Base Form of Verb	
Who			write	about?
What			do	yesterday?
When	did	I you we they he she it	finish	our report?
Where			visit	on vacation?
Why			start	a company?
How			save	enough money?

Past Progressive

Statements

AFFIRMATIVE			NEGATIVE		
Subject	Past of *Be*	Verb + *-ing*	Subject	Past of *Be* + *Not*	Verb + *-ing*
I He She It	**was**	**working.**	I He She It	**was not /** **wasn't**	**working.**
You We They	**were**		You We They	**were not /** **weren't**	

Yes / No Questions

Past of *Be*	Subject	Verb + *-ing*
Was	I he she it	**working?**
Were	you we they	**working?**

Short Answers

AFFIRMATIVE				NEGATIVE		
	Subject	Past of *Be*			Subject	Past of *Be* + *Not*
Yes,	I he she it	**was.**		No,	I he she it	**was not.** **wasn't.**
	you we they	**were.**			you we they	**were not.** **weren't.**

Information Questions

Wh- Word	Past of *Be*	Subject	Verb + *-ing*
Who	**was**	I he she it	**studying?**
What			**doing?**
When			**researching?**
Where	**were**	you we they	**working?**
Why			**experimenting?**
How			**feeling?**

Wh- Word as Subject	Past of *Be*	Verb + *-ing*
Who	**was**	**talking?**
What	**was**	**happening?**

Future: *Be Going To*

Statements

AFFIRMATIVE				
Subject	*Be*	*Going To*	Base Form of Verb	
I	**am**			
You We They	**are**	**going to**	get	a job.
He She It	**is**			

NEGATIVE				
Subject	*Be + Not*	*Going To*	Base Form of Verb	
I	**am not**			
You We They	**are not**	**going to**	get	a job.
He She It	**is not**			

Yes / No Questions

Be	Subject	*Going To*	Base Form of Verb	
Am	I			
Are	you we they	**going to**	get	a job?
Is	he she it			

Short Answers

AFFIRMATIVE		
	Subject	*Be*
Yes,	I	**am.**
	you we they	**are.**
	he she it	**is.**

NEGATIVE		
	Subject	*Be + Not*
No,	I	**'m not.**
	you we they	**aren't.**
	he she it	**isn't.**

Information Questions

Wh- Word	*Be*	Subject	*Going To*	Base Form of Verb	
Who	am	I		interview	tomorrow?
What	are	you we they	**going to**	do	after graduation?
When				leave	for New York?
Where				work	after college?
Why	is	he she it		move	to Canada?
How				pay	his loans?

Information Questions

Wh- Word as Subject	Be	Going To	Base Form of Verb	
Who	is	going to	get	a job after college?
What			happen	after school?

Future: *Will*

Statements

AFFIRMATIVE			
Subject	Will	Base Form of Verb	
I You We They He She It	will 'll	have	a healthy life.

NEGATIVE			
Subject	Will + Not	Base Form of Verb	
I You We They He She It	will not won't	have	a healthy life.

Yes / No Questions

Will	Subject	Base Form of Verb	
Will	I you we they he she it	have	a healthy life?

Short Answers

AFFIRMATIVE	
Yes, I Yes, you Yes, we Yes, they Yes, he Yes, she Yes, it	will.

NEGATIVE	
No, I No, you No, we No, they No, he No, she No, it	won't.

Information Questions

Wh- Word	Will	Subject	Base Form of Verb	
Who			meet	at the interview tomorrow?
What		I you we they he she it	do	in your training program?
When	will		return	your documents?
Where			find	information about careers?
Why			travel	to South America?
How			build	new apartments?

Imperatives

Statements

AFFIRMATIVE		NEGATIVE		
Base Form of Verb		Do + Not	Base Form of Verb	
Smile	and be helpful.	**Don't / Do not**	**interrupt**	people who are very busy.
Look	at people when you talk to them.		**do**	this in the beginning.

4. Common Regular and Irregular Verbs

Regular

Base Form	Past Form
call	called
decide	decided
happen	happened
like	liked
live	lived
look	looked
move	moved
start	started
talk	talked
try	tried
work	worked

Irregular

Base Form	Past Form
come	came
do	did
get	got
go	went
have	had
make	made
put	put
read	read
say	said
see	saw

5. Irregular Verbs

Base Form	Simple Past	Base Form	Simple Past
be	was / were	keep	kept
become	became	know	knew
begin	began	leave	left
bite	bit	lose	lost
blow	blew	make	made
break	broke	meet	met
bring	brought	pay	paid
build	built	put	put
buy	bought	read	read
catch	caught	ride	rode
choose	chose	run	ran
come	came	say	said
cost	cost	see	saw
cut	cut	sell	sold
do	did	send	sent
draw	drew	set	set
drink	drank	shake	shook
drive	drove	show	showed
eat	ate	shut	shut
fall	fell	sing	sang
feed	fed	sit	sat
feel	felt	sleep	slept
fight	fought	speak	spoke
find	found	spend	spent
fly	flew	stand	stood
forget	forgot	steal	stole
forgive	forgave	swim	swam
get	got	take	took
give	gave	teach	taught
go	went	tell	told
grow	grew	think	thought
have	had	throw	threw
hear	heard	understand	understood
hide	hid	wake	woke
hit	hit	wear	wore
hold	held	win	won
hurt	hurt	write	wrote

6. Spelling Rules for Possessive Nouns

1. Add *'s* to singular nouns to show possession.	The **manager's** name is Mr. Patel. (one manager) The **boss's** ideas are helpful. (one boss)
2. Add an apostrophe (') to plural nouns ending in *-s* to show possession.	The **managers'** names are hard to remember. (more than one manager) The **bosses'** ideas are very good. (more than one boss)
3. For irregular plural nouns, add *'s* to show possession.	The **men's** uniforms are heavy. (more than one man) The **children's** room is messy. (more than one child)
4. *My, your, his, her, our,* and *their* can come before a possessive noun.	**My friend's** sister is in Peru. **Our parents'** names are short.

7. Noncount Nouns and Containers

Common Noncount Nouns

Food and Liquids		Materials	School Subjects	Weather	Other
beef	rice	leather	algebra	fog	advice
bread	salt	metal	art	ice	furniture
butter	seafood	oil	biology	rain	garbage
cheese	shrimp	plastic	economics	snow	help
coffee	soup	silk	English	weather	homework
fish	spinach	wood	geography		information
ice cream	sugar		history		jewelry
meat	tea		music		mail
milk	water		physics		money
olive oil			psychology		noise
			science		traffic
					vocabulary
					work

Measurement Words and Containers			
a bag of potatoes rice	**a glass** of water soda	**a bowl** of soup pasta	**a piece** of cake meat
a bar of chocolate soap	**a head** of lettuce cabbage	**a bunch** of grapes bananas	**a plate** of eggs chicken
a bottle of oil ketchup	**a jar** of mustard pickles	**a can** of beans tuna	**a pound** of butter cheese
a box of cereal candy	**a loaf** of bread	**a carton** of milk juice	**a slice** of pie pizza

8. Metric Conversion

1 ounce = 28 grams	1 mile = 1.6 kilometers
1 gram = .04 ounce	1 kilometer = .62 mile
1 pound = .45 kilogram	1 foot = .30 meter
1 kilogram = 2.2 pounds	1 meter = 3.3 feet
1 liter = .26 gallon	1 inch = 2.54 centimeters
1 gallon = 3.8 liters	1 centimeter = .39 inch

9. Subject and Object Pronouns

Subject Pronoun	Possessive Adjective	Object Pronoun	
I	my	me	*I* can't find the calculator. **My** desk is so messy. My boss is unhappy with **me**.
you	your	you	*You* are very organized. **Your** desk is so neat. I want to be like **you**.
he	his	him	*He* is a new employee. **His** old job was in Hong Kong. This is very exciting to **him**.
she	her	her	*She* went home. **Her** computer is off. I'll call **her**.
it	its	it	*It's* a new company. **Its** president is Mr. Janesh. He wants **it** to be successful.
we	our	us	*We* are looking for the reports. **Our** boss wants to read them. The reports are important to **us**.
they	their	them	*They* are writing a report. **Their** team members will help **them**.

10. Indefinite and Definite Articles

Indefinite Article	
1. Use *a/an* with singular count nouns.	*She made **a decision** about her job.* ***An analyst** examines something in detail.*
2. Use *a* when the noun begins with a consonant sound.	*She made **a decision** about her job.*
3. Use *an* when the noun begins with a vowel sound.	***An analyst** examines something in detail.*
4. Use *a* before adjectives or adverbs that begin with a consonant sound.	*Tony found **a great** apartment in Chicago.*
5. Use *a* before words that begin with *u* when the *u* makes a "you" sound.	*James went to **a university** in Boston.* *The economy is **a universal** concern.*
6. Use *a/an* to introduce a person or thing for the first time to a listener. When you mention the person or thing again, use *the*.	*Tom bought **a car**.* (The listener does not know about this car.) ***The car** was not very expensive.* (Now the listener knows about this car.)

Definite Article

1. You can use *the* before singular or plural count nouns, and before noncount nouns.
***The job** is a good one.*
***The choices** were interesting.*
***The information** is very useful.*

2. Use *the* to talk about people or things that both the listener and speaker know about.
***The president** discussed **the plan**.* (Everyone knows the president and the plan.)
***The moon** and **the stars** were beautiful last night.* (Everyone knows the moon and the stars.)

3. Use *the* to talk about a specific noun.
*"**The teacher** gave us difficult homework tonight."* (The speaker and listener know this teacher.)
*"**The game** was interesting."*   *"I agree."* (The speaker and listener are thinking of the same game.)

11. Spelling Rules for Verbs Ending in *-ing*

1. For most verbs, add *-ing**.

go → going   say → saying   talk → talking

2. if the verb ends in a silent *-e*, delete *e* and add *-ing*.

live → living   make → making   write → writing

3. For *be* and *see,* don't drop the *e* because it is not silent.

be → being   see → seeing

4. If the verb ends in *-ie*, change the *ie* to *y* and add *-ing*.

die → dying   lie → lying

5. If the verb has one syllable and follows the pattern consonant, vowel, consonant (CVC), double the last letter and add *-ing*.

get → getting   put → putting   sit → sitting

6. Do not double the consonant if the verb ends in *-w, -x,* or *-y*.

grow → growing   fix → fixing   say → saying

7. If the verb has two syllables, ends in the pattern CVC, and is stressed on the last syllable, double the last letter and add *-ing*.

beGIN → begin**n**ing

8. If the verb has two syllables and is stressed on the first syllable, do not double the last letter.

LISten → listening   TRAVel → traveling   VISit → visiting

* Verbs that end in *-ing* are also called *gerunds* when they are used as a noun. The same spelling rules above apply to gerunds as well.

12. Spelling and Pronunciation Rules for Simple Present

Spelling of Third-Person Singular Verbs

1. Add *-s* to most verbs.
Add *-s* to verbs ending in a vowel* + *-y*.
drink**s**, ride**s**, run**s**, see**s**, sleep**s**   buy**s**, pay**s**, say**s**

2. Add *-es* to verbs ending in *-ch, -sh, -ss, -x*.
Add *-es* to verbs ending in a consonant** + *-o*.
teach**es**, push**es**, miss**es**, fix**es**   do**es**, go**es**

3. For verbs that end in a consonant + *-y*, change the *y* to *i* and add *-es*.
cry → cr**ies**   study → stud**ies**

4. Some verbs are irregular.
be → am / are / is   have → has

* **Vowels:** the letters *a, e, i, o, u*
** **Consonants:** the letters *b, c, d, f, g, h, j, k, l, m, n, p, q, r, s, t, v, w, x, y, z*

Pronunciation of Third-Person Singular Verbs

1. Say /s/ after /f/, /k/, /p/, and /t/ sounds.
laughs, drinks, walks, sleeps, writes, gets

2. Say /z/ after /b/, /d/, /g/, /v/, /m/, /n/, /l/, and /r/ sounds and all vowel sounds.
grabs, rides, hugs, lives, comes, runs, smiles, hears, sees, plays, buys, goes, studies

3. Say /əz/ after /tʃ/, /ʃ/, /s/, /ks/, /z/, and /dʒ/ sounds.
teaches, pushes, kisses, fixes, uses, changes

4. Pronounce the vowel sound in *does* and *says* differently from *do* and *say*.
do /duː/ → *does* /dʌz/
say /seɪ/ → *says* /sez/

13. Spelling and Pronunciation Rules for Regular Verbs in Simple Past

Spelling of Regular Verbs

1. For most verbs, add *-ed*.	*work* → *worked*
2. For verbs ending in *-e*, add *-d*.	*live* → *lived*
3. For verbs ending in consonant + *-y*, change the *y* to *i* and add *-ed*.	*study* → *studied*
4. For verbs ending in vowel + *-y*, add *-ed*.	*play* → *played*
5. For one-syllable verbs ending in consonant-vowel-consonant (CVC), double the consonant.	*plan* → *planned*
6. Do not double the consonant if the verb ends in *-x* or *-w*.	*show* → *showed*
7. For two-syllable verbs ending in CVC and stressed on the first syllable, do not double the consonant.	*TRAvel* → *TRAveled*
8. For two-syllable verbs ending in CVC and stressed on the second syllable, double the consonant.	*conTROL* → *conTROLLED*

Pronunciation of Regular Verbs

1. When the verb ends in /t/ or /d/, say *-ed* as /ɪd/ or /əd/.	*wait* → *waited*	*decide* → *decided*
2. When the verb ends in /f/, /k/, /p/, /s/, /ʃ/, and /tʃ/, say *-ed* as /t/.	*laugh* → *laughed* *look* → *looked* *stop* → *stopped*	*miss* → *missed* *finish* → *finished* *watch* → *watched*
3. For verbs that end in other consonant and vowel sounds, say *-ed* as /d/.	*agree* → *agreed* *borrow* → *borrowed* *change* → *changed*	*listen* → *listened* *live* → *lived* *play* → *played*

14. Adjectives and Adverbs: Comparative and Superlative Forms

	Adjective	Comparative	Superlative
1. One-Syllable Adjectives			
a. Add -er and -est to one-syllable adjectives.	cheap new old small strong tall young	cheaper newer older smaller stronger taller younger	the cheapest the newest the oldest the smallest the strongest the tallest the youngest
b. If the adjective ends with one vowel + one consonant, double the last letter and add -er or -est. Do not double the consonant w.	big hot sad thin	bigger hotter sadder thinner	the biggest the hottest the saddest the thinnest
2. Two-Syllable Adjectives			
a. Add more or the most to most two-syllable adjectives.	boring famous handsome patient	more boring more famous more handsome more patient	the most boring the most famous the most handsome the most patient
b. Some two-syllable adjectives have two forms.	narrow simple	narrower / more narrow simpler / more simple	the narrowest / the most narrow the simplest / the most simple
c. If the adjective has two syllables and ends in -y, change the y to i and add -er or -est.	angry easy friendly happy lucky pretty silly	angrier easier friendlier happier luckier prettier sillier	the angriest the easiest the friendliest the happiest the luckiest the prettiest the silliest

Adjectives and Adverbs: Comparative and Superlative Forms *(continued)*

	Adjective	Comparative	Superlative
3. Three-or-More-Syllable Adjectives Add *more* or *the most* to adjectives with three or more syllables.	beautiful difficult enjoyable expensive important serious	more beautiful more difficult more enjoyable more expensive more important more serious	the most beautiful the most difficult the most enjoyable the most expensive the most important the most serious
4. Irregular Adjectives Some adjectives have irregular forms.	bad far good	worse farther / further better	the worst the farthest / the furthest the best

	Adverb	Comparative	Superlative
1. -ly Adverbs Most adverbs end in *-ly*.	patiently quickly quietly slowly	more patiently more quickly more quietly more slowly	(the) most patiently (the) most quickly (the) most quietly (the) most slowly
2. One-Syllable Adverbs A few adverbs do not end in *-ly*. Add *-er* and *-est* to these adverbs.	fast hard	faster harder	(the) fastest (the) hardest
3. Irregular Adverbs Some adverbs have irregular forms.	badly far well	worse farther / further better	(the) worst (the) farthest / furthest (the) best

People usually only use *the* with superlative adverbs in formal writing and speaking.

15. Adverbs with -ly

Adjective	Adverb	Adjective	Adverb
bad	badly	loud	loudly
beautiful	beautifully	nervous	nervously
careful	carefully	nice	nicely
clear	clearly	patient	patiently
close	closely	polite	politely
confident	confidently	proper	properly
deep	deeply	quick	quickly
fluent	fluently	quiet	quietly
honest	honestly	slow	slowly
interesting	interestingly	strong	strongly
late	lately		

Spelling Rules for Adverbs

	Adjectives	Adverbs
1. After most adjectives, add -ly.	accidental interesting nice peaceful	accidentally interestingly nicely peacefully
2. After -y, delete y and add -ily.	easy happy	easily happily
3. After -ic, add -ally.	automatic terrific	automatically terrifically
4. After a consonant + -le, drop the e and add -y.	gentle terrible	gently terribly

16. Modal Verbs and Modal-like Expressions

Modals are helper verbs. Most modals have multiple meanings.

Function	Modal Verb	Time	Example
Ability	can	present	I **can** speak three languages.
	could	past	She **couldn't** attend class yesterday.
	be able to	present, past	I'**m not able** to help you tomorrow.
	know how to	present, past	I **know how to** speak two languages.
Possibility	can	present	I **can** meet you at 3:00 for coffee.
	could	past	People **could** read the newspaper online many years ago.
Requests less formal	can	present, future	**Can** you stop that noise now?
more formal	could would	present, future	**Could** you turn off your cell phone, please? **Would** you please come to my party?
Permission less formal	can could	present, future	You **can** give me your answer next week. Yes, you **could** watch TV now.
more formal	may	present, future	You **may** leave now.
Advice	should ought to might want to	present, future	What **should** you do if you live in a noisy place? You really **ought to** save your money. You **might want to** wait until next month.
Suggestions	Why don't Let's	present, future	**Why don't** we study together? **Let's** read the chapter together.
Necessity	have to need to must	past, present, future	We **had to** cancel our date at the last minute. She **needs to** make a schedule. All students **must** send their applications out on time.
Conclusion	must	present, future	Today is Monday, so tomorrow **must** be Tuesday.

17. Stative (Non-Action) Verbs

1. Stative verbs describe states, not actions.

These are stative verbs: *love, know, want, need, seem, mean,* and *agree.*

Use the simple present with stative verbs, not the present progressive.

I **don't like** rude people. NOT I'm not liking rude people.

What **do** you **know** about this? NOT What are you knowing?

They **seem** upset. NOT They are seeming upset.

Experts **don't agree** on the meaning of some gestures.

NOT Experts are not agreeing on the meaning of some gestures.

2. Some verbs have a stative meaning and an action meaning.

STATIVE	I **think** grammar is fun. (= an opinion)	ACTION	I**'m thinking** about my homework. (= using my mind)
STATIVE	The book **looks** interesting. (= appears)	ACTION	We**'re looking** at the book right now. (= using our eyes) appears)
STATIVE	**Do** you **have** a dog? (= own)	ACTION	**Are** you **having** a good time? (= experiencing)

3. You can use *feel* with the same meaning in the simple present and the present progressive.

I **feel** tired today.   OR   I**'m feeling** tired today.

How **do** you **feel**?   OR   How **are** you **feeling**?

18. Verbs + Gerunds and Infinitives

Verbs Followed by a Gerund Only	
admit	keep (= continue)
avoid	mind (= object to)
consider	miss
delay	postpone
deny	practice
discuss	quit
enjoy	recall (= remember)
finish	risk
imagine	suggest
involve	understand

Verbs Followed by an Infinitive Only		
afford	help	pretend
agree	hope	promise
arrange	intend	refuse
attempt	learn	seem
decide	manage	tend (= be likely)
deserve	need	threaten
expect	offer	volunteer
fail	plan	want
forget	prepare	

Verbs Followed by a Gerund or an Infinitive		
begin	like	start
continue	love	
hate	prefer	

19. Academic Word List (AWL) Words and Definitions

Academic Word	Definition
academic (adj) [U1] [U22]	relating to schools, especially colleges and universities
adult (n) [U11]	person who has grown to his or her full size and strength; not a child
affect (v) [U16]	have an influence on someone or something
analyst (n) [U18]	someone who studies or examines something in detail, such as finances, computer systems, or the economy
appropriate (adj) [U30]	correct or right for a particular situation
area (n) [U7] [U8] [U33]	specific part of a country, city, town, etc.
assignment (n) [U28]	specific job or responsibility that someone gives you
available (adj) [U30]	ready to use or get, such as an apartment or a parking space
challenge (n) [U16]	something that requires a lot of mental or physical effort
chapter (n) [U29]	separate part of a book that divides it into sections
comment (n) [U7] [U21]	an opinion or remark
communicate (v) [U21] [U23]	give messages or information to others through speech, writing, body movements, or signals
communication (n) [U23] [U29] [U32]	way of sending messages or information to others through speaking, writing, using body movement, or sending signals
community (n) [U5] [U14]	the people who live in a particular area; also a neighborhood
computer (n) [U1] [U2] [U14] [U26] [U28] [U32]	an electronic device that can store large amounts of information
concentrate (v) [U29]	direct your attention and thought to an activity or subject
concept (n) [U13]	idea
conference (n) [U4]	large formal meeting
contact (v) [U5] (n) [U17] [U23] [U31]	communicate with someone
contract (n) [U12]	written legal agreement
corporation (n) [U32]	large company
create (v) [U11] [U25] [U30]	make something new or imaginative
credit (n) [U15]	method of buying items or services and paying for them in the future
crucial (adj) [U23]	extremely important
culture (n) [U7] [U23] [U27]	the way of life of a particular people
definitely (adv) [U29]	without doubt, certainly
design (n) [U26] [U27]	the details or features of a picture or building
designer (n) [U27]	person who imagines how to make something and creates a plan for it
distribute (v) [U13]	give something to many people
economy (n) [U18]	the system of trade and industry in a city, region, or country

Academic Word	Definition
editor (n) [U27]	person who corrects and makes changes to texts, such as books or magazines
eventually (adv) [U14]	happening at a later time
expand (v) [U13]	make something bigger
expert (n) [U23]	person with a high level of knowledge or skill about a particular subject
export (v) [U17] (n) [U33]	send items to another country for sale or use
feature (n) [U3] [U11]	an important characteristic
fee (n) [U15]	money you pay for a service
file (n) [U3]	collection of information in a computer stored as one unit with one name
finally (adv) [U12] [U16] [U18] [U27]	at the end or after some delay
financial (adj) [U22]	relating to money
focus (v) [U29]	direct attention toward something or someone
foundation (n) [U9]	organization that provides financial support for activities and groups
global (adj) [U32]	relating to the whole world
goal (n) [U5] [U22] [U29]	purpose, something you want to achieve
grade (n) [U29]	measure of the quality of a student's schoolwork
grant (n) [U30]	sum of money that a university, government, or an organization gives to someone for a purpose, such as to do research or study
intelligent (adj) [U14]	able to understand and learn well; for example, an intelligent person
issues (n) [U22]	current subjects or problems that people are talking about, such as climate change, terrorism, etc.
job (n) [U5] [U18] [U20] [U22] [U27] [U28]	regular work that a person does to earn money
link (n) [U5]	word or image on a website that can take you to another document or website
major (n) [U1] [U22] [U27] [U29]	the main subject that a college student is studying
networking (n) [U5] [U21] [U26]	the process of meeting and talking to people who might be useful to know, especially in your job
persistent (adj) [U30]	having the ability to continue doing something even when there are difficulties
physical (adj) [U19]	relating to the body
positive (adj) [U23] [U31]	happy or hopeful
processed (adj) [U25]	treated with chemicals that preserve or give food extra taste or color
professional (n) [U5]	person who does work that needs special training
promote (v) [U25]	encourage or support something

Academic Word	Definition
publishing (n) [U27]	the business of making books, magazines, and newspapers
region (n) [U10]	particular area or part of a state, country, or the earth's surface
relax (v) [U8] [U31]	become calm and comfortable, and not worried
research (n) [U16] [U29]	the study of a subject in order to discover information
researcher (n) [U8] [U16] [U24]	person who studies something to learn detailed information about it
respond (v) [U18]	answer in words or actions
schedule (n) [U3] [U11] [U25] [U30]	list of planned activities or things to do at a certain time
site (n) [U5] [U21] [U26]	place
specific (adj) [U30]	relating to one thing and not others
stable (adj) [U18]	safe, not likely to change
stressed (adj) [U8] [U11] [U30]	very nervous or worried
survey (n) [U9]	set of questions to find out people's habits or beliefs about something
symbolize (v) [U10]	use a sign or mark to represent something
task (n) [U11] [U29]	small job or something you have to do
team (n) [U4]	number of people who act together as a group, such as a sports team
technology (n) [U21] [U32]	the different ways we use scientific discoveries for a practical purpose, such as a computer or cell phone
text (v) [U3] [U21] [U29]	send messages through a cell phone
topic (n) [U10] [U21]	subject or theme
tradition (n) [U10]	something that has existed for a long time in a culture, such as beliefs, stories, and songs
traditional (adj) [U7]	existing for a long time
vary (v) [U23]	change or cause to be different
virtual (adj) [U28]	describes a set of images or sounds a computer can make to represent a real place or situation, such as a virtual classroom
volunteer (adj) [U8] [U14]	consisting of people who work without receiving money

20. Pronunciation Table International Phonetic Alphabet (IPA)

Vowels	
Key Words	**International Phonetic Alphabet**
cake, mail, pay	/eɪ/
pan, bat, hand	/æ/
tea, feet, key	/iː/
ten, well, red	/e/
ice, pie, night	/aɪ/
is, fish, will	/ɪ/
cone, road, know	/oʊ/
top, rock, stop	/ɑ/
blue, school, new, cube, few	/uː/
cup, us, love	/ʌ/
house, our, cow	/aʊ/
saw, talk, applause	/ɔː/
boy, coin, join	/ɔɪ/
put, book, woman	/ʊ/
alone, open, pencil, atom, ketchup	/ə/

Consonants

Key Words	International Phonetic Alphabet
bid, jo**b**	/b/
do, fee**d**	/d/
food, sa**f**e	/f/
go, do**g**	/g/
home, be**h**ind	/h/
kiss, ba**ck**	/k/
load, poo**l**	/l/
man, plu**m**	/m/
need, ope**n**	/n/
pen, ho**p**e	/p/
road, ca**r**d	/r/
see, re**c**ent	/s/
show, na**ti**on	/ʃ/
team, mee**t**	/t/
choose, wa**tch**	/tʃ/
think, bo**th**	/θ/
this, fa**th**er	/ð/
visit, sa**v**e	/v/
watch, a**w**ay	/w/
yes, oni**o**n	/j/
zoo, the**s**e	/z/
bei**g**e, mea**s**ure	/ʒ/
jump, bri**dg**e	/dʒ/

Glossary of Grammar Terms

action verb a verb that describes an action.
> I **eat** breakfast every day.
> The band **played** in clubs every week.

adjective a word that describes or modifies a noun.
> That's a **beautiful** hat.

adverb a word that describes or modifies a verb, another adverb, or an adjective. Adverbs often end in -ly.
> Please drive **carefully**.

adverb of manner an adverb that describes how an action happens.
> I studied **hard** for our English test.

article the words a / an and the. An article introduces or identifies a noun.
> I bought **a** new MP3 player. **The** price was reasonable.

auxiliary verb (helping verb) a verb that comes before a main verb in a sentence. Modals are one kind of auxiliary verb. Do, have, and be can act as auxiliary verbs.
> **Does** he want to go to the library later?   The package **will** arrive today.

base form of the verb the form of a verb without any endings (-s or -ed) or to.
> come   go   take

clause a group of words that has a subject and a verb.
> SUBJECT   VERB
> My husband works every day.

comparative the form of an adjective or adverb that shows how two people, places, or things are different.
> My daughter is **older than** my son. (adjective)
> She does her work **more quickly** than he does. (adverb)

conjunction the words and, but, and or. They connect single words, phrases, or clauses.
> I bought my groceries **and** went home.

consonant a sound represented in writing by these letters of the alphabet: **b, c, d, f, g, h, j, k, l, m, n, p, q, r, s, t, v, w, x, y,** and **z**.

count noun a noun that you can count. Count nouns have a plural form.
> There are three **banks** on Oak Street.

definite article the is a definite article. Use the with a person, place, or thing that is familiar to you and your listener. Also, use the when the noun is unique – there is only one (the sun, the moon, the Internet).
> **The** movie we saw last week was very good.
> **The** moon and the stars were beautiful last night.

demonstrative a word that "points to" things and people. The demonstratives are *this, that, these,* and *those.*

This is my English book. ***That** one is yours.*

determiner a word that comes before a noun to limit its meaning in some way. Some common determiners are *some, any, this, that, these, those, a, an, the, much,* and *many.* Possessive adjectives – *my, your, his, her, our, their* – are also determiners.

*These computers have **many** parts.*

*Please give me **my** book.*

formal language a style of writing you use when you don't know the other person very well or where it is not appropriate to show familiarity, such as in a business, a job interview, speaking to a stranger, or speaking to an older person who you respect.

Good evening. I'd like to speak with Ms. Smith. Is she available?

future a verb form that describes a time that hasn't come yet. In English, we express the future with *will, be going to,* and the present.

*I'**ll meet** you tomorrow.*

*I'**m going to visit** my uncle and aunt next weekend.*

*We'**re taking** the test tomorrow.*

gerund the base form of a verb + *-ing,* for example, *going, watching, working.* Gerunds follow some verbs or can act as the subject of a sentence.

*She enjoyed **making** things.*   *Salsa **dancing** is a lot of fun.*

helping verb see **auxiliary verb**.

imperative a type of clause that tells people to do something. It gives instructions, directions to a place, or advice. It usually starts with the base form of a verb. The negative form begins with *Don't.*

***Listen** to the conversation.*

***Don't open** your books.*

indefinite article *a/an* are the indefinite articles. Use *a/an* with a singular person, place, or thing when you and your listener are not familiar with it, or when the specific name of it is not important. Use *a* with consonant sounds. Use *an* with vowel sounds.

*She's going to see **a** doctor today.*   *I had **an** egg for breakfast.*

indefinite pronoun a pronoun that refers to people or things that are not specific, not known, or not the focus of the sentence. *Something, anything, nothing, somebody, anybody, someone,* and *anyone* are indefinite pronouns.

***Everyone** knows fruit is good for you.*   *Does **anybody** want dessert?*

infinitive *to* + the base form of a verb.

*I need **to get** home early tonight.*

informal language a style of speaking or writing to friends, family, and children.

Hey, there. Nice to see you again.

information question (also called *Wh-* question) a question that begins with a *wh*-word (*who, what, when, where, why, how*). To answer this type of question, you need to provide information rather than answer *yes* or *no.*

***Where** were you yesterday?*

***How** much does that cost?*

G2

irregular adjective an adjective that does not change its form in the usual way. For example, you do not make the comparative form by adding *-er*.

good → better

irregular adverb an adverb that does not change its form in the usual way. For example, you do not make the comparative form by adding *-er*.

badly → worse

irregular verb a verb that does not change its form in the usual way. For example, it does not form the simple past with *-d* or *-ed*. It has its own special form.

go → *went*   *ride* → *rode*   *hit* → *hit*

linking verb a verb that links the subject with an adjective. Linking verbs are *be, get, seem, look, feel, sound, smell,* and *taste.*

*That coffee **smells good**.*

main clause a clause that can be used alone as a complete sentence.

*While he was working, **he discovered the cure**.*

main verb a verb that functions alone in a sentence or with an auxiliary verb.

*They **had** a meeting last week.*

*They **didn't have** many meetings this month.*

measurement word a word or phrase that shows the amount of something. Measurement words can be singular or plural.

*I bought **a box** of cereal, and Sonia bought **five pounds** of apples.*

modal a verb such as *can, could, be able to, know how to, would, may, should, ought to, might want to, have to, need to,* and *must.* Modals modify the main verb to show ability, possibility, requests, permission, suggestions, advice, necessity, or obligation.

*It **might** rain later today.*

*You **should** study harder if you want to pass this course.*

non-action verb see **stative verb**.

noncount noun a noun that you cannot count. Noncount nouns use a singular verb and do not have a plural form.

***Fish** is good for you.*

noun a word for a person, place, or thing. There are common nouns and proper nouns.

COMMON NOUN   PROPER NOUN

*I stayed in a **hotel** on my trip to New York.*   *I stayed at the **Pennsylvania Hotel**.*

object the person or thing that receives the action of the verb.

*I remember **James**.*

object pronoun a word that replaces a noun in the object position. Object pronouns are *me, you, him, her, it, us,* and *them.*

*Sara loves exercise classes. She takes **them** three times a week.*

past progressive a verb form that describes events in progress at a time in the past. The emphasis is on the action.

*They **were watching** TV until late last night.*

plural noun a noun that refers to more than one person, place, or thing.

students   women   roads

G3

possessive a word that shows that someone owns or has something. The word can be an adjective, a noun, or a pronoun.

A: *Is this **Diane's** desk?*

B: *No, it's **my** desk. **Her** desk is in the other office. **Her boss's** desk is in that office, too.*

possessive determiner *my, your, his, her, its, our,* and *their* are words that can come before a noun to show possession.

possessive pronoun a word that tells who owns something. Possessive pronouns are *mine, yours, his, hers, ours,* and *theirs.*

*That coffee is **mine**. (mine = my coffee)*   *I think this one is **yours**. (yours = your coffee)*

preposition a word such as *above, at, below, for, in, next to, on, to,* or *with* that goes before a noun or pronoun to show location, time, or direction.

*The shoes are **under** the bed.*   *I'll see you **on** July 1.*   *The man is **in front of** the bakery.*

prepositional phrase a phrase that begins with a preposition; a noun or noun phrase follows the preposition.

*Class starts **in five minutes**.*

present progressive a verb form that describes an action or situation that is in progress now or around the present time. It is also used to indicate the near future.

*What **are** you **doing** right now?*

*I**'m leaving** for Spain next week.*

pronoun a word that replaces a noun or noun phrase. Some examples are *I, you, we, him, hers,* and *it.*

proper noun a noun that is the name of a specific person, place, or thing. It begins with a capital letter.

***Central Park** is in **New York City**.*

punctuation mark a symbol used in writing, such as a period (.), a comma (,), a question mark (?), or an exclamation point (!).

quantifier a word that tells the amount of something, such as *some, any, a lot of, a little, a few, much,* and *many.* Quantifiers can refer to large or small amounts.

*"Do we have **any** eggs?"*   *"Yes, I think we have **some**."*

regular verb a verb that changes its form in the usual way.

live ➞ live**s**

wash ➞ wash**ed**

sentence a complete thought or idea that has a subject and a main verb. In writing, it begins with a capital letter and has a punctuation mark at the end (. ? !). In an imperative sentence, the subject (you) is not usually stated.

This sentence is a complete thought.   *Turn to page 168 in your books.*

simple past a verb form that describes completed actions or events in the past.

*They **grew up** in Washington, D.C.*

*They **attended** Howard University and **graduated** in 2011.*

simple present a verb form that describes things that regularly happen, such as habits and routines (usual and regular activities). It also describes facts and general truths.

*I **play** games online every night.* (routine)
*They **have** many friends.* (fact)

singular noun a noun that refers to one person, place, or thing.

*He is my best **friend**.*

statement a sentence that gives information. It can be spoken or written.

Today is Thursday.

stative (non-action) verb a verb that describes a state or situation, not an action. It is usually in the simple present or simple past.

*I **remember** your friend.*

subject the person, place, or thing that performs the action of the verb.

***People** should eat lots of fruit and vegetables.*

subject pronoun a pronoun that replaces a noun in the subject position. Subject pronouns are *I, you, he, she, it, we,* and *they.*

***We** (Sara and I) are taking exercise classes.*

superlative the form of an adjective or adverb that compares one person, place, or thing to others in a group.

*The **most important** day is tomorrow.* (adjective)
*Who arrives **the earliest** at school every day?* (adverb)

third-person singular refers to *he, she,* and *it,* or a singular noun. In the simple present, the third-person singular form ends in *-s* or *-es.*

***It looks** warm and sunny today.*   ***He washes** the laundry on Saturdays.*

time clause a clause that shows the order of events and begins with a time word such as *when, before, after,* or *while.*

*I met Joanna **when I was living in Houston**.*

verb a word that describes the action or state of a subject.

*Alex **wears** jeans and a T-shirt to school.*

vowel a sound represented in writing by these letters of the alphabet: *a, e, i, o,* and *u.*

Wh- question see **information question**.

Yes / No question a question that begins with a form of *be* or an auxiliary verb. You can answer this question with *yes* or *no.*

*"**Are** they going to the movies?"*   *"**No**, they're not."*
*"**Can** you give me some help?"*   *"**Yes**, I can."*

Index

Art Credits

Illustration

Pat Byrnes: 10, 11, 43, 92, 106, 202 *(bottom)*, 236, 255, 269, 278, 290, 291, 308, 354, 356, 381, 392, 393; **Ed Fotheringham:** 21, 70, 328, 379; **Ben Hasler:** 6, 7, 14, 63, 64, 146, 165, 206, 243, 274, 286, 314, 367; **Michael Mantel:** 202 *(top)*, 296, 302; **Maria Rabinky:** 10, 66, 245, 403; **Monika Roe:** 2, 18, 38, 62, 93, 128, 164, 198, 214, 242, 259, 268, 282, 298, 305, 310, 330, 348, 353, 368, 391; **Rob Schuster:** 26, 28, 180, 188, 189, 229; **Richard Williams:** 42, 65, 105, 174, 175, 219, 260, 281, 303, 304, 318, 340, 355, 394

Photography

5 ©Peter Cade/Getty Images; 9 *(left to right)* ©Jacqueline Veissid/Getty Images; ©Alamy; 19 ©Media Bakery; 31 ©Yellow Dog Productions Inc./Getty Images; 32 *(clockwise from top left)* ©Alamy; ©Istock Photos; ©Superstock; ©Andersen Ross/Getty Images; ©Alamy; ©Getty Images; ©Age Fotostock; 35 ©Sean Justice/Getty Images; 36 ©Keren Su/Getty Images; 46 ©Alamy; 47 ©Shutterstock; 48 *(left to right)* ©Media Bakery; ©Getty Images; ©Moodboard/Getty Images; 52 ©Shutterstock; 58 ©Media Bakery; 60 *(both)* ©Media Bakery; 61 ©Media Bakery; 69 ©Cheryl Clegg Photography; 76 *(all)* ©Alamy; 79 ©Wendy Connett/Getty Images; 81 *(clockwise from top left)* ©Media Bakery; ©Shutterstock; ©Tom Brosnahan; 82 *(top to bottom)* ©Photo Library; ©Alamy; 86 ©Media Bakery; 88 *(both)* ©Alamy; 98 *(left to right)* ©Media Bakery; ©Alamy; ©Media Bakery; 99 ©Alamy; 102 *(top to bottom)* ©Howard Berman/Getty Images; ©White Packert/Getty Images; 107 ©Absodels/Getty Images; 110 ©Alamy; 113 *(left to right)* ©Pontino/Alamy; ©Alamy; ©Media Bakery; 115 *(left to right)* ©Eric Fowke/Alamy; ©Michael Dwyer/Alamy; ©Jerry Driendl/Getty Images; 122 ©Shutterstock; 126 ©Media Bakery; 131 ©Shutterstock; 133 ©Media Bakery; 134 ©Shutterstock; 137 ©NY Daily News/Getty Images; 138 *(top to bottom)* ©World History Archive/Alamy; ©Pat Gaines/Getty Images; 140 *(left to right)* Istock Photos; ©Lebrecht Music and Arts Photo Library/Alamy; 144 *(left to right)* ©FPG/Getty Images; ©Jeremy Sutton-Hibbert/Alamy; ©Pictorial Press Ltd/Alamy; ©Classic Image/Alamy; 145 ©Alamy; 148 ©John M. Heller/Getty Images; 150 ©Media Bakery; 154 ©Courtesy of Pinkberry; 155 ©Courtesy of Pinkberry; 158 ©Stefan Kiefer/Vario Images/Alamy; 160 ©Everett Collection Inc/Alamy; 161 *(top to bottom)* ©Red Carpet Press/Alamy; ©Everett Collection Inc/Alamy; 167 ©Jeff Fusco/Getty Images; 168 ©Getty Images; 170 ©Media Bakery; 171 *(left to right)* ©Media Bakery; ©Shutterstock; 185 *(top to bottom)* ©Media Bakery; ©Johnny Greig/Alamy; ©Getty Images; 186 *(top to bottom)* ©Shutterstock; ©Shutterstock; ©Shutterstock; ©James Jackson/Alamy; 190 ©Shutterstock; 191 *(all)* ©Shutterstock; 194 ©Andrew Twort/Alamy; 197 *(top to bottom)* ©Media Bakery; ©Shutterstock; ©Shutterstock; 203 ©Robert Daemmrich/Getty Images; 210 ©Media Bakery; 213 ©AbleStock/Thinkstock; 215 ©Getty Images; 216 ©Media Bakery; 218 ©Alamy; 220 *(left to right)* ©Larry Lilac/Alamy; ©Shutterstock; 224 *(top to bottom)* ©Robert Harding Picture Library Ltd/Alamy; ©Susan Marie Andersson/Getty Images; ©Gastromedia/Alamy; 228 *(top to bottom)* ©Danita Delimont/Alamy; ©David Gee/Alamy ©David Hanson/Getty Images; 230 *(top to bottom)* ©Dirk Freder/Getty Images; ©Alamy; 233 *(top to bottom)* Media Bakery; ©Kathrin Ziegler/Getty Images; 238 ©Media Bakery 241 ©Blend Images/Alamy; 246 *(top to bottom)* ©Octavio Campos Salles/Alamy; ©John W Banagan/Getty Images; 248 ©Tony Peacock/Alamy; 250 ©MBI/Alamy; 253 ©Hola Images/Getty Images; 264 ©Angela Hampton Picture Library/Alamy; 271 *(left to right)* ©Andres Rodriguez/Alamy; ©Alamy; ©Media Bakery; ©William King/Getty Images; 273 ©Media Bakery; 283 ©Photo Alto/Alamy; 294 ©Tom Mc Nemar/Alamy; 311 ©Burke/Triolo Productions/Getty Images; 316 *(both)* ©Media Bakery; 320 ©Courtesy of Ashley Qualls; 323 ©Media Bakery; 324 ©Somos Images/Alamy; 328 ©Getty Images; 334 ©Media Bakery; 338 *(left to right)* ©Picture Partners/Photo Library; ©Ulrike Preuss/Photo Library; ©Echo/Getty Images; 339 *(top to bottom)* ©Alan Copson/Getty Images; ©Media Bakery; 343 *(top to bottom)* ©Angelo Hornak/Alamy; ©Frances Roberts/Alamy; 351 ©Photo Alto/Alamy; 360 ©UpperCut Images/Alamy; 364 ©Media Bakery; 367 ©Alamy; 372 ©Blend Images/Alamy; 376 ©Thomas Barwick/Getty Images; 378 ©Getty Images; 384 ©Media Bakery; 387 ©Media Bakery; 388 *(top to bottom)* ©Radius Images/Alamy; ©QxQ Images/Datacraft/Getty Images; 398 *(top to bottom)* ©Media Bakery; ©Getty Images; 402 *(left to right)* ©Alamy; ©Adrian Lyon/Alamy; 412 *(clockwise from top left)* ©Antony Giblin/Getty Images; ©Robert Harding/Getty Images; ©Nik Wheeler/Alamy; ©Jon Arnold Images Ltd/Alamy; 416 ©TAO Images Limited/Alamy; 418 ©RubberBall/Alamy; 423 *(all)* ©Alamy